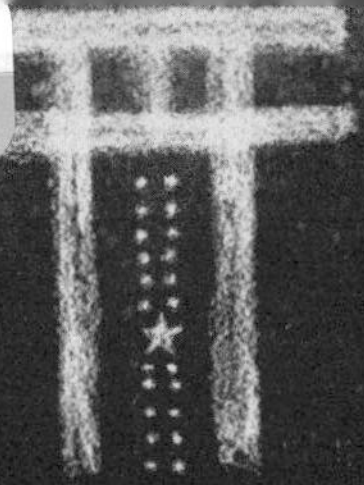

From my speeding car
I catch a glimpse through the trees of what looks like the
ocean.
Hope…a premonition…

Every month, as I write, I am visited by such moments.

The scene that follows is sometimes an ocean brighter
than anything I could have imagined,
sometimes a barren seashore littered with rocks,
sometimes a place I once visited,
sometimes a road that ends up going nowhere.

I would like to end up at a heartbreakingly beautiful sea.

—Hiroyuki Asada, 2010

Hiroyuki Asada made his debut in *Monthly Shonen Jump* in
1986. He's best known for his basketball manga *I'll*.
He's a contributor to artist Range Murata's quarterly manga
anthology *Robot*. *Tegami Bachi: Letter Bee*
is his most recent series.

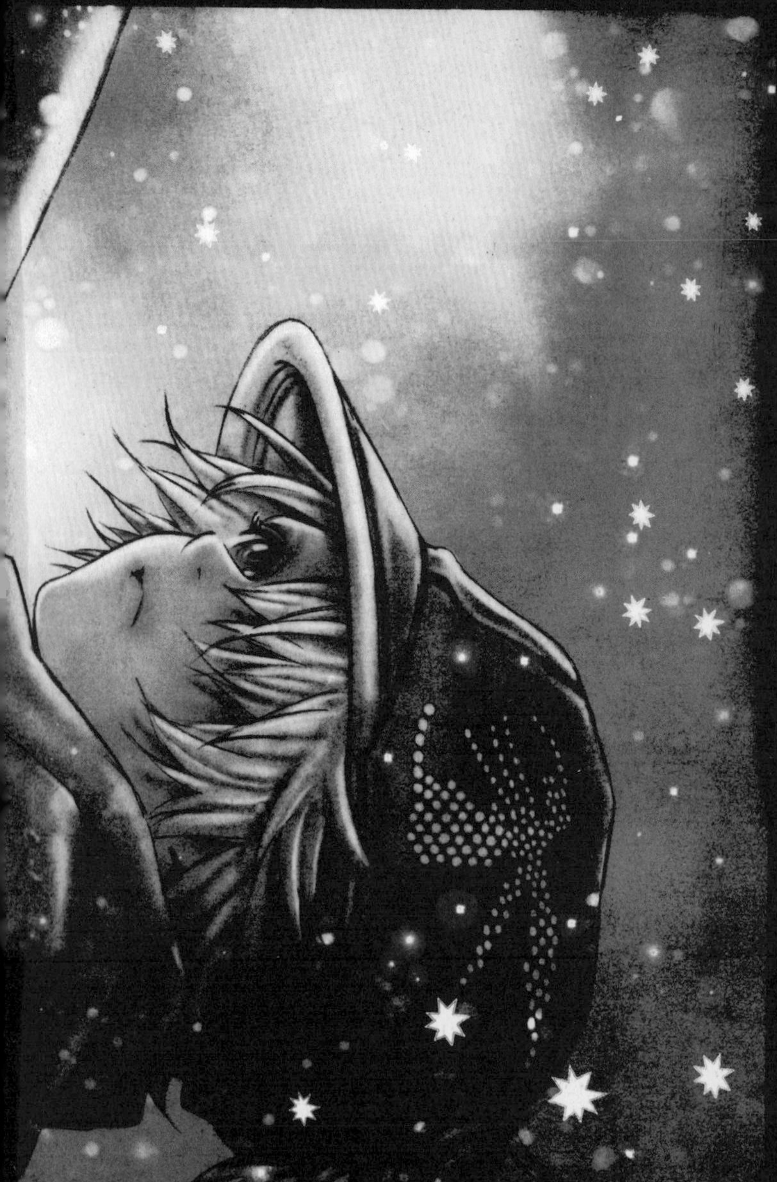

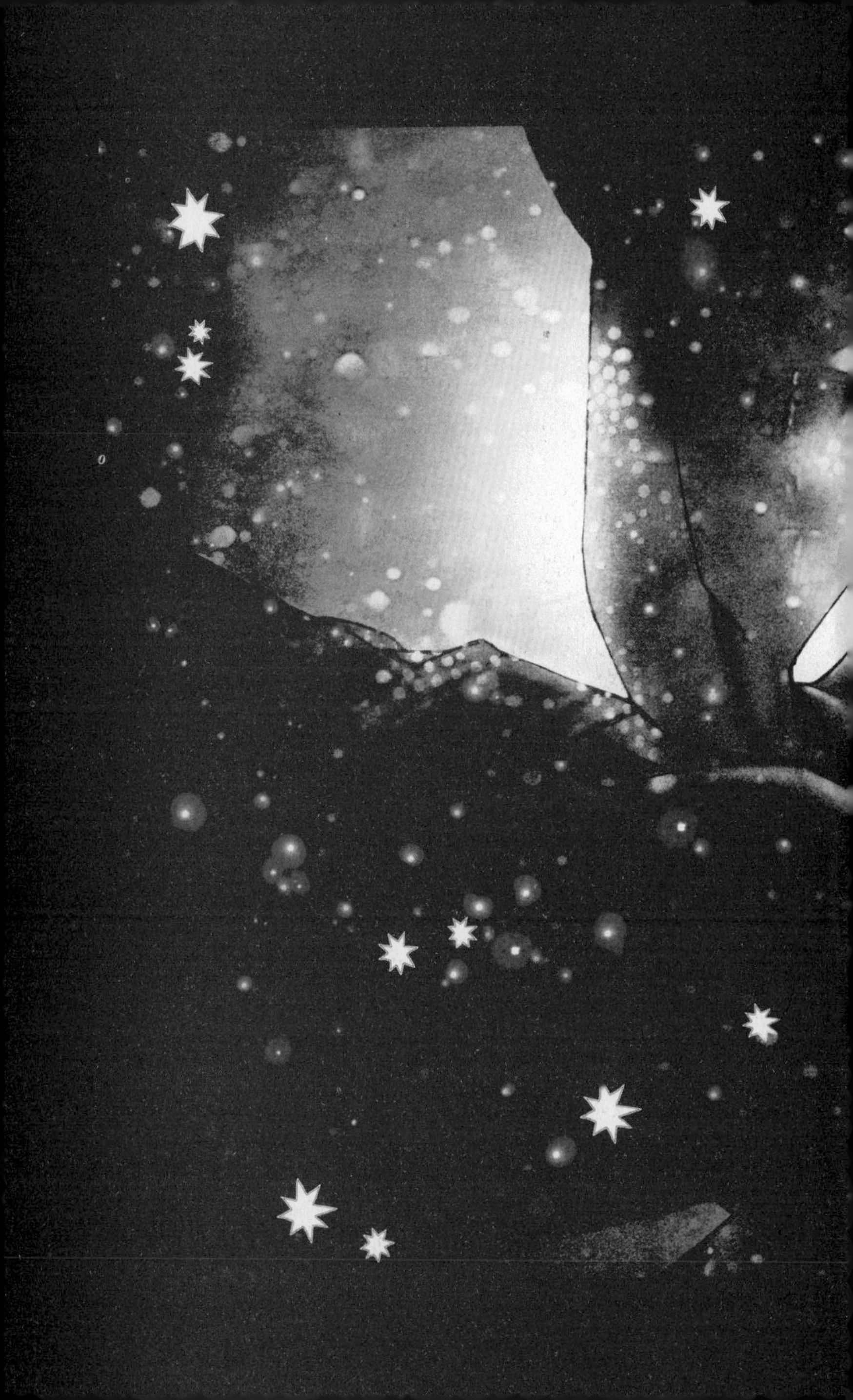

Tegami Bachi
LETTER · BEE

Volume 10

SHONEN JUMP Manga Edition

Story and Art by Hiroyuki Asada

English Adaptation/Rich Amtower
Translation/JN Productions
Touch-up & Lettering/Annaliese Christman
Design/Amy Martin
Editor/Shaenon K. Garrity

TEGAMIBACHI © 2006 by Hiroyuki Asada. All rights reserved.
First published in Japan in 2006 by SHUEISHA Inc., Tokyo. English
translation rights arranged by SHUEISHA Inc.

The rights of the author(s) of the work(s) in this publication to be so
identified have been asserted in accordance with the Copyright, Designs
and Patents Act 1988. A CIP catalogue record for this book is available
from the British Library.

Printed in Canada

Published by VIZ Media, LLC
P.O. Box 77010
San Francisco, CA 94107

10 9 8 7 6 5 4 3 2 1
First printing, August 2012

Tegami Bachi
LETTER · BEE

VOLUME 10

The·Shining Eye

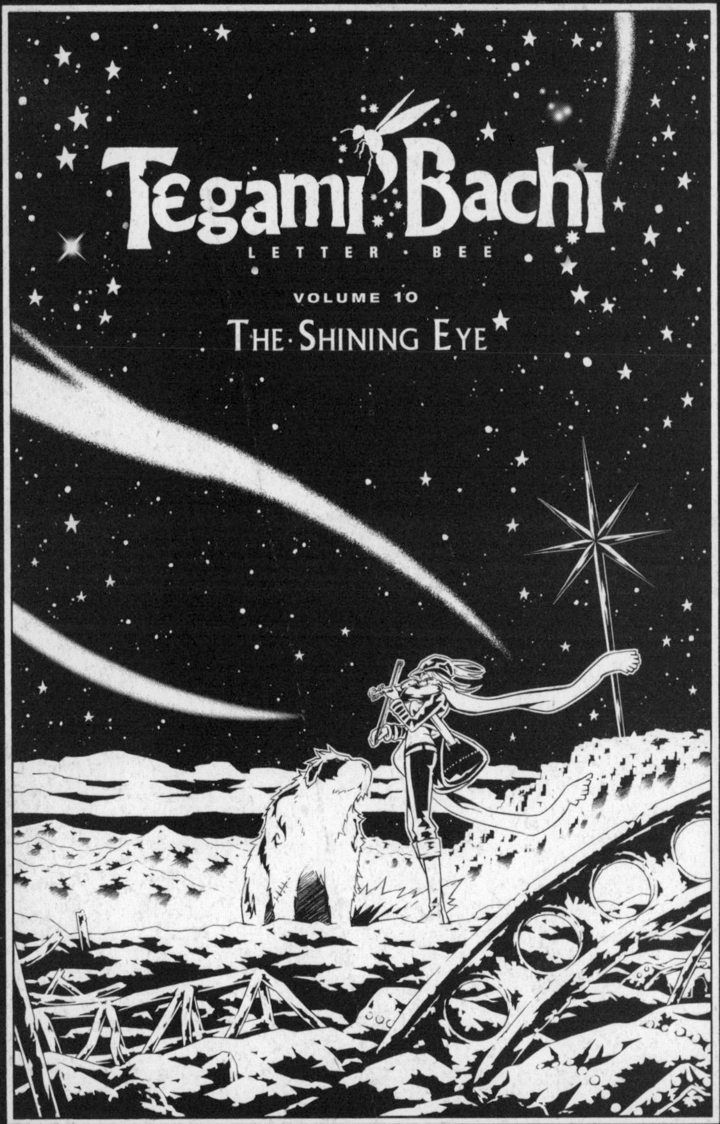

STORY AND ART BY

HIROYUKI ASADA

This is a country known as Amberground, where night never ends.

Its capital, Akatsuki, is illuminated by a man-made sun. The farther one strays from the capital, the weaker the light. The Yuusari region is cast in twilight; the Yodaka region survives only on pale moonlight.

Letter Bee Gauche Suede and young Lag Seeing meet in the Yodaka region— a postal worker and the "letter" he must deliver. In their short time together, they form a fast friendship, but when the journey ends, each departs down his own path. Gauche longs to become Head Bee, while Lag himself wants to be a Letter Bee, like Gauche.

In time, Lag becomes a Letter Bee. He learns that Gauche has lost his *heart* and become a marauder named Noir, working for the rebel organization Reverse. After many adventures, Lag returns with the unconscious Gauche, throwing the Beehive into an uproar.

Two inspectors from the Capital, the ex-Bee Garrard and his ex-dingo Valentine, are sent to investigate the matter. They fire Director Largo Lloyd and put Lag and Assistant Director Aria Link to work at the Dead Letter Office. There, Aria and Lag must process the thousands of letters the Beehive has marked "undeliverable." Undaunted, Lag continues to make deliveries, but the strain is catching up to him…

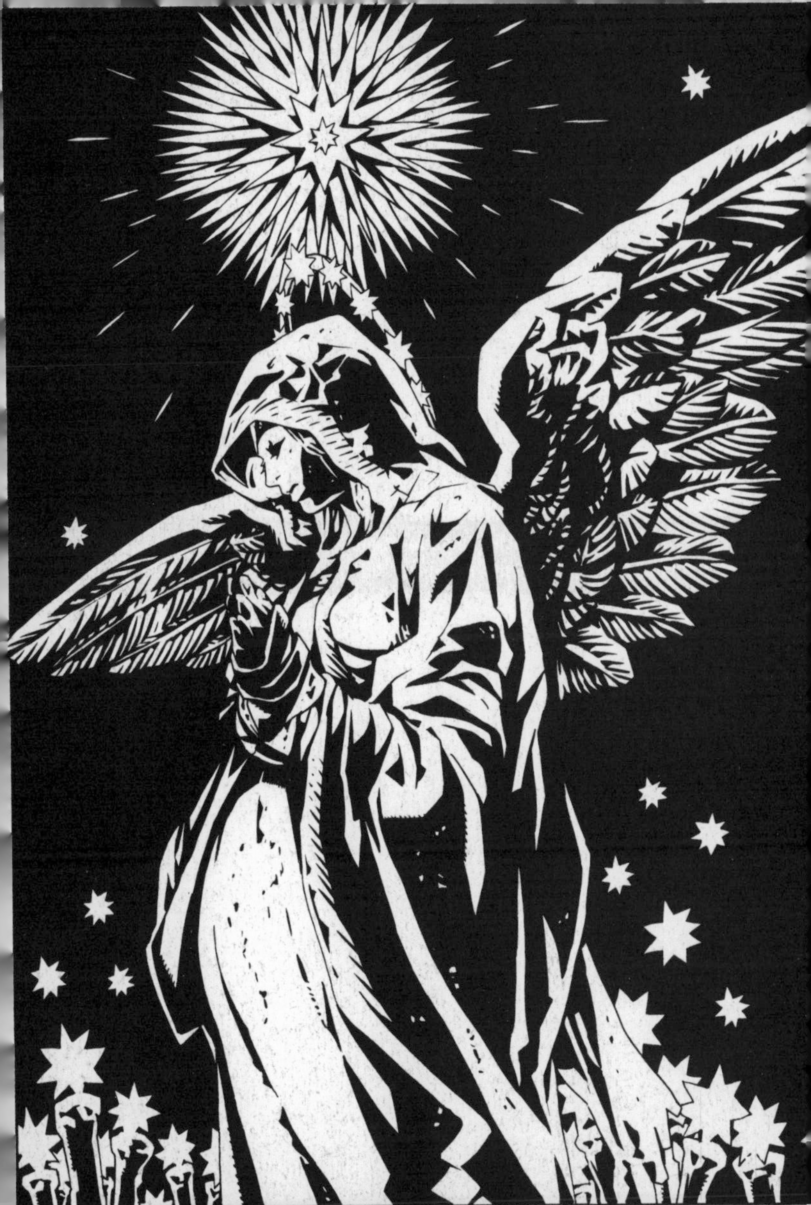

List of Characters

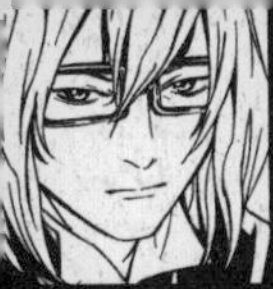

LARGO LLOYD
Beehive Director

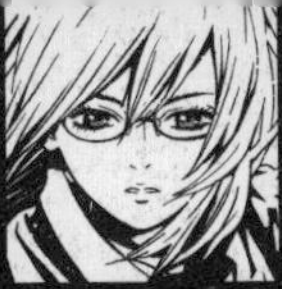

ARIA LINK
Beehive Assistant Director

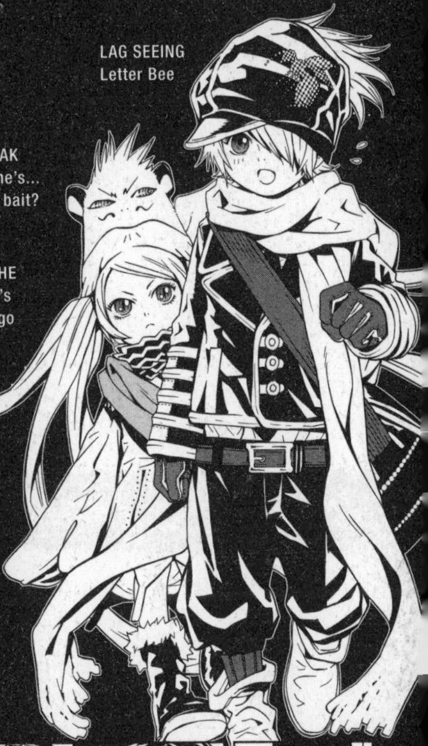

LAG SEEING
Letter Bee

STEAK
Niche's... live bait?

NICHE
Lag's Dingo

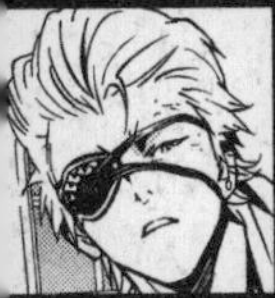

DR. THUNDERLAND, JR.
Member of the AG Biological Science Advisory Board, Third Division and head doctor at the Beehive

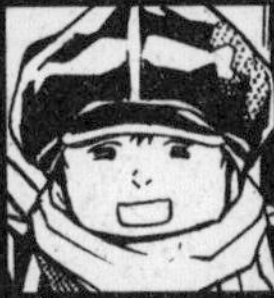

CONNOR KLUFF
Letter Bee

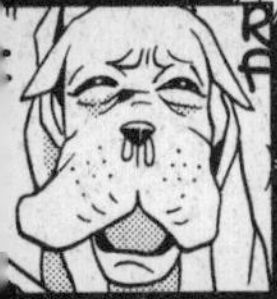

GUS
Connor's Dingo

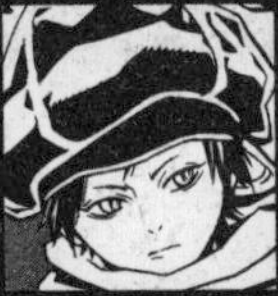

ZAZIE
Letter Bee

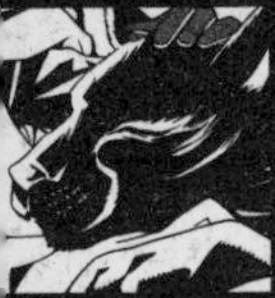

VASIOLKA
Zazie's Dingo

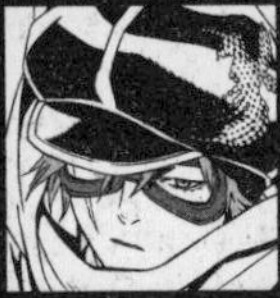

JIGGY PEPPER
Express Delivery Letter Bee

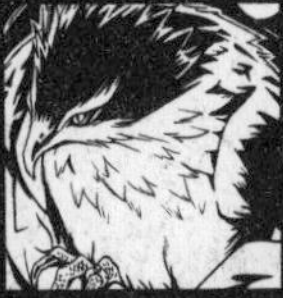

HARRY
Jiggy's Dingo

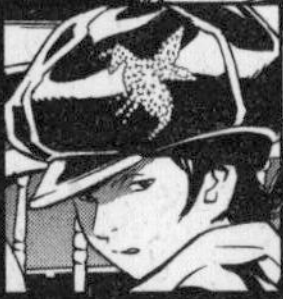

MOC SULLIVAN
Letter Bee

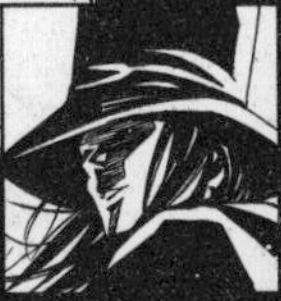

THE MAN WHO COULD NOT BECOME SPIRIT
The ringleader of Reverse

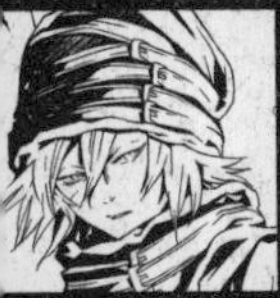

NOIR (FORMERLY GAUCHE SUEDE)
Marauder for Reverse and an ex–Letter Bee

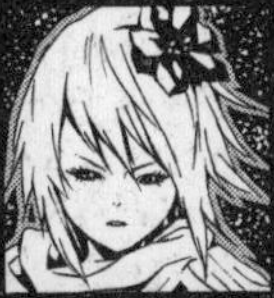

RODA
Noir's Dingo

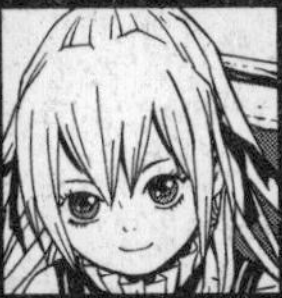

SYLVETTE SUEDE
Gauche's Sister

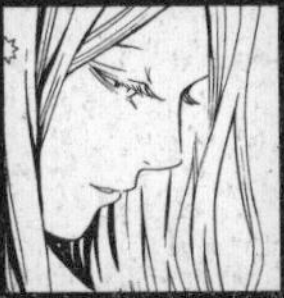

ANNE SEEING
Lag's Mother (Missing)

Tegami Bachi

LETTER · BEE

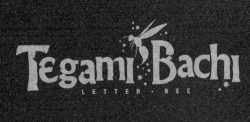

VOLUME 10

The Shining Eye

In all things... the heart must take precedence.

The heart rules over all things...

...and all things come from the heart.

—THE SCRIPTURES OF AMBERGROUND, 1st verse

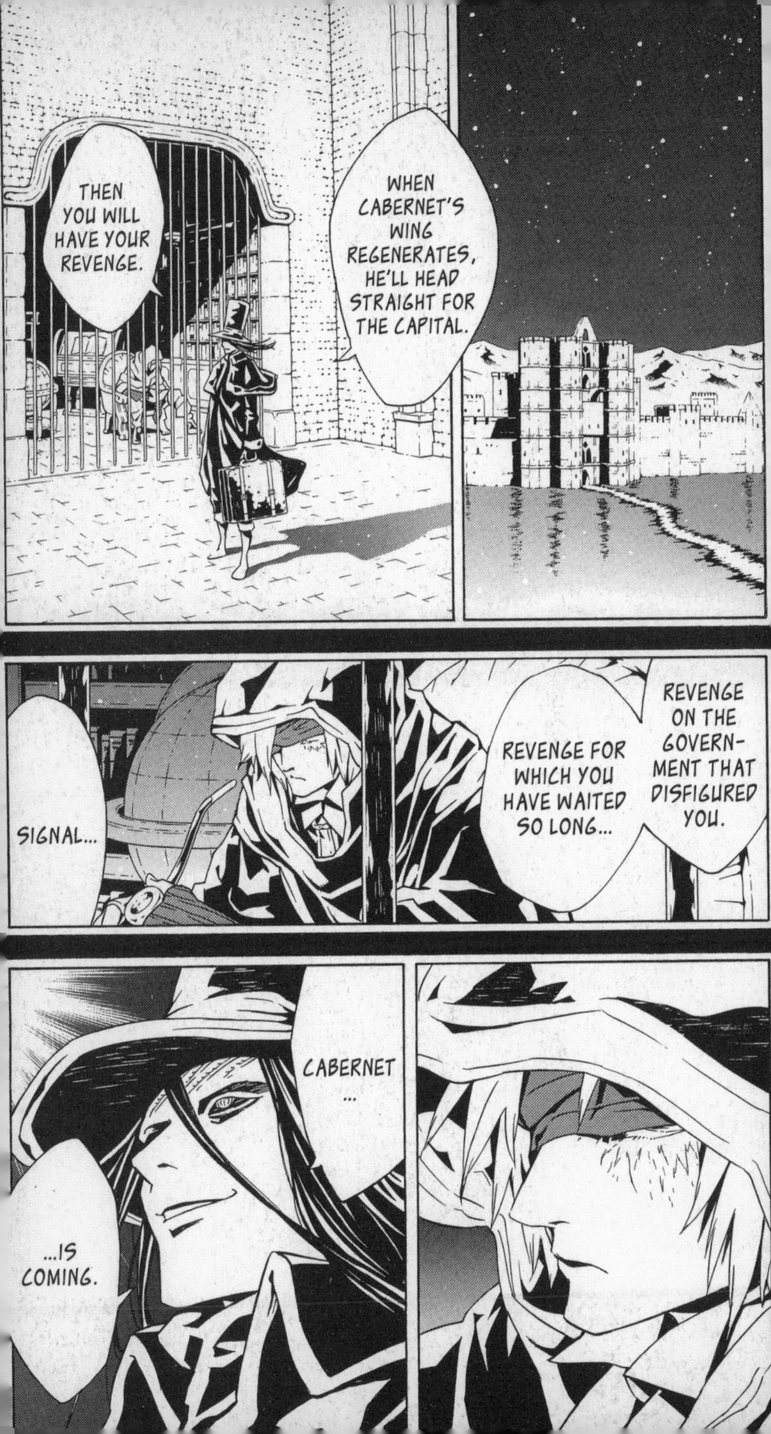
WHEN CABERNET'S WING REGENERATES, HE'LL HEAD STRAIGHT FOR THE CAPITAL.
THEN YOU WILL HAVE YOUR REVENGE.
REVENGE ON THE GOVERN-MENT THAT DISFIGURED YOU.
REVENGE FOR WHICH YOU HAVE WAITED SO LONG...
SIGNAL...
CABERNET ...
...IS COMING.

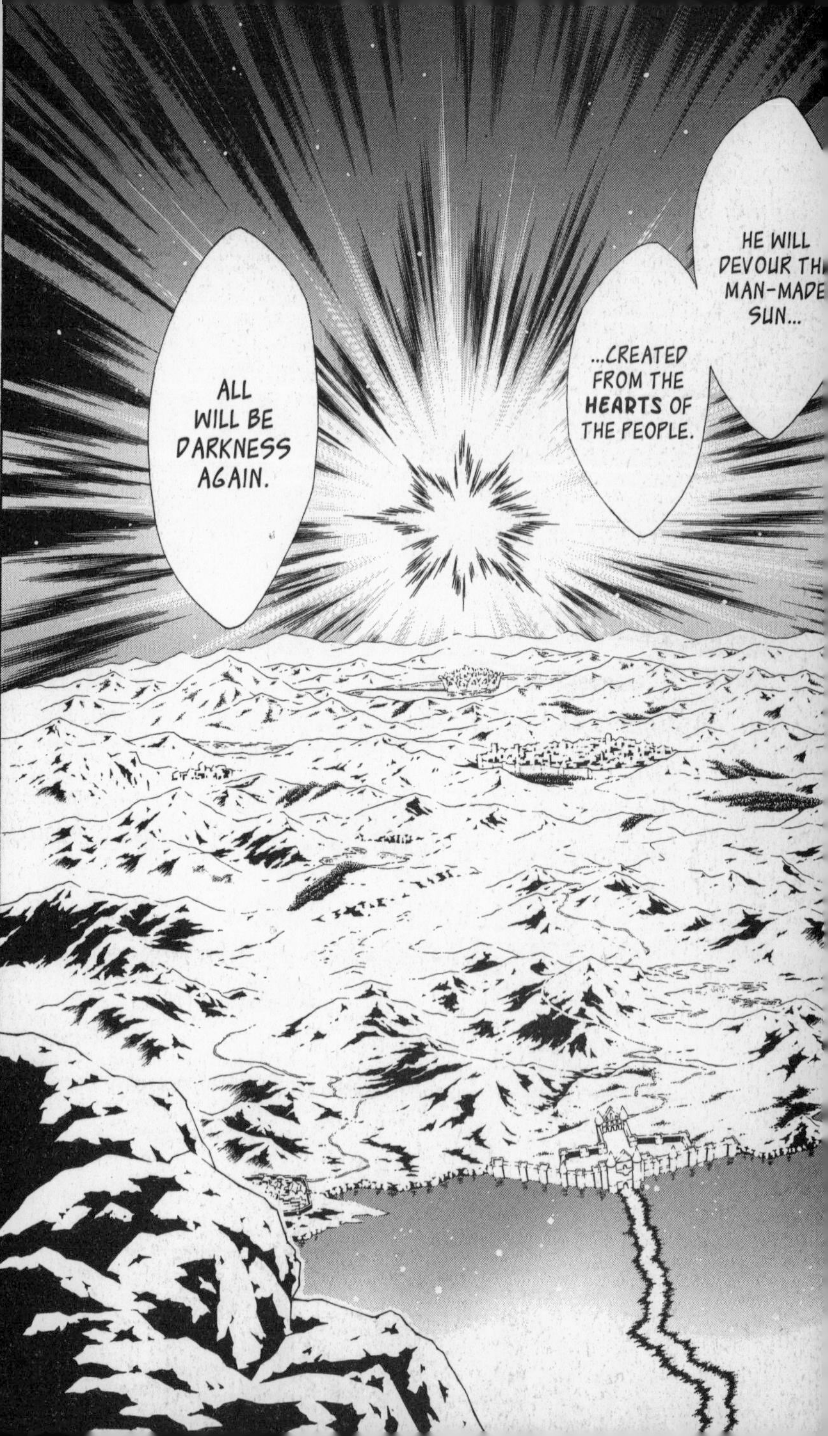
HE WILL DEVOUR TH MAN-MADE SUN...
...CREATED FROM THE **HEARTS** OF THE PEOPLE.
ALL WILL BE DARKNESS AGAIN.

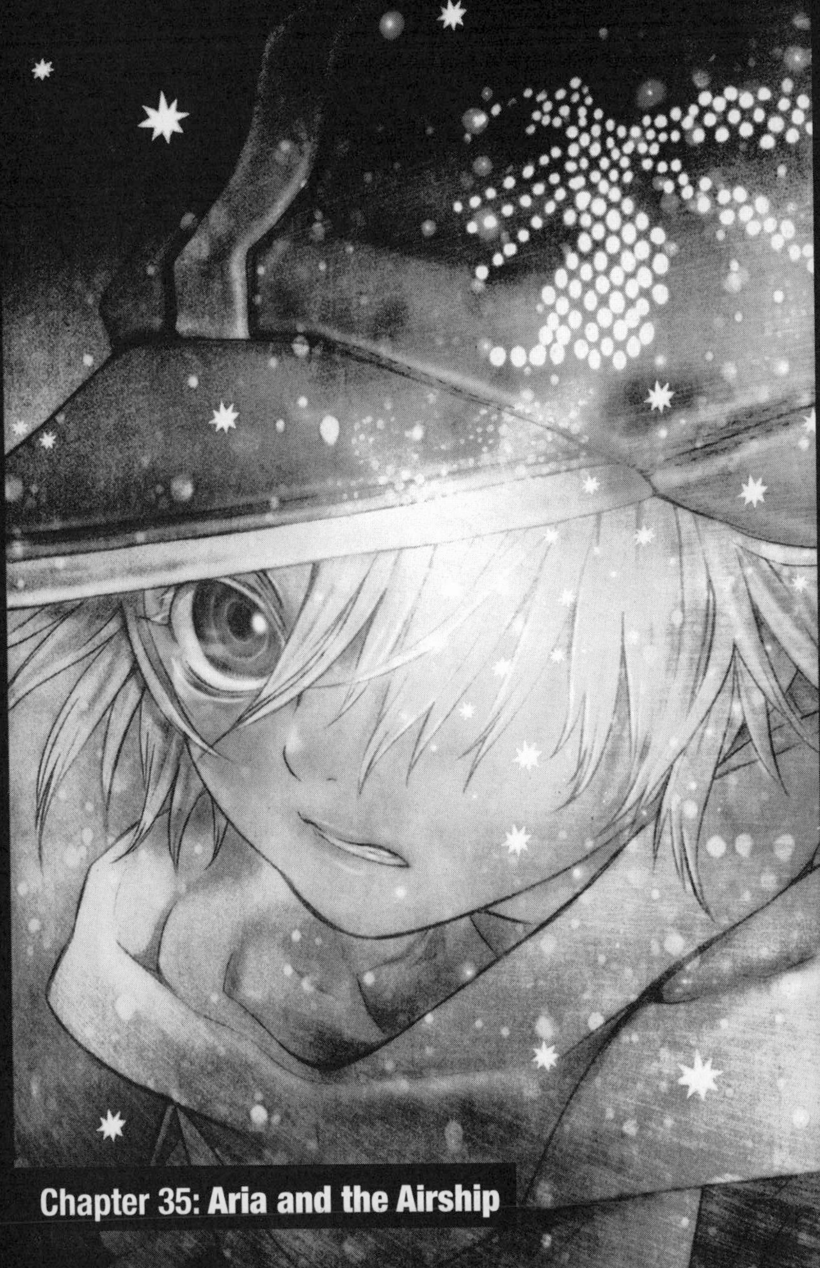

Chapter 35: Aria and the Airship

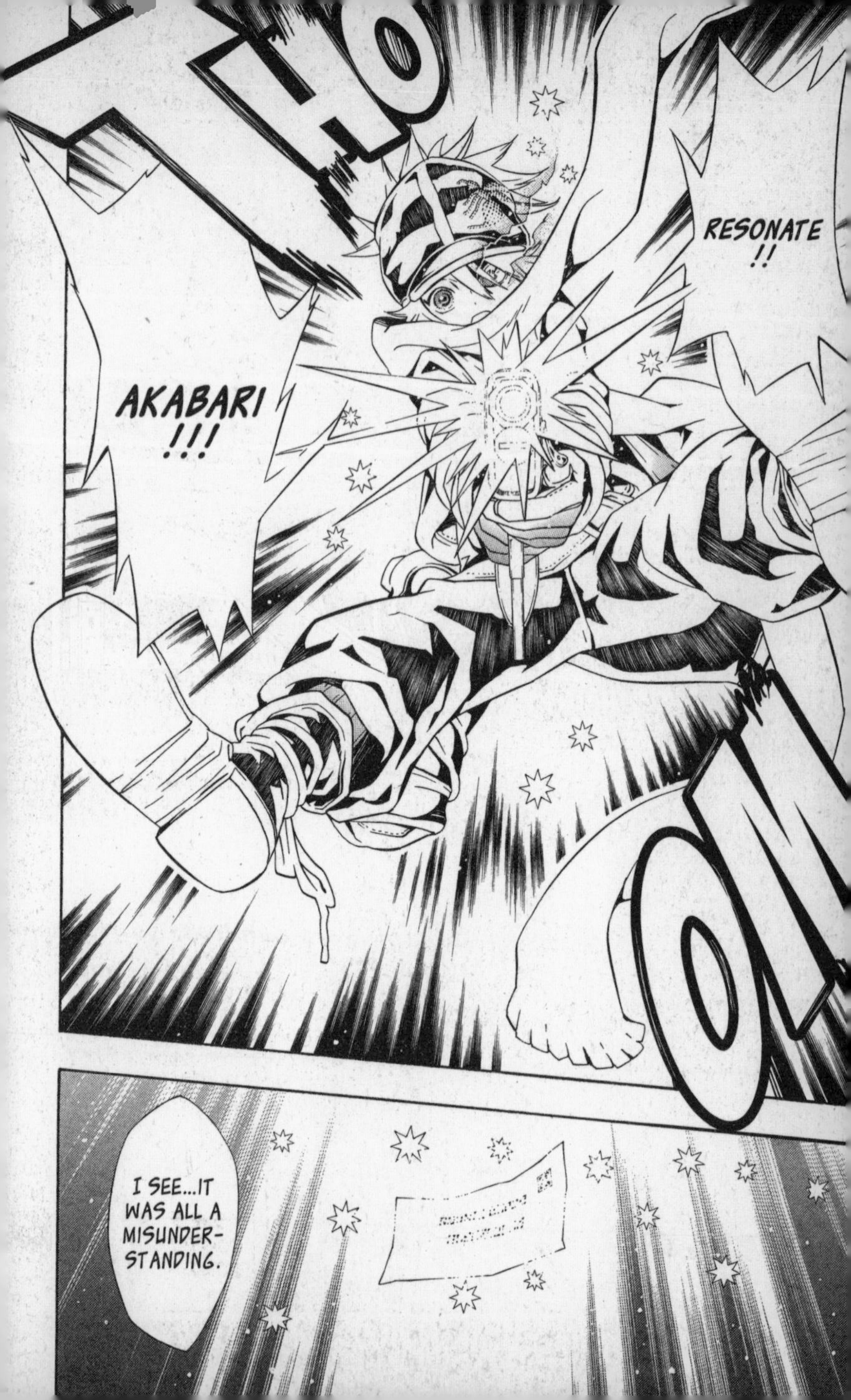
RESONATE !!
AKABARI !!!
I SEE...IT WAS ALL A MISUNDER-STANDING.

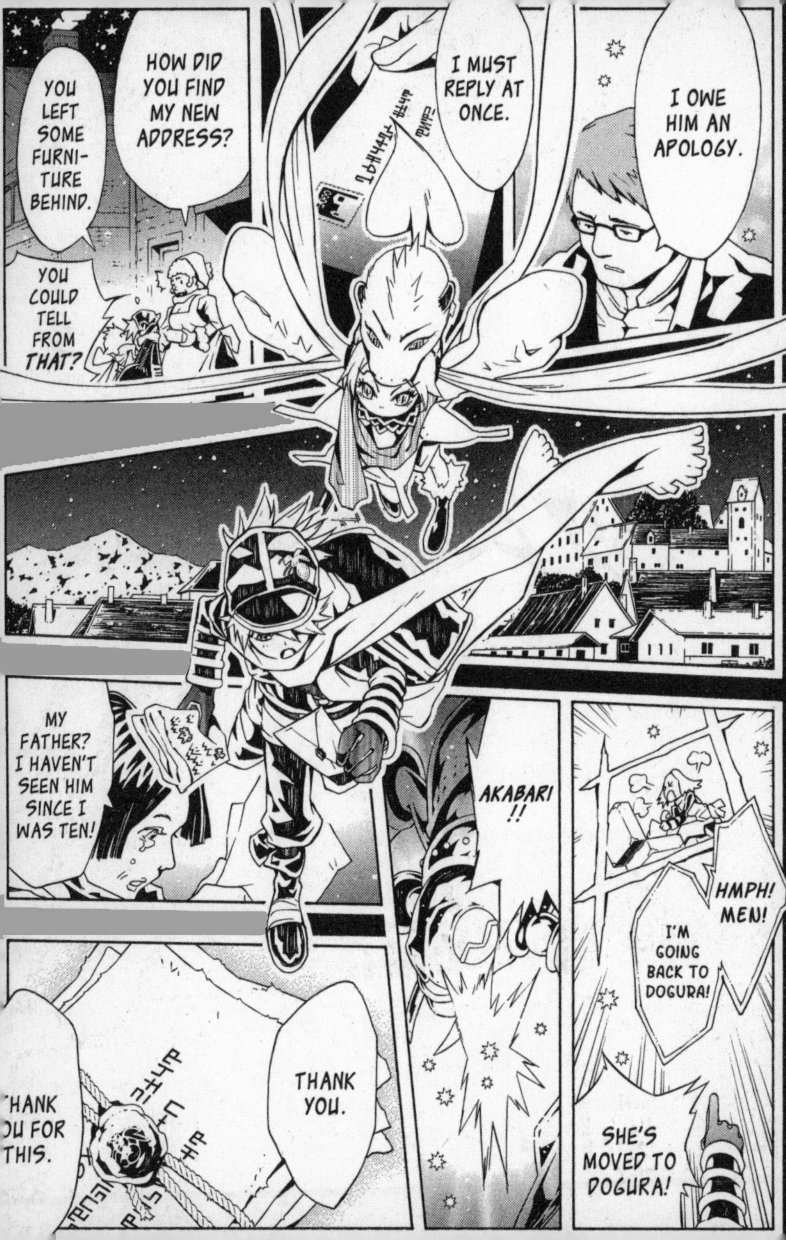
I OWE HIM AN APOLOGY.
I MUST REPLY AT ONCE.
HOW DID YOU FIND MY NEW ADDRESS?
YOU LEFT SOME FURNITURE BEHIND.
YOU COULD TELL FROM *THAT?*
HMPH! MEN!
I'M GOING BACK TO DOGURA!
SHE'S MOVED TO DOGURA!
AKABARI!!
MY FATHER? I HAVEN'T SEEN HIM SINCE I WAS TEN!
THANK YOU.
THANK OU FOR THIS.

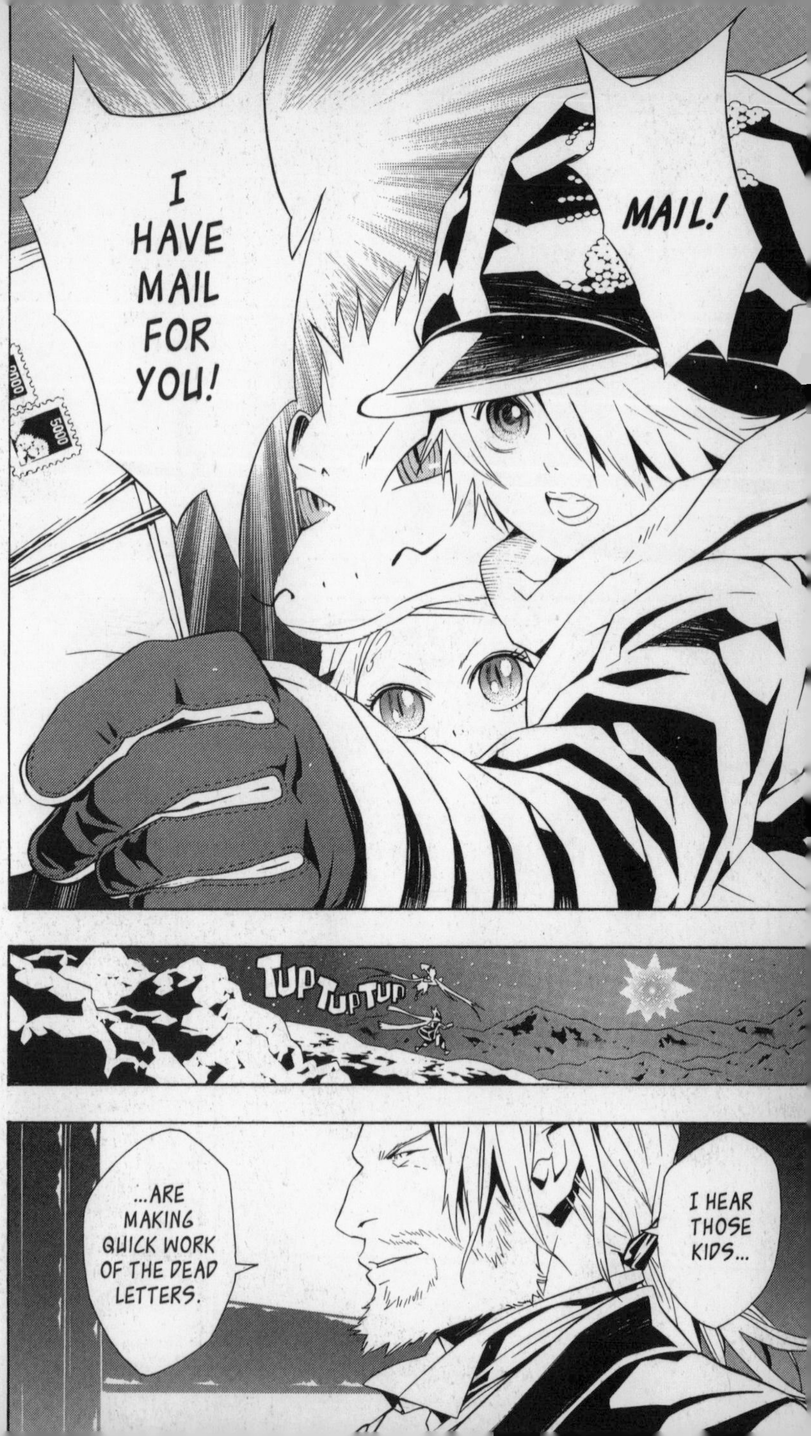
MAIL!
I HAVE MAIL FOR YOU!
TUP TUP TUP
I HEAR THOSE KIDS...
...ARE MAKING QUICK WORK OF THE DEAD LETTERS.

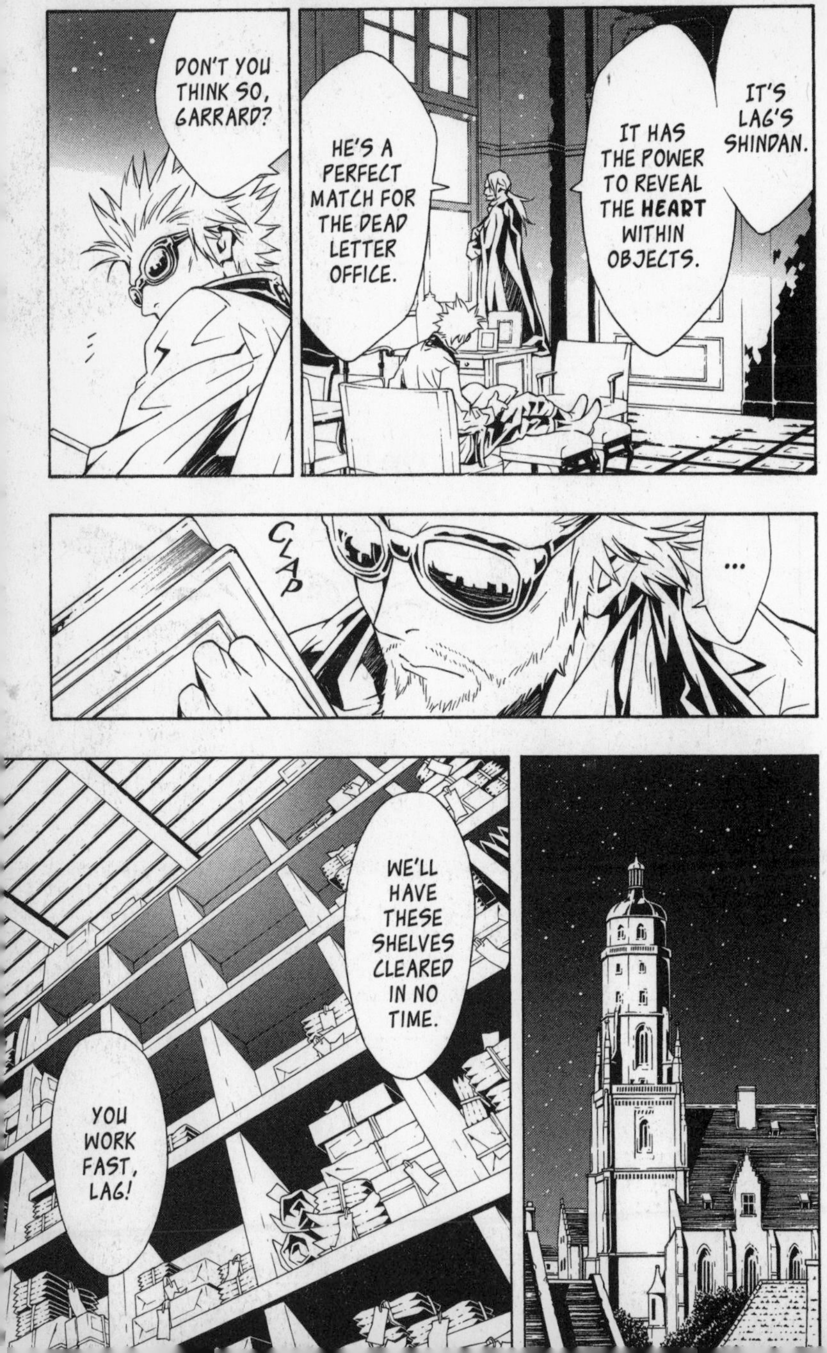
IT'S LAG'S SHINDAN.
IT HAS THE POWER TO REVEAL THE **HEART** WITHIN OBJECTS.
HE'S A PERFECT MATCH FOR THE DEAD LETTER OFFICE.
DON'T YOU THINK SO, GARRARD?
...
CLAP
WE'LL HAVE THESE SHELVES CLEARED IN NO TIME.
YOU WORK FAST, LAG!

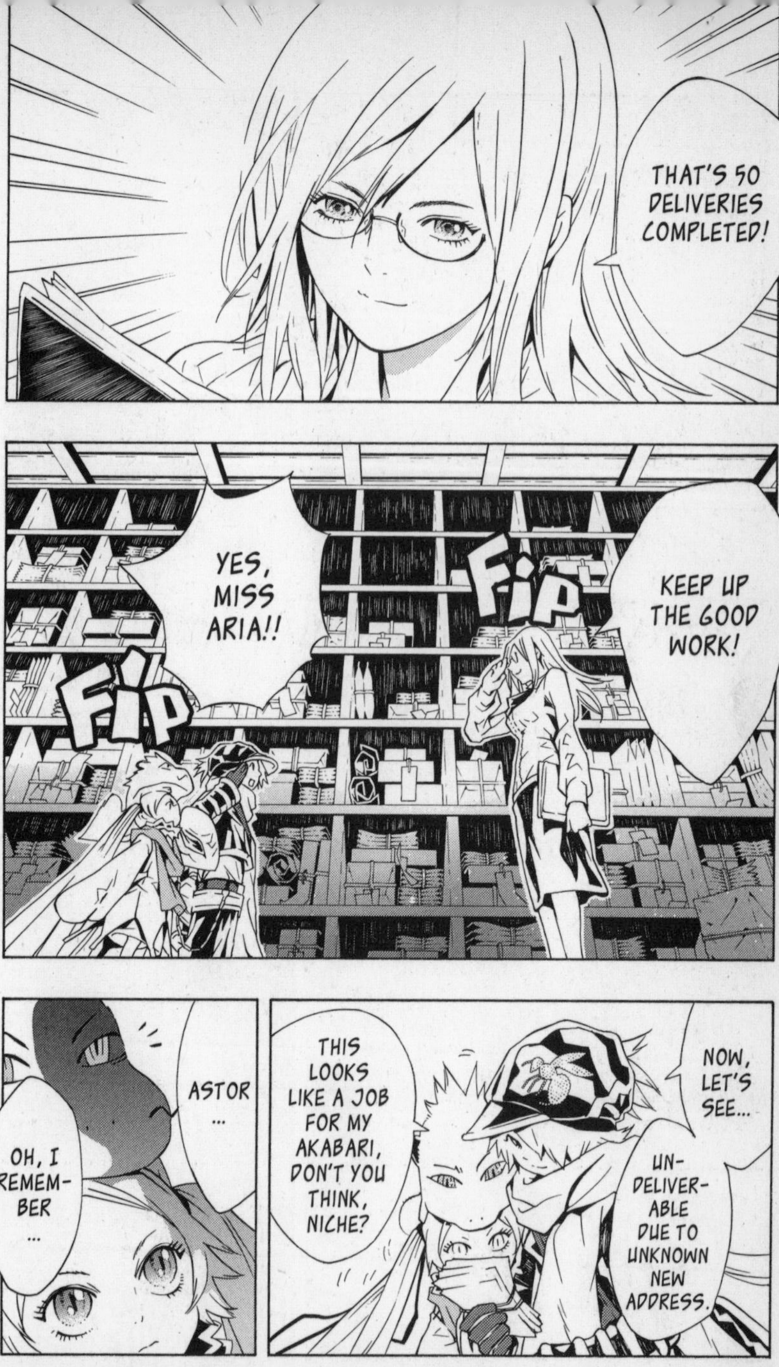
THAT'S 50 DELIVERIES COMPLETED!
KEEP UP THE GOOD WORK!
FIP
YES, MISS ARIA!!
FIP
NOW, LET'S SEE...
UN-DELIVER-ABLE DUE TO UNKNOWN NEW ADDRESS.
THIS LOOKS LIKE A JOB FOR MY AKABARI, DON'T YOU THINK, NICHE?
ASTOR ...
OH, I REMEMBER ...

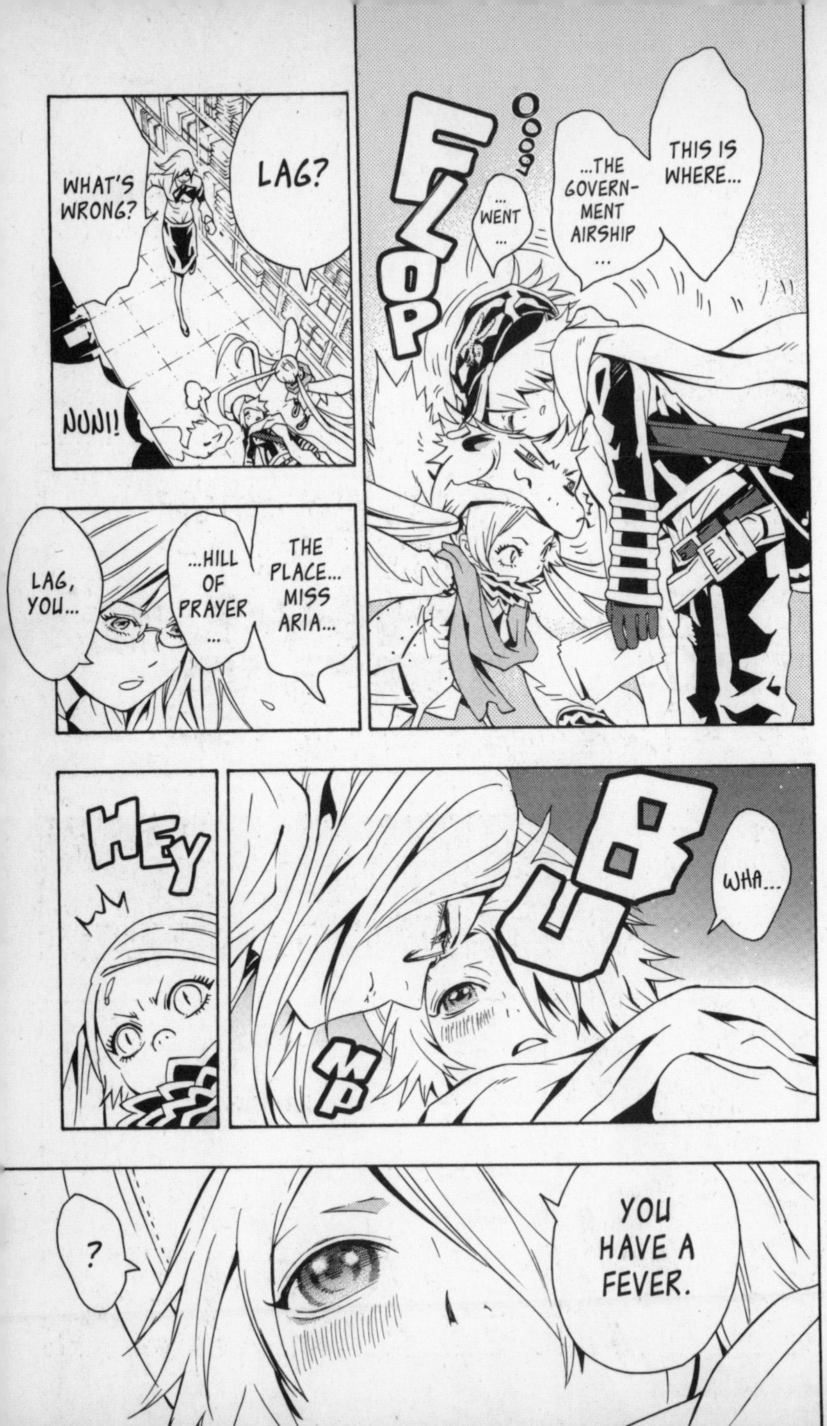
THIS IS WHERE...
...THE GOVERN-MENT AIRSHIP ...
... WENT ...
OOOG
FLOP
LAG?
WHAT'S WRONG?
NUNI!
THE PLACE... MISS ARIA...
...HILL OF PRAYER ...
LAG, YOU...
WHA...
BUMP
HEY
YOU HAVE A FEVER.
?

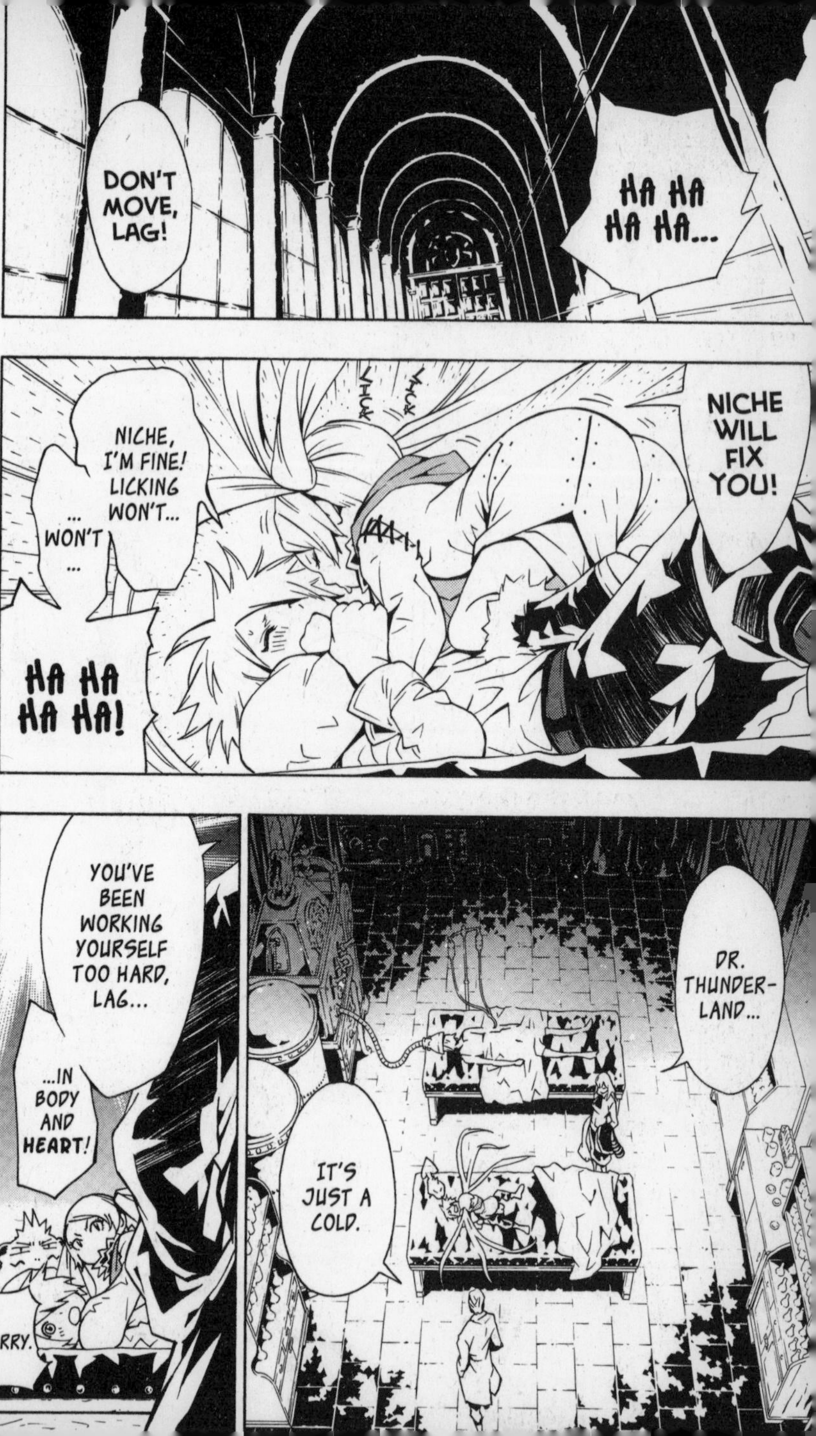
HA HA HA HA...
DON'T MOVE, LAG!
NICHE WILL FIX YOU!
LICK LICK
NICHE, I'M FINE! LICKING WON'T...
... WON'T ...
HA HA HA HA!
DR. THUNDER-LAND...
IT'S JUST A COLD.
YOU'VE BEEN WORKING YOURSELF TOO HARD, LAG...
...IN BODY AND HEART!
SORRY.

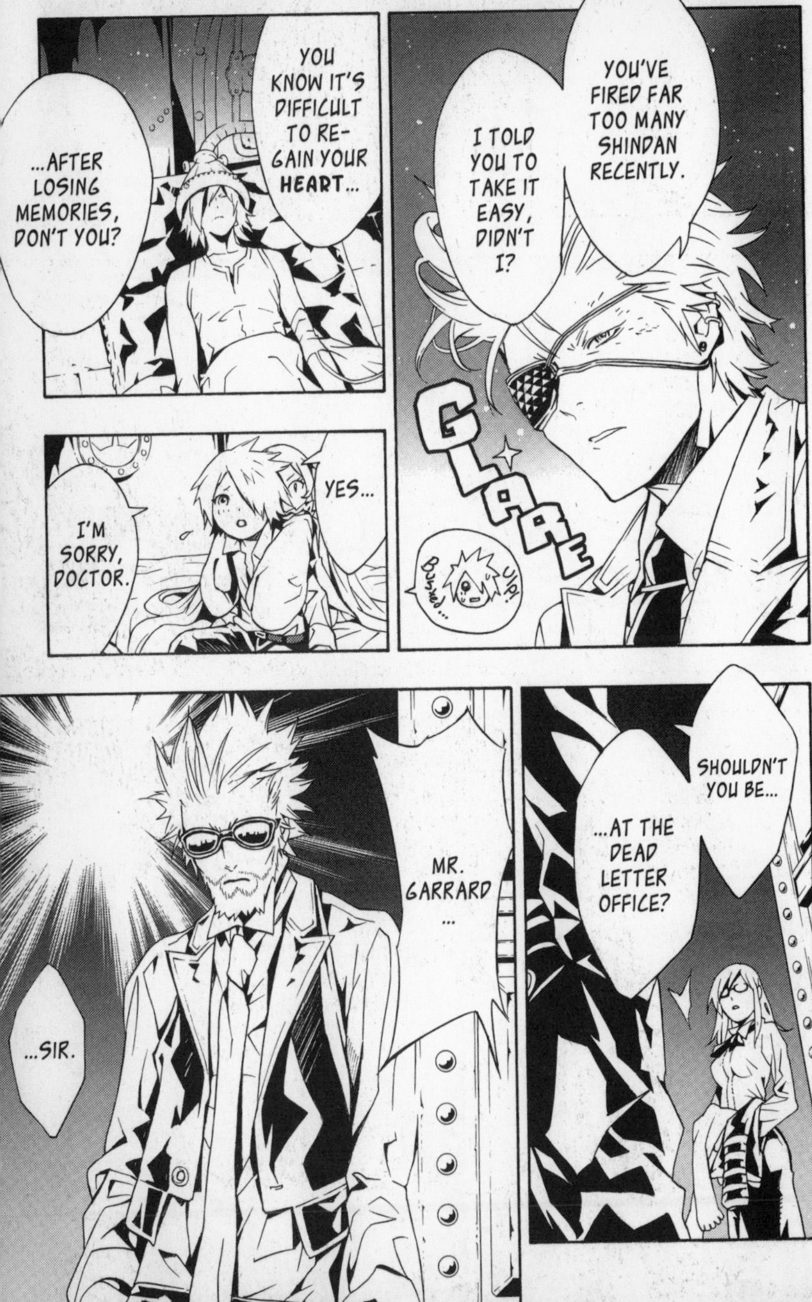
YOU'VE FIRED FAR TOO MANY SHINDAN RECENTLY.
I TOLD YOU TO TAKE IT EASY, DIDN'T I?
GLARE
Ulp!
Busted...
YOU KNOW IT'S DIFFICULT TO RE-GAIN YOUR HEART...
...AFTER LOSING MEMORIES, DON'T YOU?
YES...
I'M SORRY, DOCTOR.
SHOULDN'T YOU BE...
...AT THE DEAD LETTER OFFICE?
MR. GARRARD ...
...SIR.

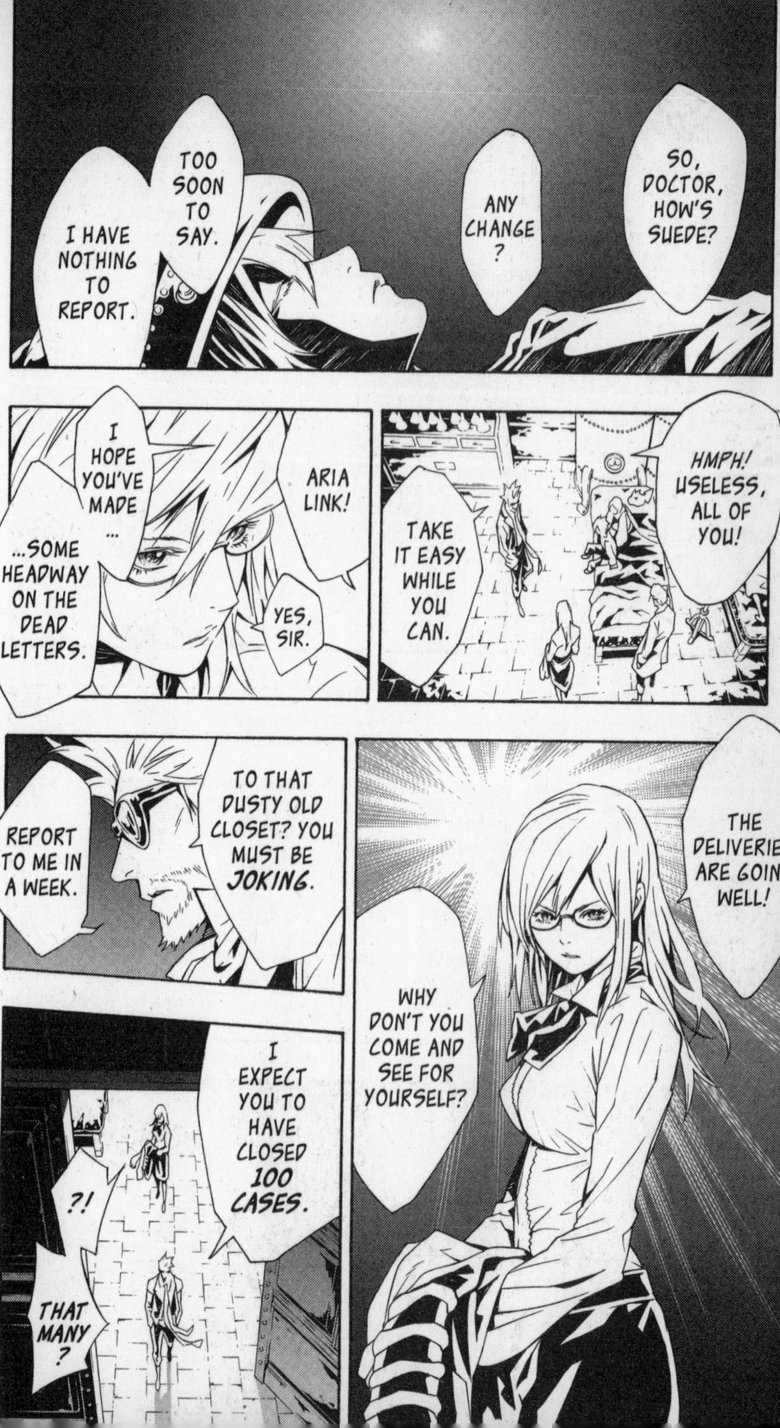
SO, DOCTOR, HOW'S SUEDE?
ANY CHANGE ?
TOO SOON TO SAY.
I HAVE NOTHING TO REPORT.
HMPH! USELESS, ALL OF YOU!
TAKE IT EASY WHILE YOU CAN.
ARIA LINK!
YES, SIR.
I HOPE YOU'VE MADE ...
...SOME HEADWAY ON THE DEAD LETTERS.
THE DELIVERIES ARE GOING WELL!
WHY DON'T YOU COME AND SEE FOR YOURSELF?
TO THAT DUSTY OLD CLOSET? YOU MUST BE JOKING.
REPORT TO ME IN A WEEK.
I EXPECT YOU TO HAVE CLOSED 100 CASES.
?!
THAT MANY ?

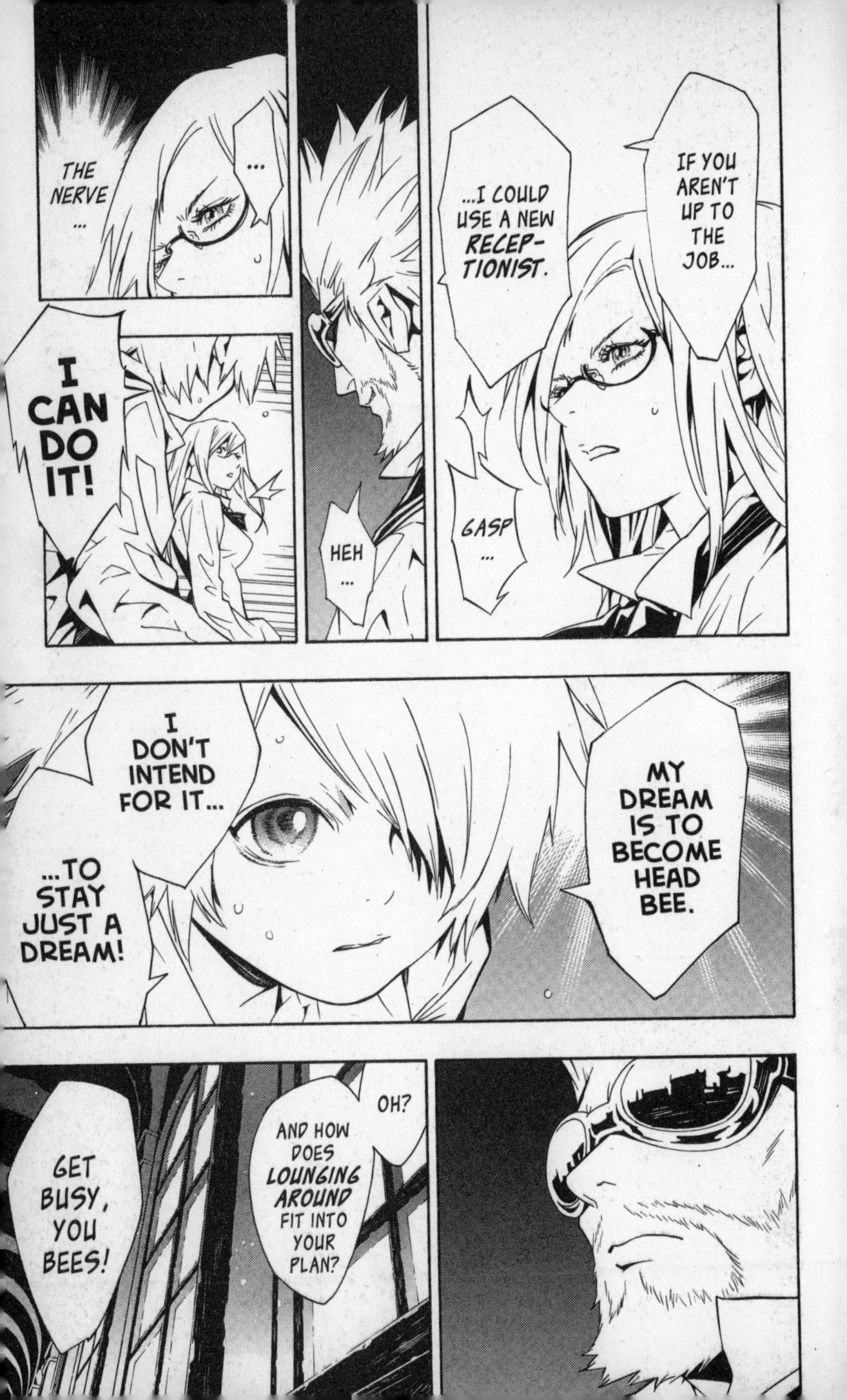
IF YOU AREN'T UP TO THE JOB...
...I COULD USE A NEW RECEPTIONIST.
GASP...
HEH...
...
THE NERVE...
I CAN DO IT!
MY DREAM IS TO BECOME HEAD BEE.
I DON'T INTEND FOR IT...
...TO STAY JUST A DREAM!
OH?
AND HOW DOES LOUNGING AROUND FIT INTO YOUR PLAN?
GET BUSY, YOU BEES!

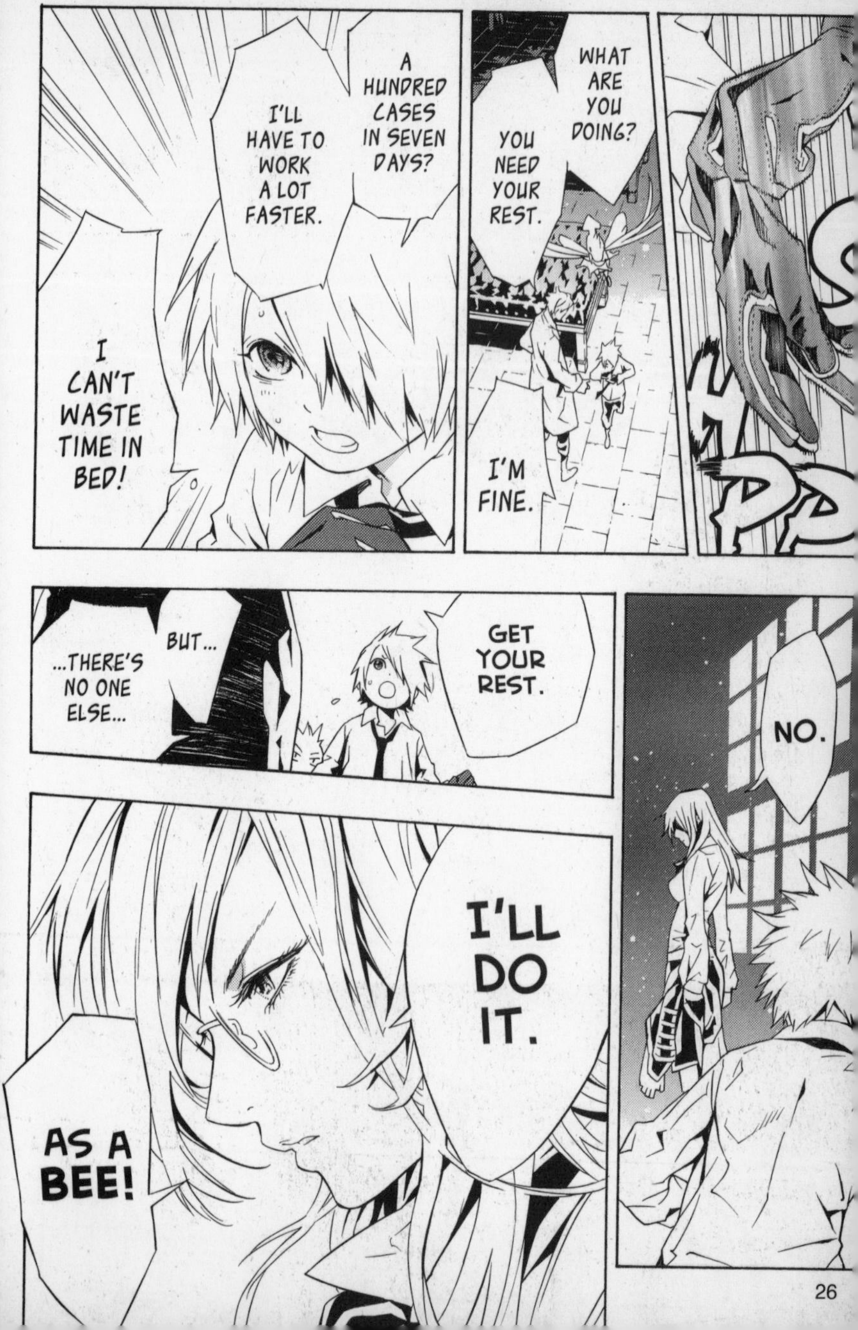
WHAT ARE YOU DOING?
YOU NEED YOUR REST.
I'M FINE.
A HUNDRED CASES IN SEVEN DAYS?
I'LL HAVE TO WORK A LOT FASTER.
I CAN'T WASTE TIME IN BED!
NO.
GET YOUR REST.
BUT...
...THERE'S NO ONE ELSE...
I'LL DO IT.
AS A BEE!

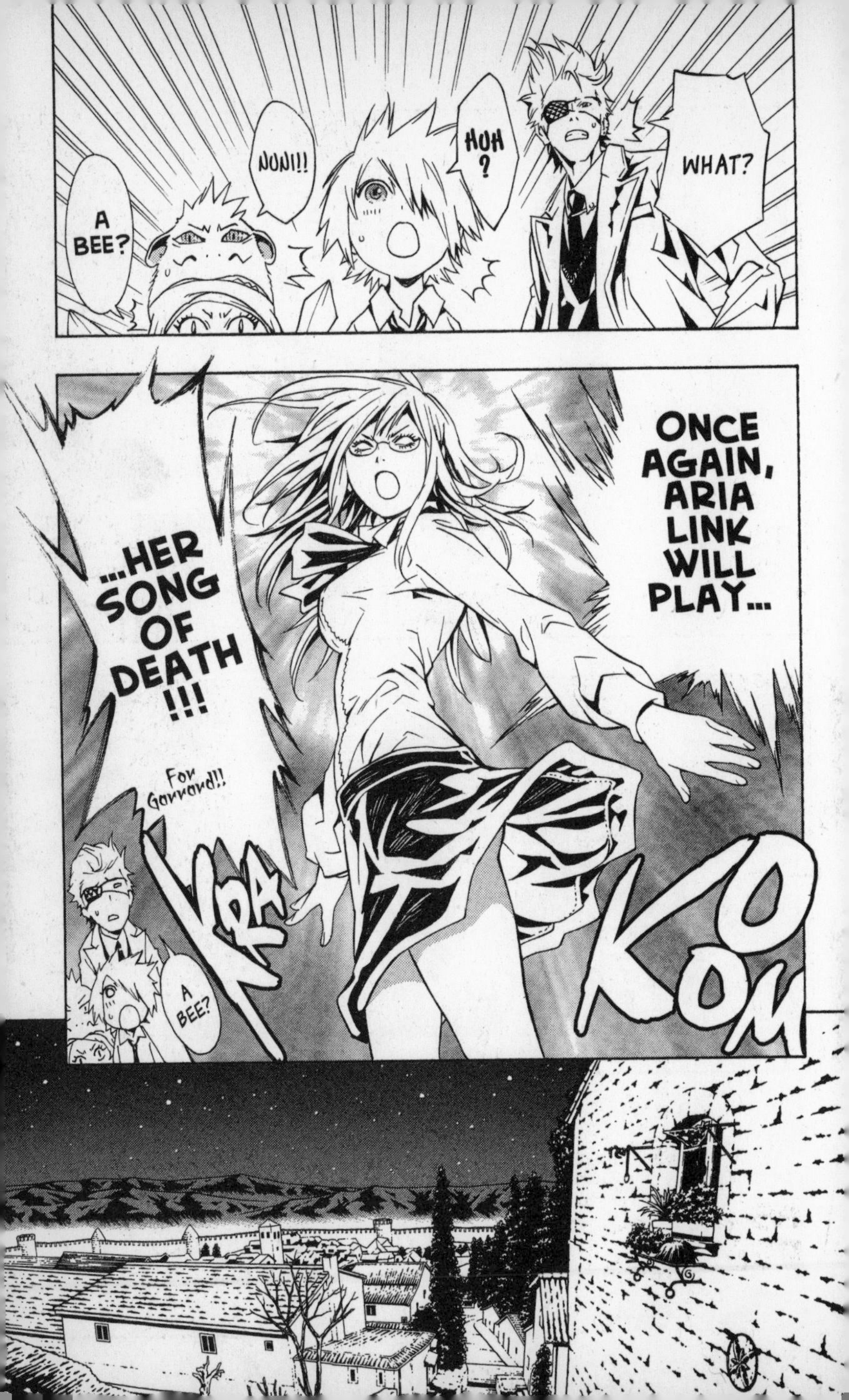
WHAT?
HUH ?
NUH!!!
A BEE?
ONCE AGAIN, ARIA LINK WILL PLAY...
...HER SONG OF DEATH !!!
For Garrard!!
A BEE?

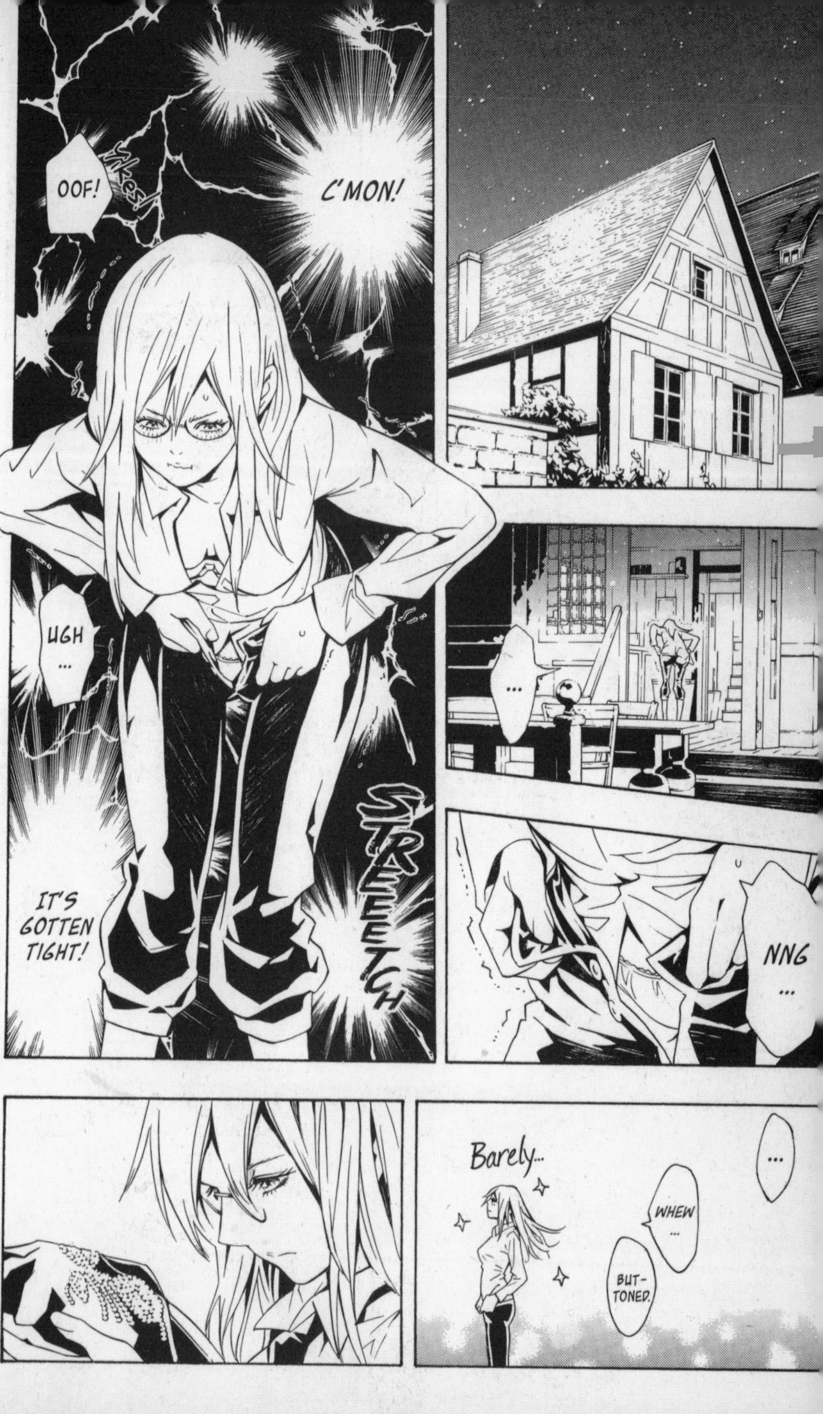
...
NNG ...
C'MON!
Yikes!
OOF!
UGH ...
STREEETCH
IT'S GOTTEN TIGHT!
...
WHEW ...
BUT-TONED.
Barely...

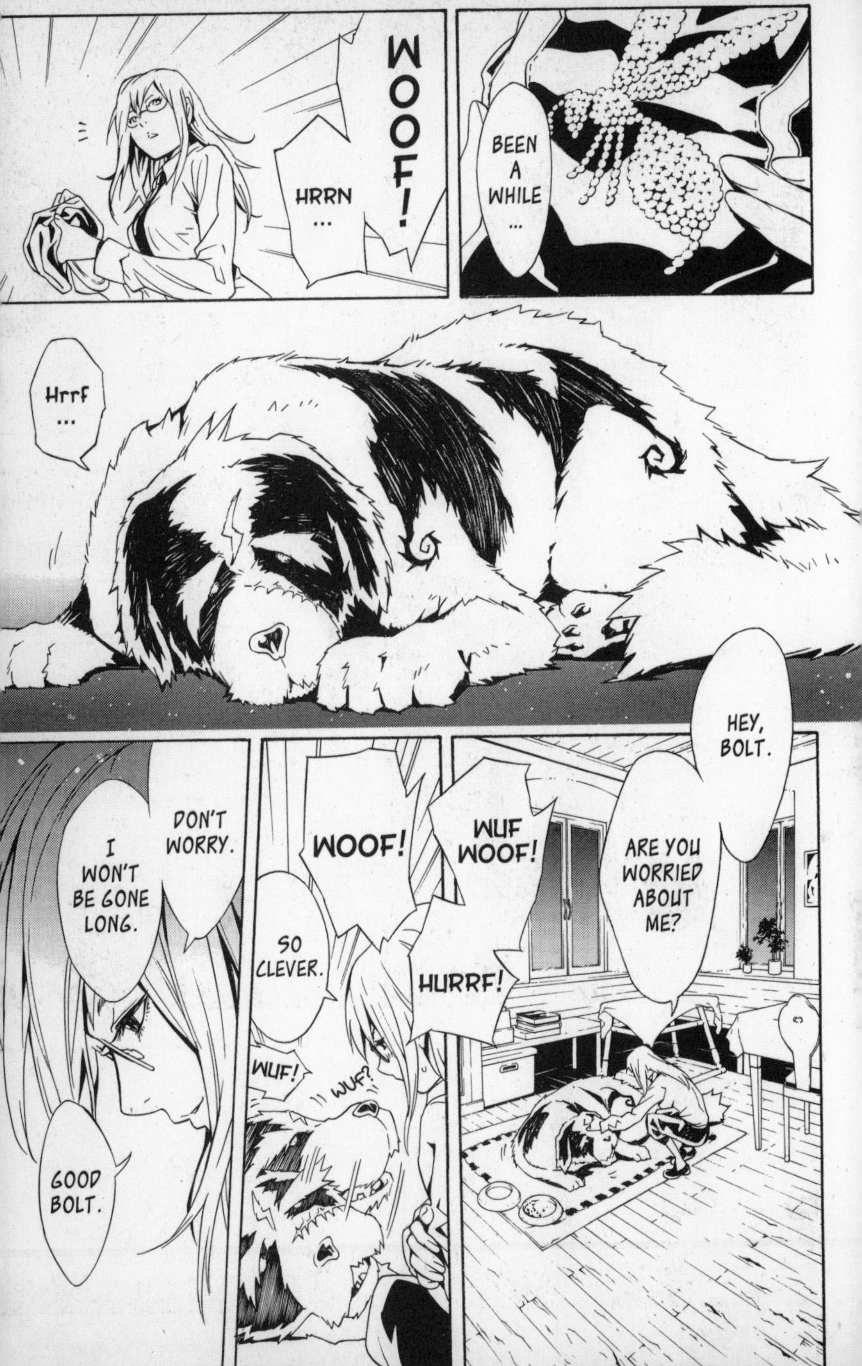
BEEN A WHILE ...
WOOF!
HRRN ...
Hrrf ...
HEY, BOLT.
ARE YOU WORRIED ABOUT ME?
WUF WOOF!
HURRF!
WOOF!
SO CLEVER.
WUF?
WUF!
DON'T WORRY.
I WON'T BE GONE LONG.
GOOD BOLT.

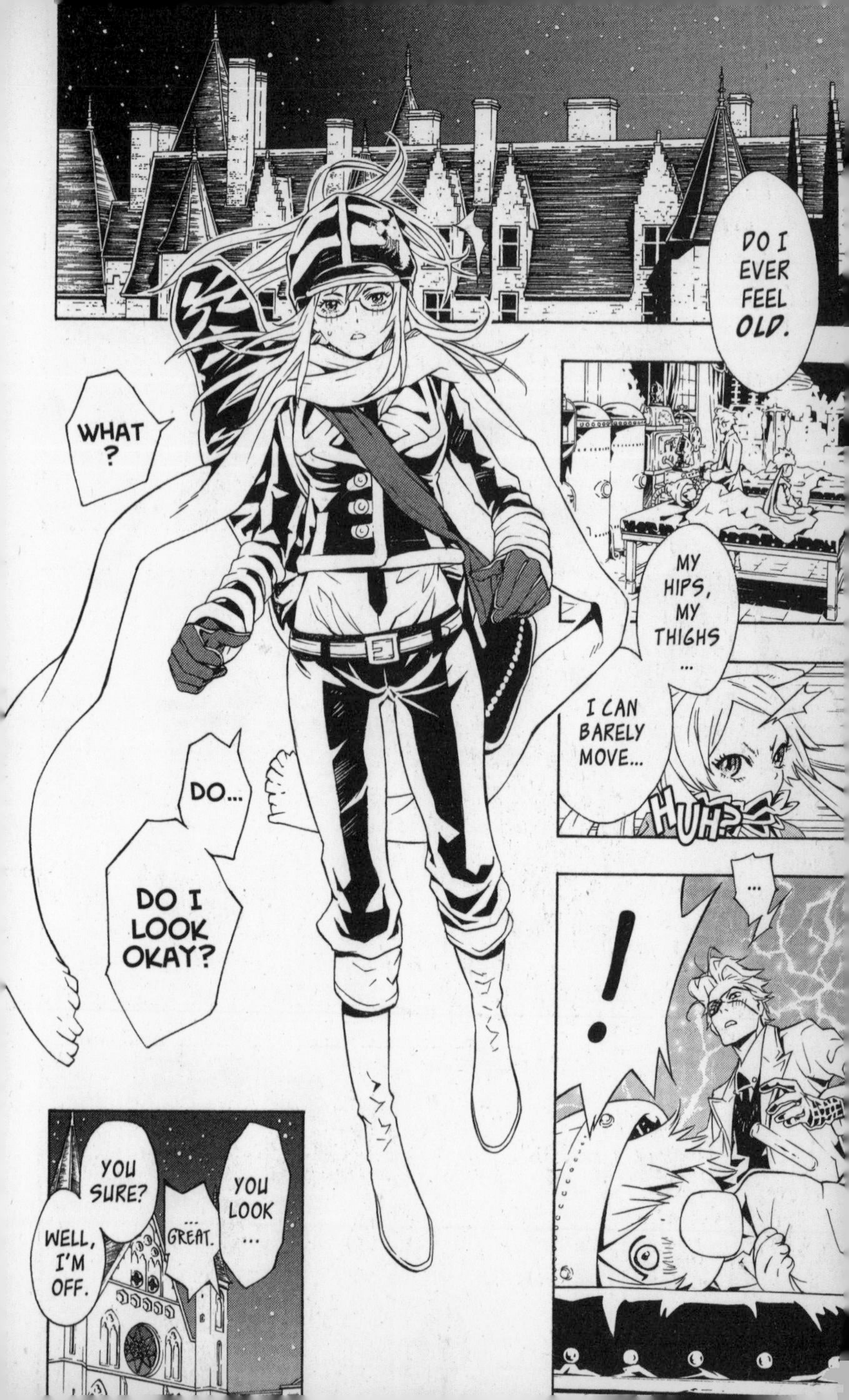
DO I EVER FEEL OLD.
MY HIPS, MY THIGHS...
I CAN BARELY MOVE...
HUH?
...
!
WHAT?
DO...
DO I LOOK OKAY?
YOU LOOK...
...GREAT.
YOU SURE?
WELL, I'M OFF.

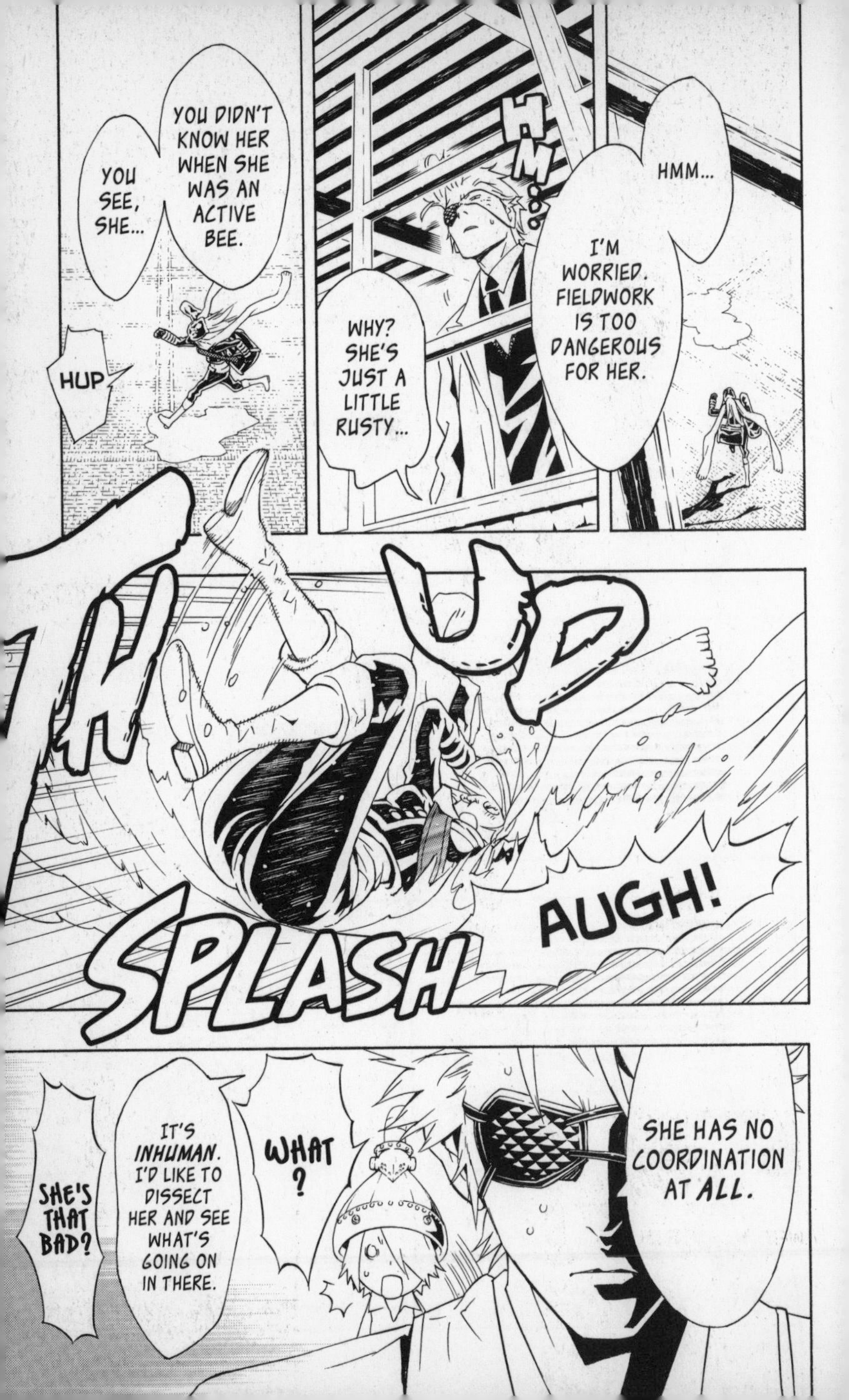
HM...
HMM...
I'M WORRIED. FIELDWORK IS TOO DANGEROUS FOR HER.
WHY? SHE'S JUST A LITTLE RUSTY...
YOU DIDN'T KNOW HER WHEN SHE WAS AN ACTIVE BEE.
YOU SEE, SHE...
HUP
THUD
AUGH!
SPLASH
SHE HAS NO COORDINATION AT *ALL*.
WHAT?
IT'S *INHUMAN*. I'D LIKE TO DISSECT HER AND SEE WHAT'S GOING ON IN THERE.
SHE'S THAT BAD?

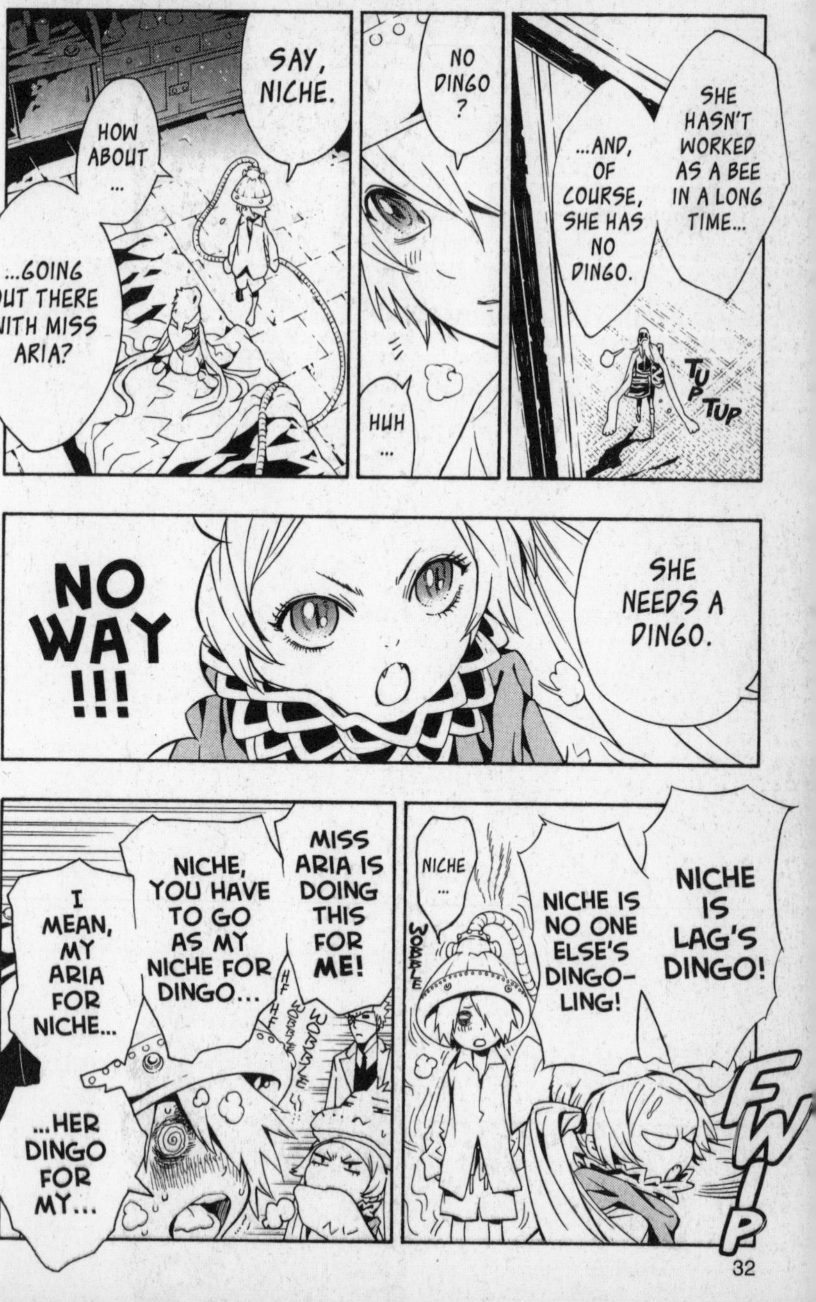
SHE HASN'T WORKED AS A BEE IN A LONG TIME...
...AND, OF COURSE, SHE HAS NO DINGO.
TUP TUP
NO DINGO ?
HUH ...
SAY, NICHE.
HOW ABOUT ...
...GOING OUT THERE WITH MISS ARIA?
SHE NEEDS A DINGO.
NO WAY !!!
NICHE IS LAG'S DINGO!
NICHE IS NO ONE ELSE'S DINGO-LING!
NICHE ...
WOBBLE
FWIP
MISS ARIA IS DOING THIS FOR ME!
NICHE, YOU HAVE TO GO AS MY NICHE FOR DINGO...
I MEAN, MY ARIA FOR NICHE...
HF HF
WOBBLE
...HER DINGO FOR MY...

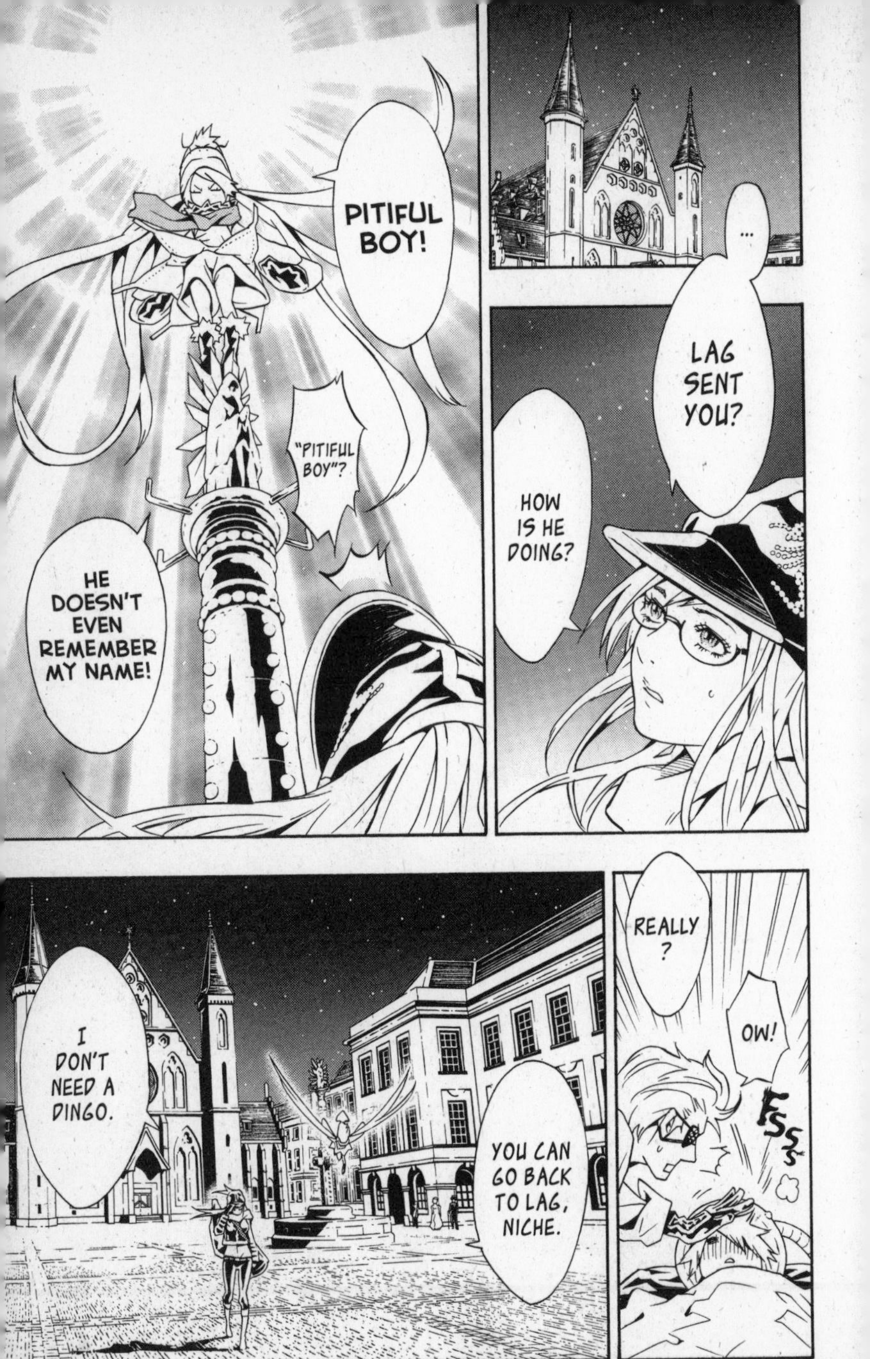
...
LAG SENT YOU?
HOW IS HE DOING?
PITIFUL BOY!
"PITIFUL BOY"?
HE DOESN'T EVEN REMEMBER MY NAME!
REALLY?
OW!
FSSS
I DON'T NEED A DINGO.
YOU CAN GO BACK TO LAG, NICHE.

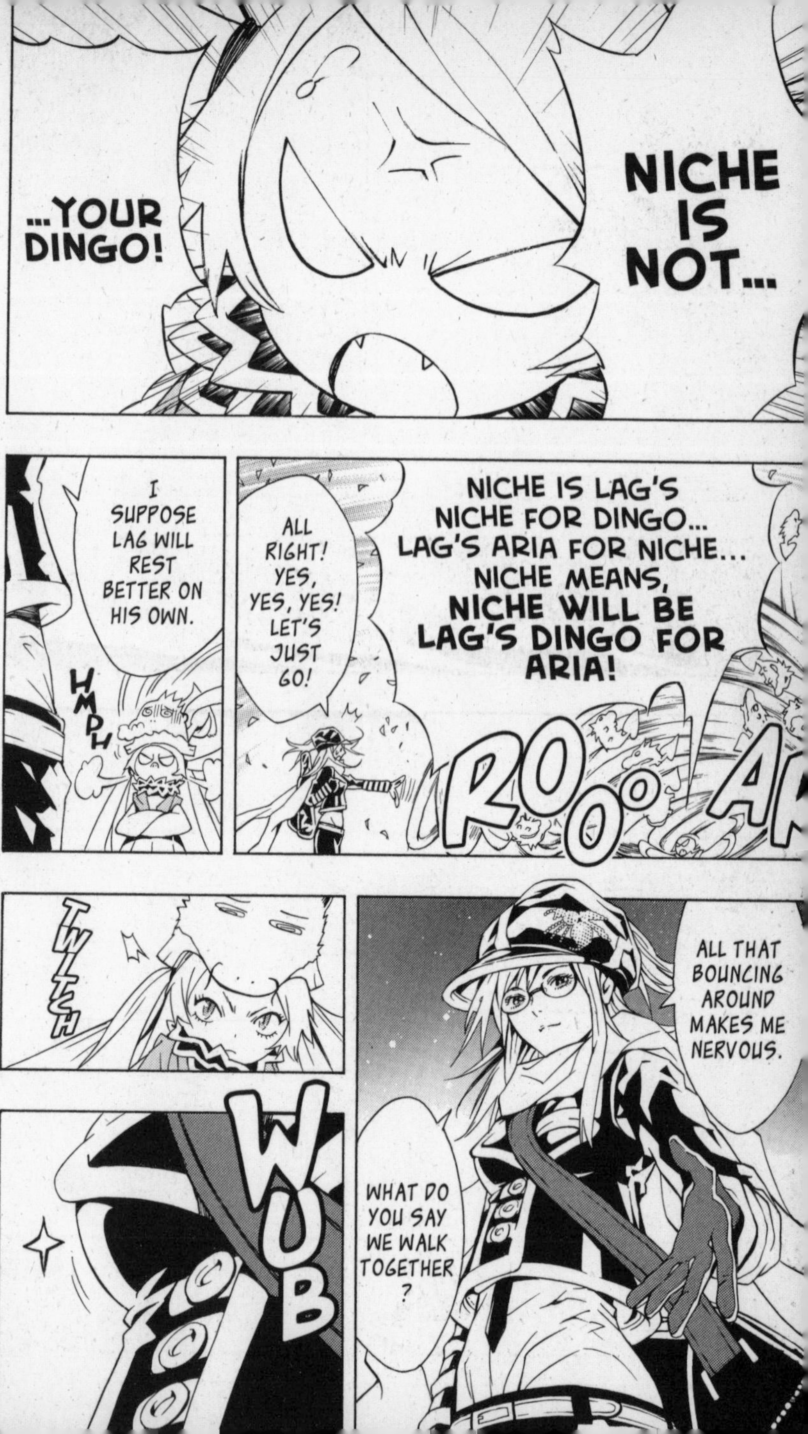
NICHE IS NOT...
...YOUR DINGO!
NICHE IS LAG'S NICHE FOR DINGO... LAG'S ARIA FOR NICHE... NICHE MEANS, NICHE WILL BE LAG'S DINGO FOR ARIA!
ROOOA
ALL RIGHT! YES, YES, YES! LET'S JUST GO!
I SUPPOSE LAG WILL REST BETTER ON HIS OWN.
HMPH
ALL THAT BOUNCING AROUND MAKES ME NERVOUS.
WHAT DO YOU SAY WE WALK TOGETHER?
TWITCH
WUB

OH DEAR ...

PWEEEEN

HMPH!

UH ... NICHE?

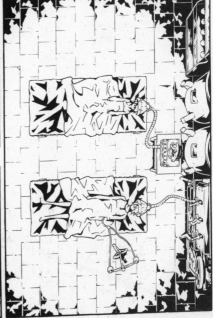

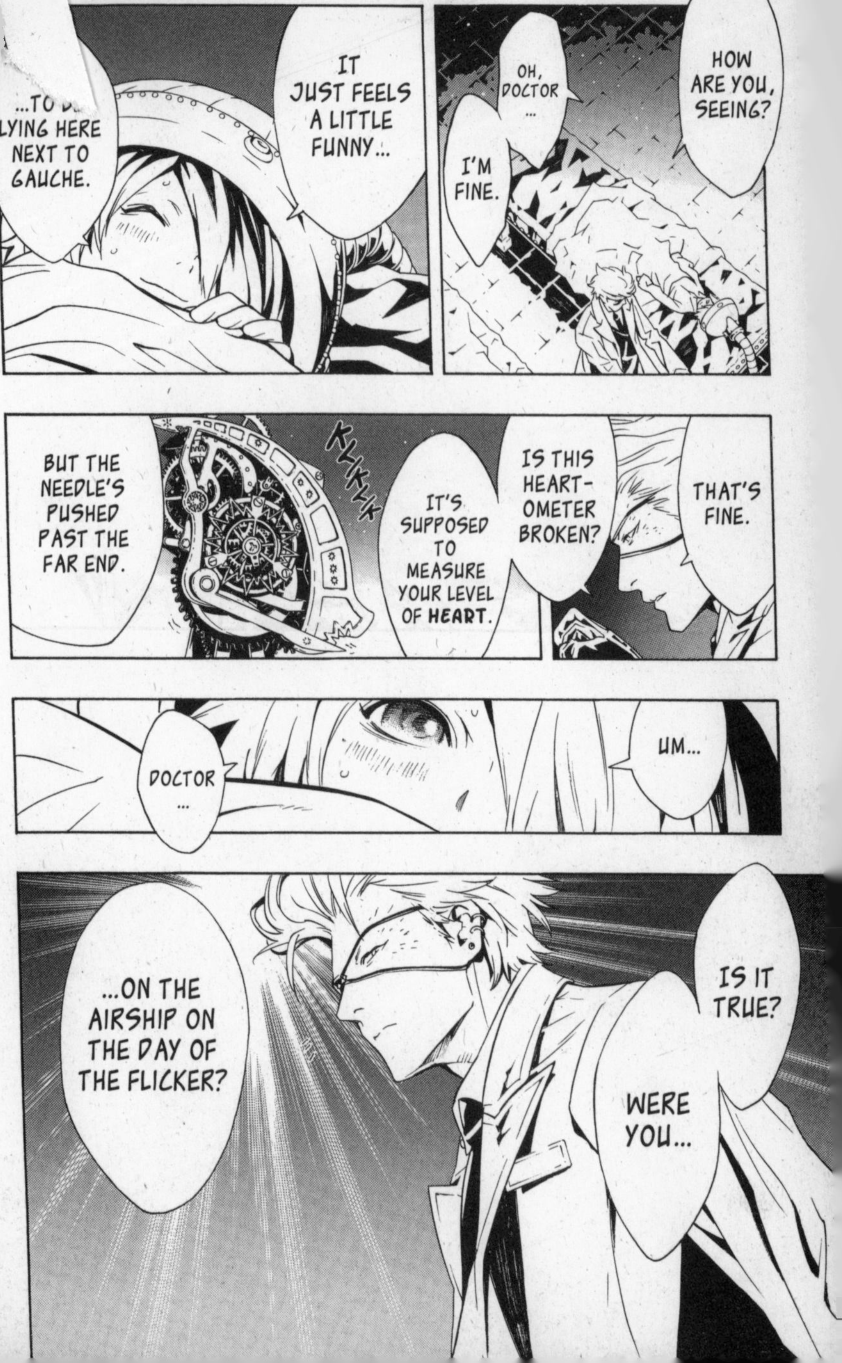
HOW ARE YOU, SEEING?
OH, DOCTOR...
I'M FINE.
IT JUST FEELS A LITTLE FUNNY...
...TO B
LYING HERE NEXT TO GAUCHE.
THAT'S FINE.
IS THIS HEART-OMETER BROKEN?
IT'S SUPPOSED TO MEASURE YOUR LEVEL OF **HEART**.
BUT THE NEEDLE'S PUSHED PAST THE FAR END.
UM...
DOCTOR...
IS IT TRUE?
WERE YOU...
...ON THE AIRSHIP ON THE DAY OF THE FLICKER?

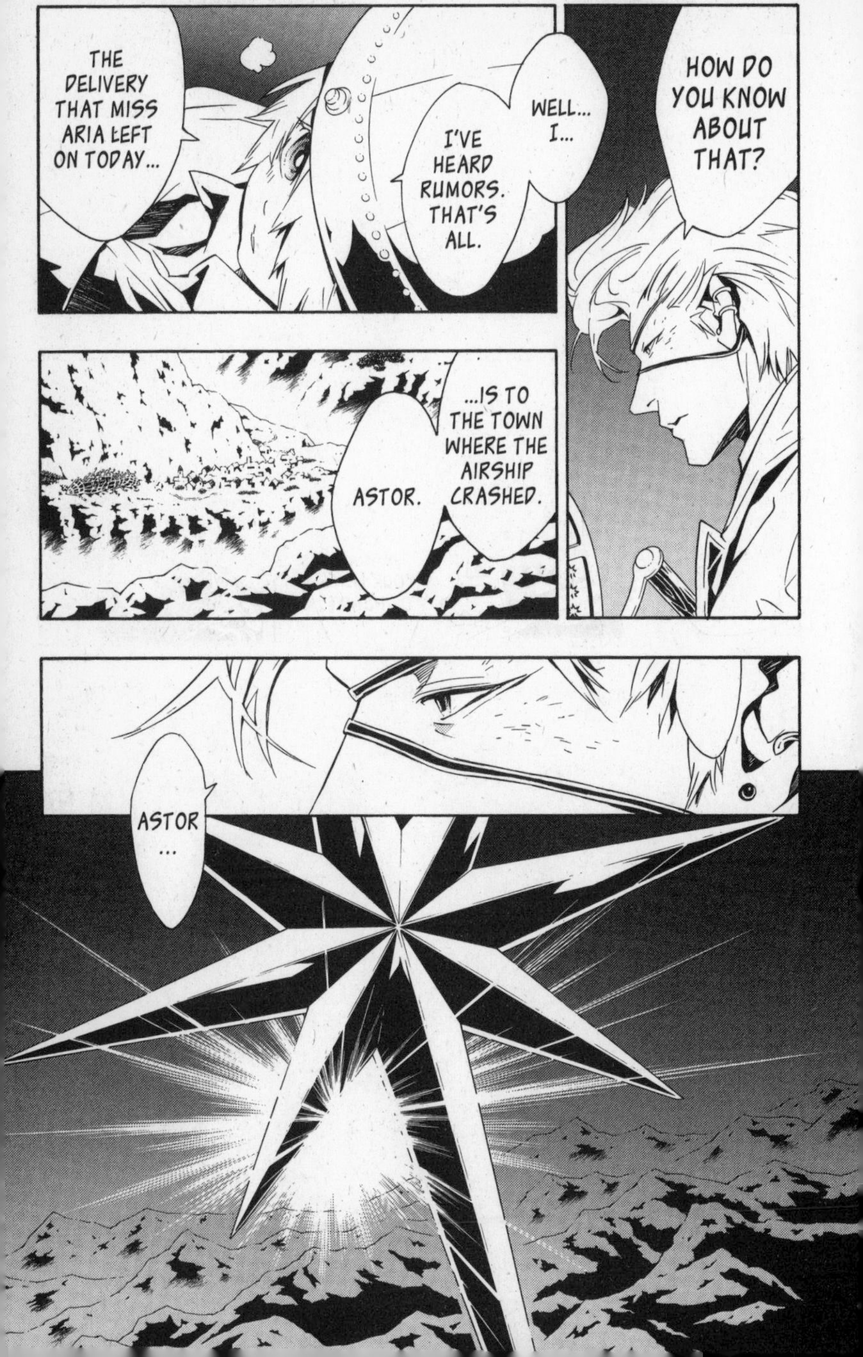
HOW DO YOU KNOW ABOUT THAT?
WELL... I...
I'VE HEARD RUMORS. THAT'S ALL.
THE DELIVERY THAT MISS ARIA LEFT ON TODAY...
...IS TO THE TOWN WHERE THE AIRSHIP CRASHED.
ASTOR.
ASTOR ...

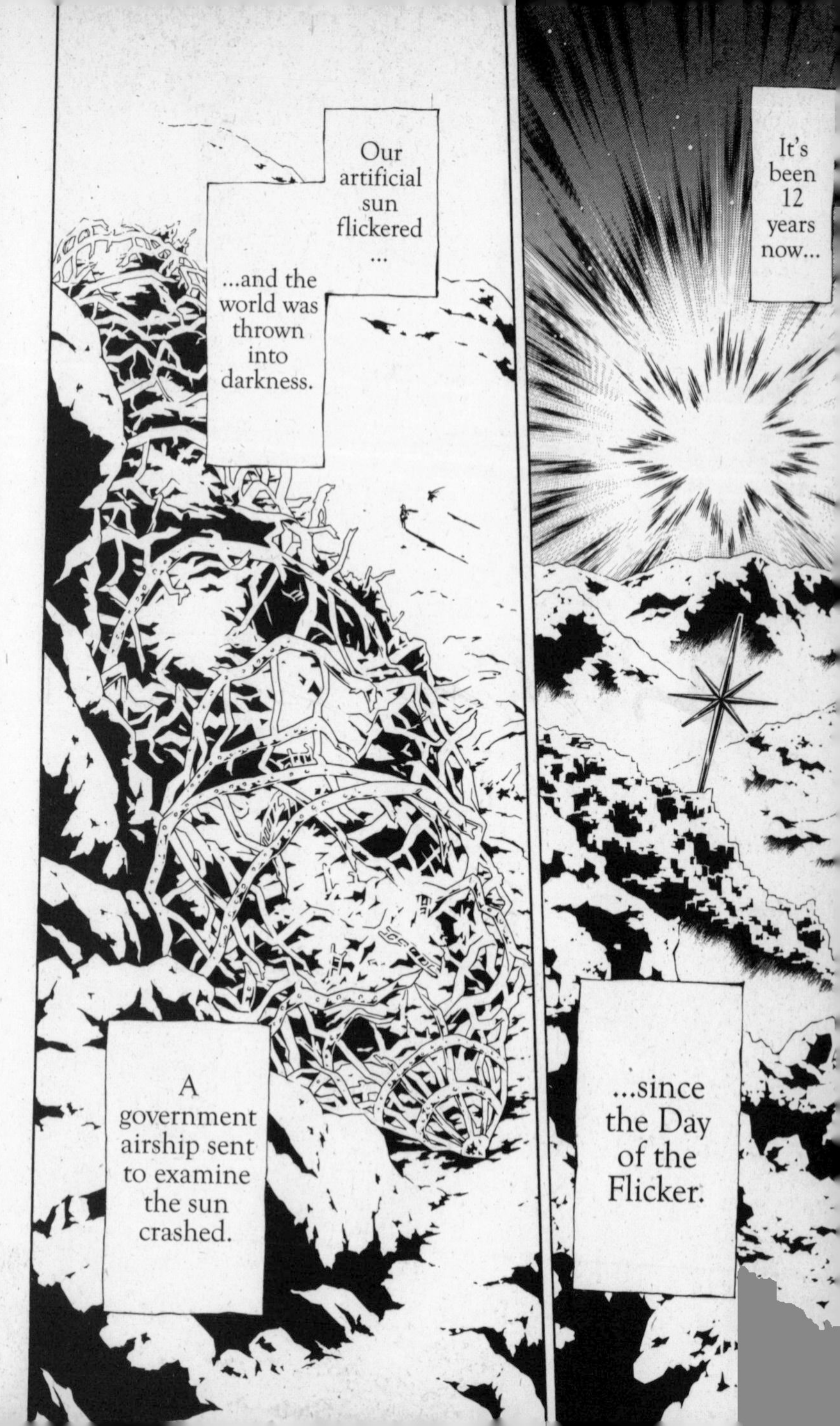
It's been 12 years now...
...since the Day of the Flicker.
Our artificial sun flickered...
...and the world was thrown into darkness.
A government airship sent to examine the sun crashed.

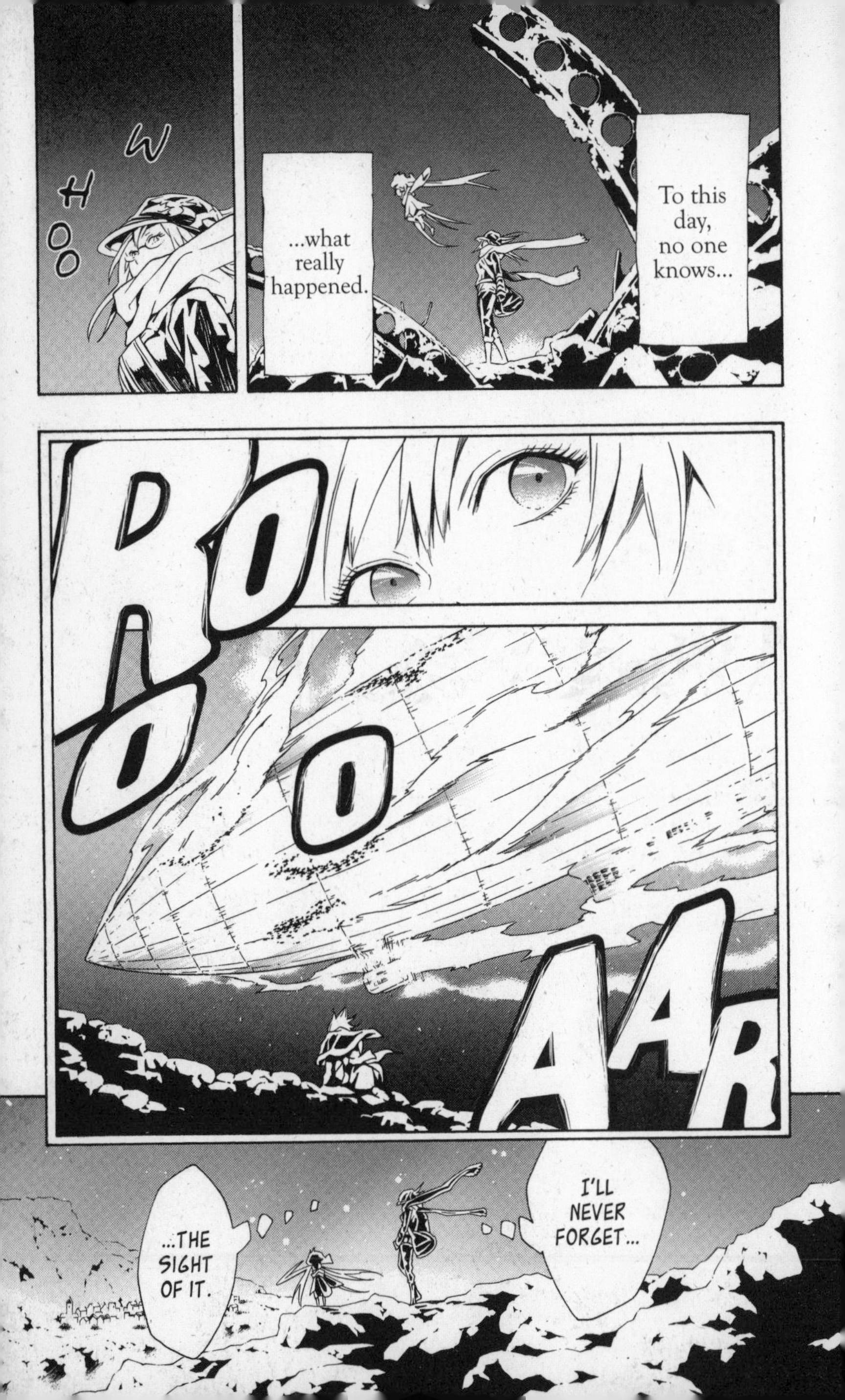
To this day, no one knows...
...what really happened.
WHOO
ROOOAAR
I'LL NEVER FORGET...
...THE SIGHT OF IT.

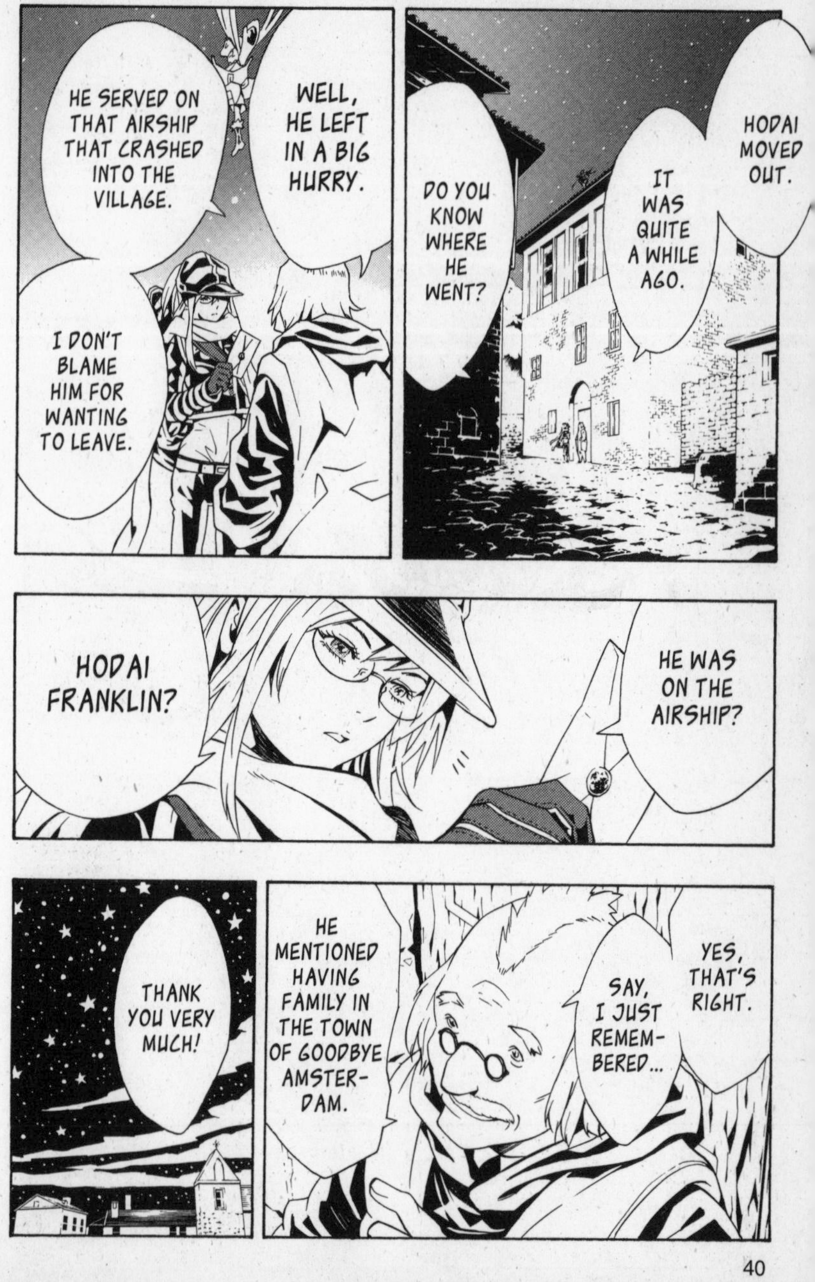
HODAI MOVED OUT.
IT WAS QUITE A WHILE AGO.
DO YOU KNOW WHERE HE WENT?
WELL, HE LEFT IN A BIG HURRY.
HE SERVED ON THAT AIRSHIP THAT CRASHED INTO THE VILLAGE.
I DON'T BLAME HIM FOR WANTING TO LEAVE.
HE WAS ON THE AIRSHIP?
HODAI FRANKLIN?
YES, THAT'S RIGHT.
SAY, I JUST REMEM-BERED...
HE MENTIONED HAVING FAMILY IN THE TOWN OF GOODBYE AMSTER-DAM.
THANK YOU VERY MUCH!

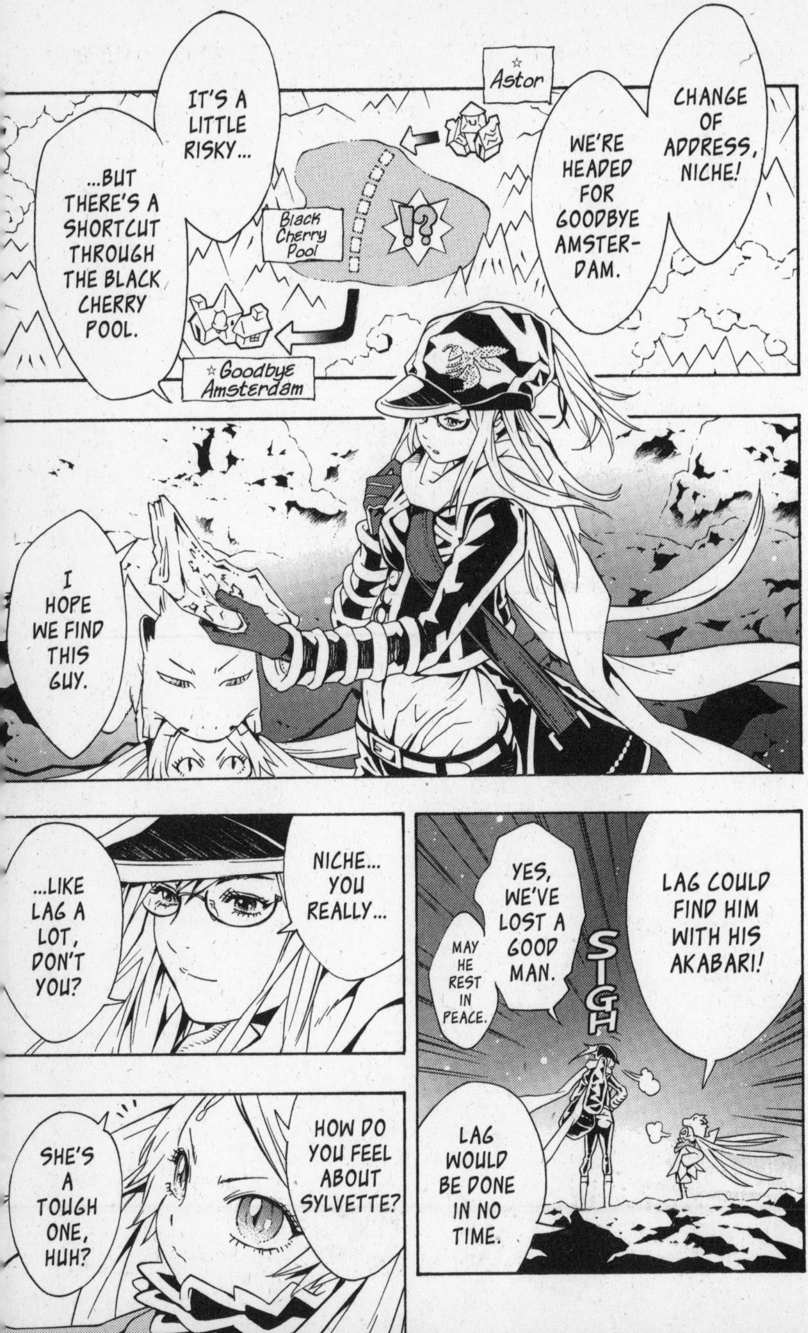
CHANGE OF ADDRESS, NICHE!
WE'RE HEADED FOR GOODBYE AMSTER-DAM.
Astor
!?
Black Cherry Pool
Goodbye Amsterdam
IT'S A LITTLE RISKY...
...BUT THERE'S A SHORTCUT THROUGH THE BLACK CHERRY POOL.
I HOPE WE FIND THIS GUY.
LAG COULD FIND HIM WITH HIS AKABARI!
SIGH
YES, WE'VE LOST A GOOD MAN.
MAY HE REST IN PEACE.
LAG WOULD BE DONE IN NO TIME.
NICHE... YOU REALLY...
...LIKE LAG A LOT, DON'T YOU?
HOW DO YOU FEEL ABOUT SYLVETTE?
SHE'S A TOUGH ONE, HUH?

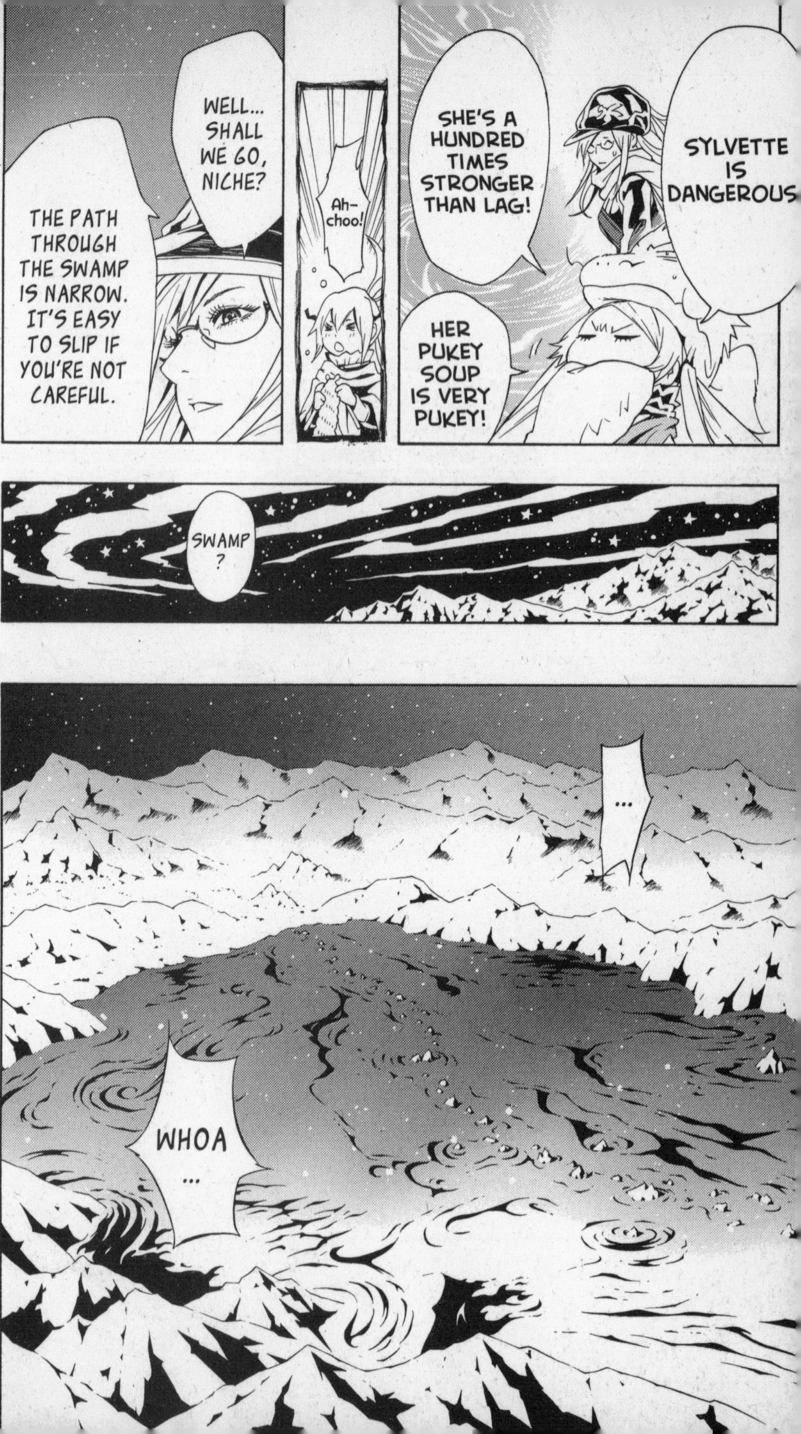
SYLVETTE IS DANGEROUS
SHE'S A HUNDRED TIMES STRONGER THAN LAG!
HER PUKEY SOUP IS VERY PUKEY!
Ah-choo!
WELL... SHALL WE GO, NICHE?
THE PATH THROUGH THE SWAMP IS NARROW. IT'S EASY TO SLIP IF YOU'RE NOT CAREFUL.
SWAMP ?
...
WHOA ...

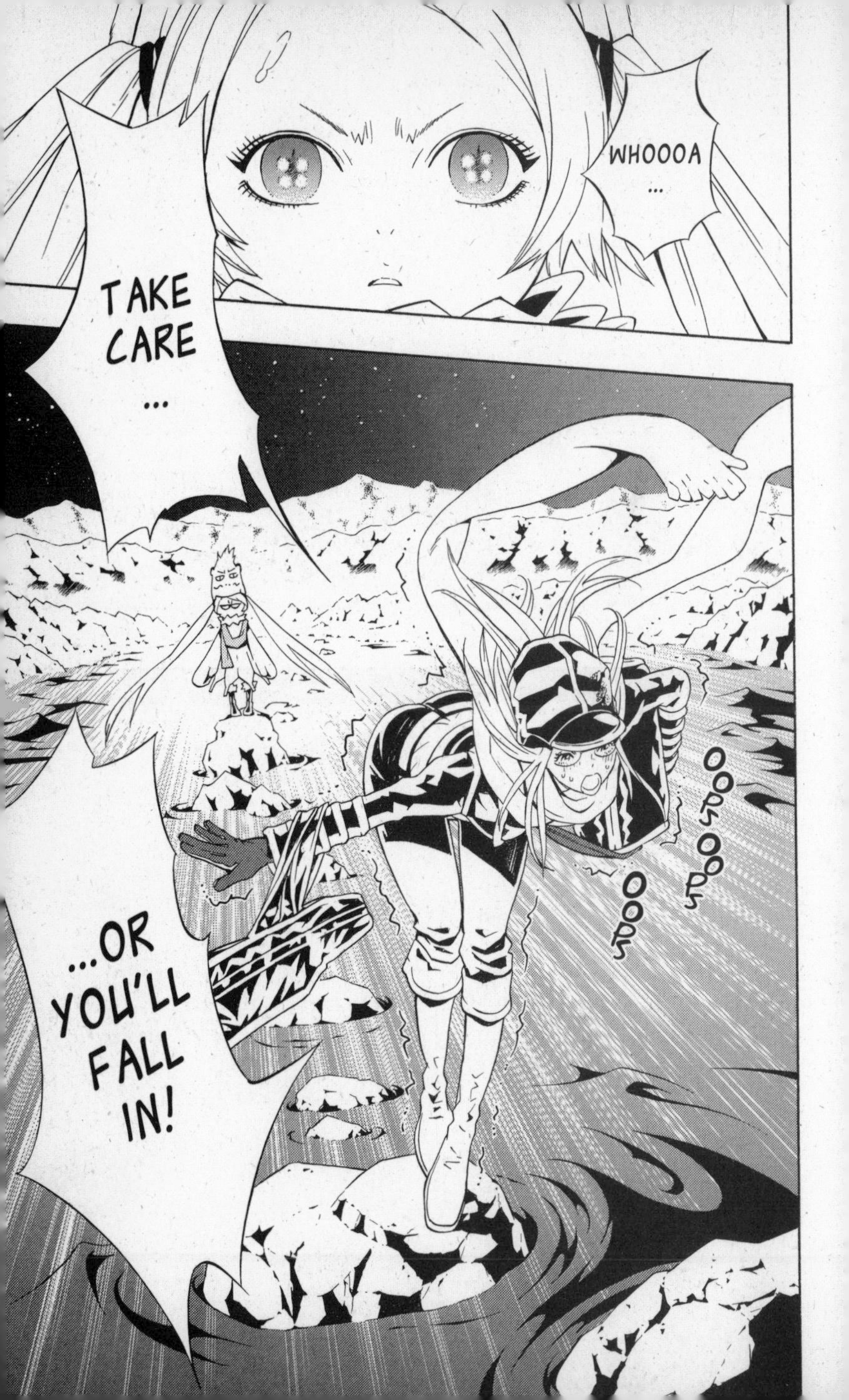
WHOOOA ...
TAKE CARE ...
OOPS OOPS
OOPS
...OR YOU'LL FALL IN!

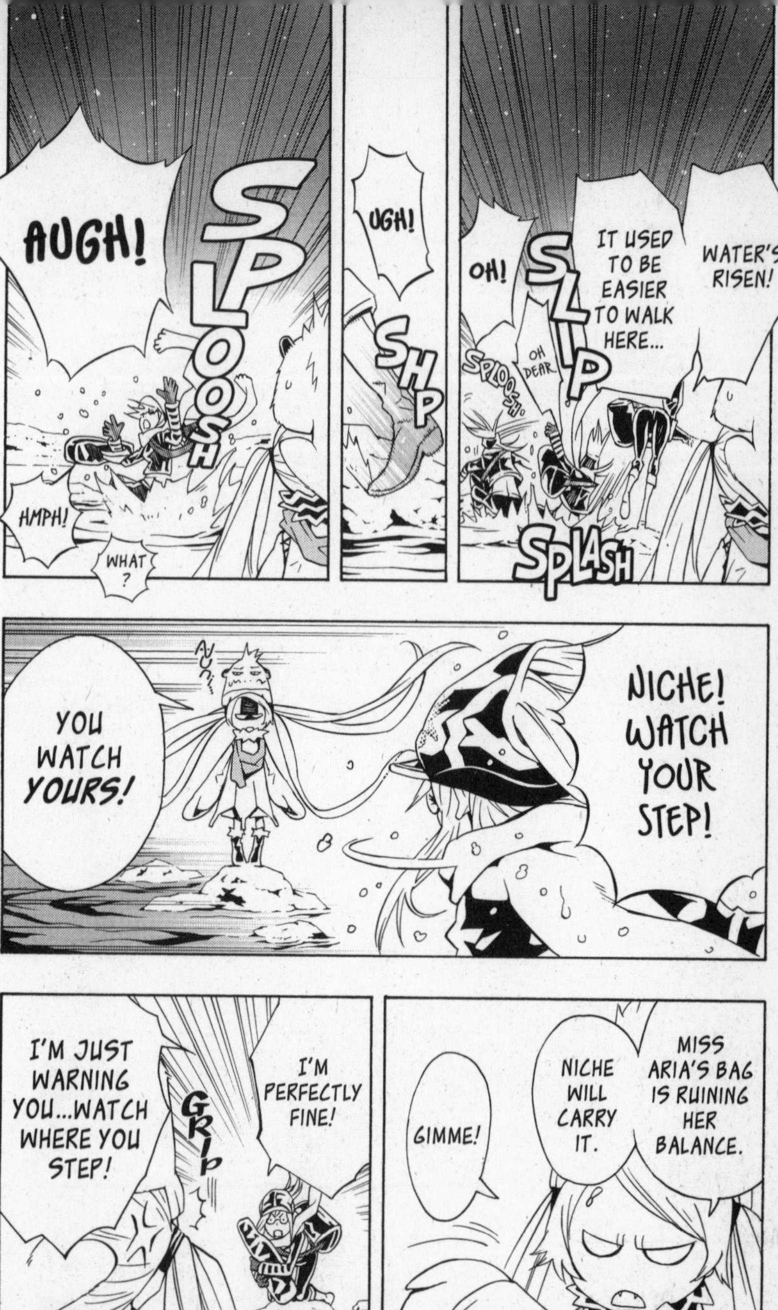
WATER'S RISEN!
IT USED TO BE EASIER TO WALK HERE...
SLIP
OH!
OH DEAR.
SPLOOSH
SPLASH
UGH!
SHP
SPLOOSH
AUGH!
HMPH!
WHAT?
NICHE! WATCH YOUR STEP!
YOU WATCH YOURS!
MISS ARIA'S BAG IS RUINING HER BALANCE.
NICHE WILL CARRY IT.
GIMME!
I'M PERFECTLY FINE!
GRIP
I'M JUST WARNING YOU...WATCH WHERE YOU STEP!

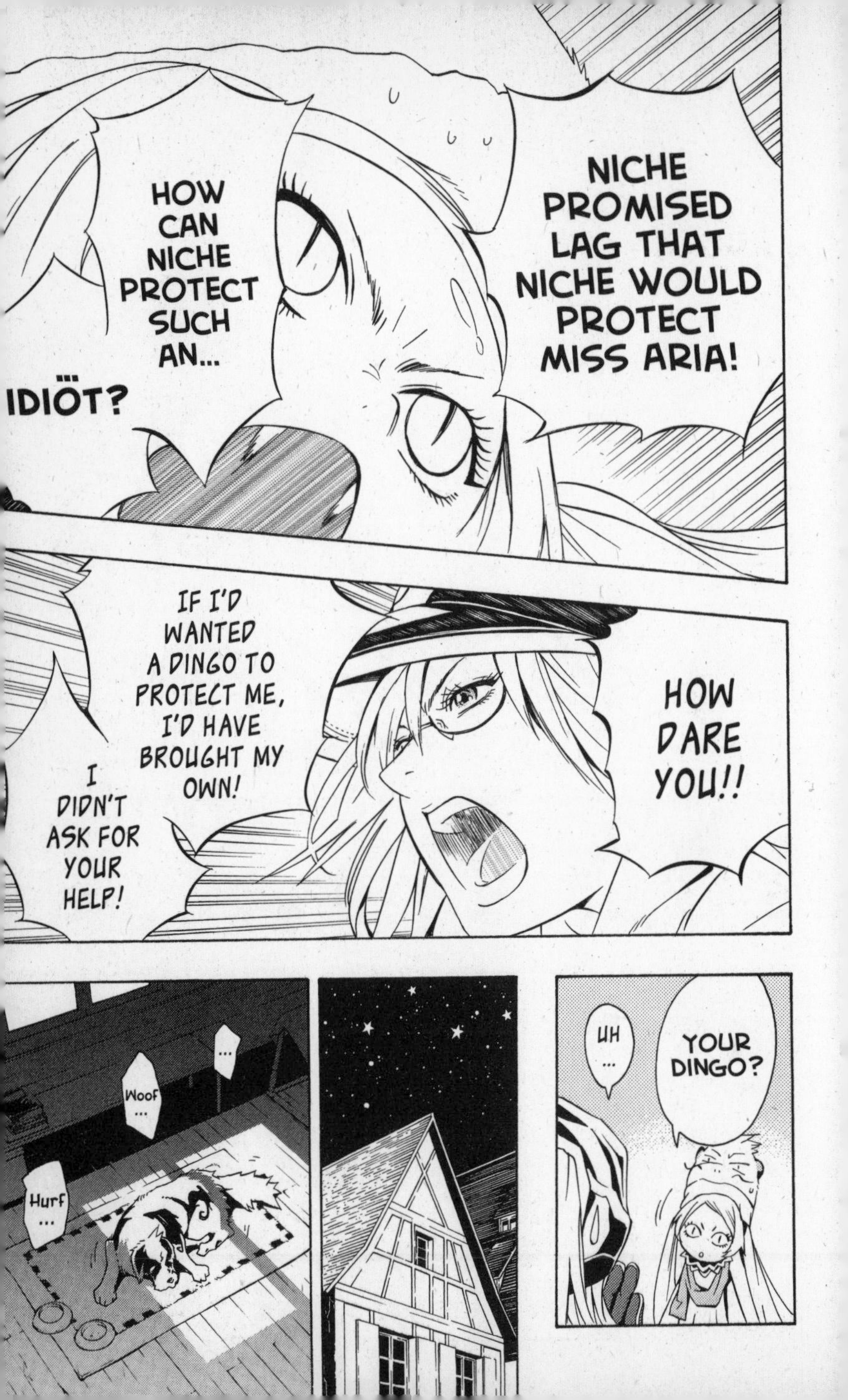
NICHE PROMISED LAG THAT NICHE WOULD PROTECT MISS ARIA!
HOW CAN NICHE PROTECT SUCH AN...
...
IDIÖT?
HOW DARE YOU!!
IF I'D WANTED A DINGO TO PROTECT ME, I'D HAVE BROUGHT MY OWN!
I DIDN'T ASK FOR YOUR HELP!
YOUR DINGO?
UH ...
...
Woof ...
Hurf ...

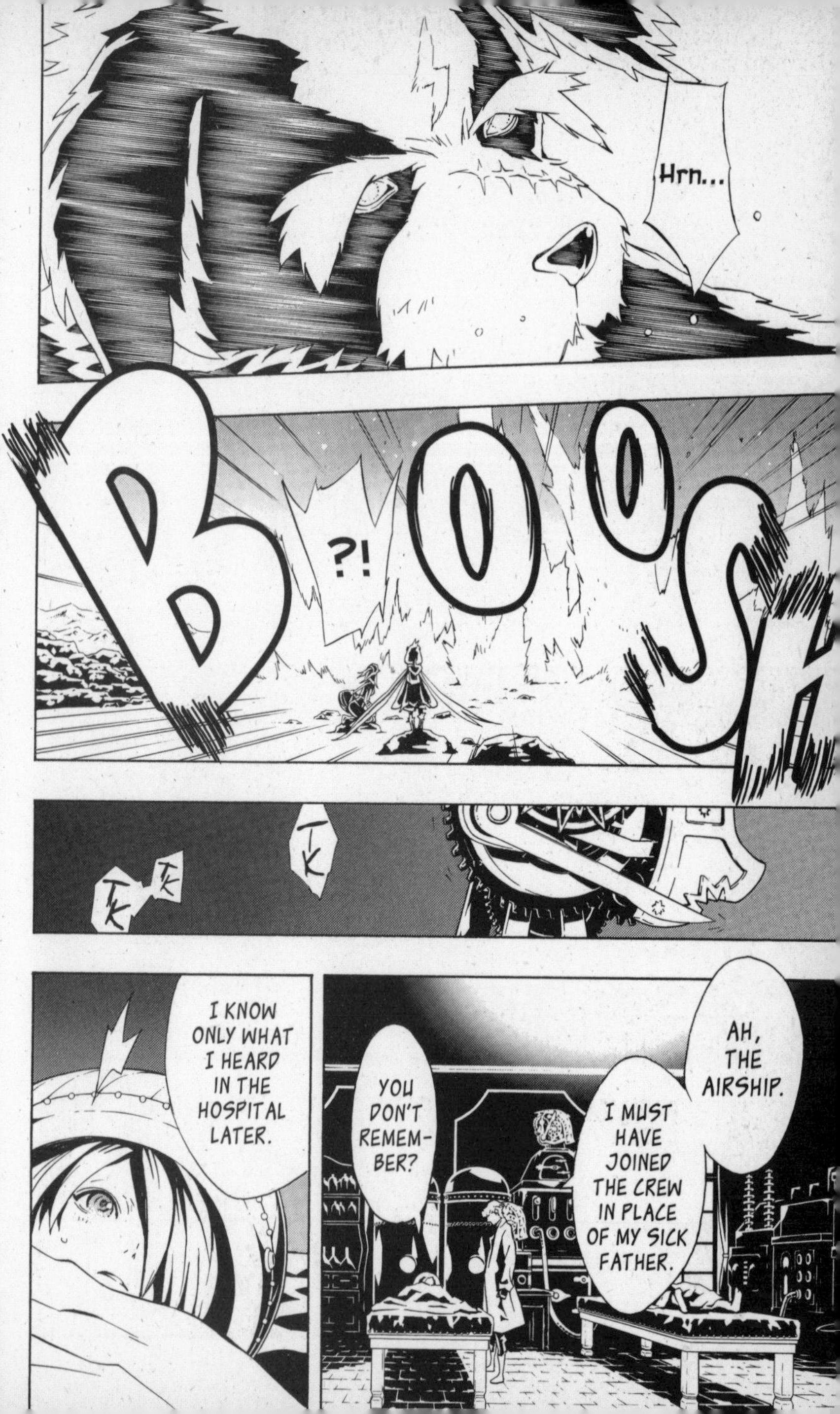
Hrn...
BOOOSH
?!
TK
TK
TK
AH, THE AIRSHIP.
I MUST HAVE JOINED THE CREW IN PLACE OF MY SICK FATHER.
YOU DON'T REMEM-BER?
I KNOW ONLY WHAT I HEARD IN THE HOSPITAL LATER.

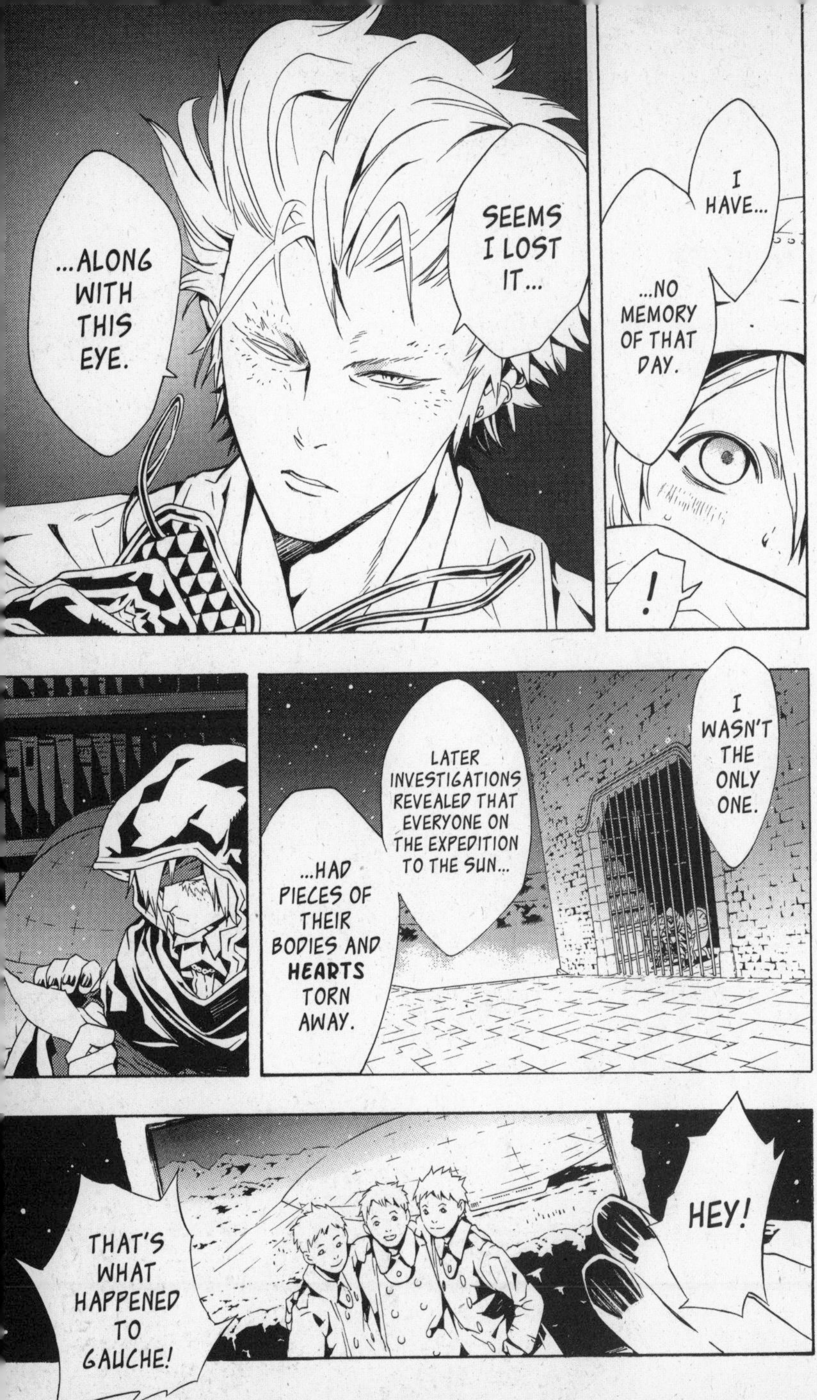
I HAVE...
...NO MEMORY OF THAT DAY.
!
SEEMS I LOST IT...
...ALONG WITH THIS EYE.
I WASN'T THE ONLY ONE.
LATER INVESTIGATIONS REVEALED THAT EVERYONE ON THE EXPEDITION TO THE SUN...
...HAD PIECES OF THEIR BODIES AND **HEARTS** TORN AWAY.
HEY!
THAT'S WHAT HAPPENED TO GAUCHE!

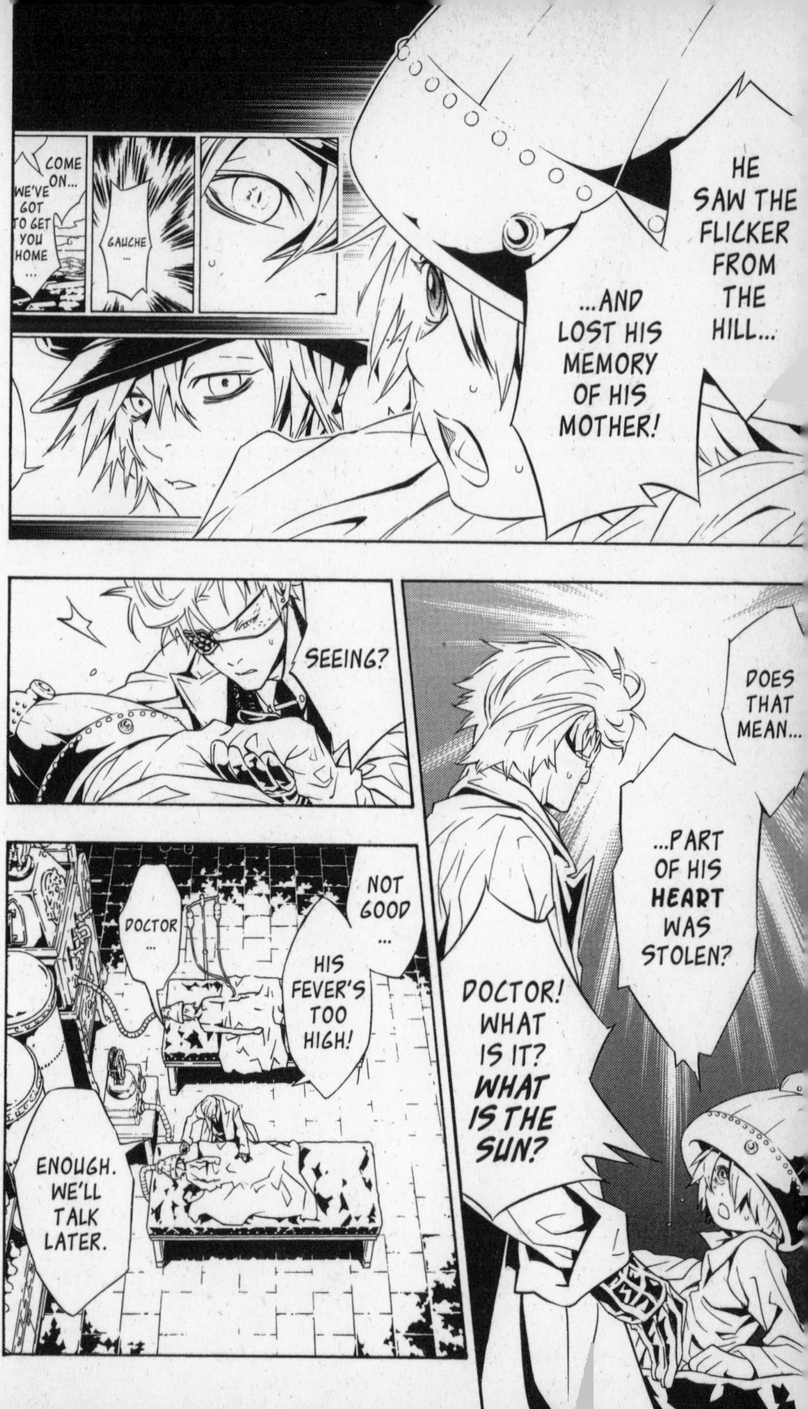
HE SAW THE FLICKER FROM THE HILL...
...AND LOST HIS MEMORY OF HIS MOTHER!
GAUCHE...
COME ON... WE'VE GOT TO GET YOU HOME...
DOES THAT MEAN...
...PART OF HIS **HEART** WAS STOLEN?
DOCTOR! WHAT IS IT? *WHAT IS THE SUN?*
SEEING?
NOT GOOD...
HIS FEVER'S TOO HIGH!
DOCTOR...
ENOUGH. WE'LL TALK LATER.

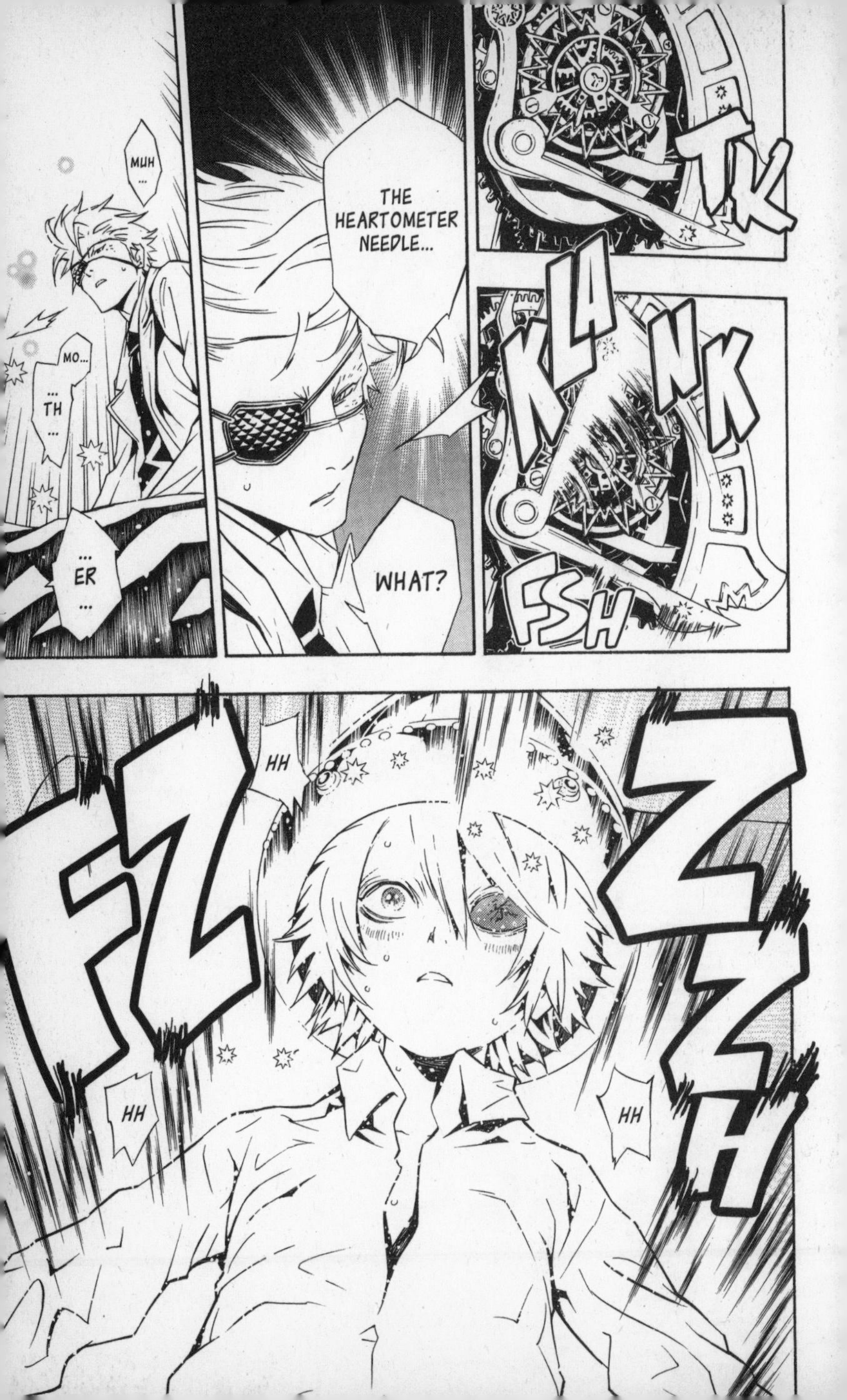

TK
KLANK
FSH
THE HEARTOMETER NEEDLE...
WHAT?
MUH...
MO...
...TH...
...ER...
FZZZZH
HH
HH
HH

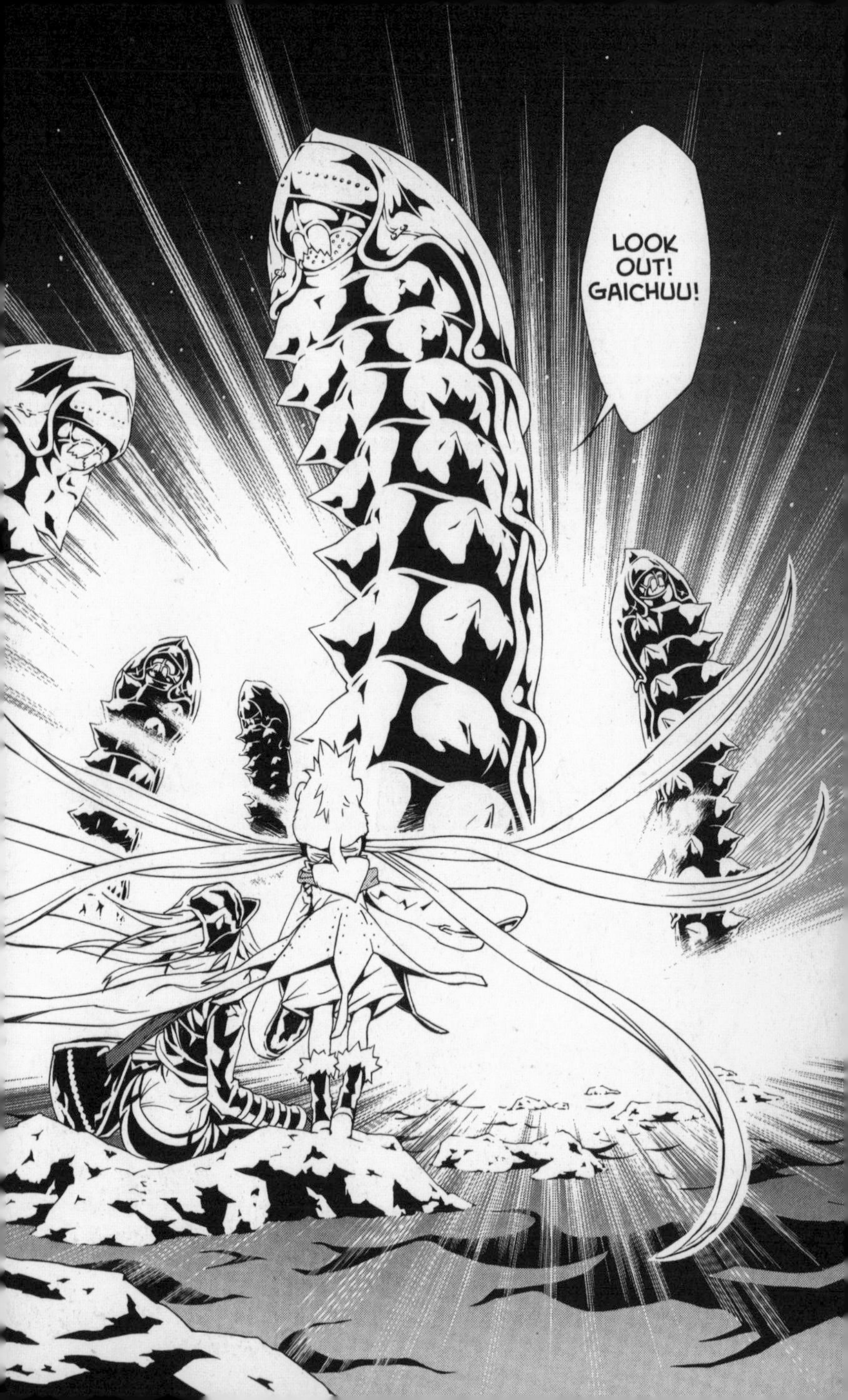
LOOK OUT! GAICHUU!

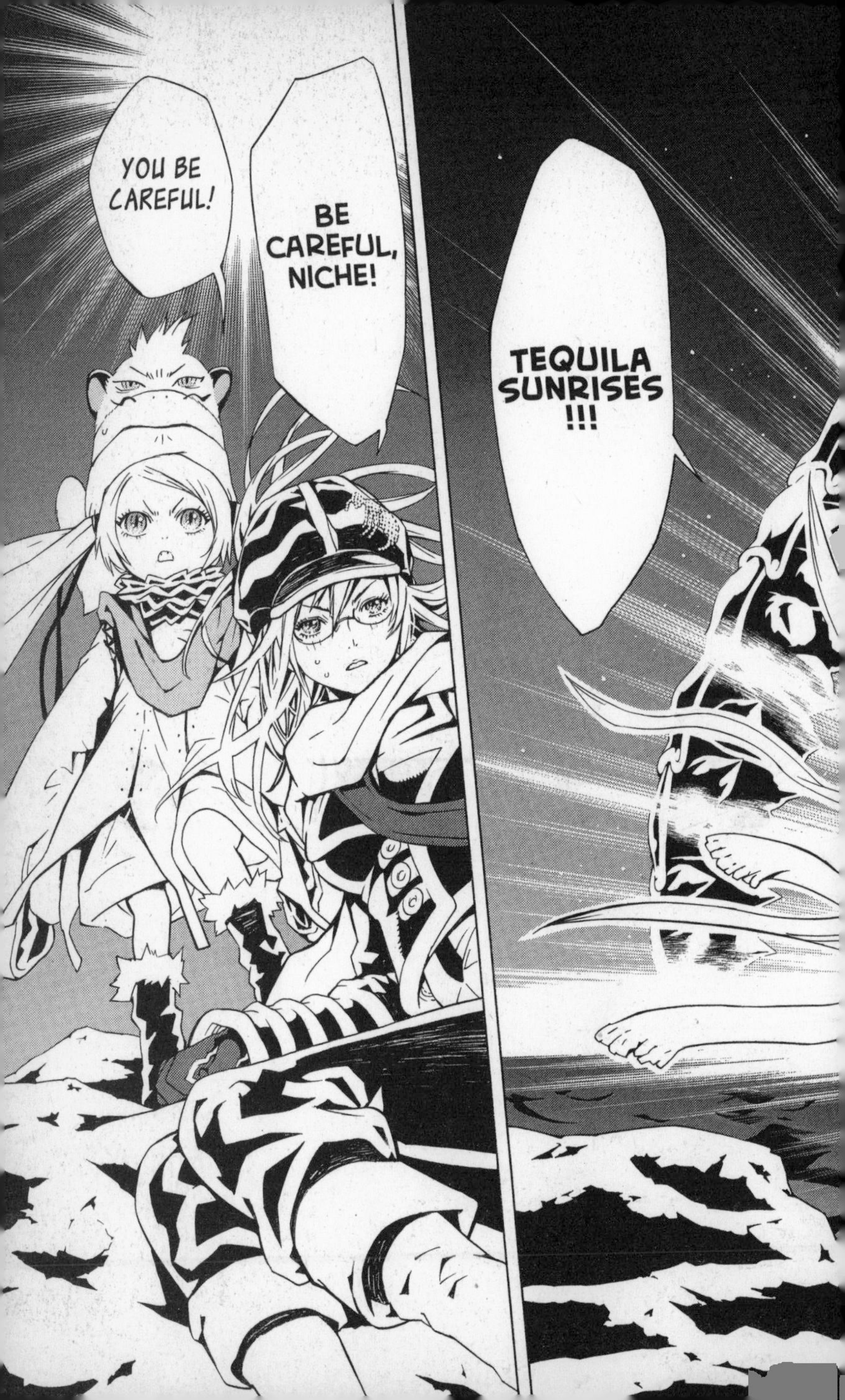
TEQUILA SUNRISES !!!
BE CAREFUL, NICHE!
YOU BE CAREFUL!

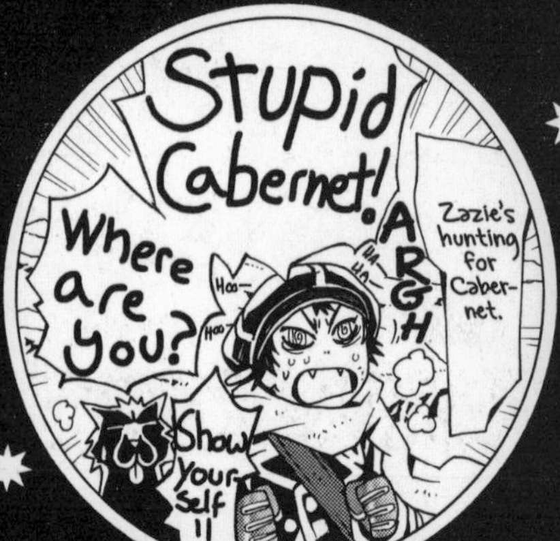
Zazie's hunting for Cabernet.
Stupid Cabernet!
ARGH
Where are you?
Show yourself!!

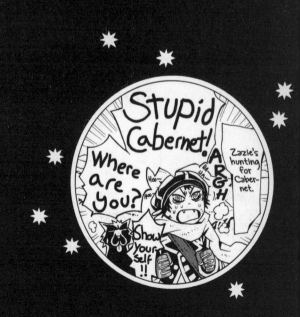

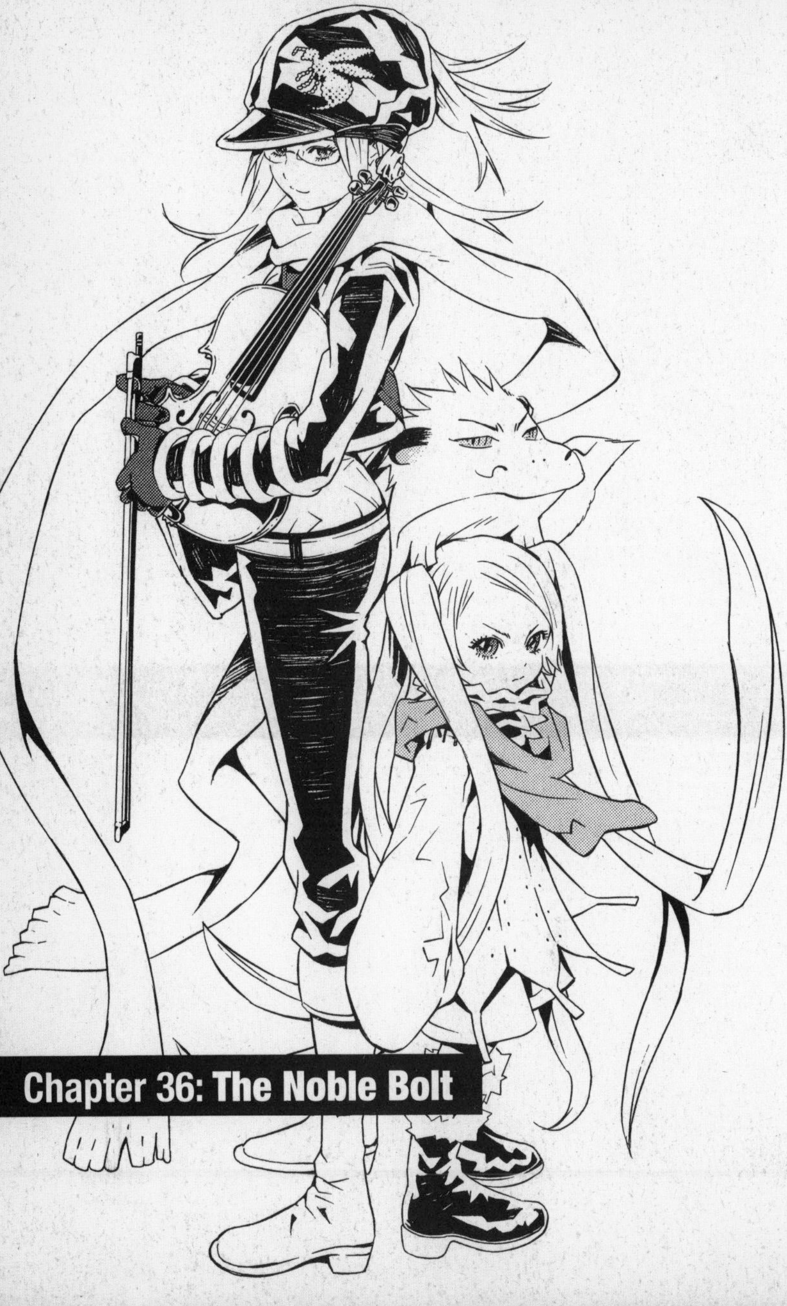

Chapter 36: The Noble Bolt

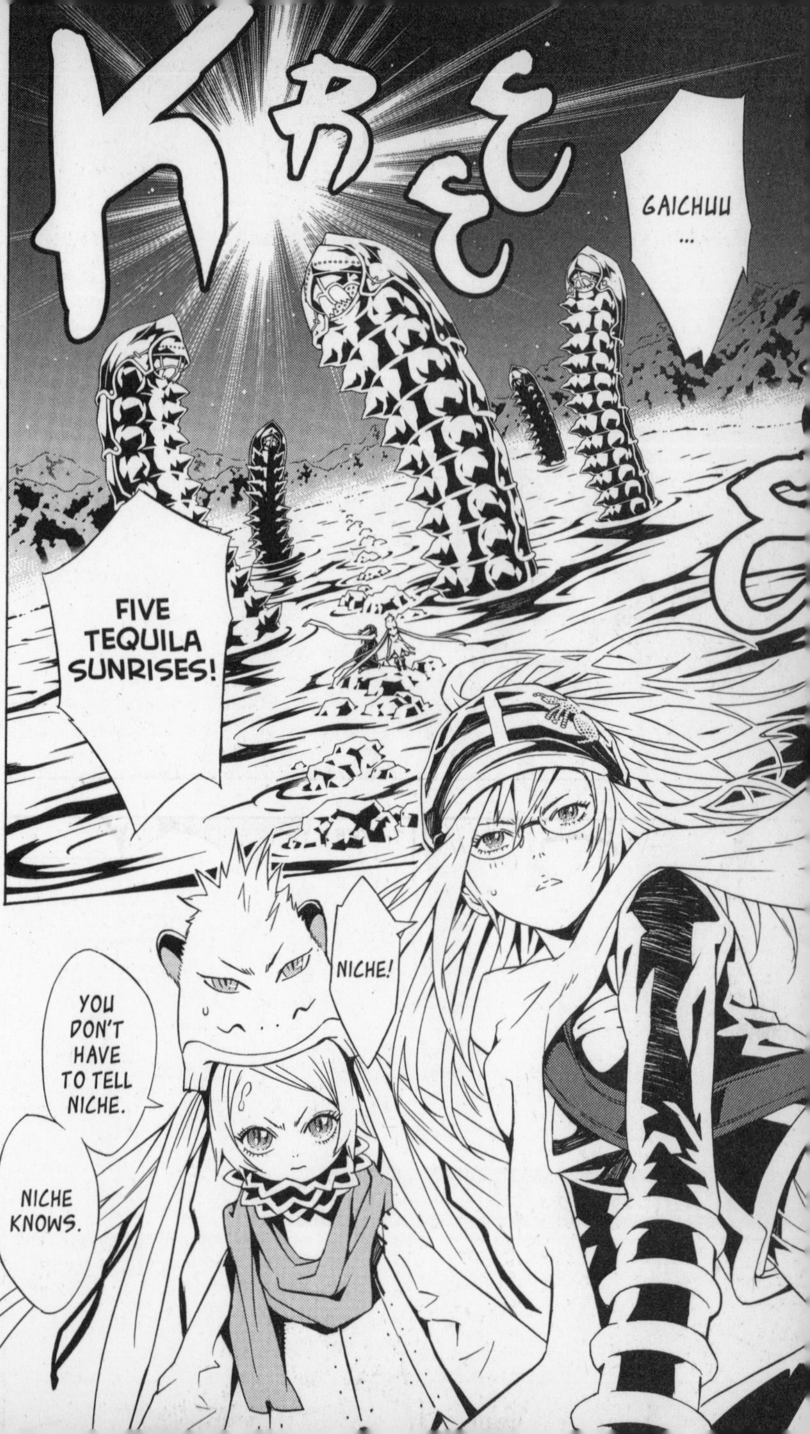
GAICHUU ...
FIVE TEQUILA SUNRISES!
NICHE!
YOU DON'T HAVE TO TELL NICHE.
NICHE KNOWS.

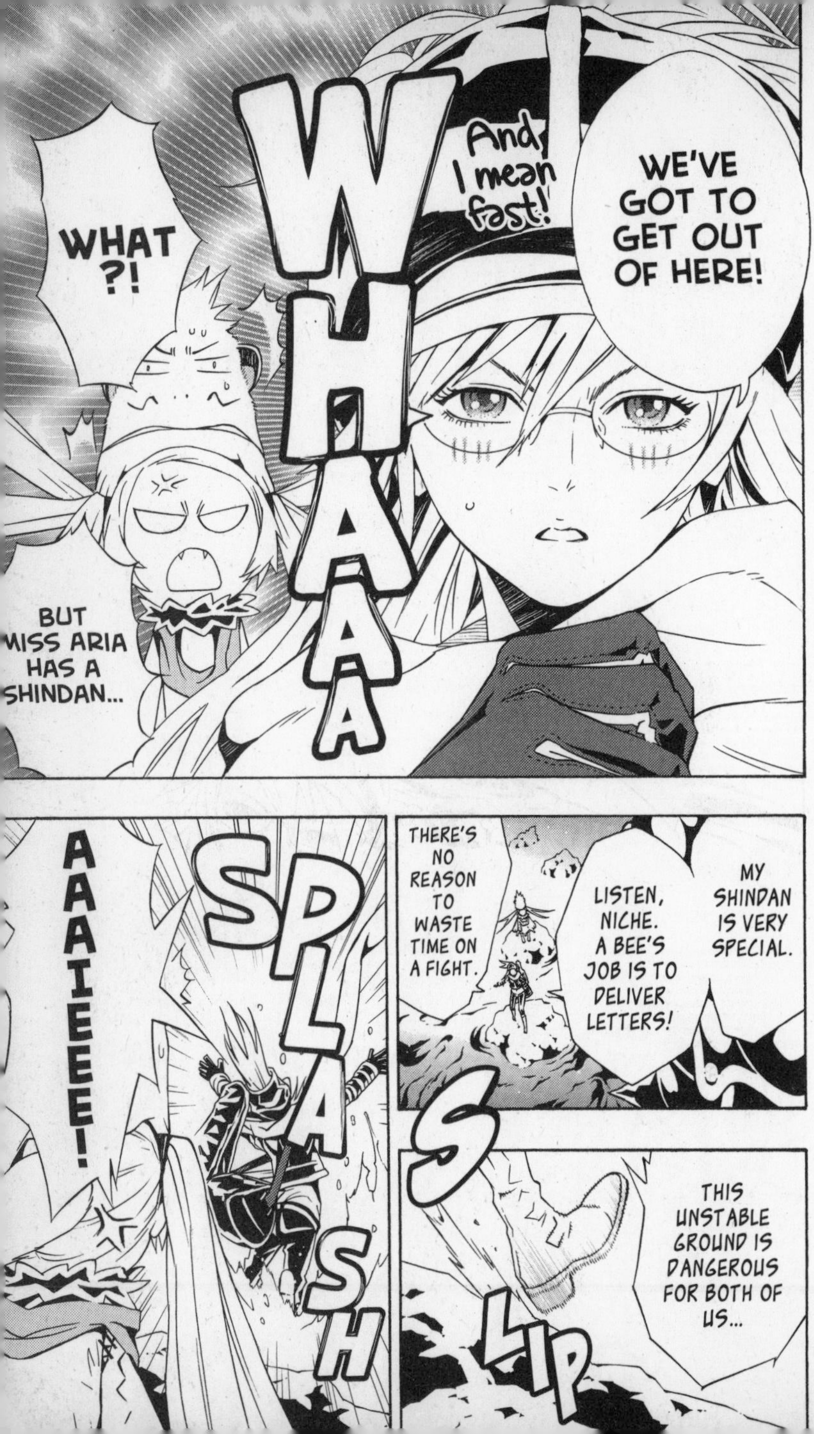
WE'VE GOT TO GET OUT OF HERE!
And, I mean fast!
WHAAAA
WHAT ?!
BUT MISS ARIA HAS A SHINDAN...
MY SHINDAN IS VERY SPECIAL.
LISTEN, NICHE. A BEE'S JOB IS TO DELIVER LETTERS!
THERE'S NO REASON TO WASTE TIME ON A FIGHT.
THIS UNSTABLE GROUND IS DANGEROUS FOR BOTH OF US...
SLIP
SPLAASH
AAAIEEEE!

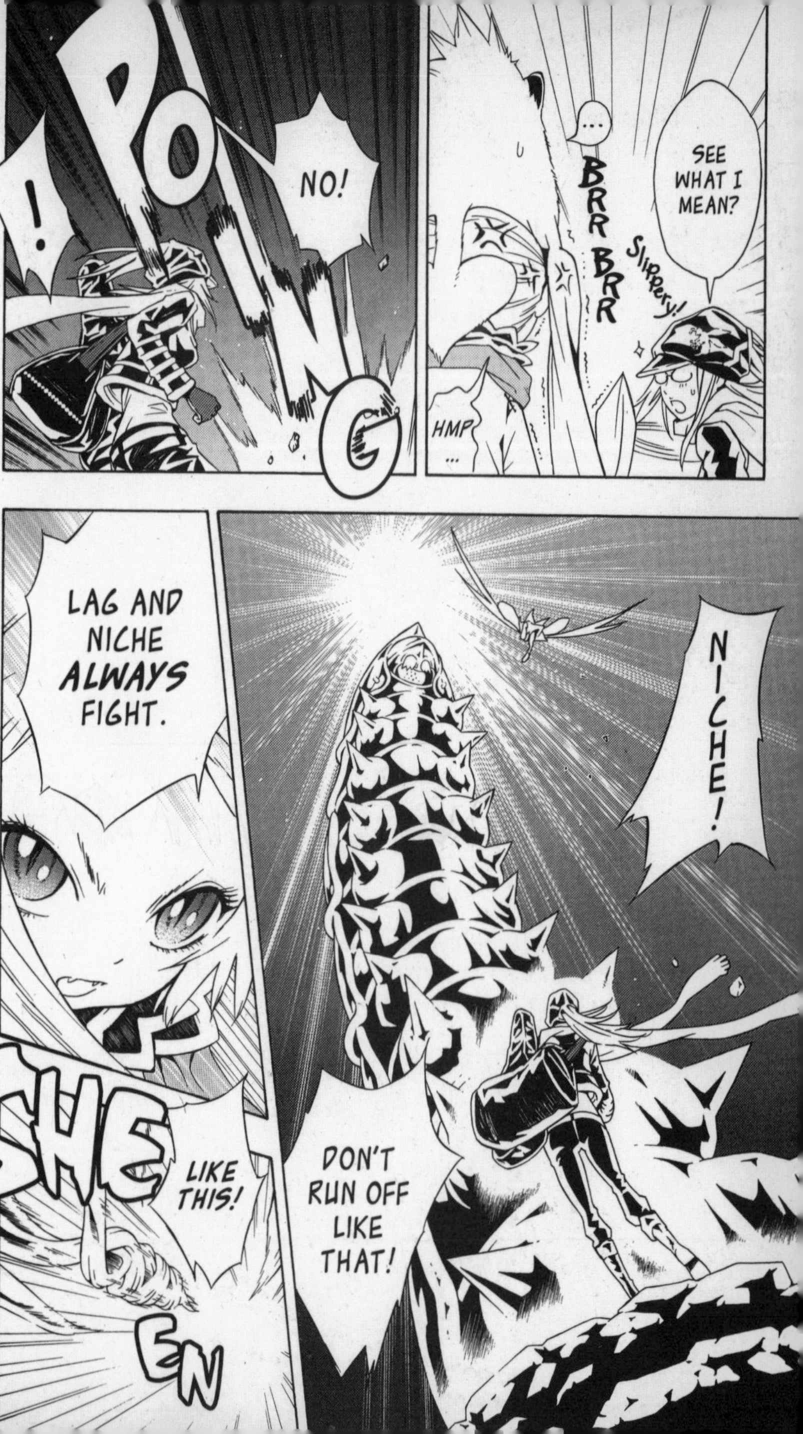

…
SEE WHAT I MEAN?
Slippery!
BRR BRR BRR
HMP …
POING
NO!
!
NICHE!
DON'T RUN OFF LIKE THAT!
LAG AND NICHE ALWAYS FIGHT.
LIKE THIS!
SHE
EN

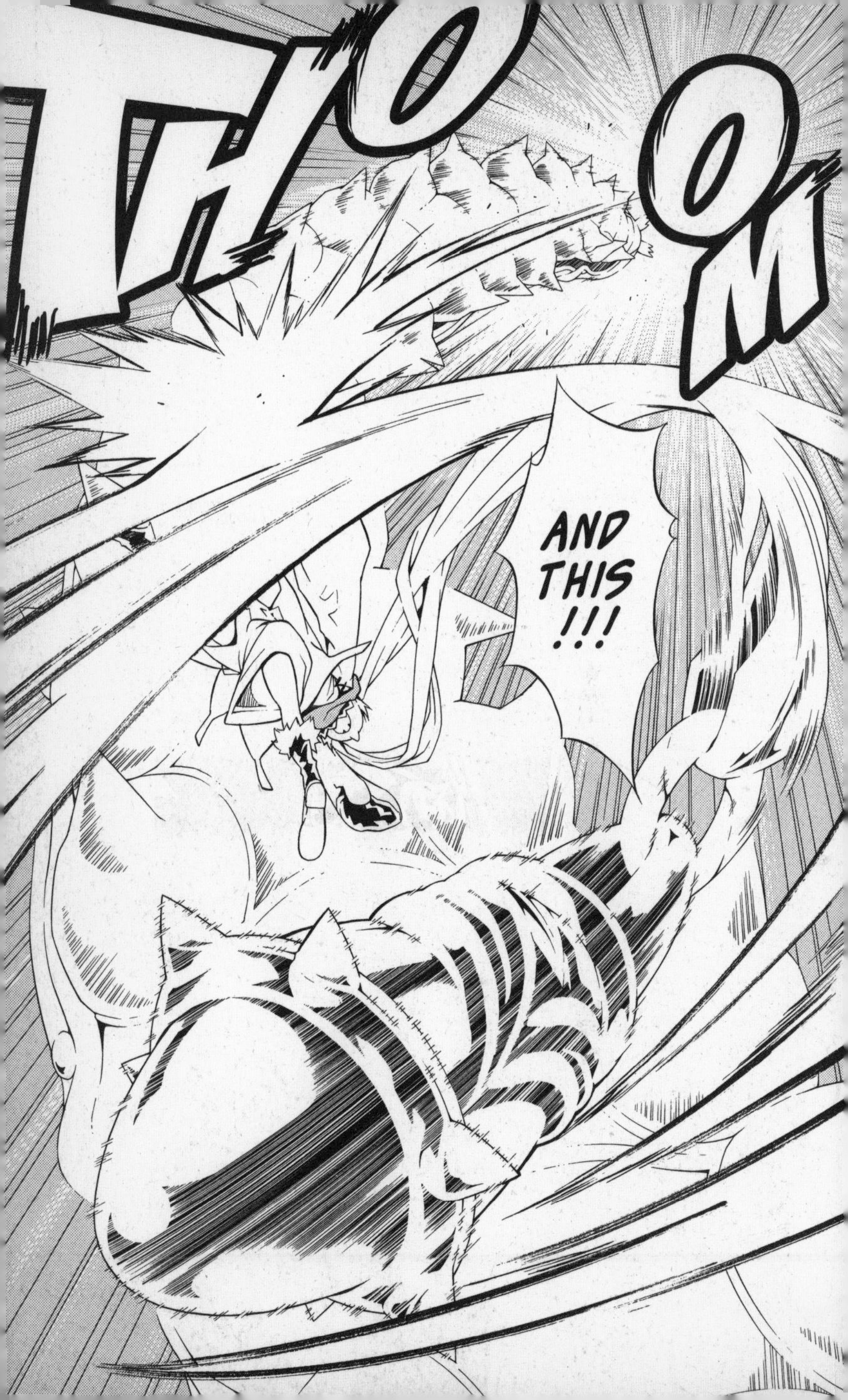
THOOM
AND THIS !!!

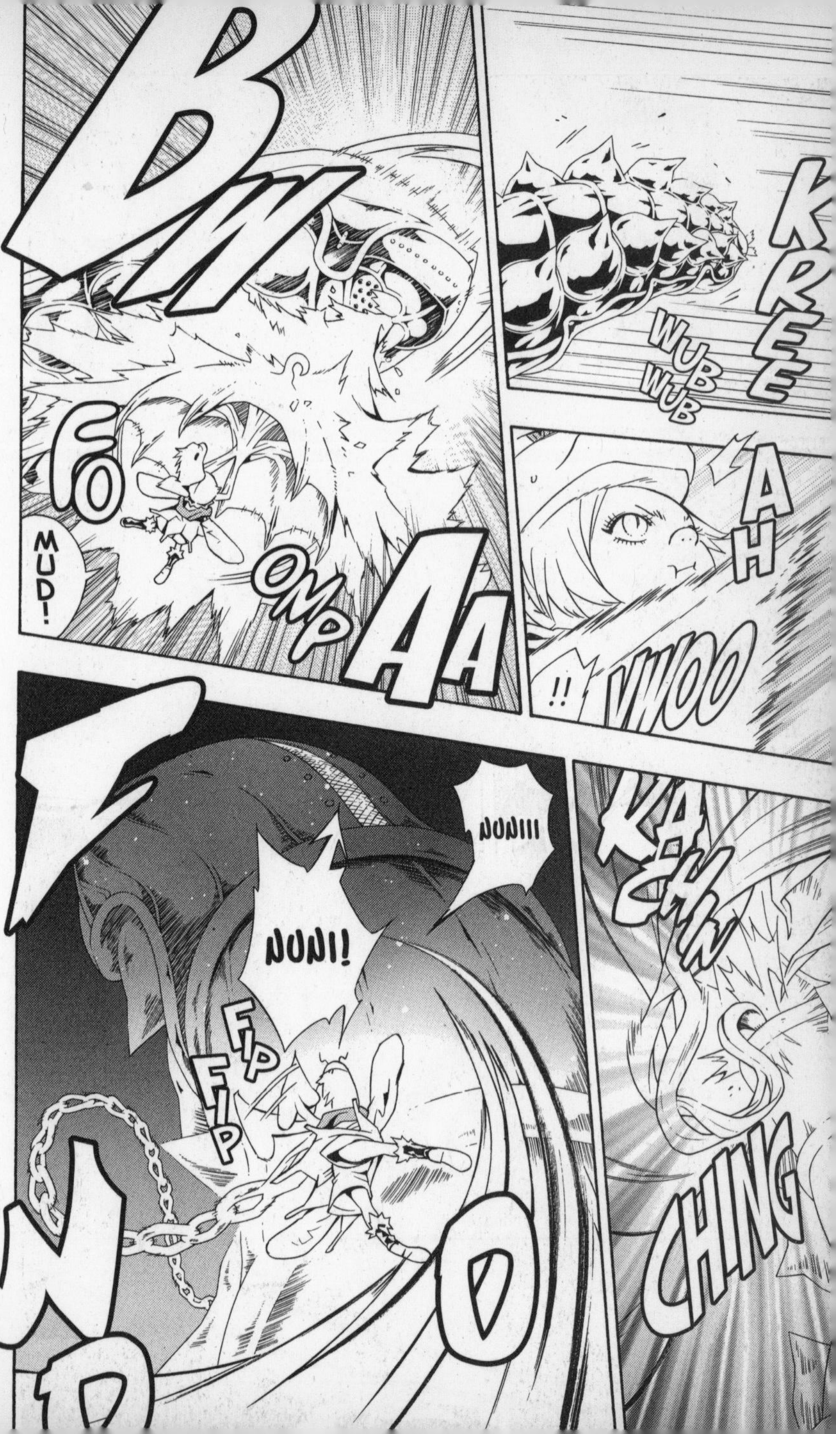
KREE
WUB WUB
AH
VWOO
!!
BW
OMP
FO
AA
MUDI!
KA CHIN
CHING
NUNI!!!
NUNI!
FIP FIP

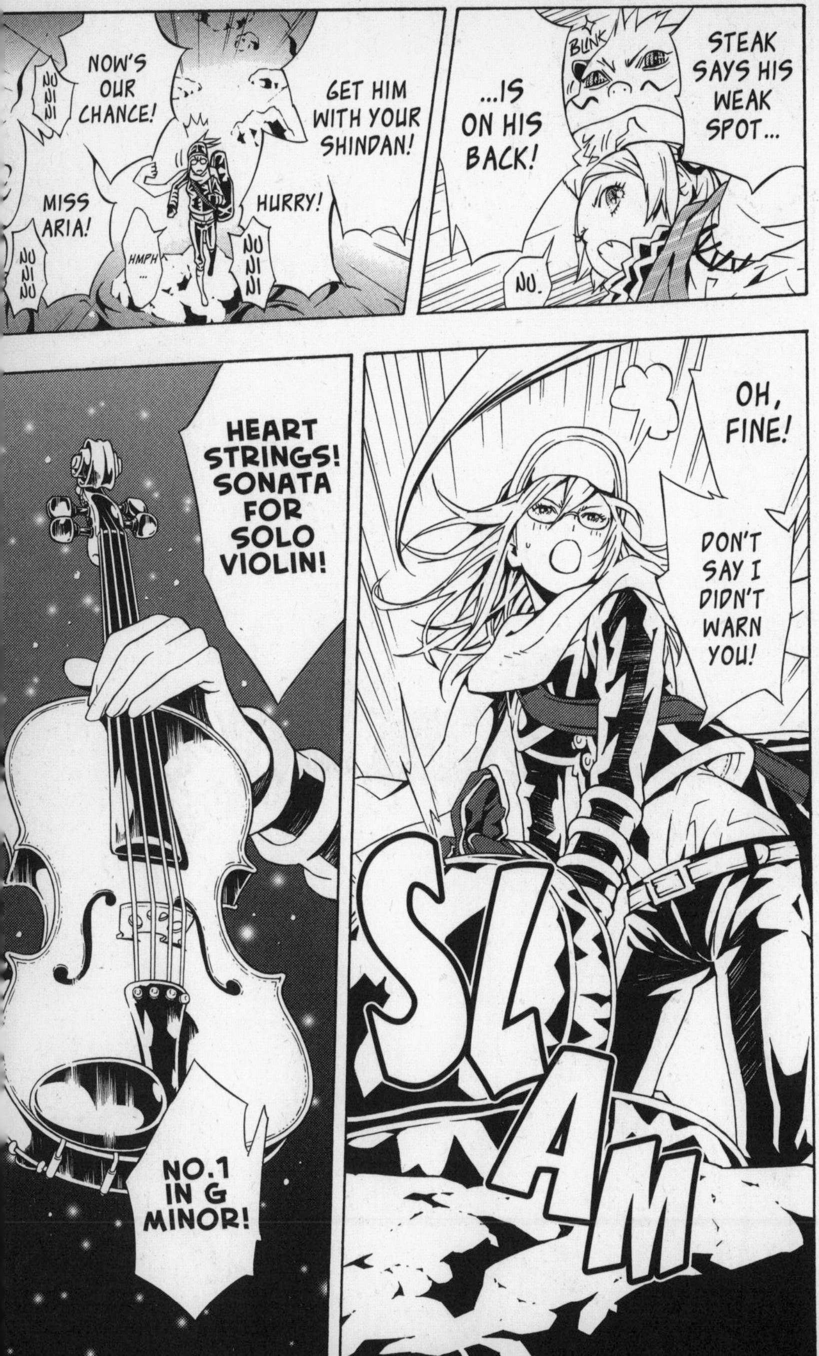
STEAK SAYS HIS WEAK SPOT...
...IS ON HIS BACK!
BLINK
NU_
GET HIM WITH YOUR SHINDAN!
NOW'S OUR CHANCE!
NU NI NI
HURRY!
NU NI NI
MISS ARIA!
NU NI NU
HMPH...
OH, FINE!
DON'T SAY I DIDN'T WARN YOU!
SLAM
HEART STRINGS! SONATA FOR SOLO VIOLIN!
NO.1 IN G MINOR!

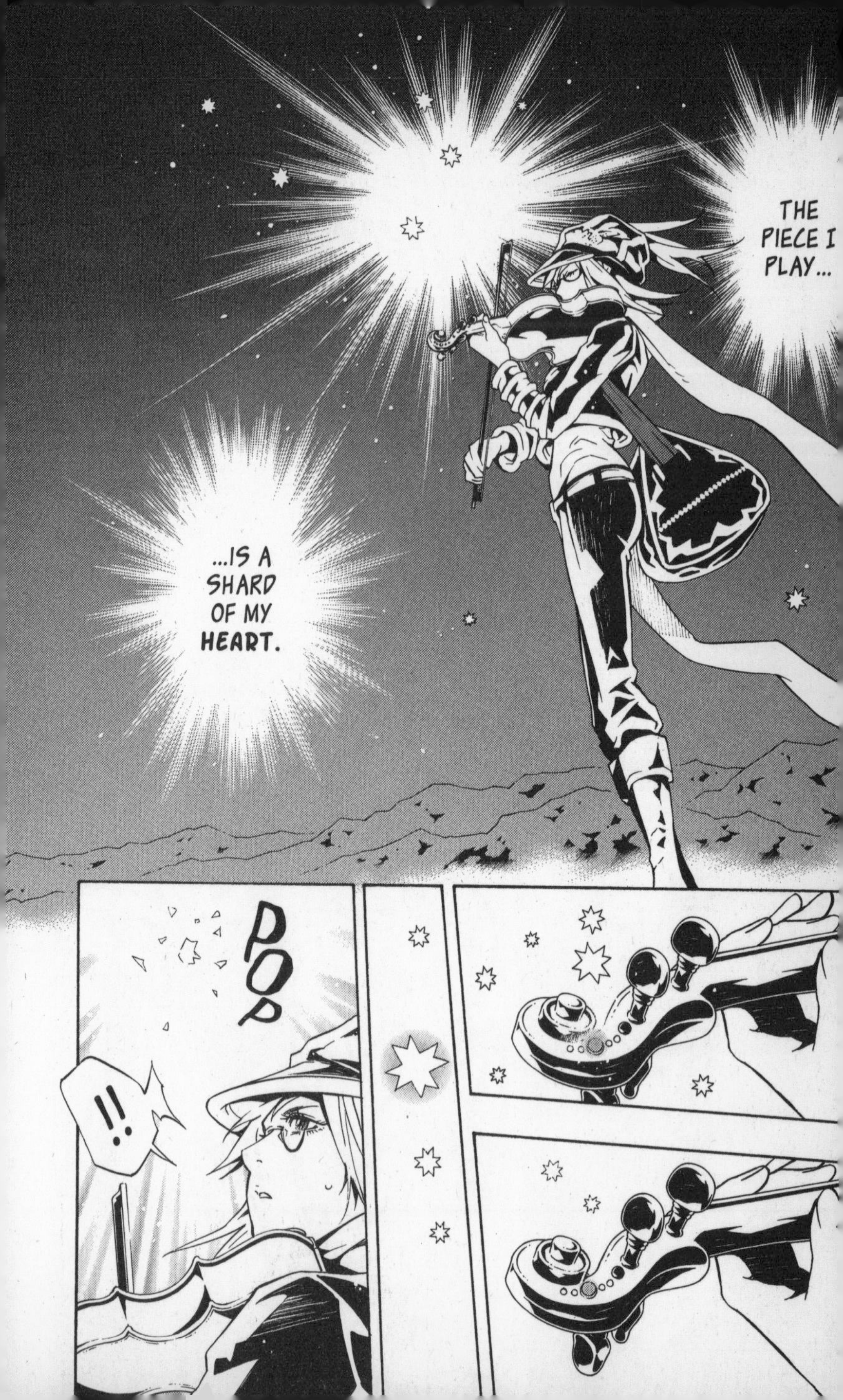
THE PIECE I PLAY...
...IS A SHARD OF MY HEART.
POP
!!

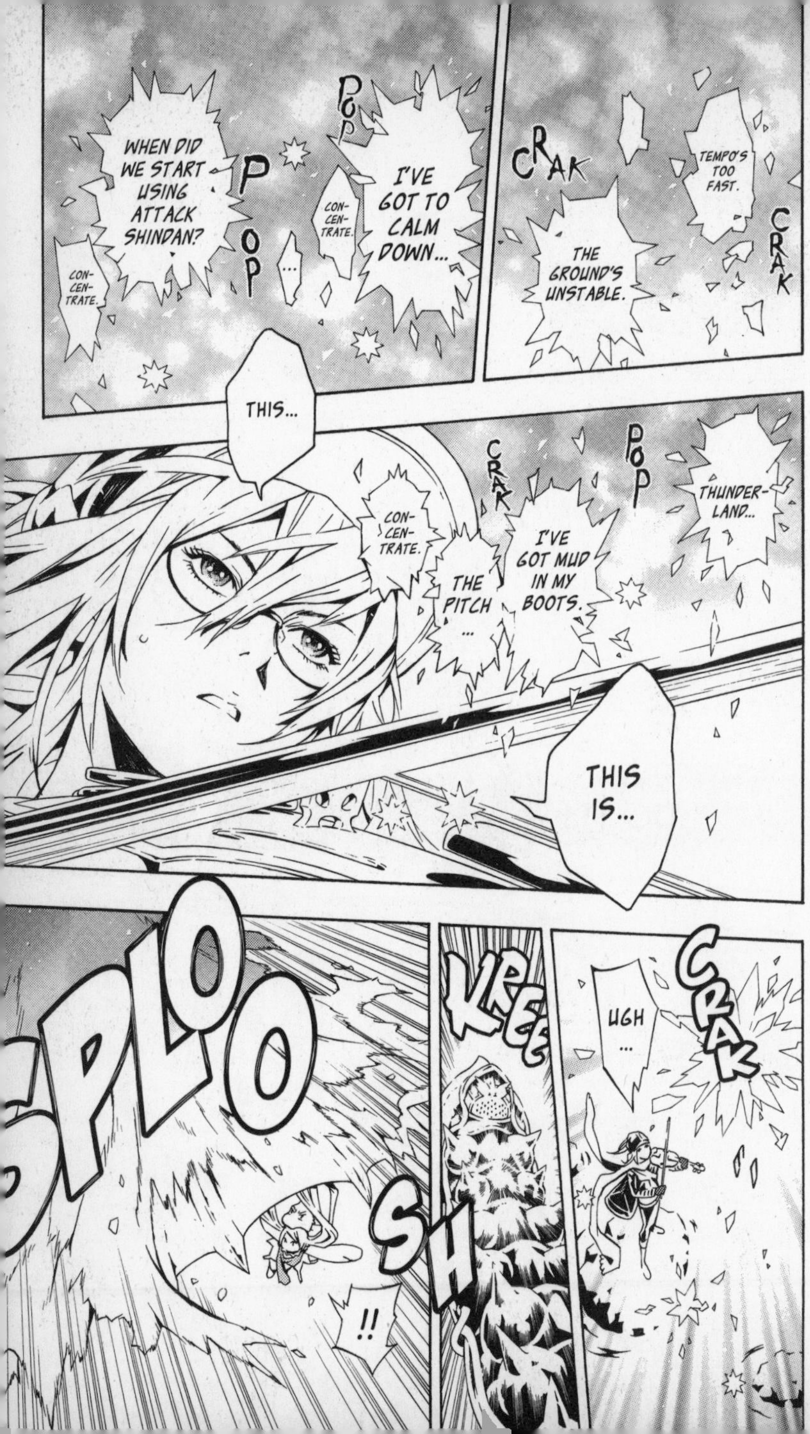
TEMPO'S TOO FAST.
CRAK
CRAK
THE GROUND'S UNSTABLE.
POP
I'VE GOT TO CALM DOWN...
CON-CEN-TRATE.
...
POP
WHEN DID WE START USING ATTACK SHINDAN?
POP
CON-CEN-TRATE.
THUNDER-LAND...
POP
I'VE GOT MUD IN MY BOOTS.
CRAK
CON-CEN-TRATE.
THE PITCH ...
THIS...
THIS IS...
CRAK
UGH ...
KREE
SH
SPLOO
!!

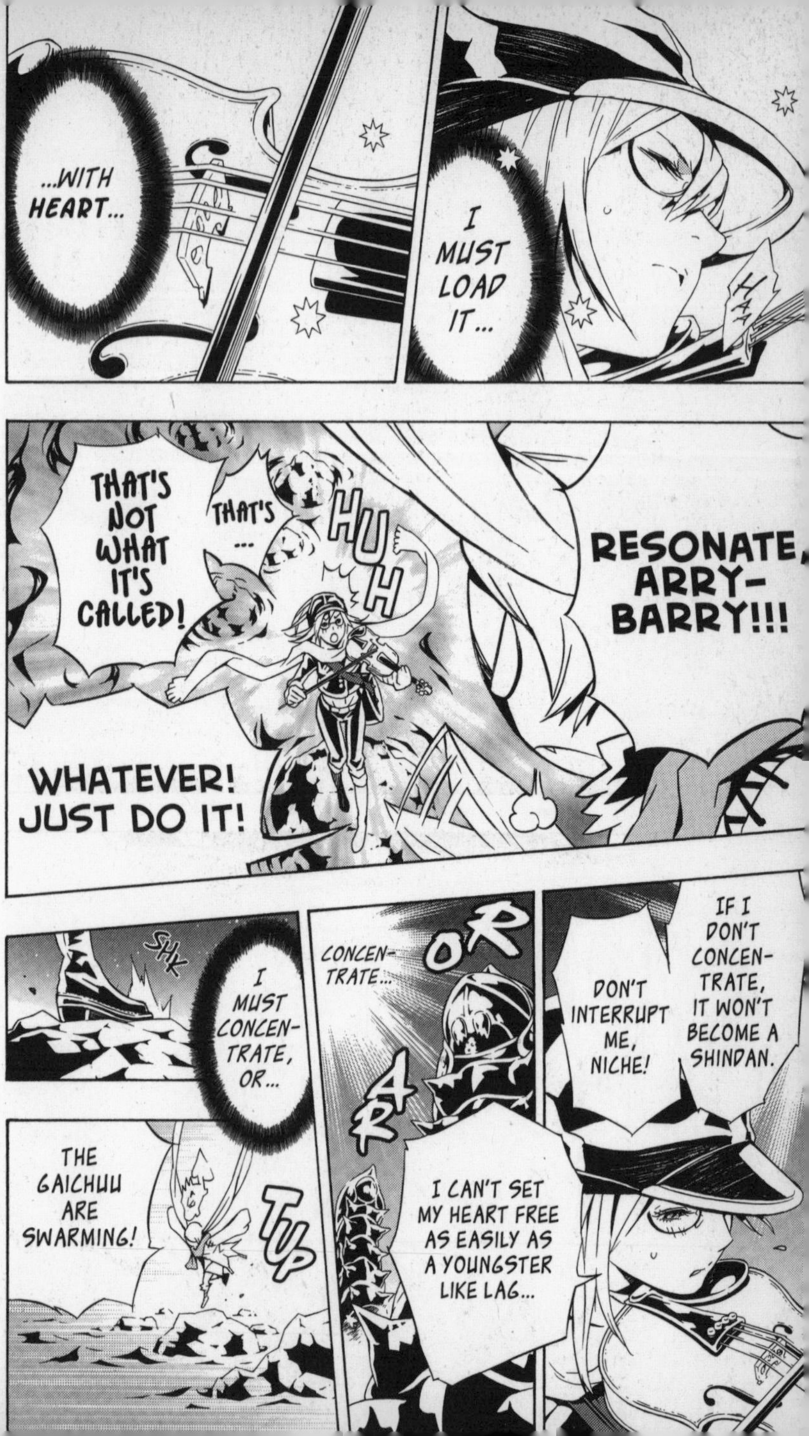
I MUST LOAD IT...
...WITH HEART...
RESONATE, ARRY-BARRY!!!
HUH
THAT'S ...
THAT'S NOT WHAT IT'S CALLED!
WHATEVER! JUST DO IT!
IF I DON'T CONCENTRATE, IT WON'T BECOME A SHINDAN.
DON'T INTERRUPT ME, NICHE!
OR
CONCENTRATE...
AR
SHK
I MUST CONCENTRATE, OR...
I CAN'T SET MY HEART FREE AS EASILY AS A YOUNGSTER LIKE LAG...
TUP
THE GAICHUU ARE SWARMING!

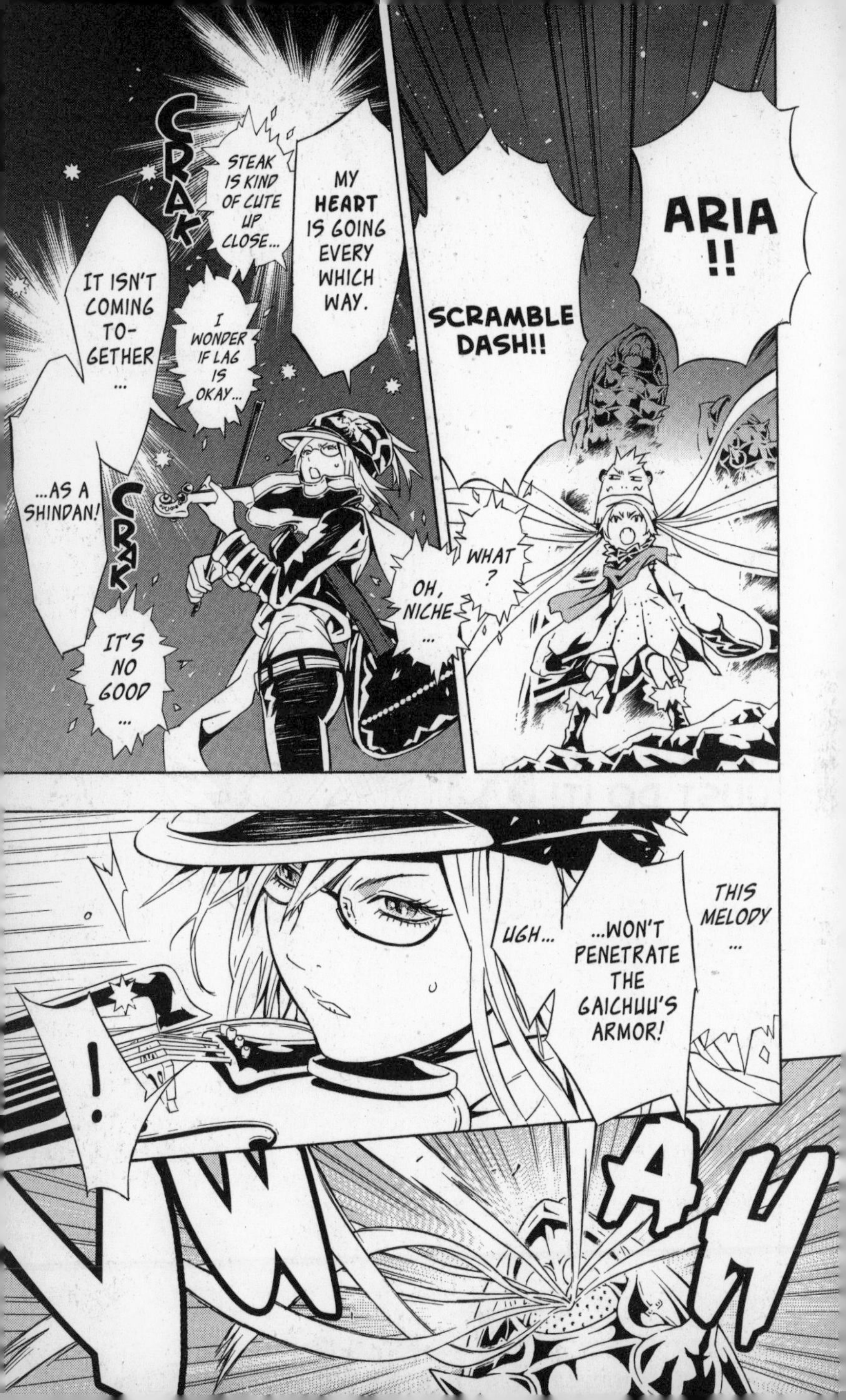
ARIA!!
SCRAMBLE DASH!!
WHAT?
OH, NICHE...
MY HEART IS GOING EVERY WHICH WAY.
STEAK IS KIND OF CUTE UP CLOSE...
CRAK
I WONDER IF LAG IS OKAY...
IT ISN'T COMING TO-GETHER...
...AS A SHINDAN!
CRAK
IT'S NO GOOD...
THIS MELODY...
...WON'T PENETRATE THE GAICHUU'S ARMOR!
UGH...
!
VWAH

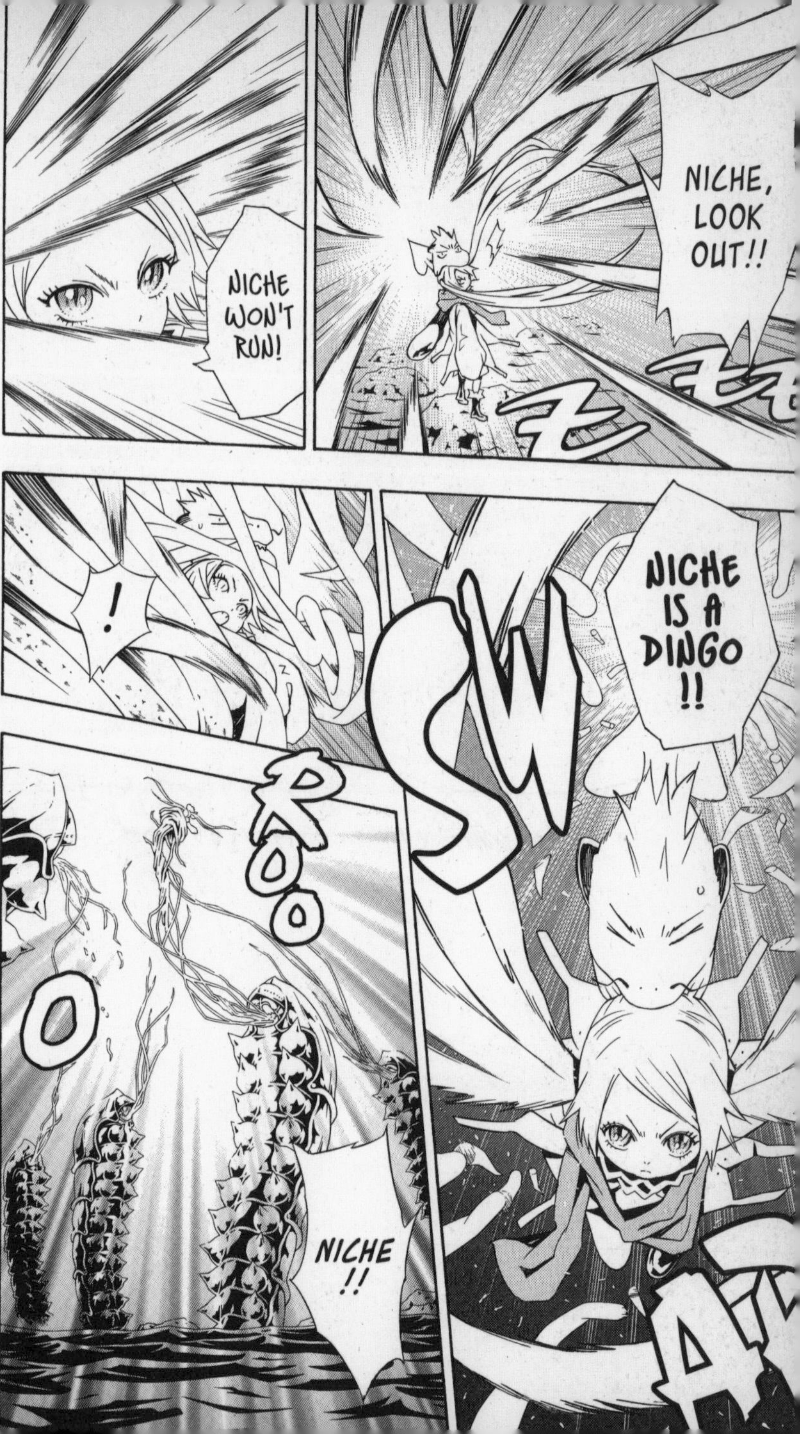
NICHE, LOOK OUT!!
NICHE WON'T RUN!
NICHE IS A DINGO !!
SW
!
ROOO
NICHE !!

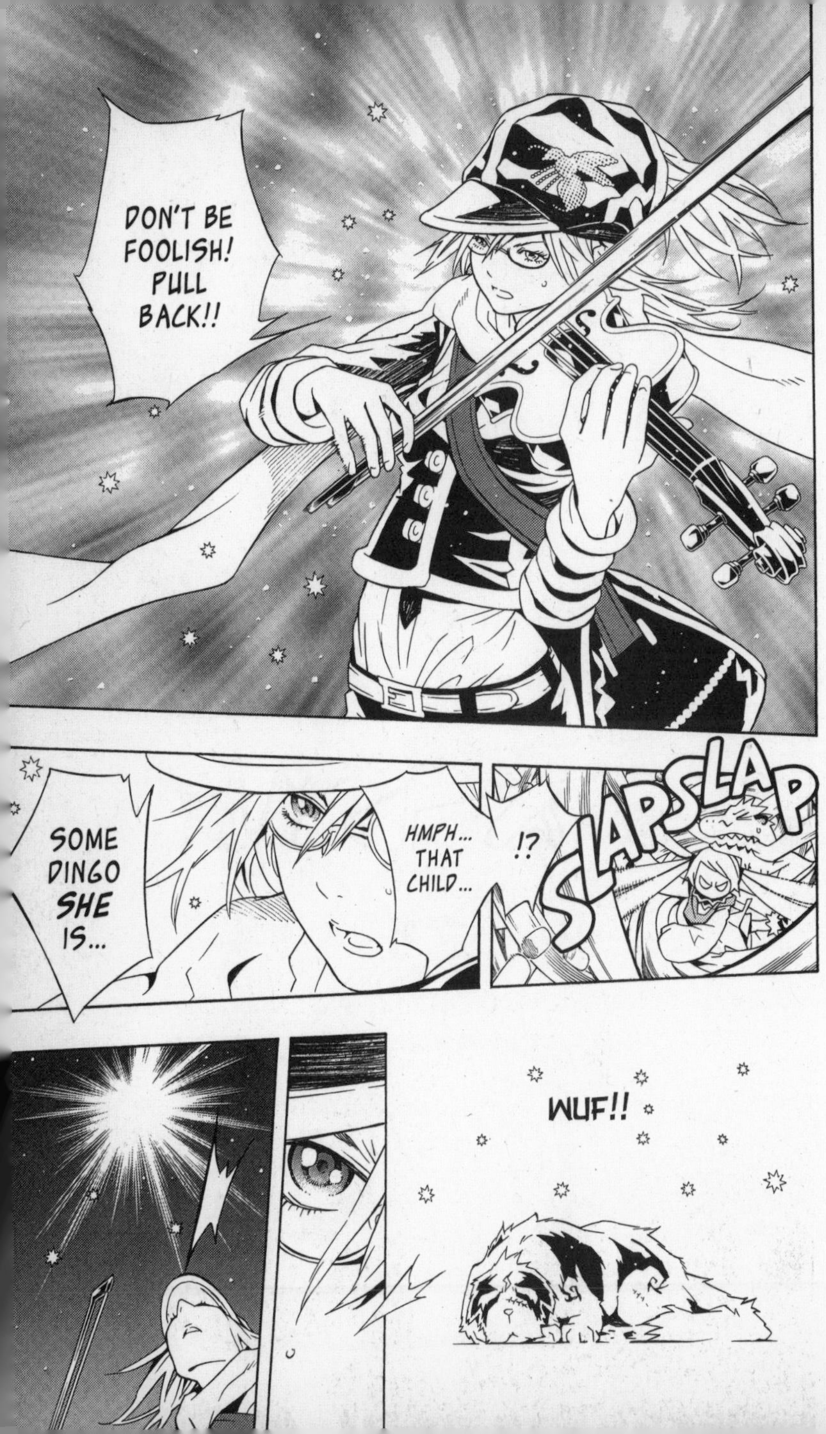
DON'T BE FOOLISH! PULL BACK!!
!?
SLAPSLAP
HMPH... THAT CHILD...
SOME DINGO SHE IS...
WUF!!

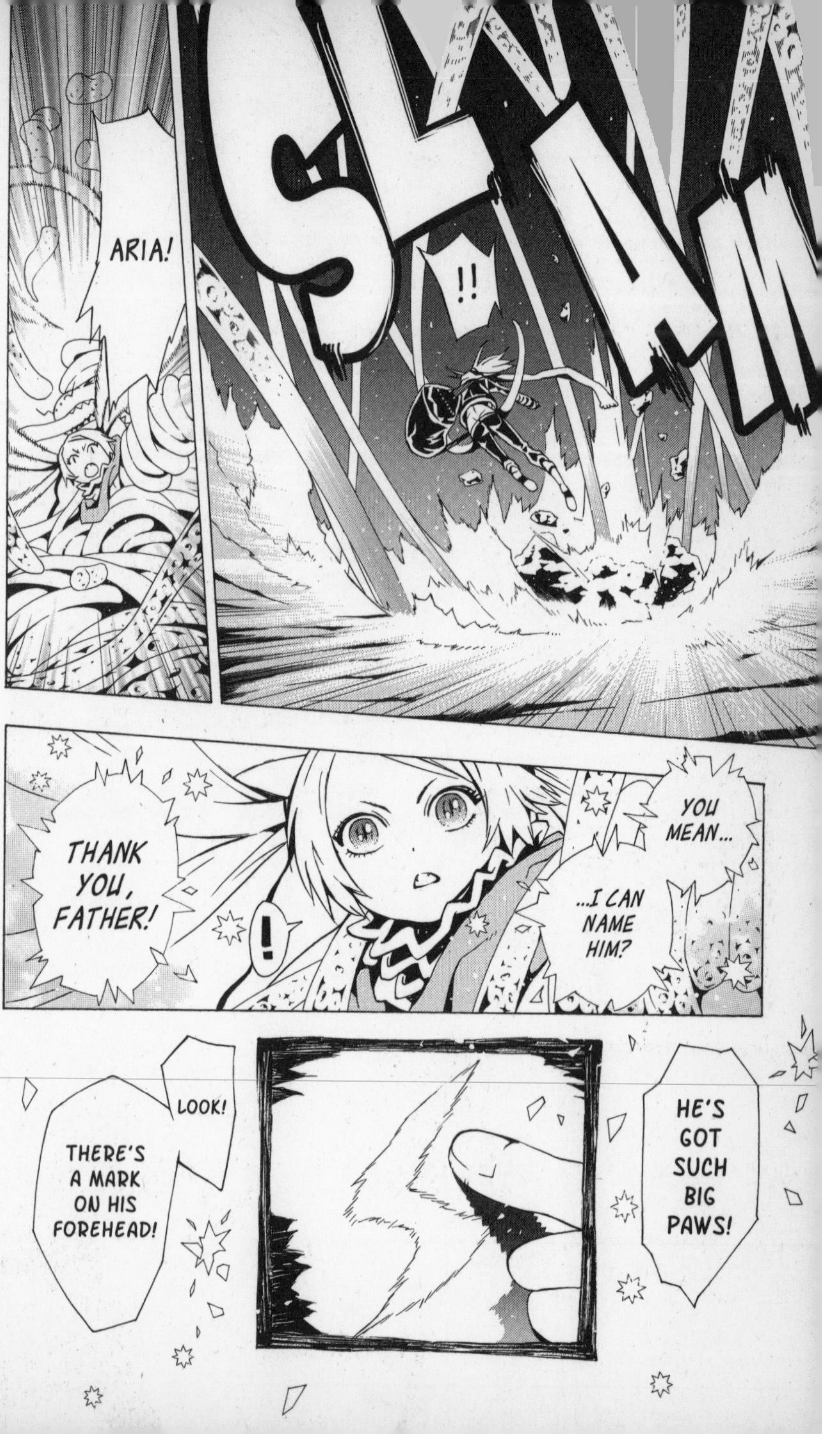
SLAM
!!
ARIA!
YOU MEAN...
...I CAN NAME HIM?
!
THANK YOU, FATHER!
HE'S GOT SUCH BIG PAWS!
LOOK!
THERE'S A MARK ON HIS FOREHEAD!

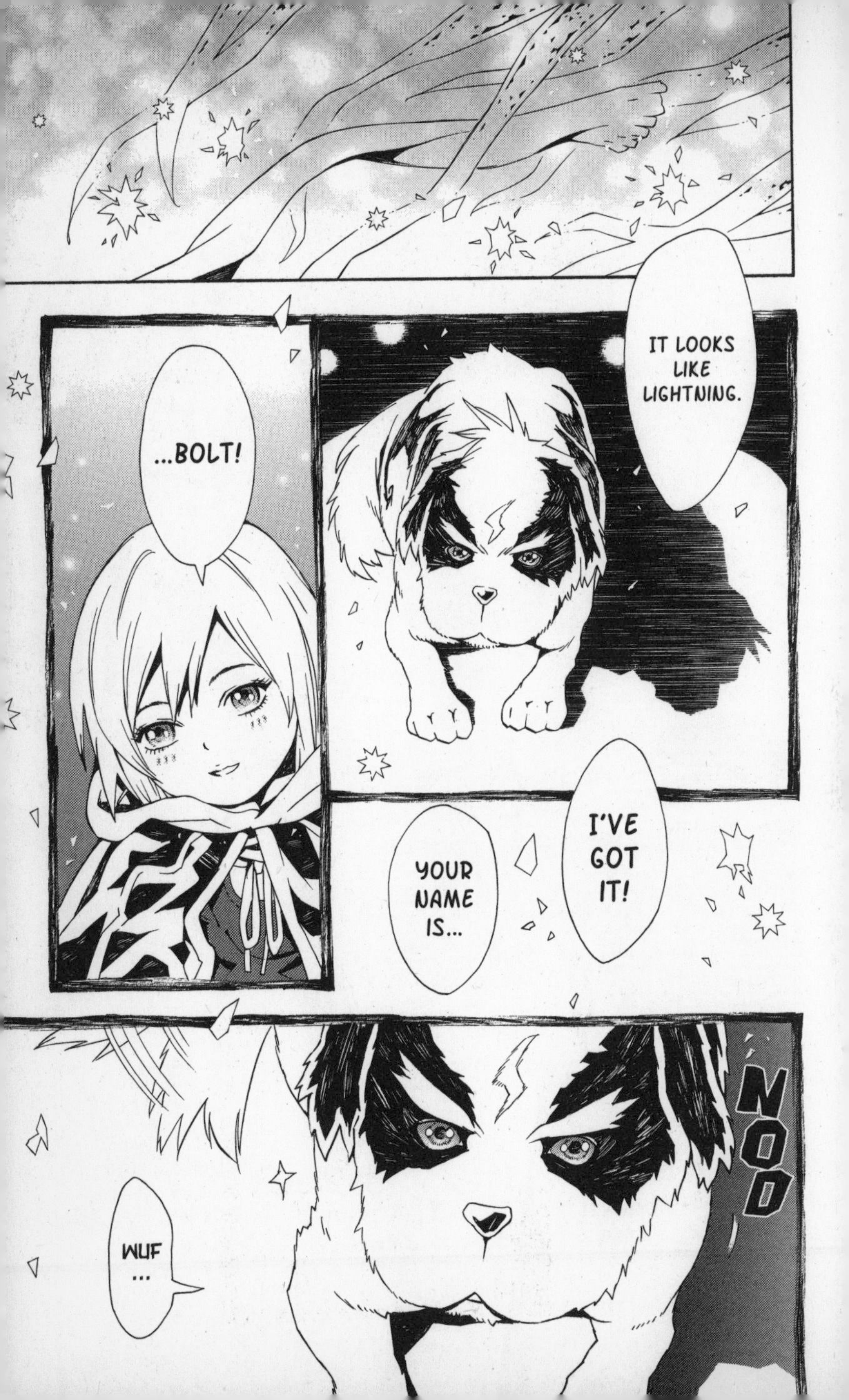
IT LOOKS LIKE LIGHTNING.
I'VE GOT IT!
YOUR NAME IS...
...BOLT!
NOD
WUF ...

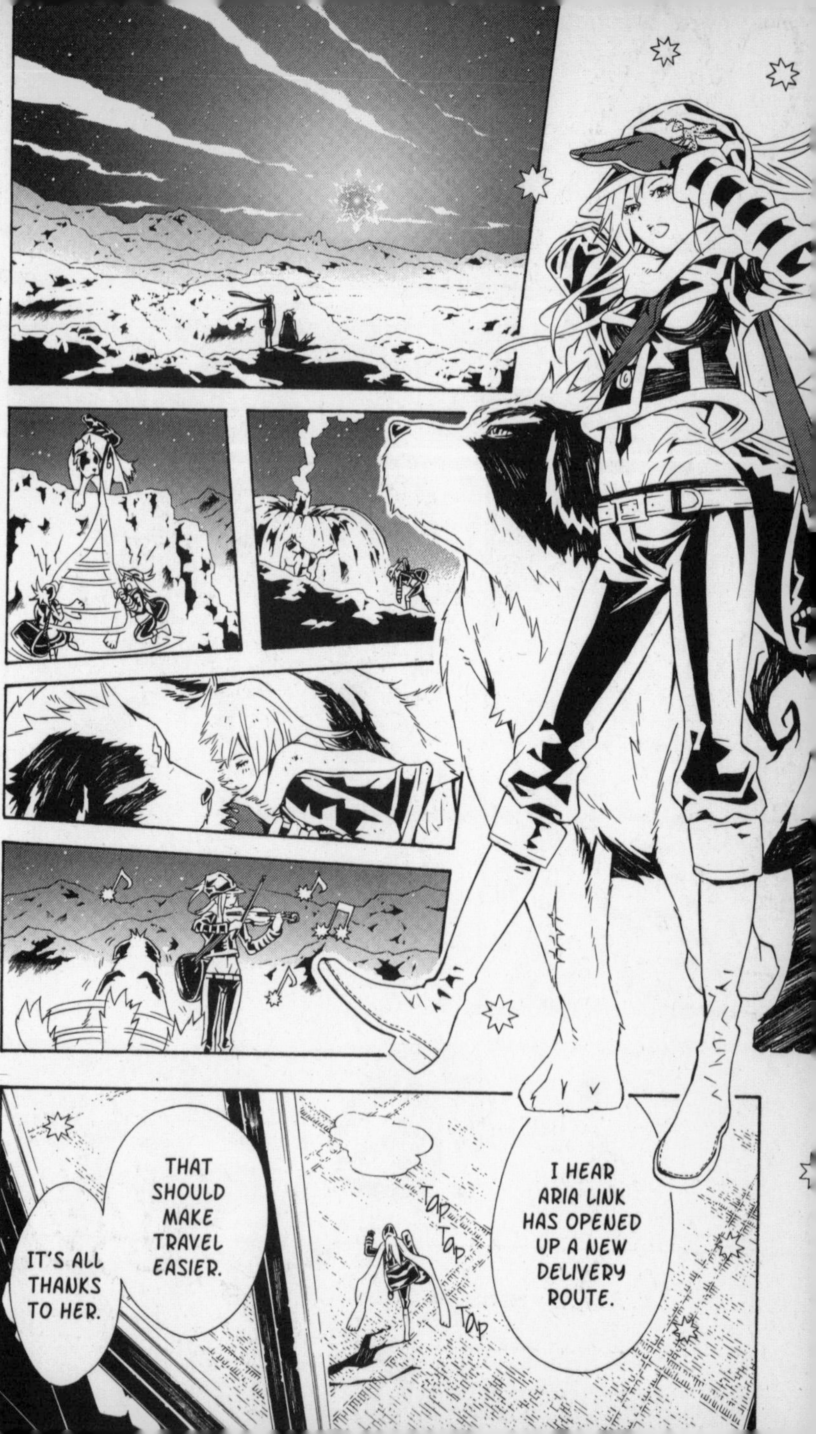
I HEAR ARIA LINK HAS OPENED UP A NEW DELIVERY ROUTE.
Tap Tap Tap
THAT SHOULD MAKE TRAVEL EASIER.
IT'S ALL THANKS TO HER.

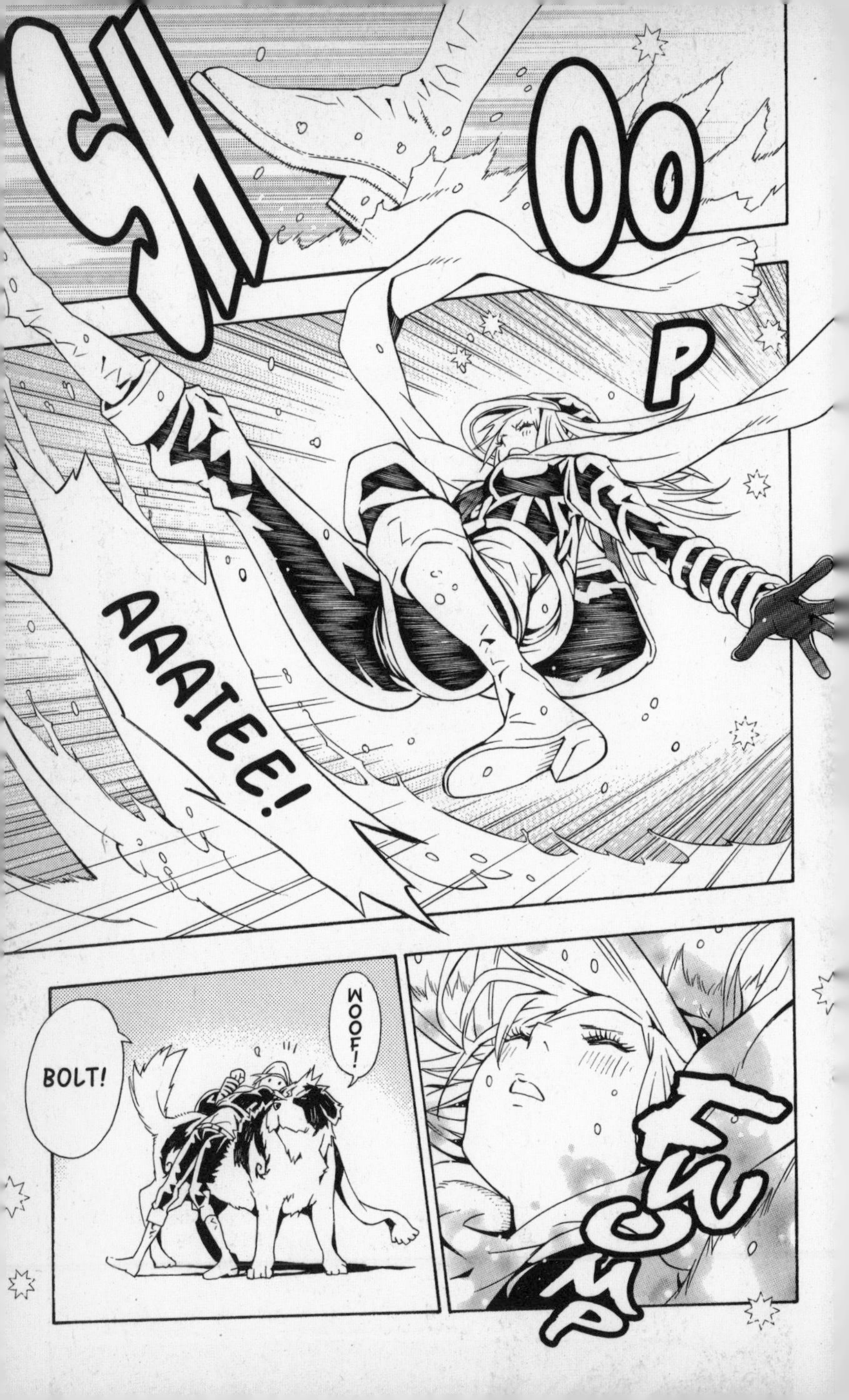
SHOOP
AAAIEEE!
THUMP
WOOF!
BOLT!

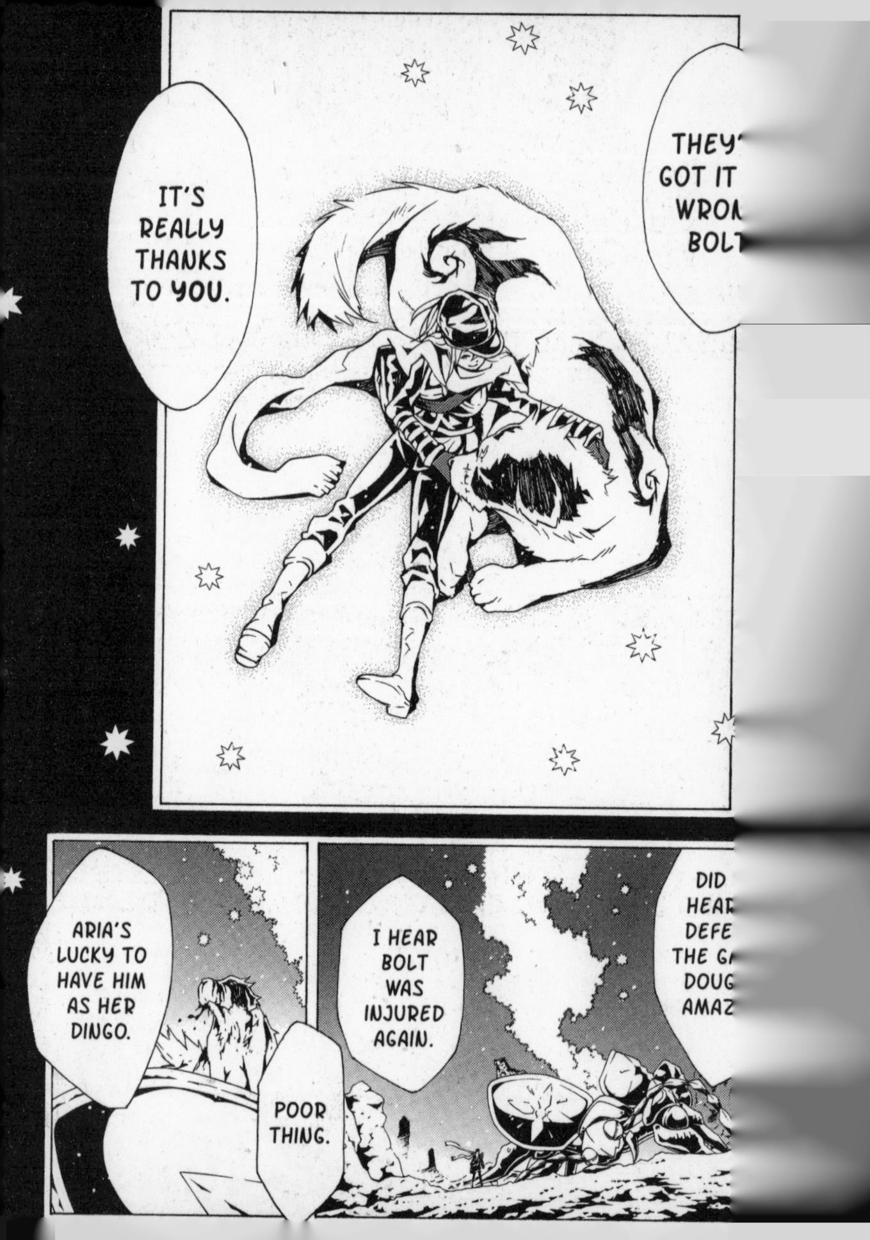
THEY' GOT IT WRON BOLT
IT'S REALLY THANKS TO YOU.
DID HEAR DEFE THE G DOUG AMAZ
I HEAR BOLT WAS INJURED AGAIN.
ARIA'S LUCKY TO HAVE HIM AS HER DINGO.
POOR THING.

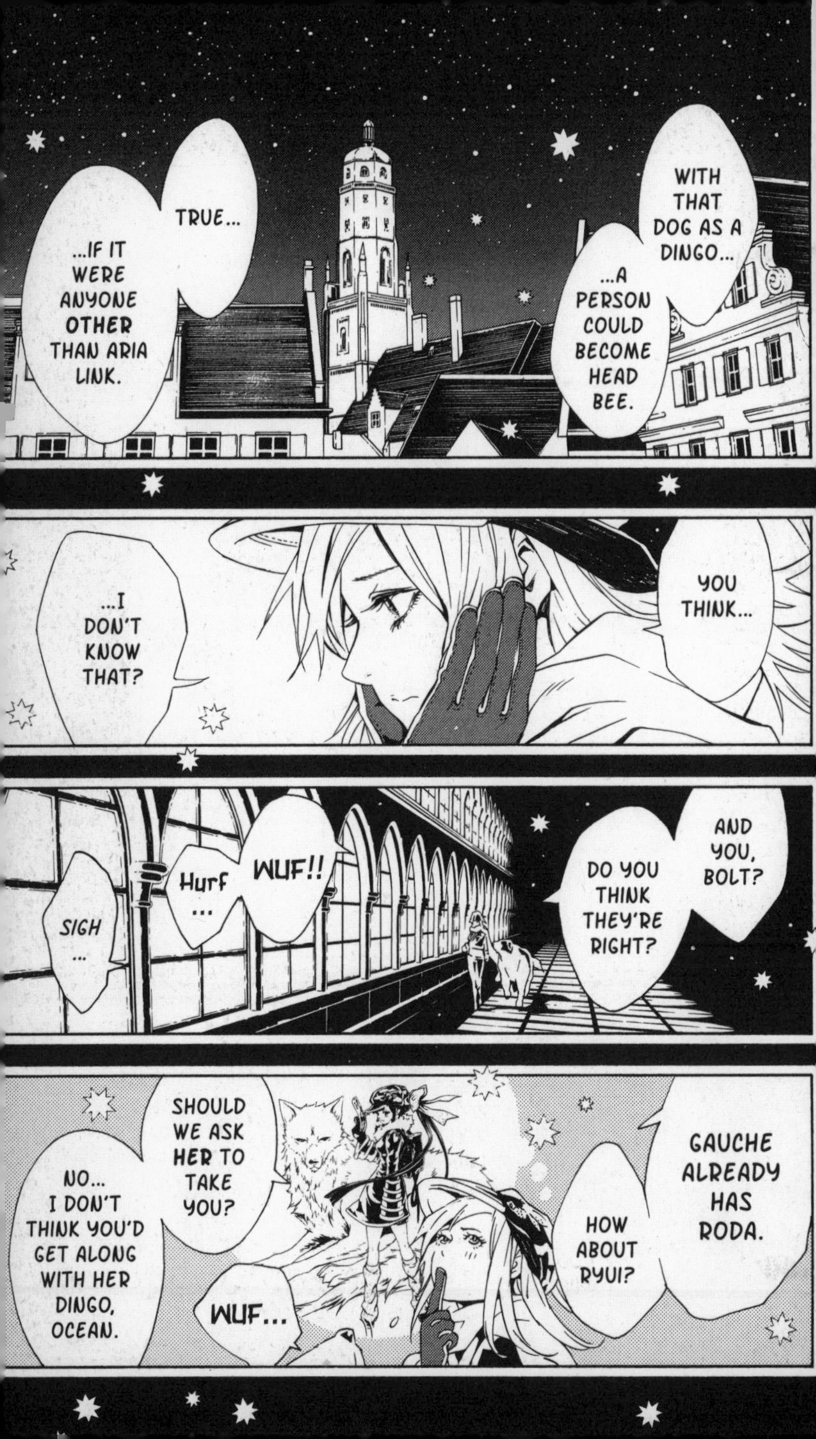
WITH THAT DOG AS A DINGO...
...A PERSON COULD BECOME HEAD BEE.
TRUE...
...IF IT WERE ANYONE OTHER THAN ARIA LINK.
YOU THINK...
...I DON'T KNOW THAT?
AND YOU, BOLT?
DO YOU THINK THEY'RE RIGHT?
WUF!!
Hurf ...
SIGH ...
GAUCHE ALREADY HAS RODA.
HOW ABOUT RYUI?
SHOULD WE ASK HER TO TAKE YOU?
WUF...
NO... I DON'T THINK YOU'D GET ALONG WITH HER DINGO, OCEAN.

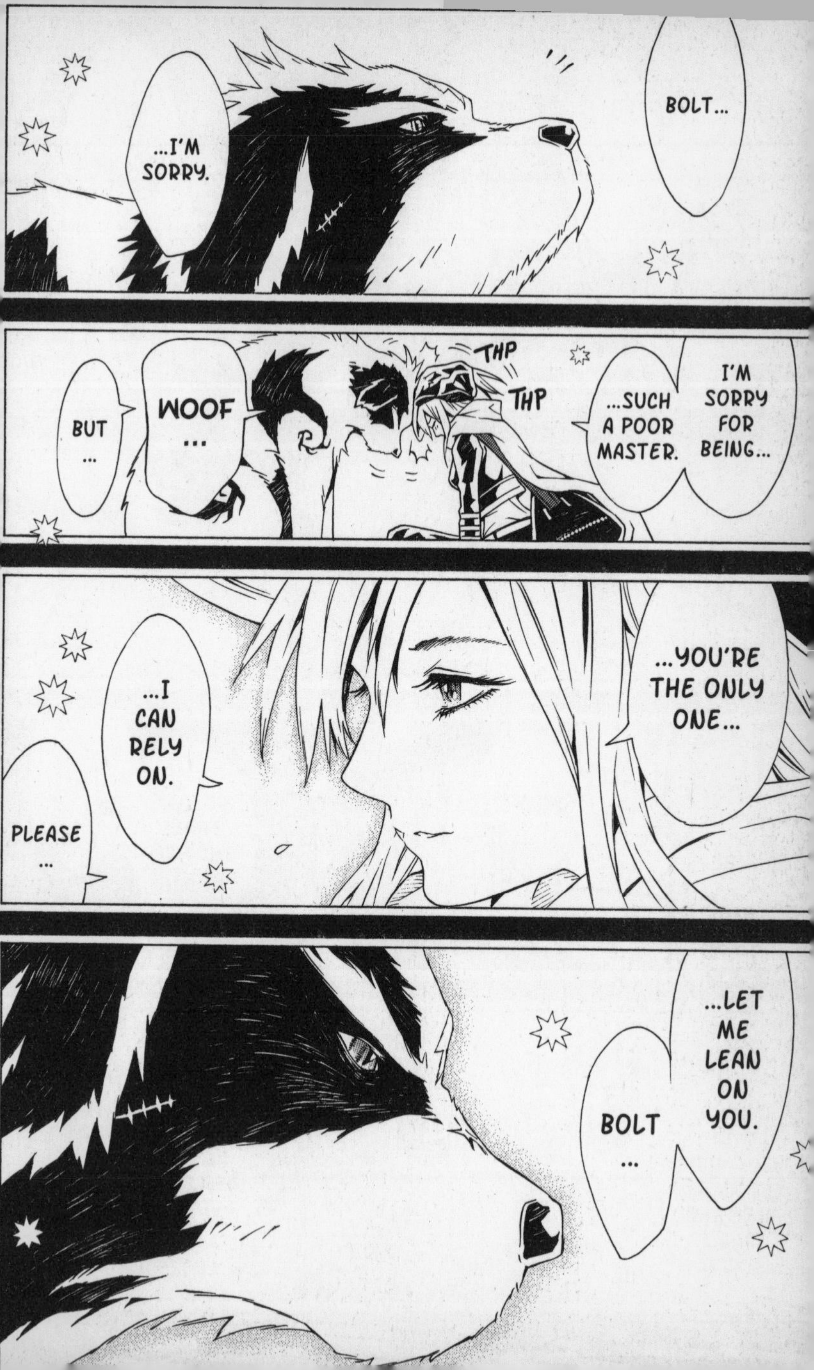
BOLT...
...I'M SORRY.
I'M SORRY FOR BEING...
...SUCH A POOR MASTER.
THP
THP
WOOF ...
BUT ...
...YOU'RE THE ONLY ONE...
...I CAN RELY ON.
PLEASE ...
...LET ME LEAN ON YOU.
BOLT ...

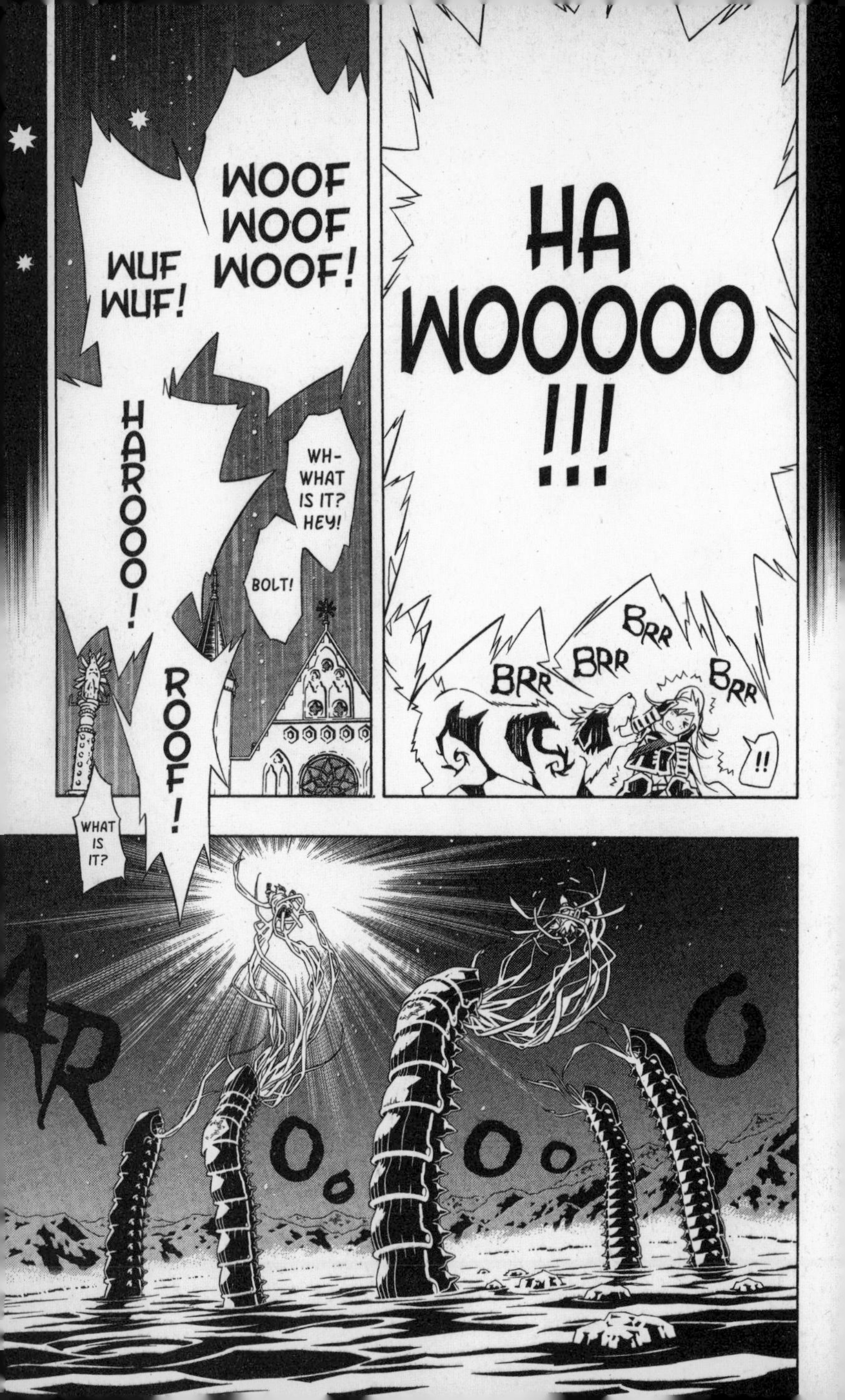
HA WOOOOO !!!
BRR
BRR
BRR
BRR
!!
WOOF WOOF WOOF!
WUF WUF!
WH- WHAT IS IT? HEY!
BOLT!
HAROOOO!
ROOF!
WHAT IS IT?

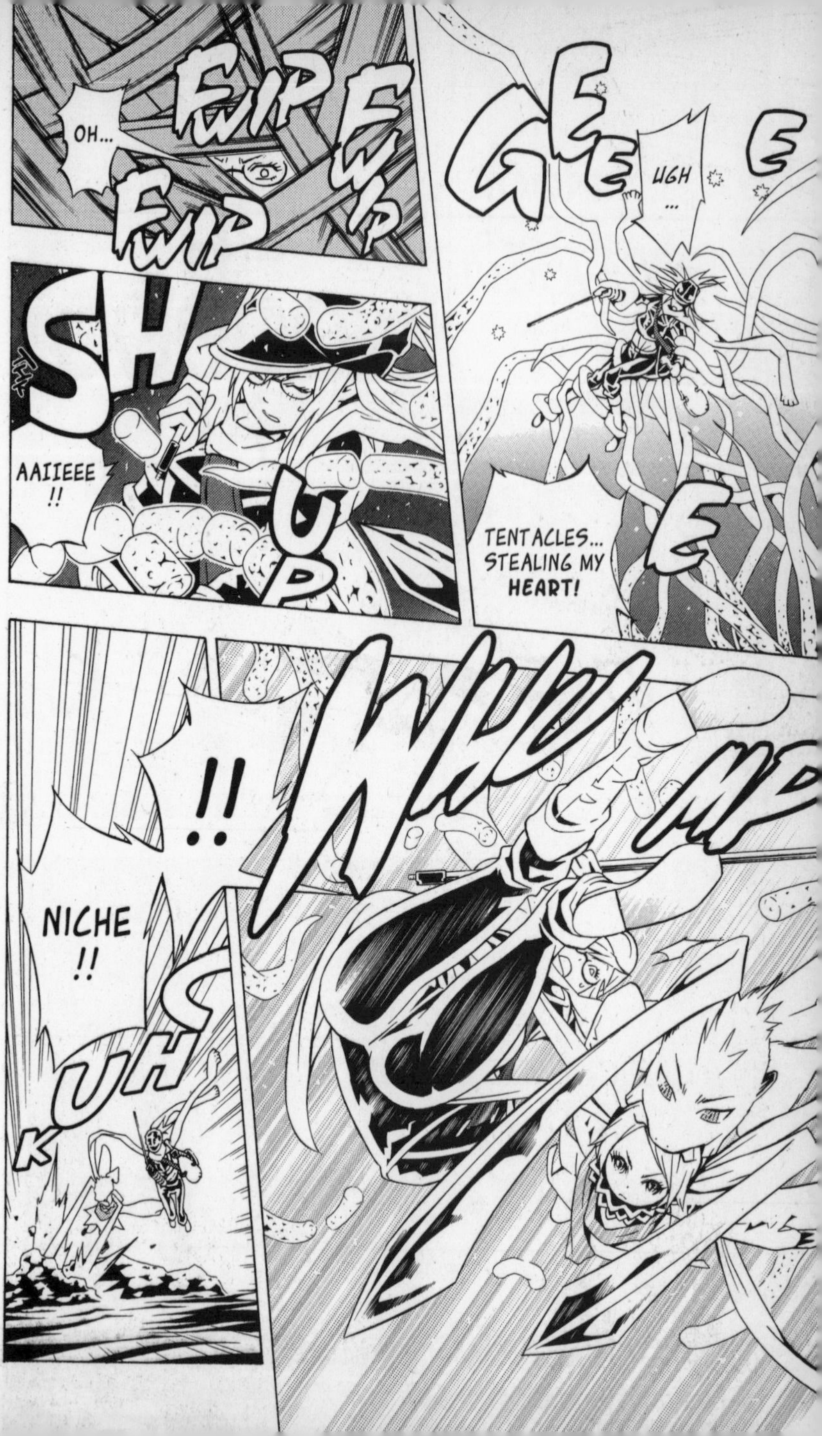
GEEE
UGH ...
E
TENTACLES... STEALING MY HEART!
E
OH...
FWIP
FWIP
FWIP
SH
UP
AAIIEEE !!
WHUMP
!!
NICHE !!
UH
K

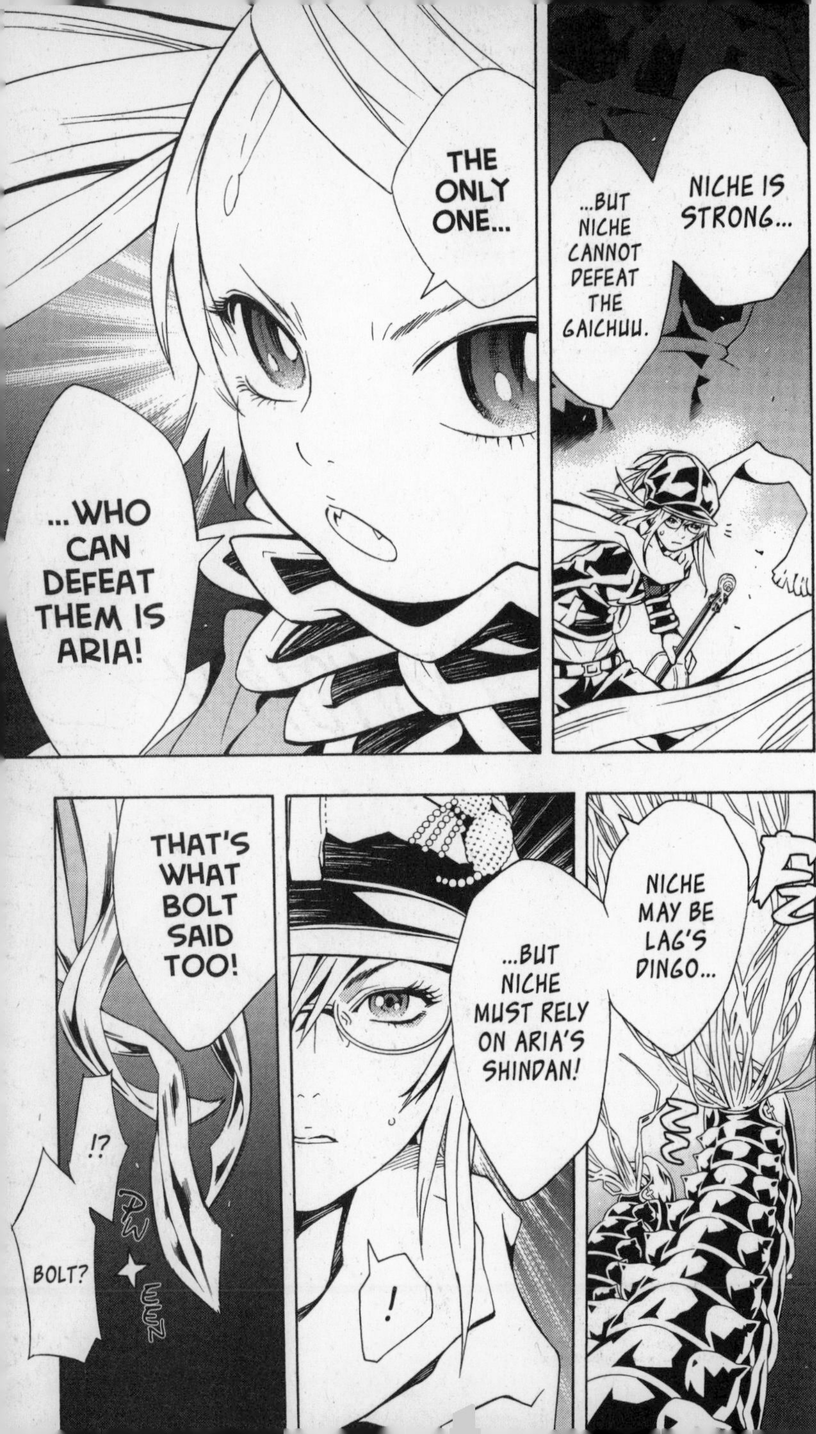
NICHE IS STRONG...
...BUT NICHE CANNOT DEFEAT THE GAICHUU.
THE ONLY ONE...
...WHO CAN DEFEAT THEM IS ARIA!
NICHE MAY BE LAG'S DINGO...
...BUT NICHE MUST RELY ON ARIA'S SHINDAN!
!
THAT'S WHAT BOLT SAID TOO!
!?
BOLT?

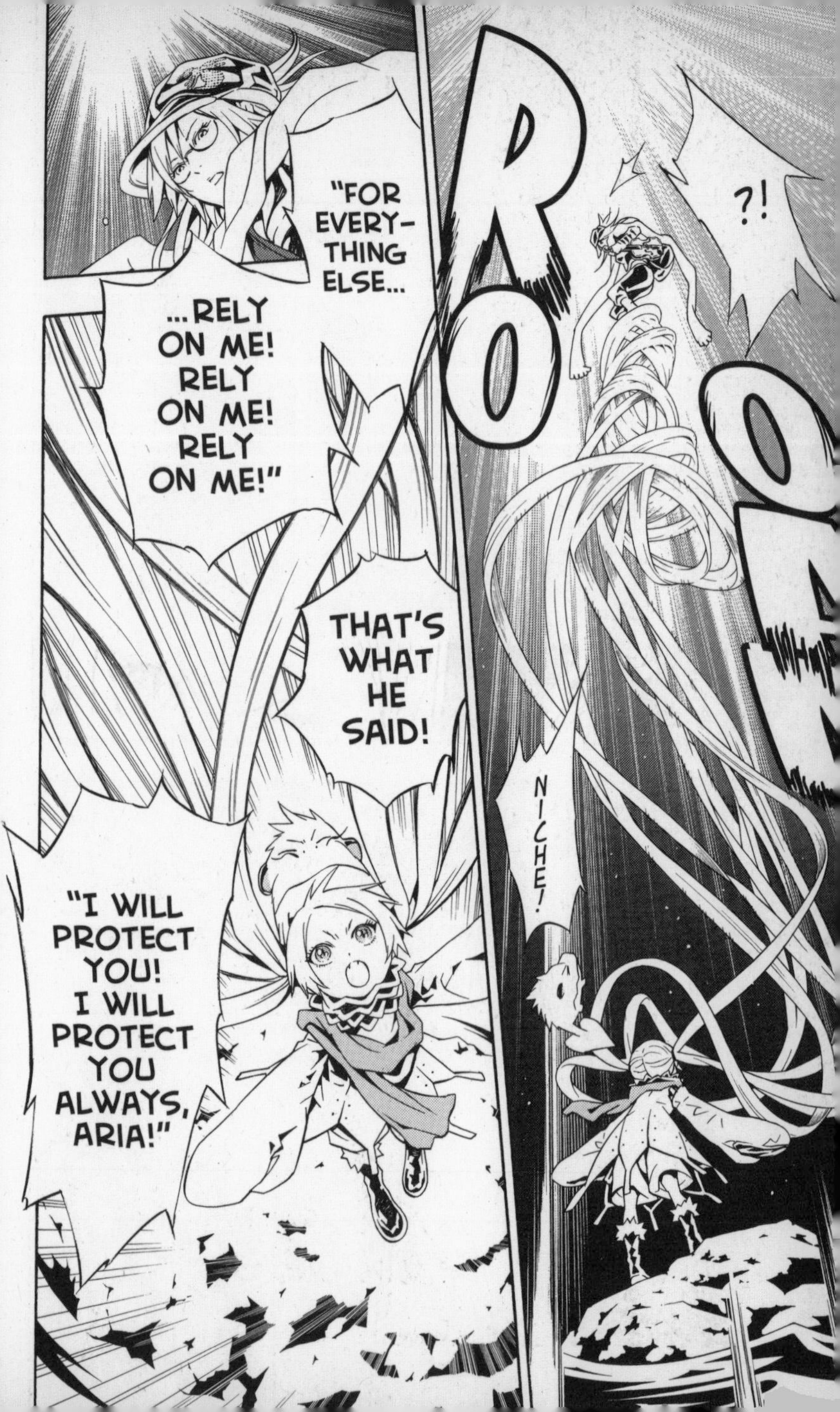
ROO
?!
NICHE!
"FOR EVERY-THING ELSE...
...RELY ON ME! RELY ON ME! RELY ON ME!"
THAT'S WHAT HE SAID!
"I WILL PROTECT YOU! I WILL PROTECT YOU ALWAYS, ARIA!"

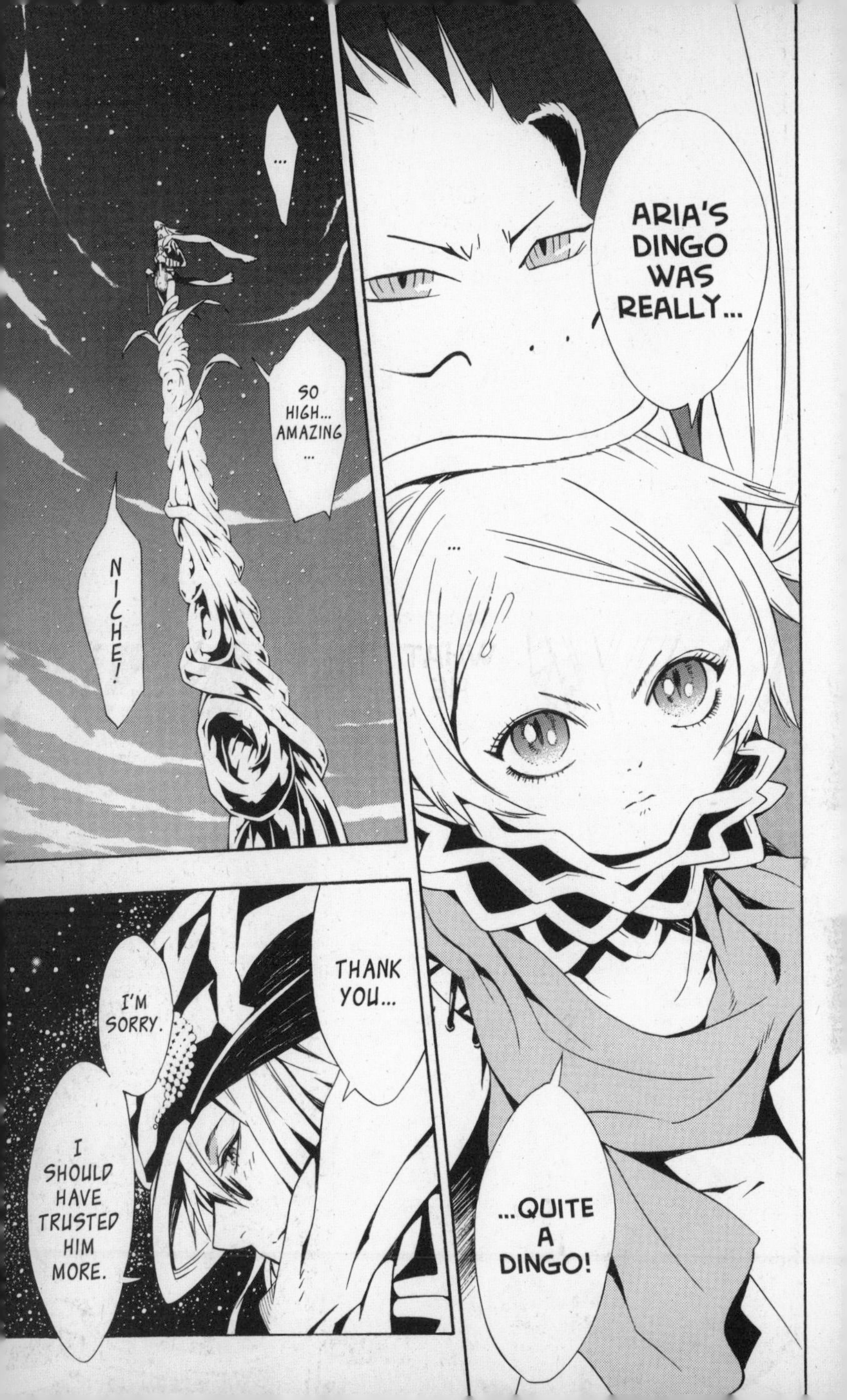
ARIA'S DINGO WAS REALLY...
...
...QUITE A DINGO!
...
SO HIGH... AMAZING...
NICHE!
THANK YOU...
I'M SORRY.
I SHOULD HAVE TRUSTED HIM MORE.

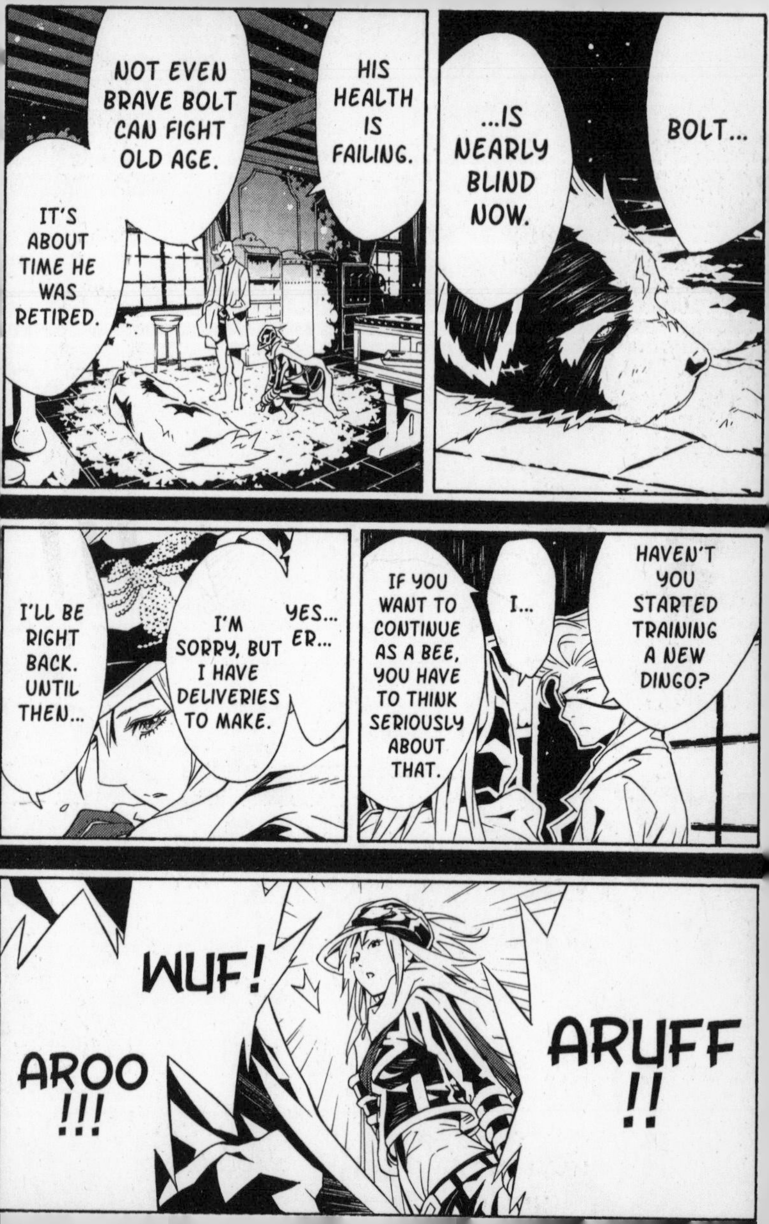
BOLT...
...IS NEARLY BLIND NOW.
HIS HEALTH IS FAILING.
NOT EVEN BRAVE BOLT CAN FIGHT OLD AGE.
IT'S ABOUT TIME HE WAS RETIRED.
HAVEN'T YOU STARTED TRAINING A NEW DINGO?
I...
IF YOU WANT TO CONTINUE AS A BEE, YOU HAVE TO THINK SERIOUSLY ABOUT THAT.
YES... ER...
I'M SORRY, BUT I HAVE DELIVERIES TO MAKE.
I'LL BE RIGHT BACK. UNTIL THEN...
ARUFF !!
WUF!
AROO !!!

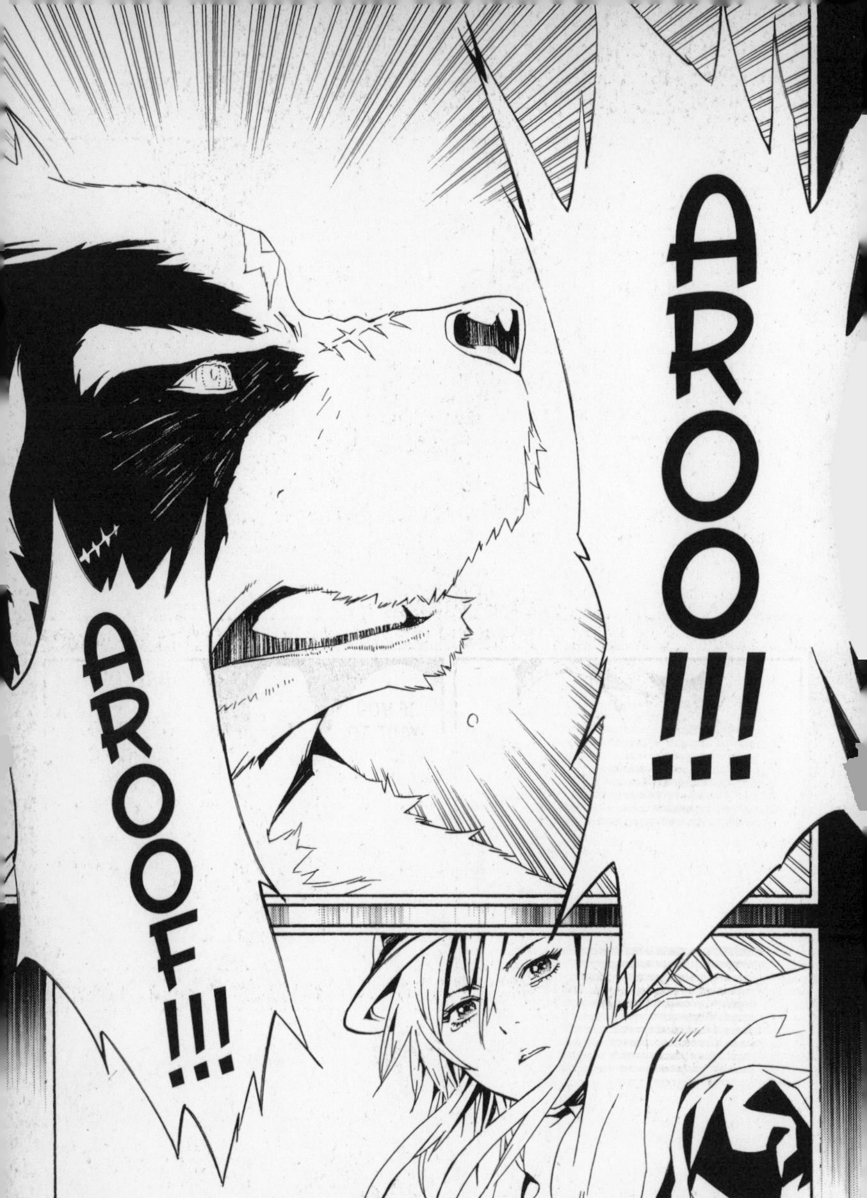
AROO!!!
AROOF!!!

Bees travel on their deliveries...

...protected by their proud dingos.

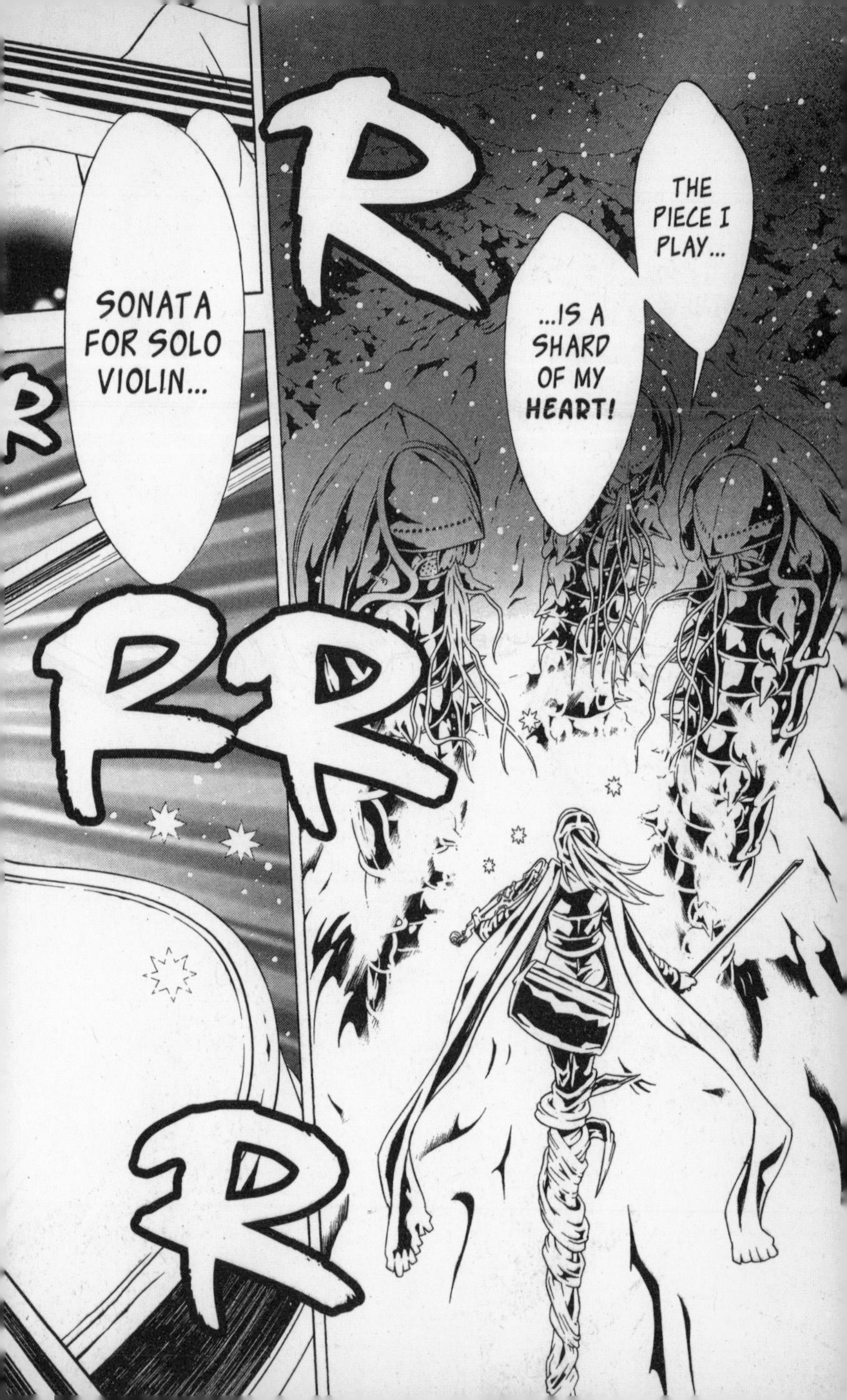
THE PIECE I PLAY...
...IS A SHARD OF MY HEART!
R
SONATA FOR SOLO VIOLIN...
RR
R

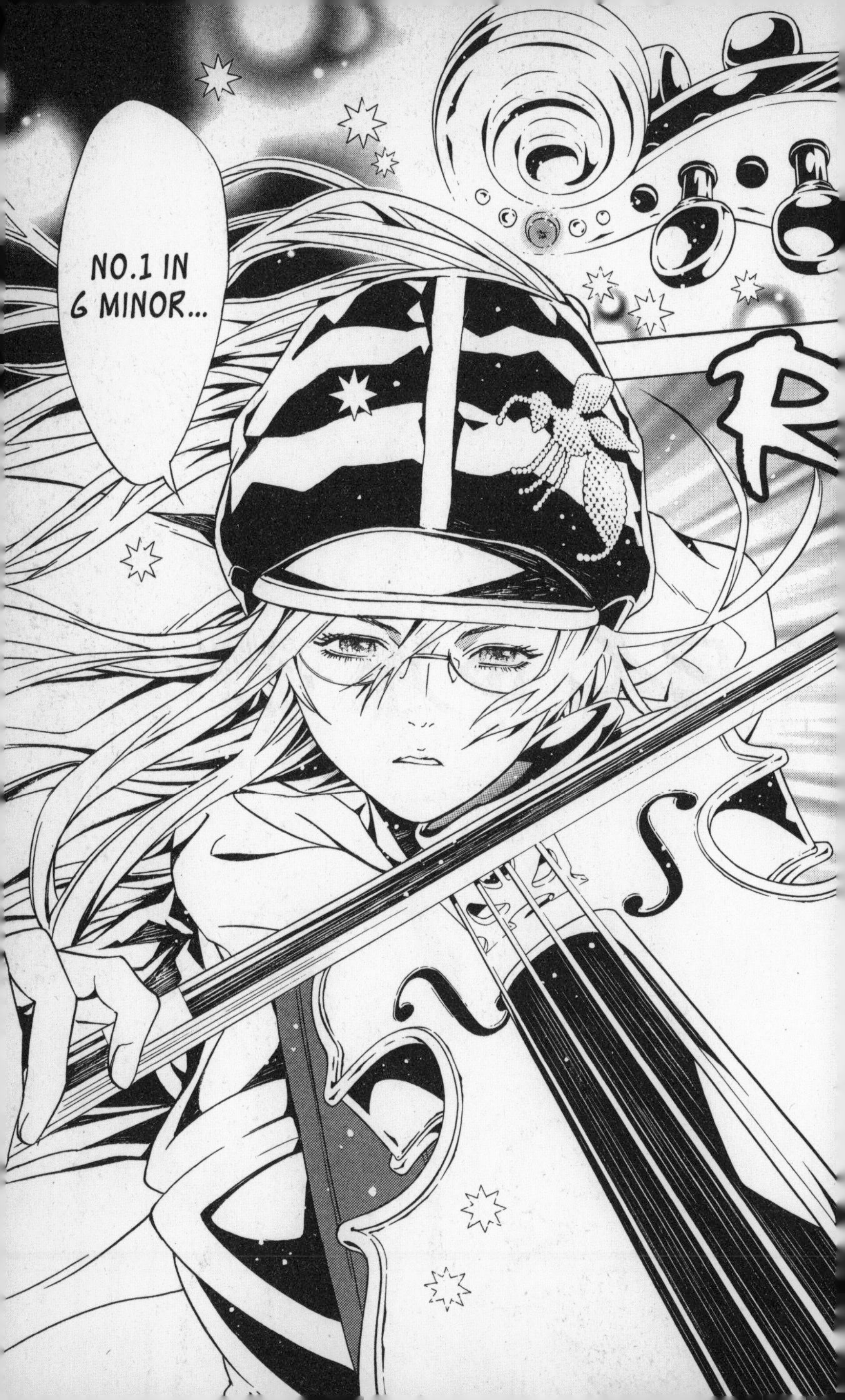
NO.1 IN G MINOR...
R

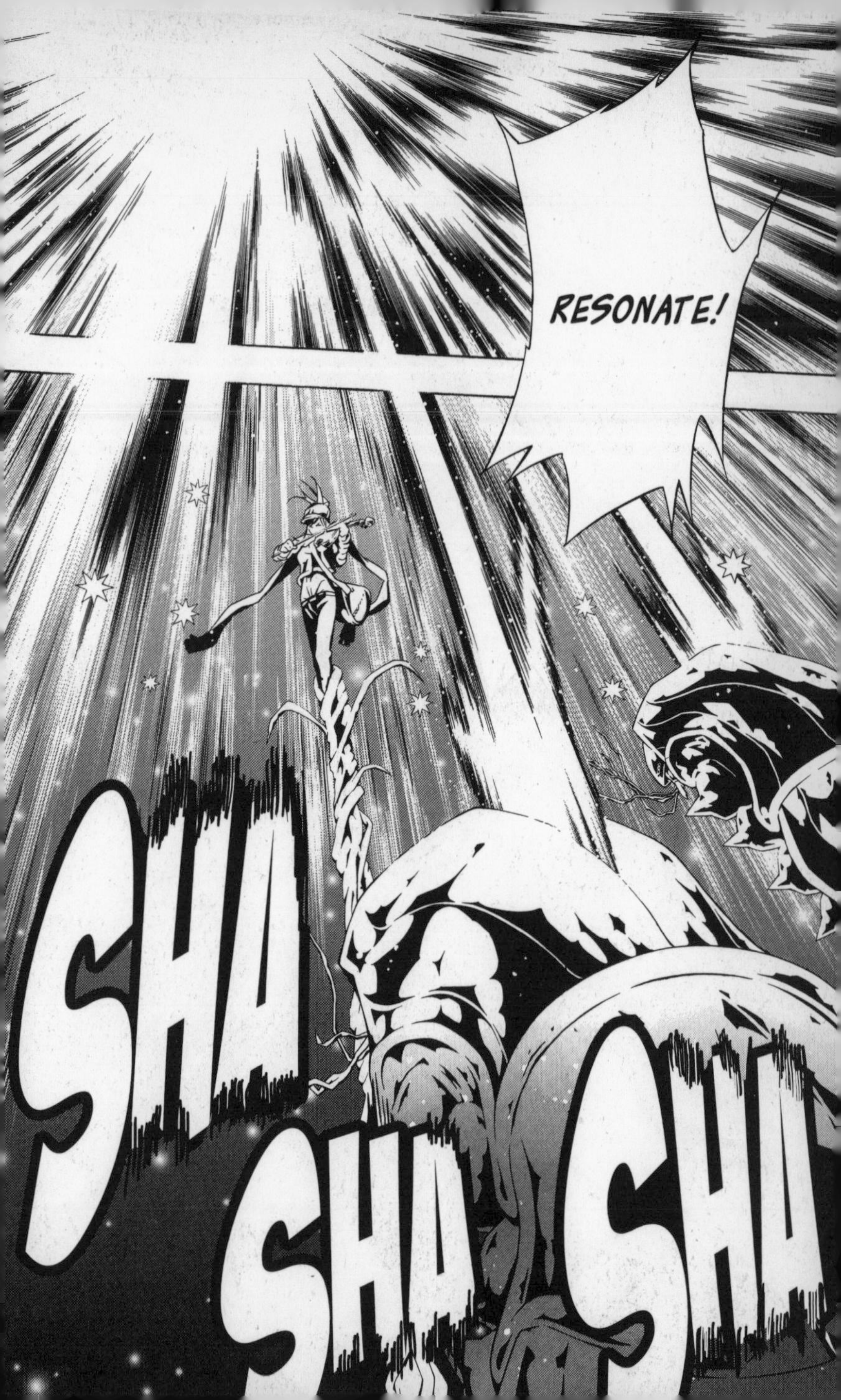
RESONATE!
SHA
SHA
SHA

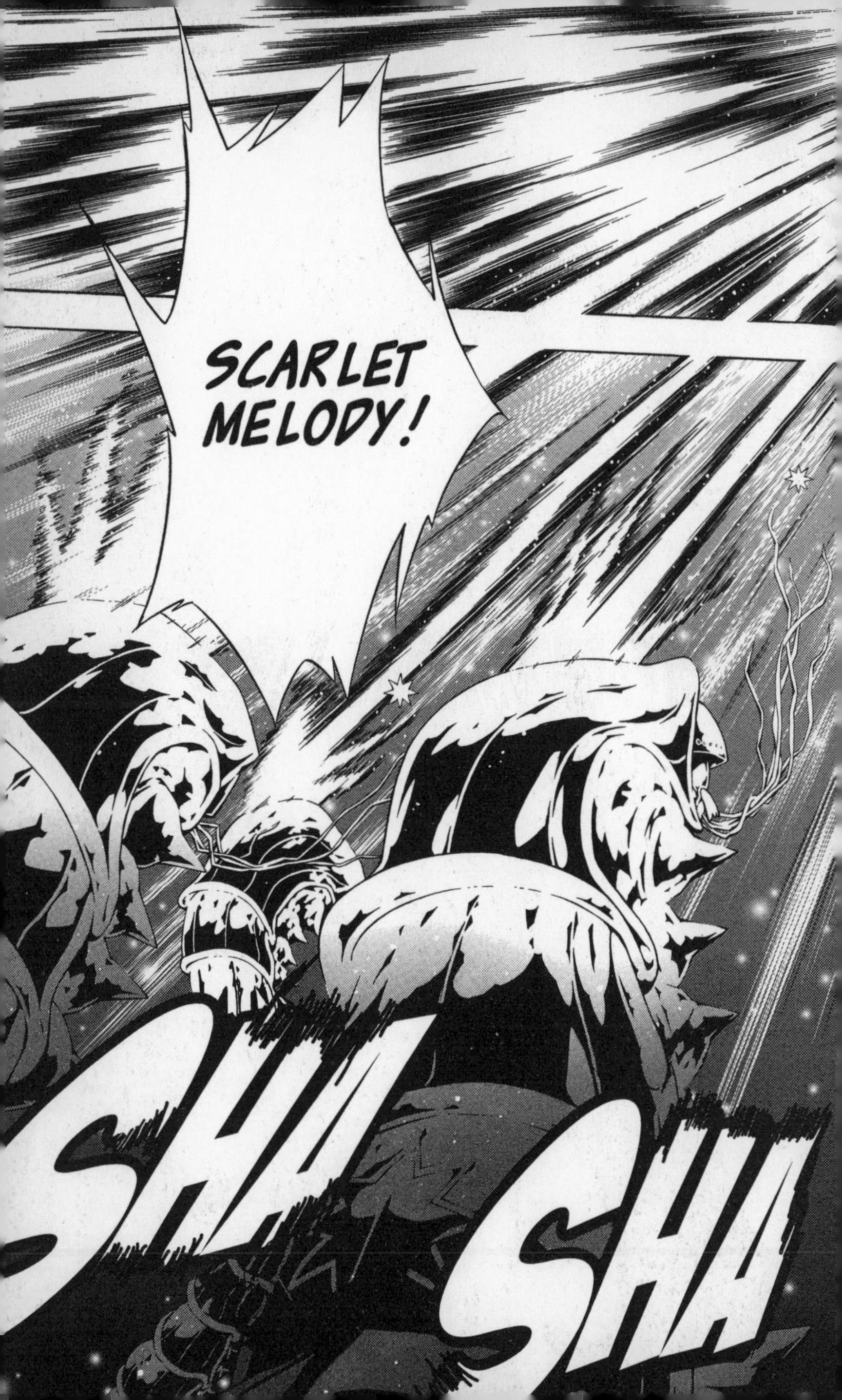
SCARLET MELODY!
SHA
SHA

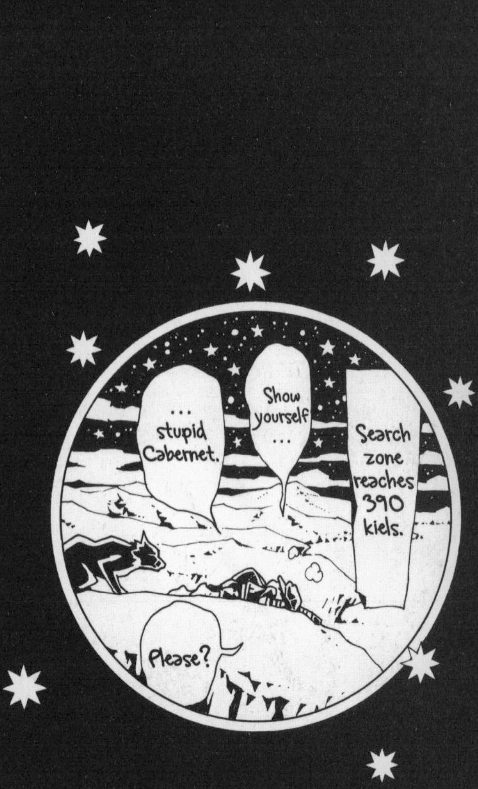
Search zone reaches 390 kiels.
Show yourself ...
... stupid Cabernet.
Please?

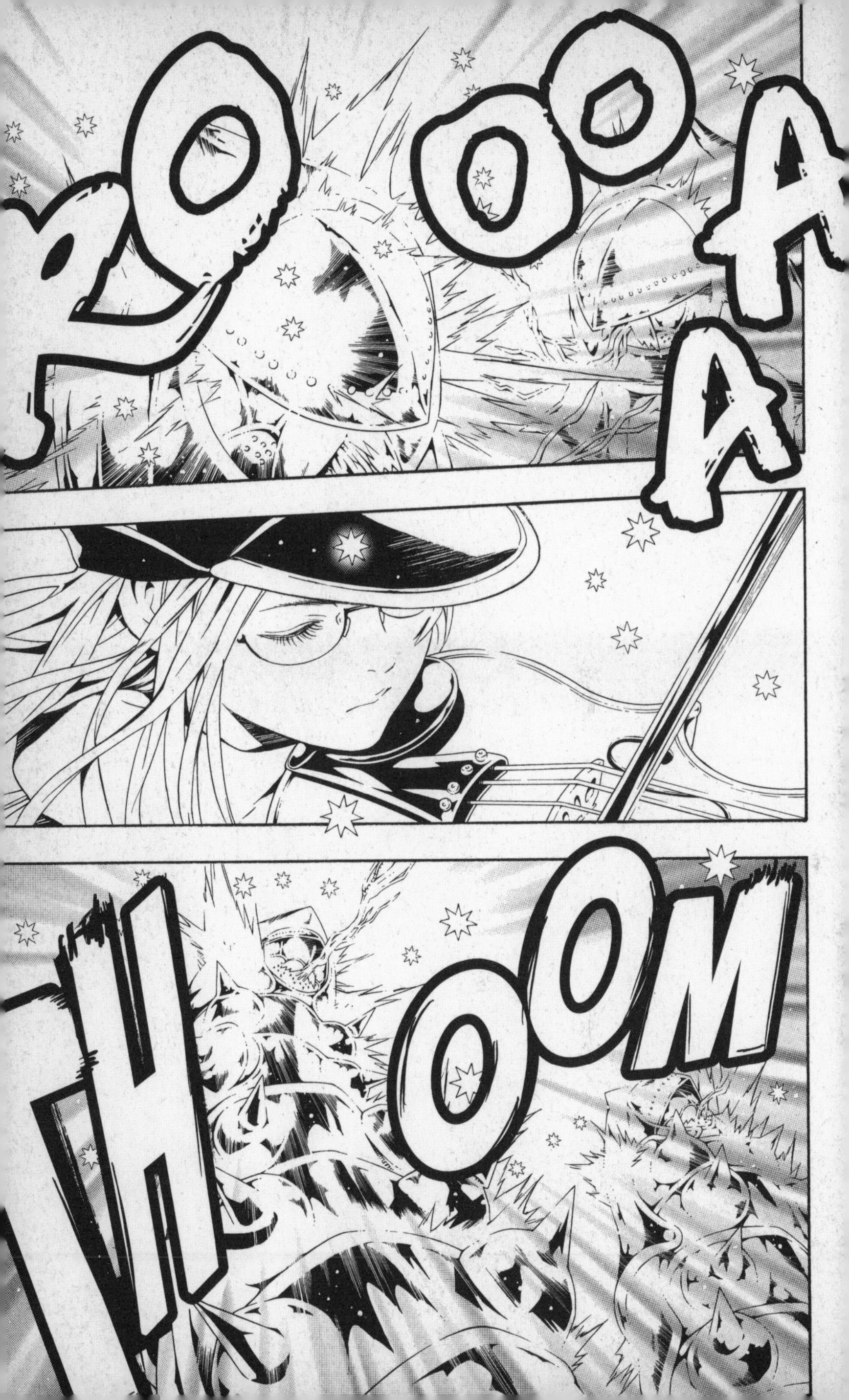
OOOAA
HOOM

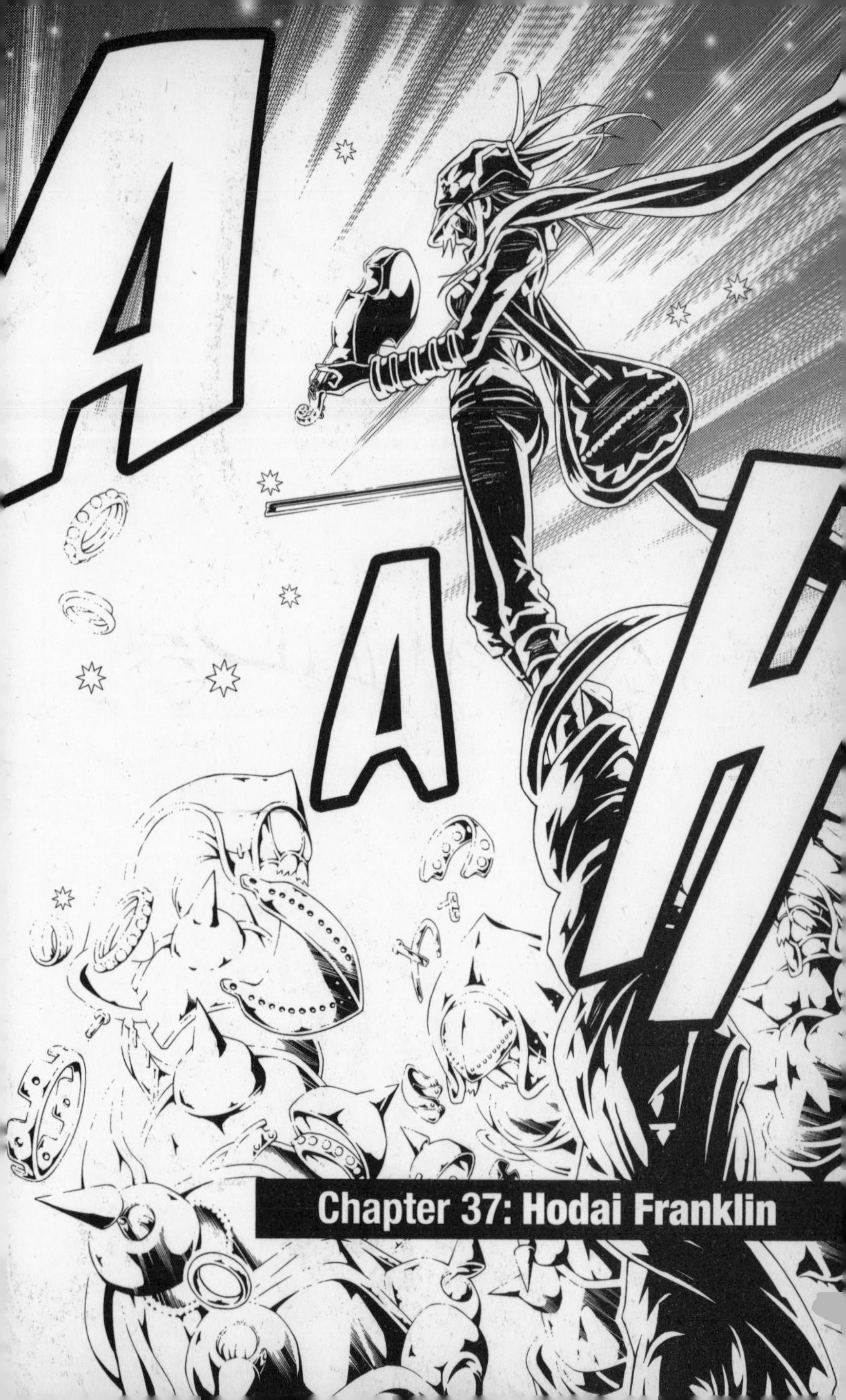
A
A

Chapter 37: Hodai Franklin

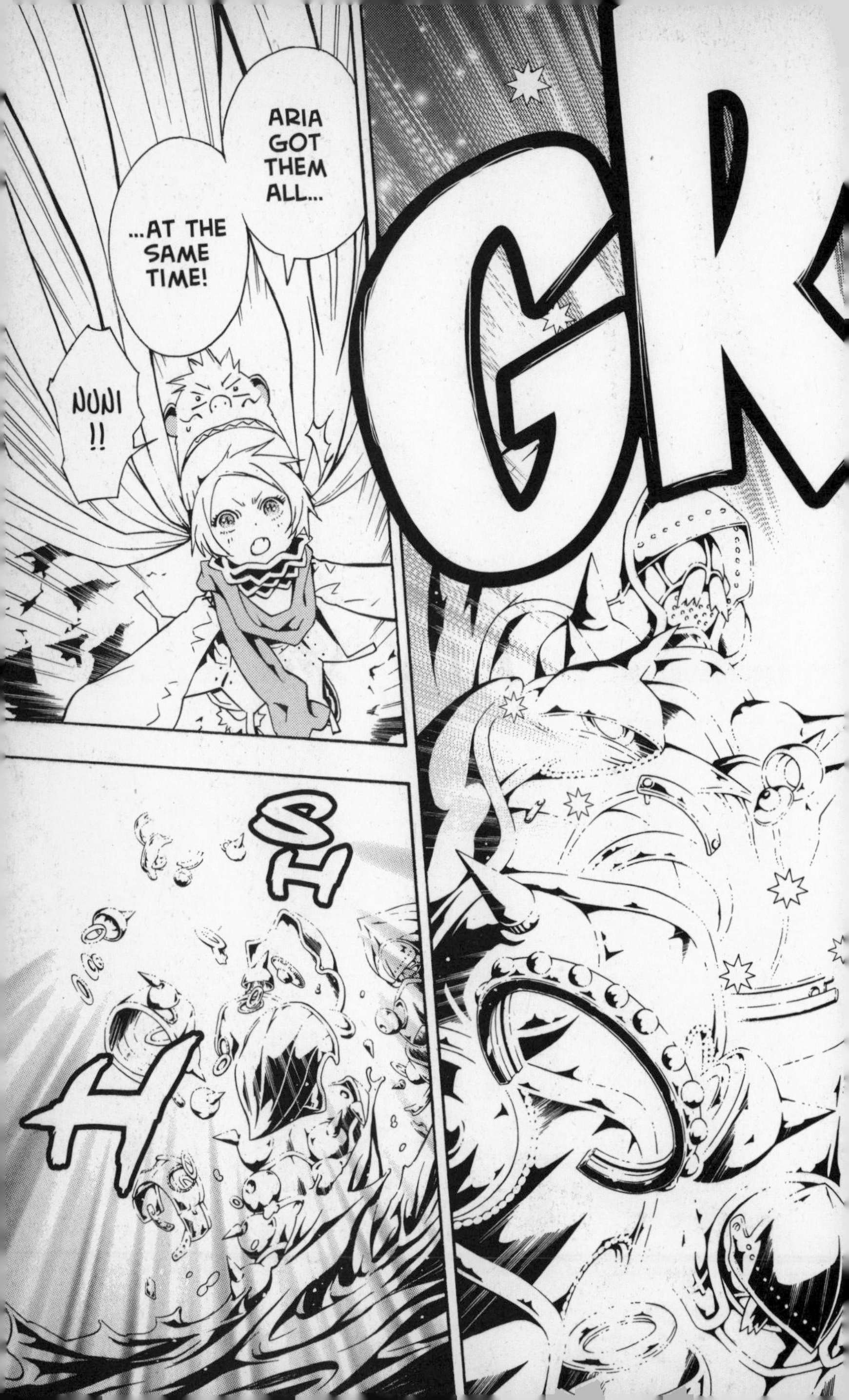
GK
ARIA GOT THEM ALL...
...AT THE SAME TIME!
NUNI !!
SHH

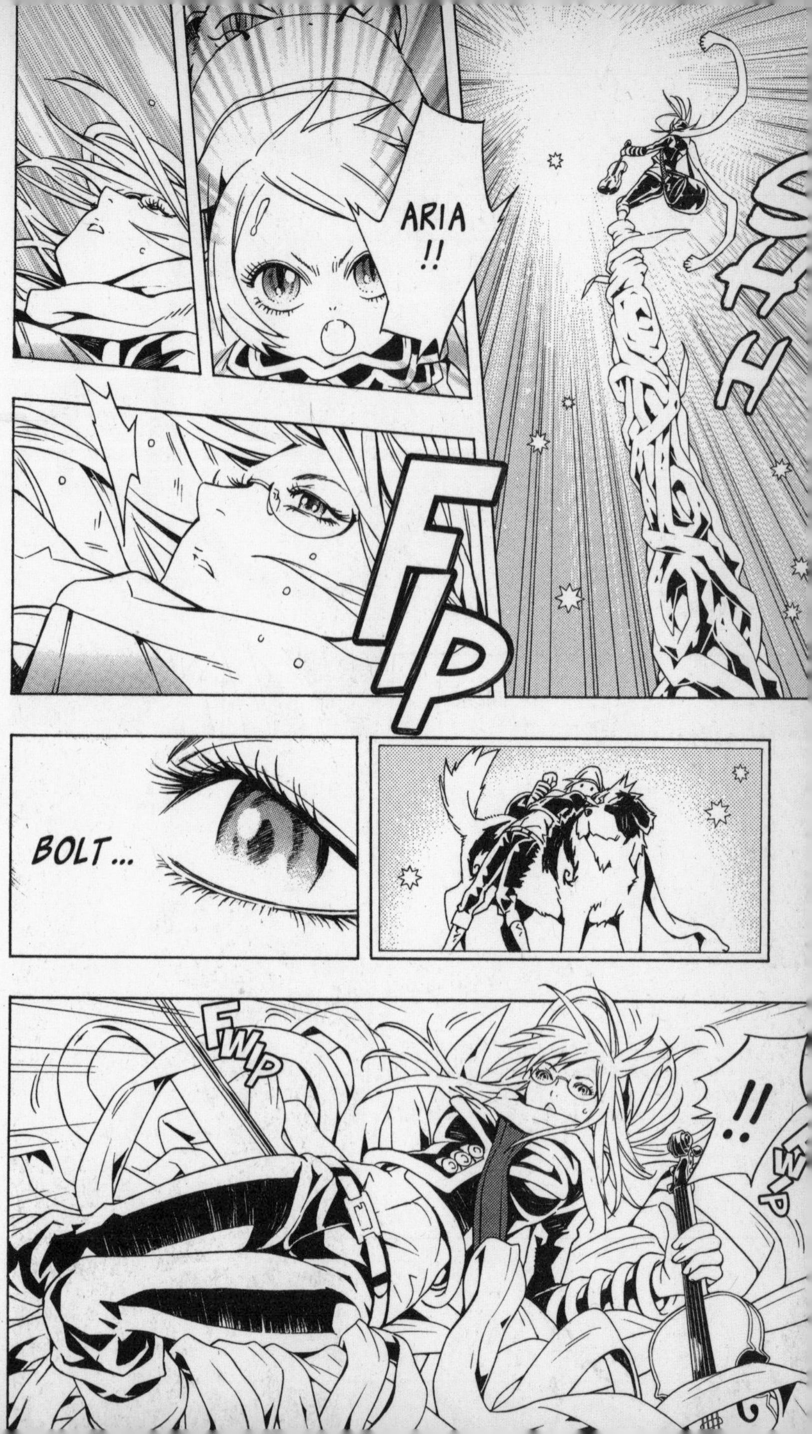
SHH
ARIA !!
FIP
BOLT...
FWIP
!!
FWIP

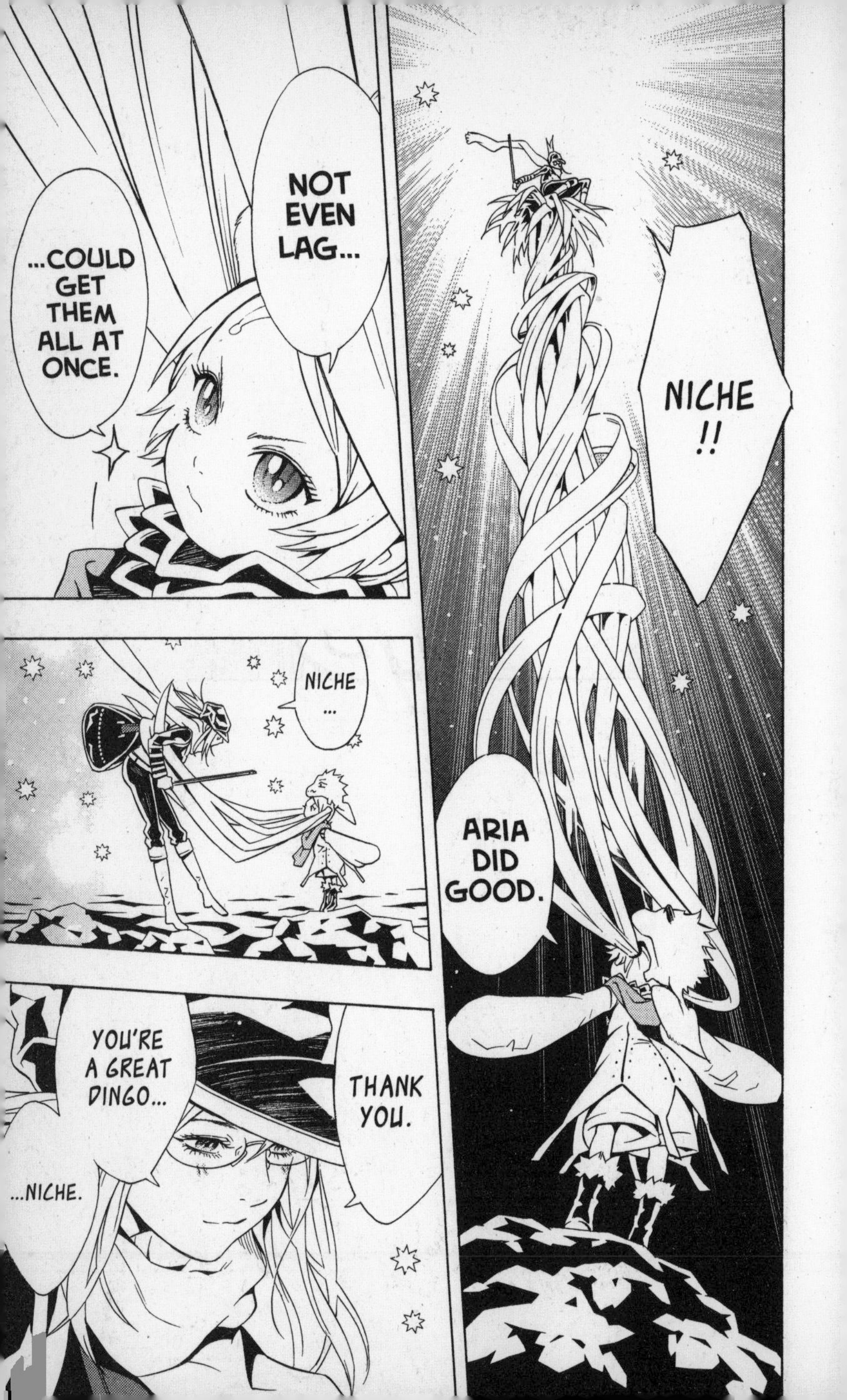
NICHE !!
ARIA DID GOOD.
NOT EVEN LAG...
...COULD GET THEM ALL AT ONCE.
NICHE ...
YOU'RE A GREAT DINGO...
...NICHE.
THANK YOU.

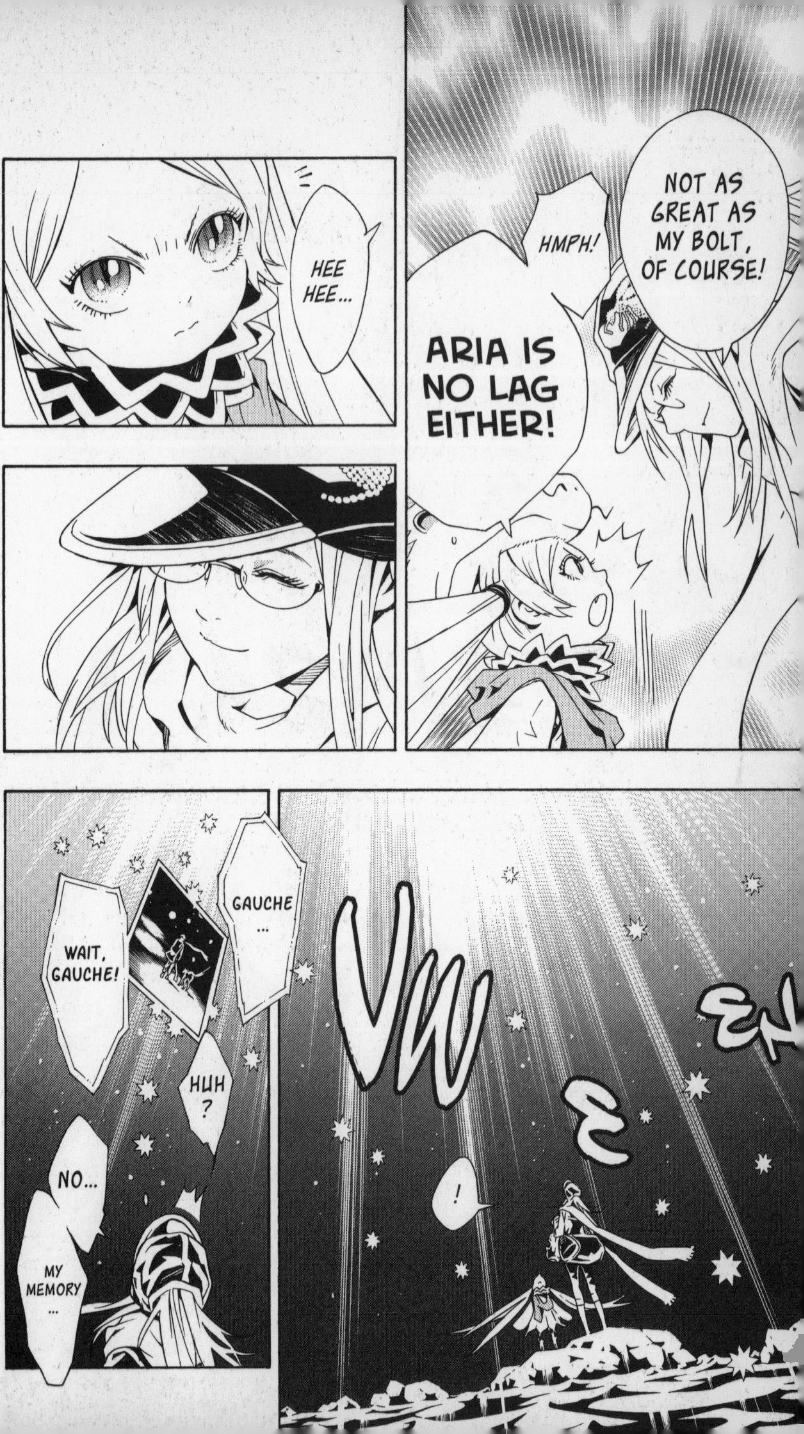
NOT AS GREAT AS MY BOLT, OF COURSE!
HMPH!
ARIA IS NO LAG EITHER!
HEE HEE...
VWEEN
!
GAUCHE...
WAIT, GAUCHE!
HUH?
NO...
MY MEMORY...

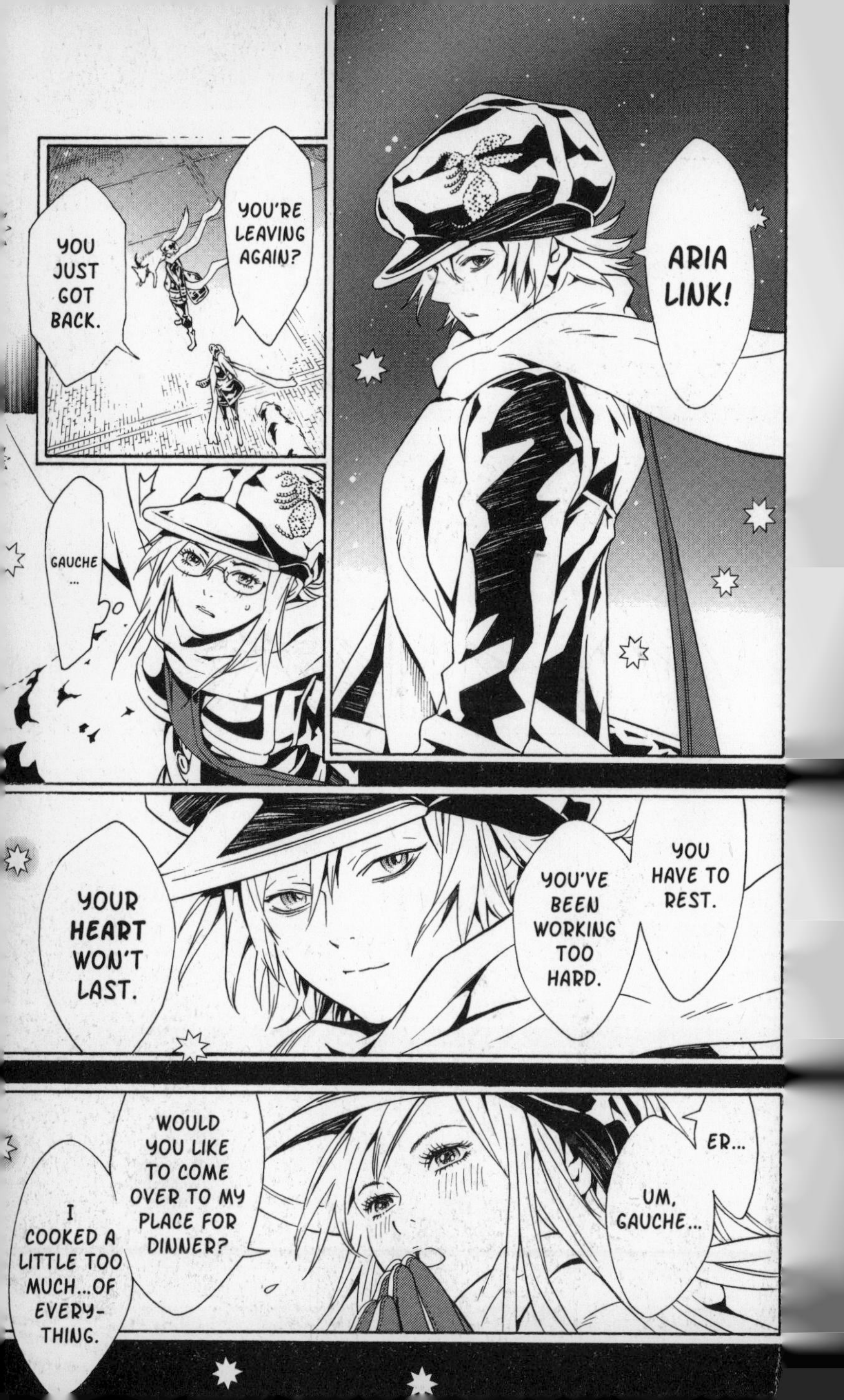
ARIA LINK!
YOU'RE LEAVING AGAIN?
YOU JUST GOT BACK.
GAUCHE ...
YOU HAVE TO REST.
YOU'VE BEEN WORKING TOO HARD.
YOUR HEART WON'T LAST.
ER...
UM, GAUCHE...
WOULD YOU LIKE TO COME OVER TO MY PLACE FOR DINNER?
I COOKED A LITTLE TOO MUCH...OF EVERY-THING.

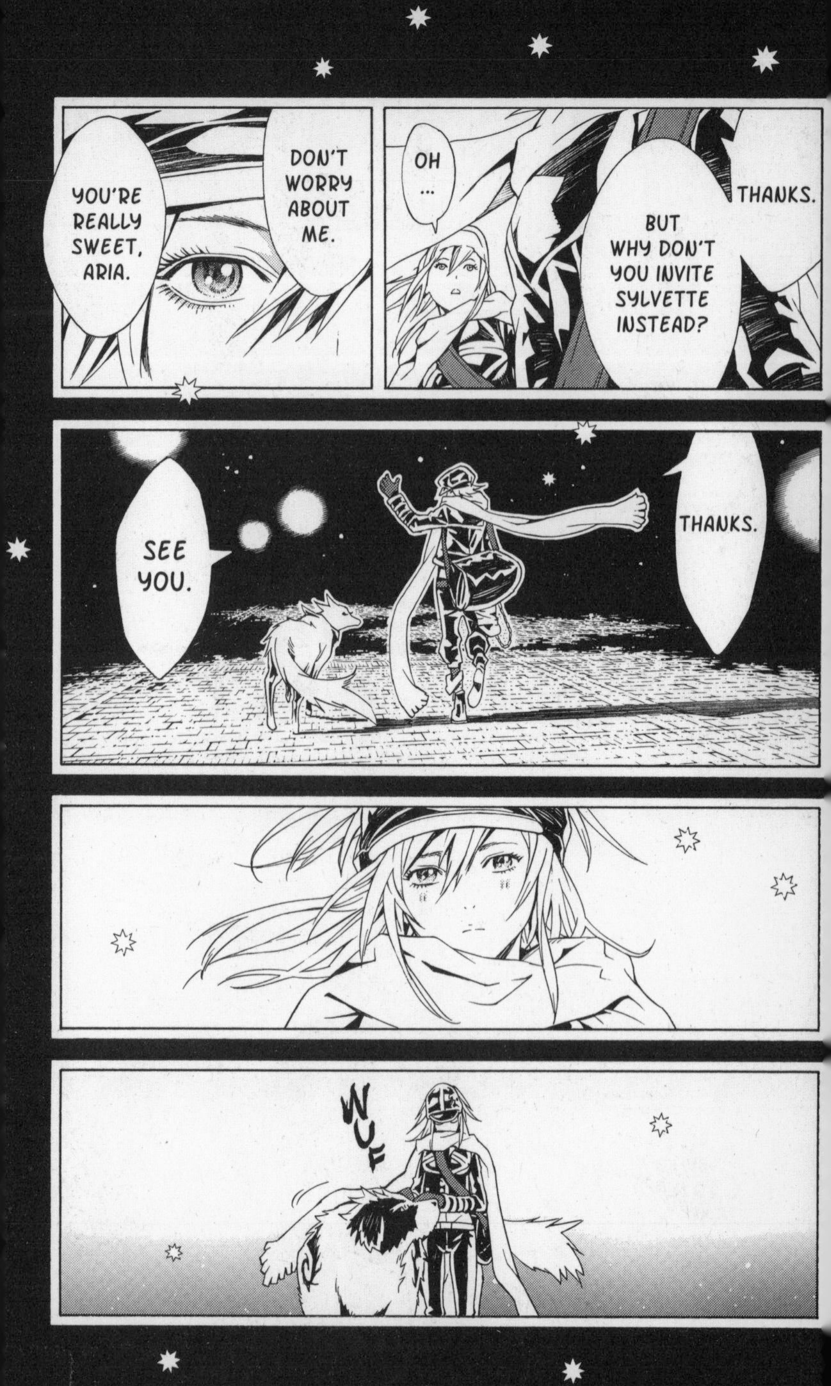
THANKS.
BUT WHY DON'T YOU INVITE SYLVETTE INSTEAD?
OH ...
DON'T WORRY ABOUT ME.
YOU'RE REALLY SWEET, ARIA.
THANKS.
SEE YOU.
WUF

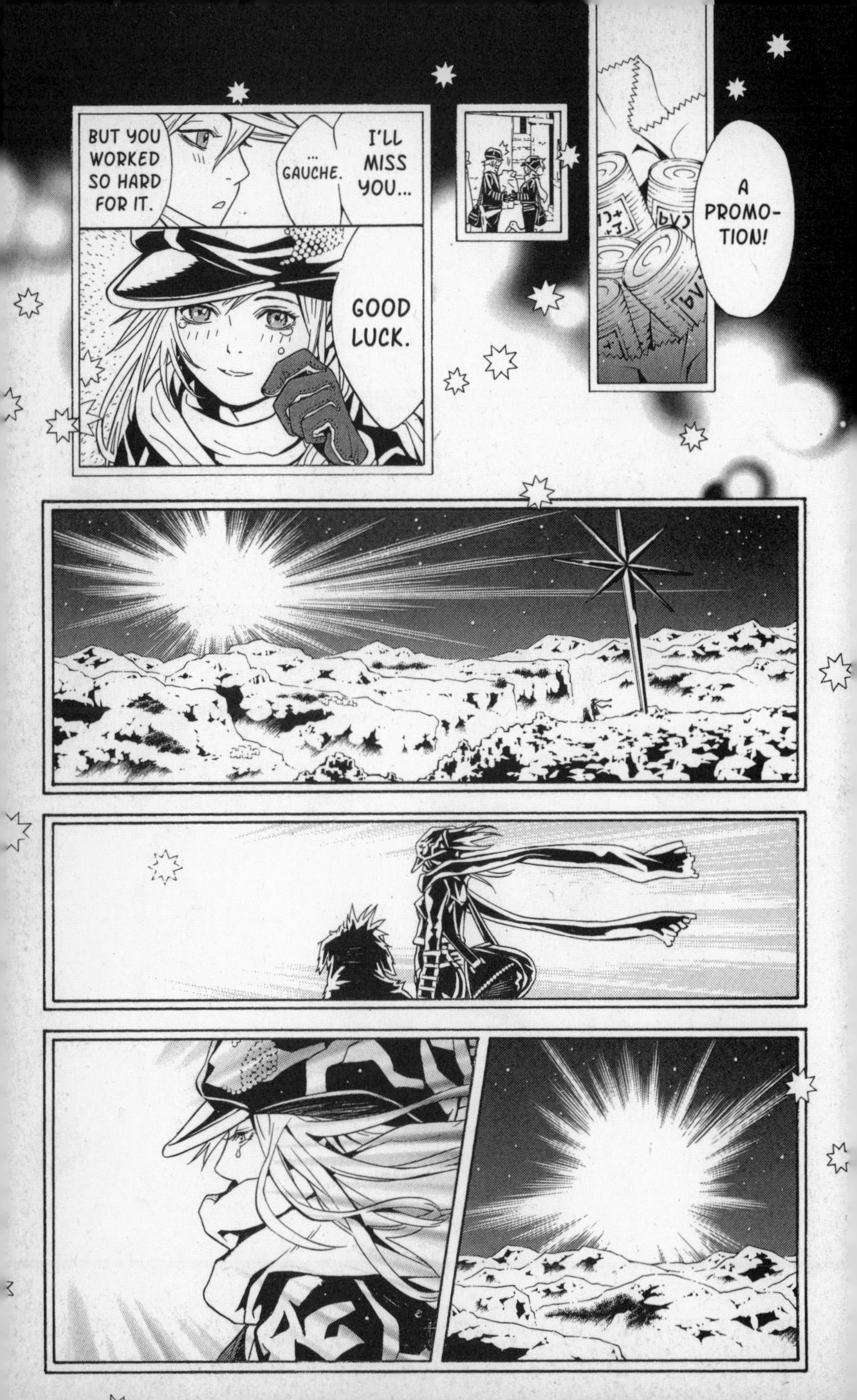
A PROMOTION!
I'LL MISS YOU...
... GAUCHE.
BUT YOU WORKED SO HARD FOR IT.
GOOD LUCK.

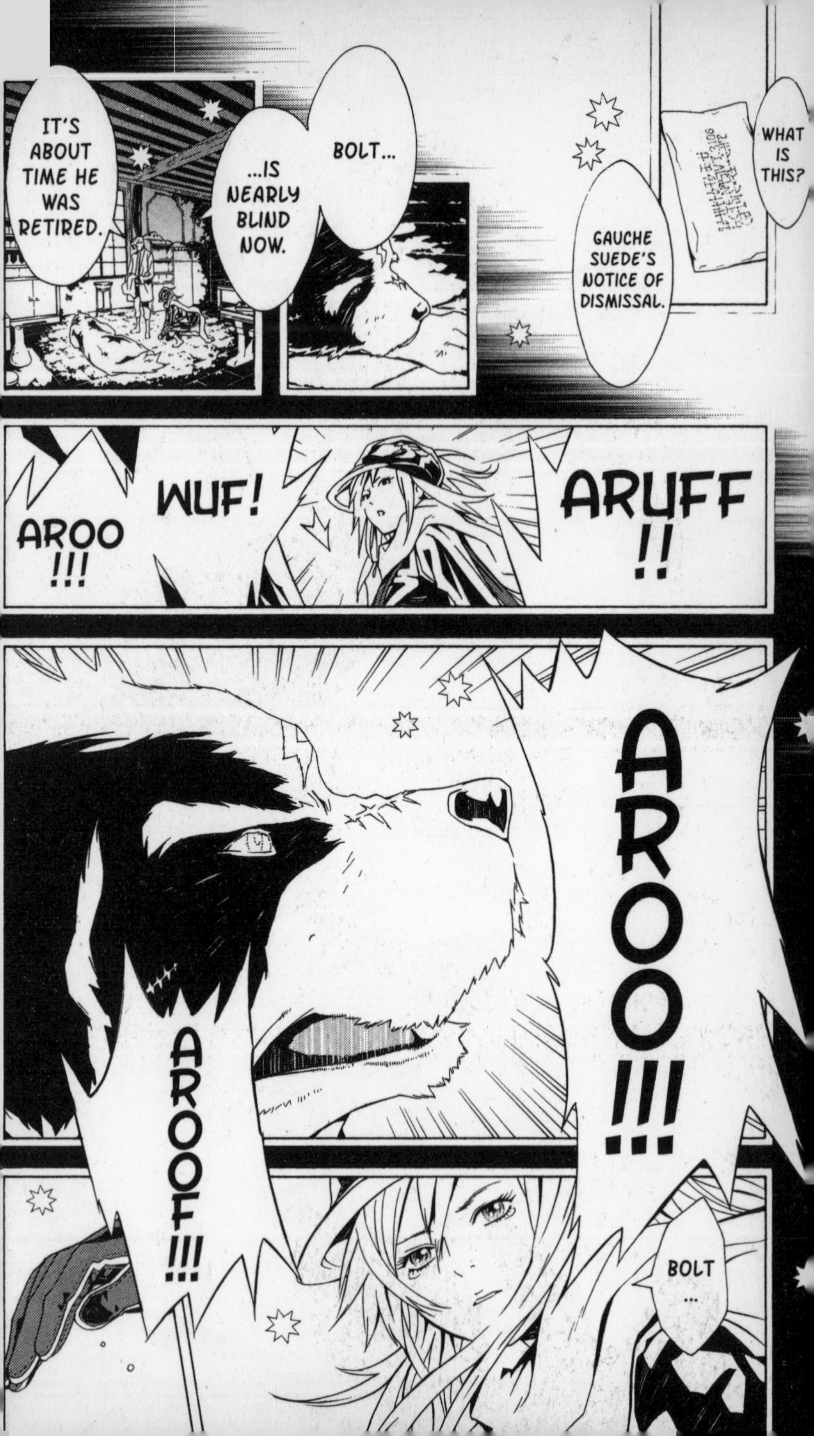
WHAT IS THIS?
GAUCHE SUEDE'S NOTICE OF DISMISSAL.
BOLT...
...IS NEARLY BLIND NOW.
IT'S ABOUT TIME HE WAS RETIRED.
ARUFF!!
WUF!
AROO!!!
AROO!!!
AROOOF!!!
BOLT...

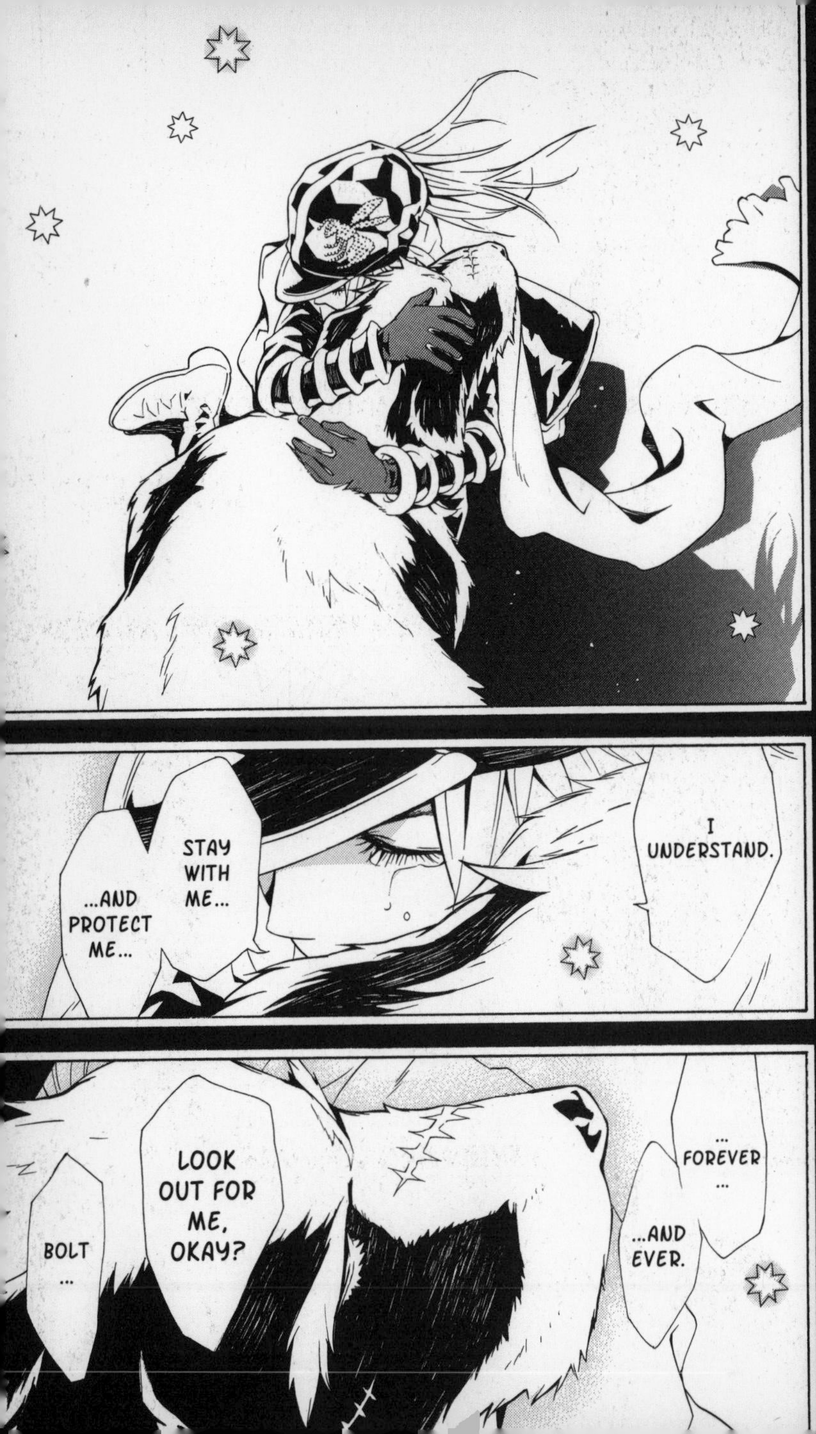
I UNDERSTAND.
STAY WITH ME...
...AND PROTECT ME...
...FOREVER...
...AND EVER.
LOOK OUT FOR ME, OKAY?
BOLT...

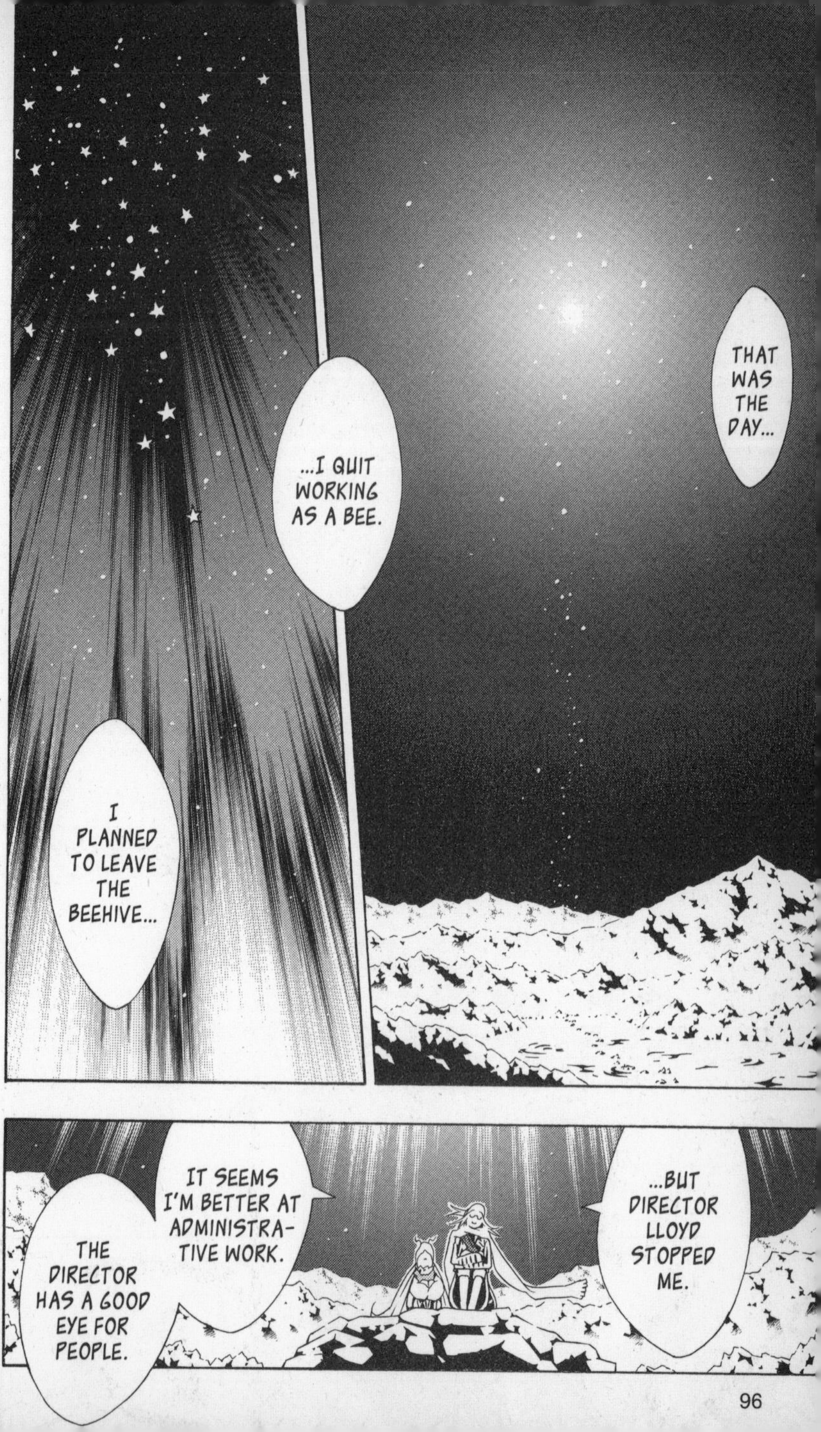
THAT WAS THE DAY...
...I QUIT WORKING AS A BEE.
I PLANNED TO LEAVE THE BEEHIVE...
...BUT DIRECTOR LLOYD STOPPED ME.
IT SEEMS I'M BETTER AT ADMINISTRATIVE WORK.
THE DIRECTOR HAS A GOOD EYE FOR PEOPLE.

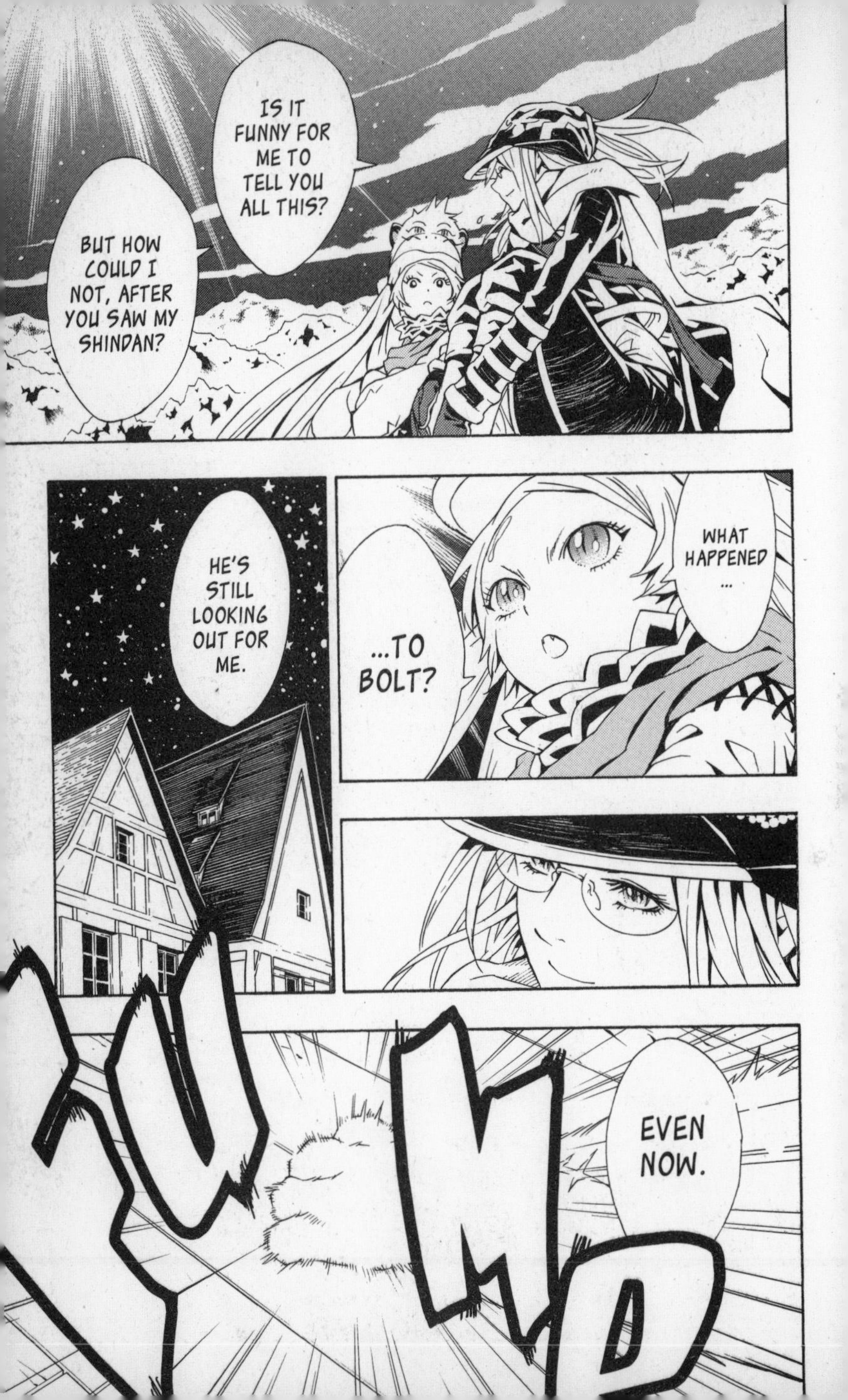
IS IT FUNNY FOR ME TO TELL YOU ALL THIS?
BUT HOW COULD I NOT, AFTER YOU SAW MY SHINDAN?
WHAT HAPPENED ...
...TO BOLT?
HE'S STILL LOOKING OUT FOR ME.
EVEN NOW.

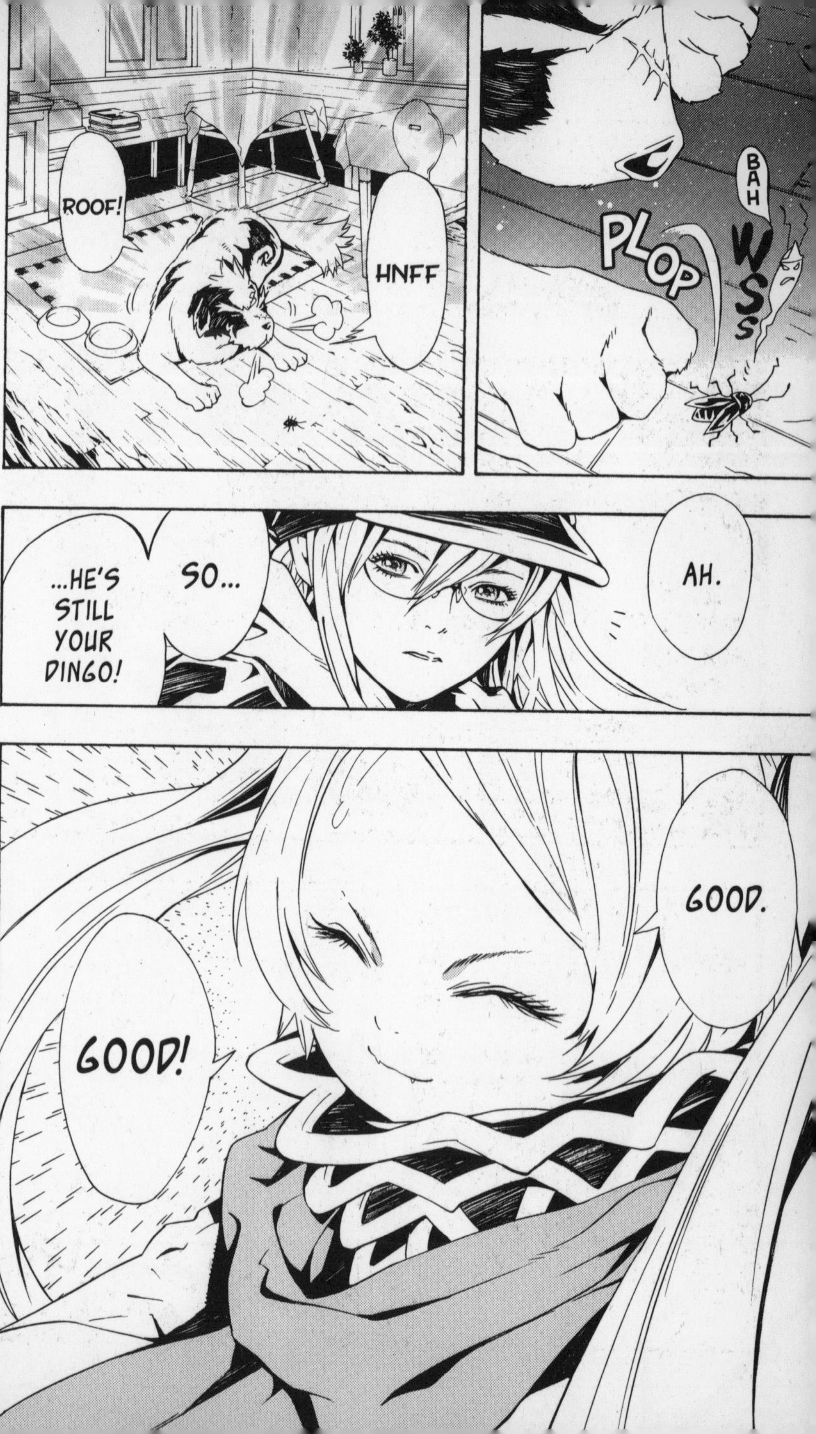

BAH
PLOP
WSS
HNFF
ROOF!
AH.
SO...
...HE'S STILL YOUR DINGO!
GOOD.
GOOD!

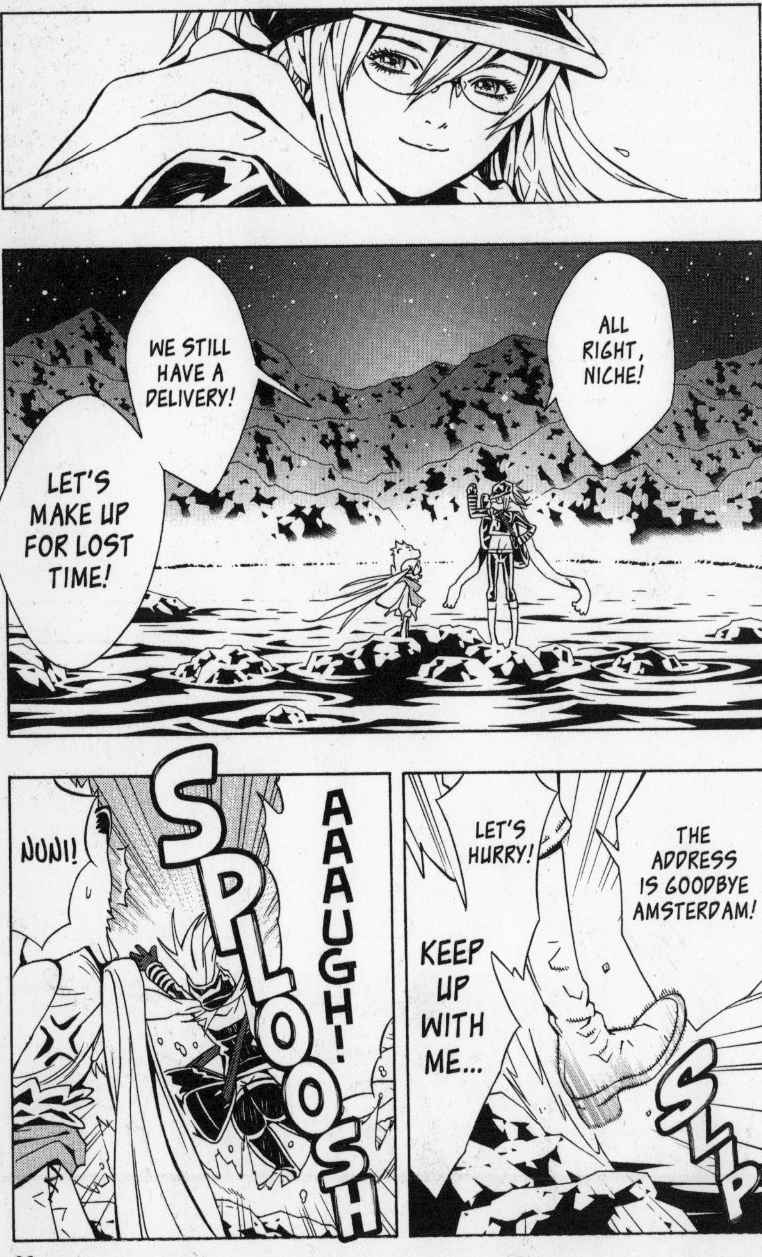
ALL RIGHT, NICHE!
WE STILL HAVE A DELIVERY!
LET'S MAKE UP FOR LOST TIME!
THE ADDRESS IS GOODBYE AMSTERDAM!
LET'S HURRY!
KEEP UP WITH ME...
SLIP
AAAUGH!
SPLOOSH
NUNI!

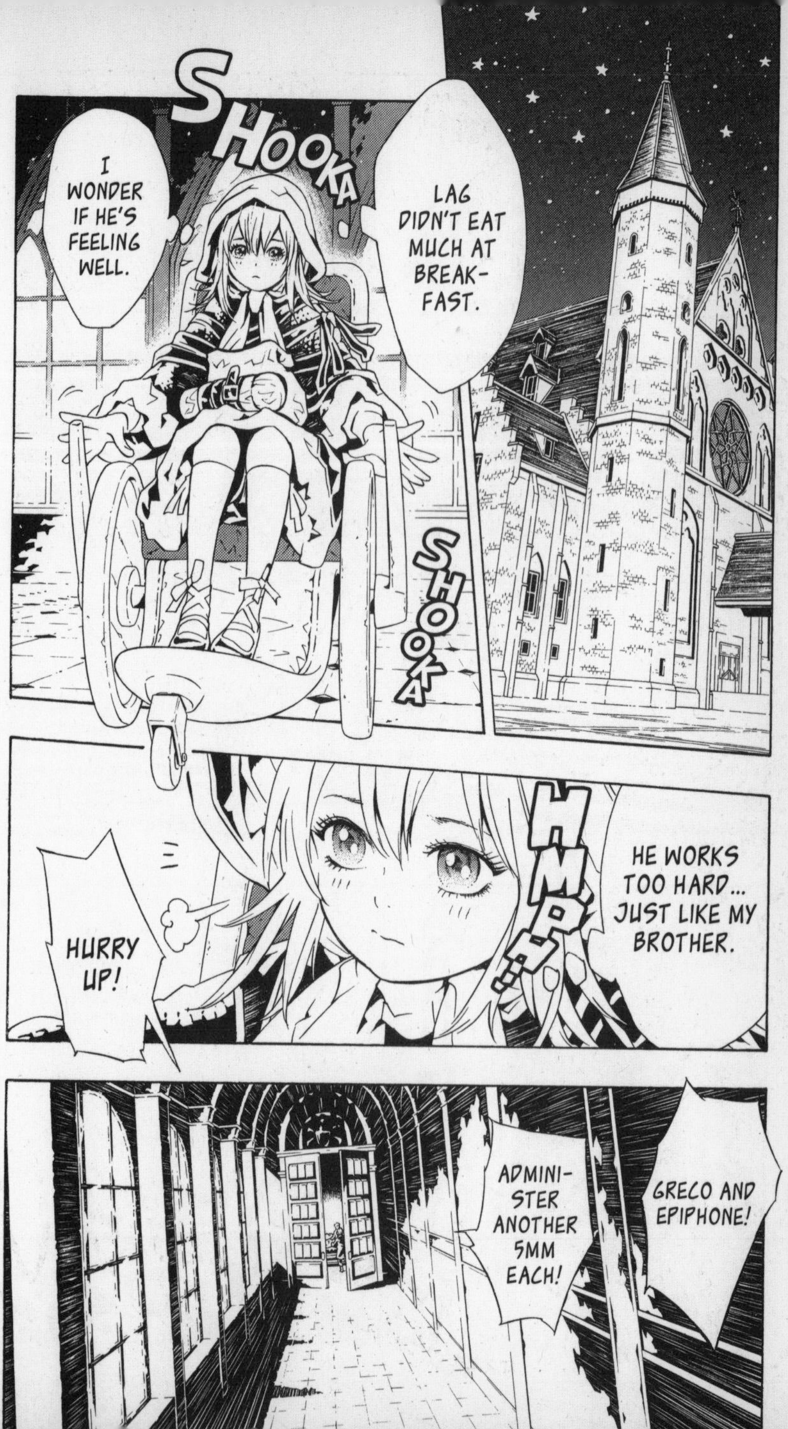
LAG DIDN'T EAT MUCH AT BREAK-FAST.
SHOOKA
I WONDER IF HE'S FEELING WELL.
SHOOKA
HE WORKS TOO HARD... JUST LIKE MY BROTHER.
HMPH!
HURRY UP!
GRECO AND EPIPHONE!
ADMINI-STER ANOTHER 5MM EACH!

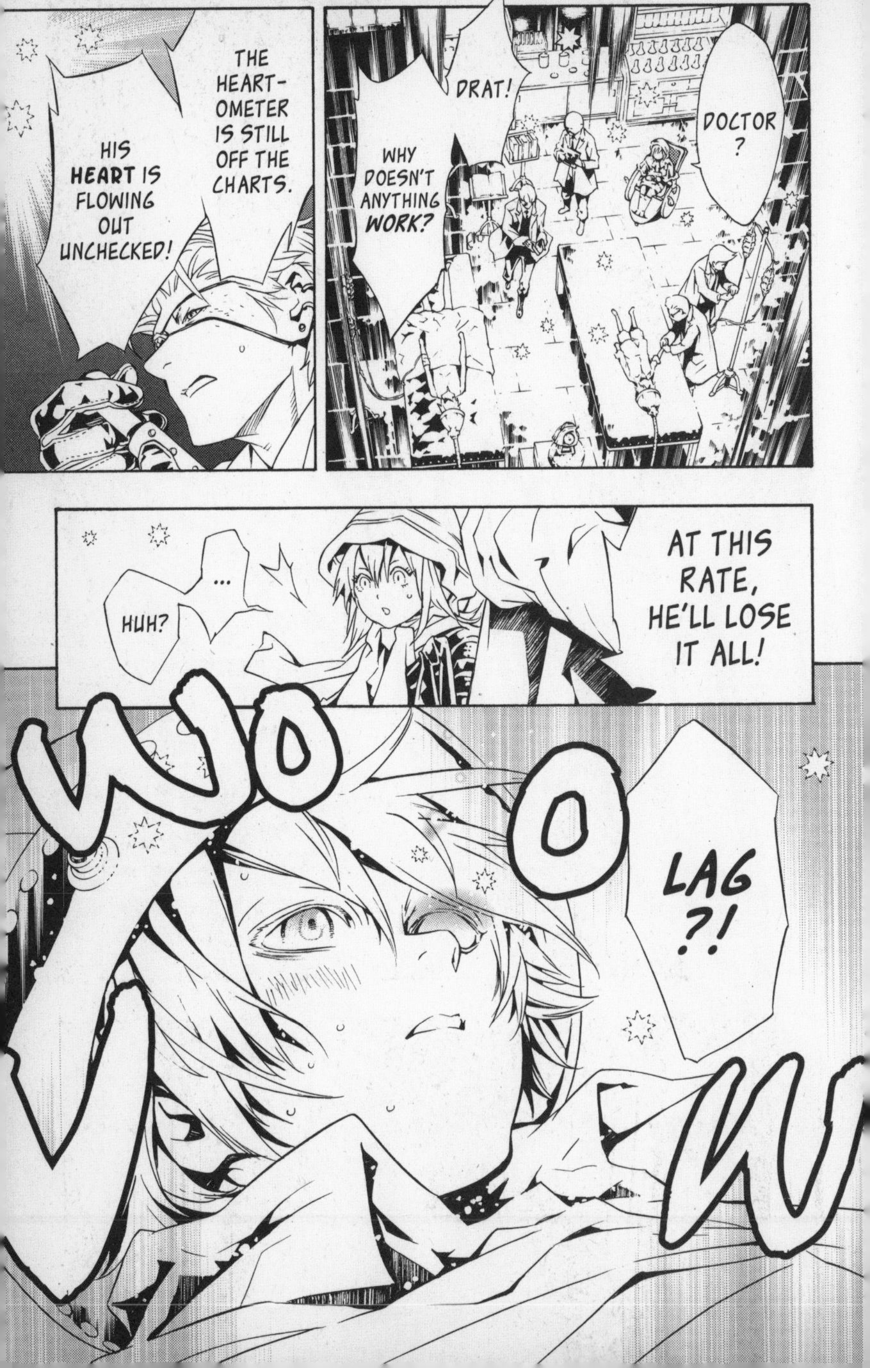
DOCTOR ?
DRAT!
WHY DOESN'T ANYTHING **WORK?**
THE HEART-OMETER IS STILL OFF THE CHARTS.
HIS **HEART** IS FLOWING OUT UNCHECKED!
AT THIS RATE, HE'LL LOSE IT ALL!
...
HUH?
LAG ?!
WOOW

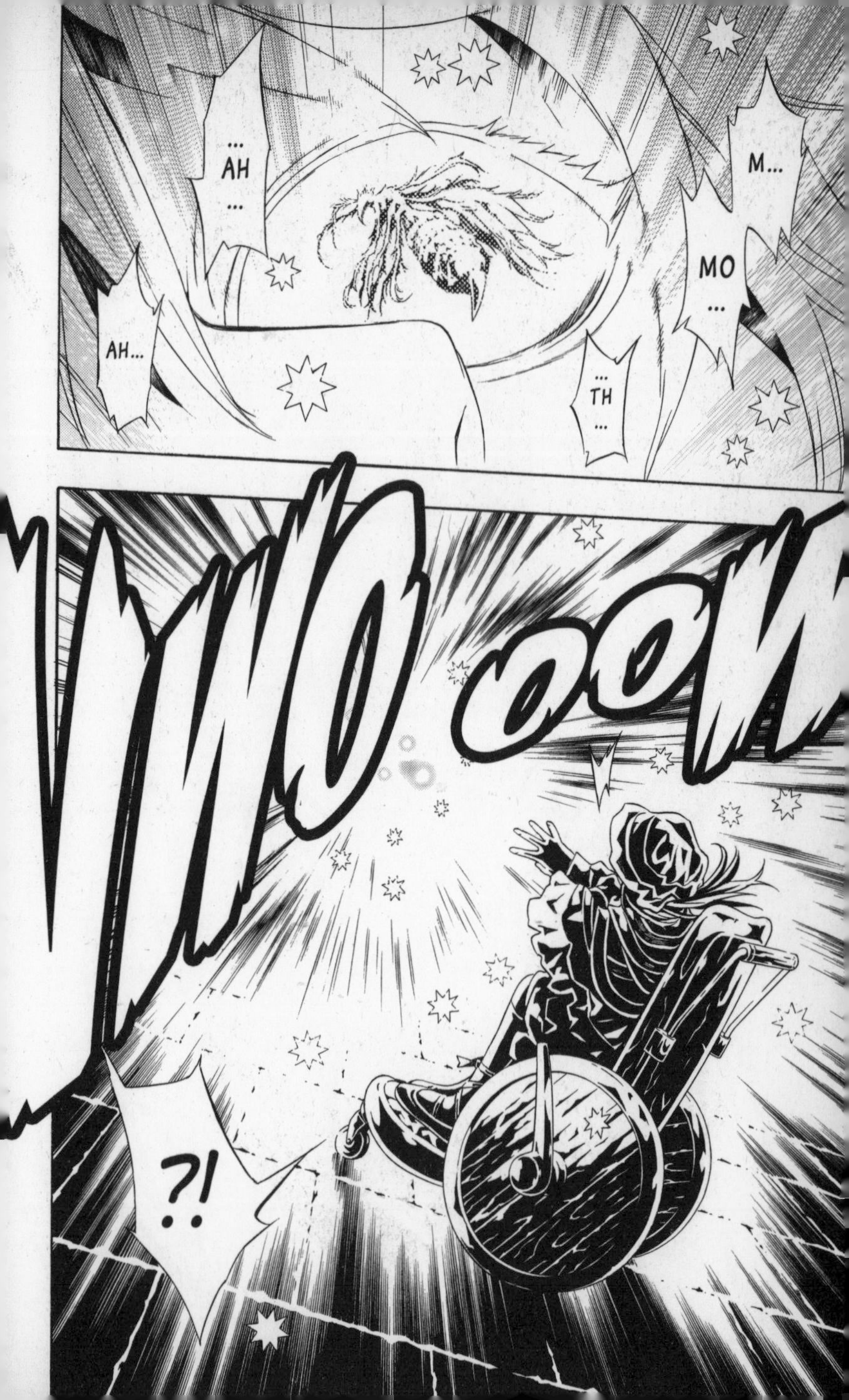
M...
MO...
...TH...
...AH...
AH...
?!

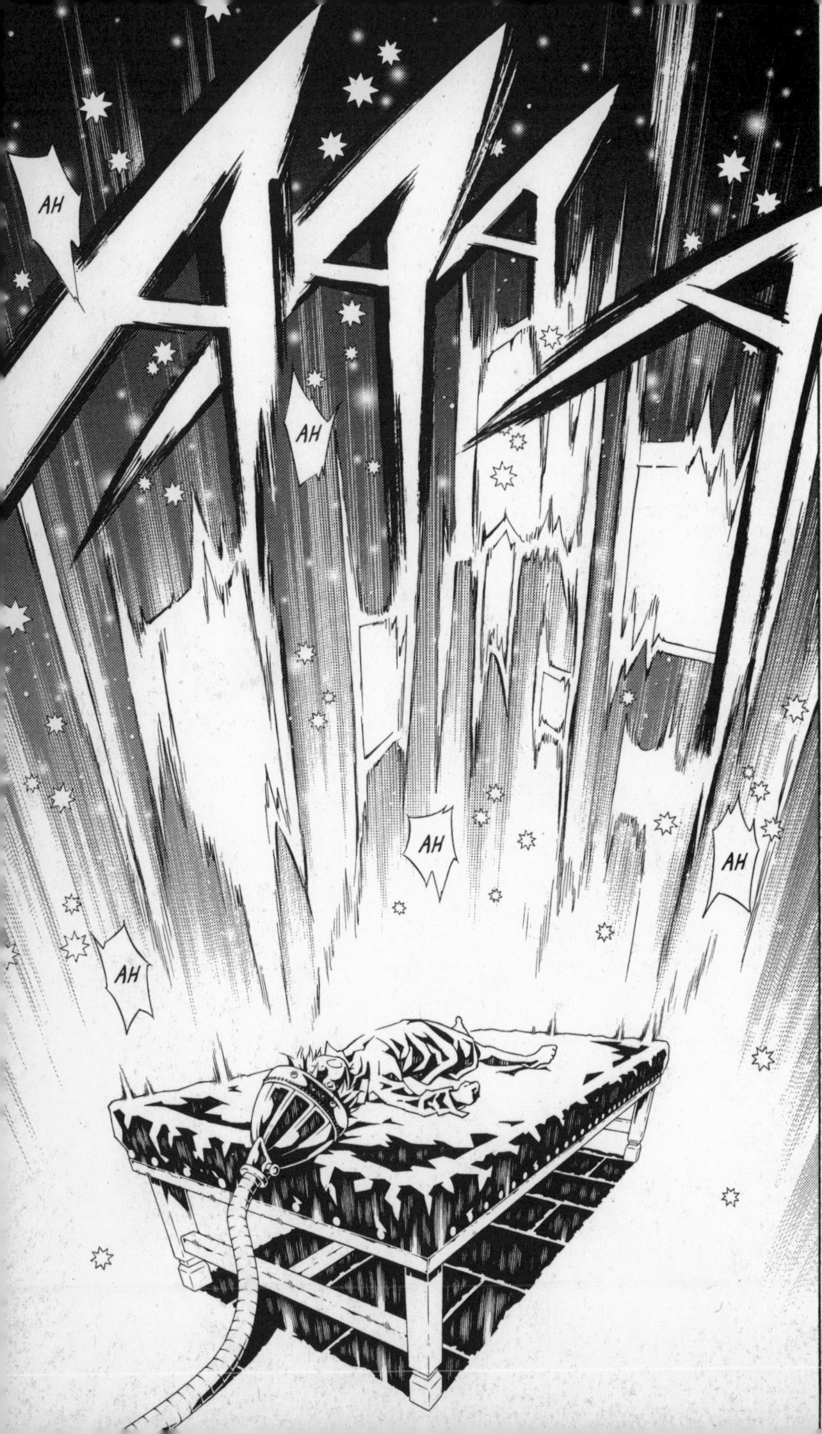
AH
AH
AH
AH
AH

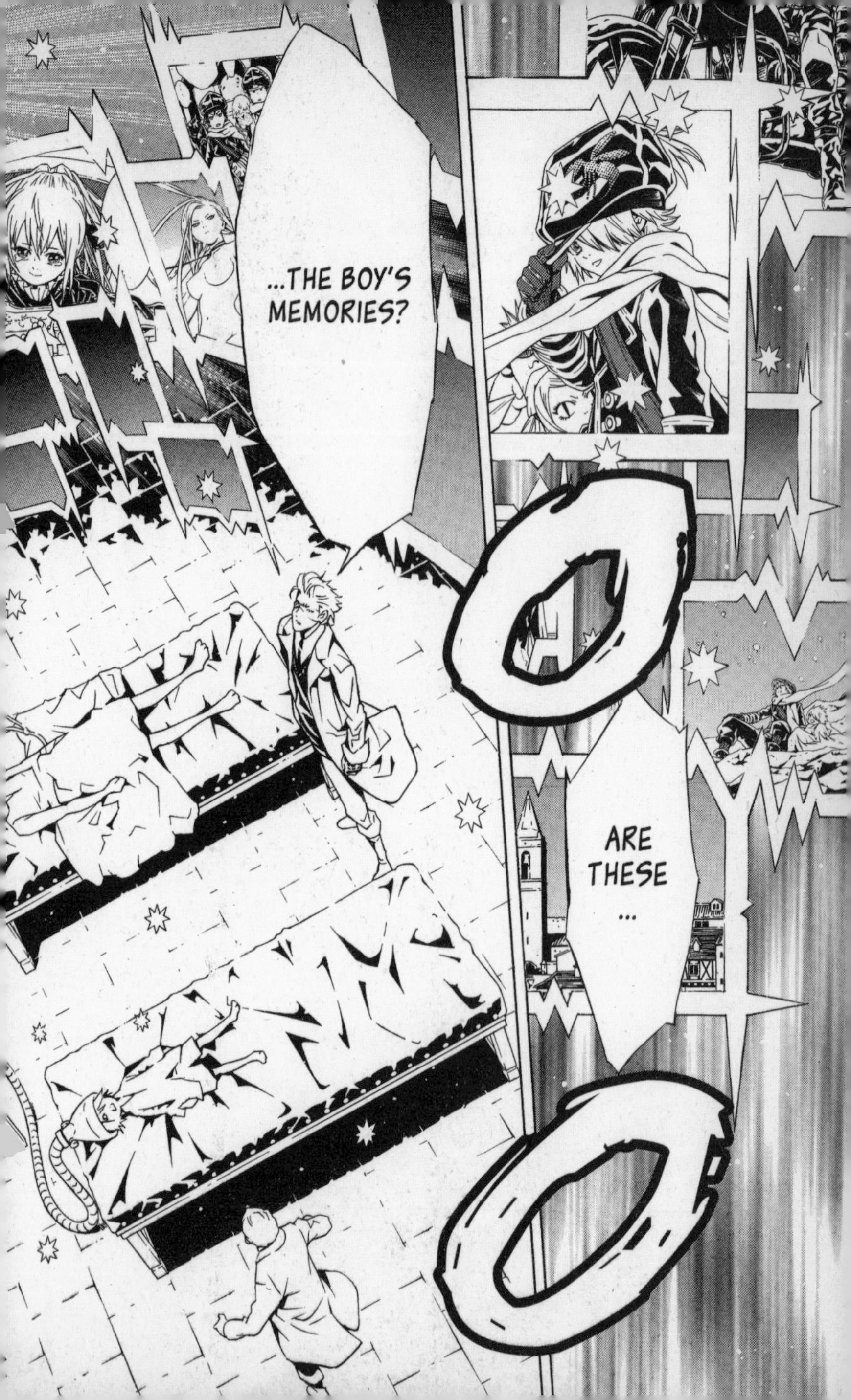
ARE THESE ...
...THE BOY'S MEMORIES?

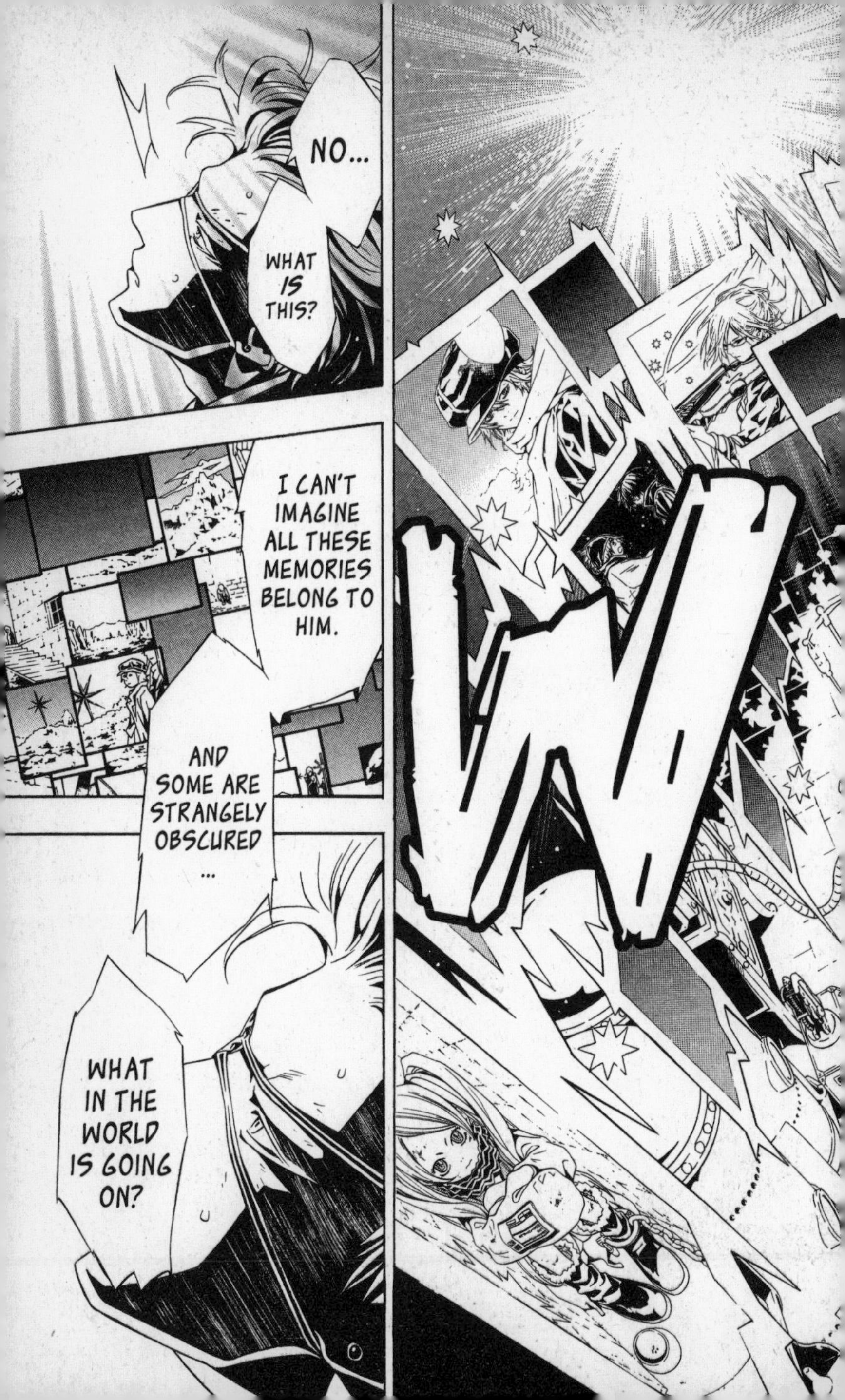
NO...
WHAT IS THIS?
I CAN'T IMAGINE ALL THESE MEMORIES BELONG TO HIM.
AND SOME ARE STRANGELY OBSCURED ...
WHAT IN THE WORLD IS GOING ON?

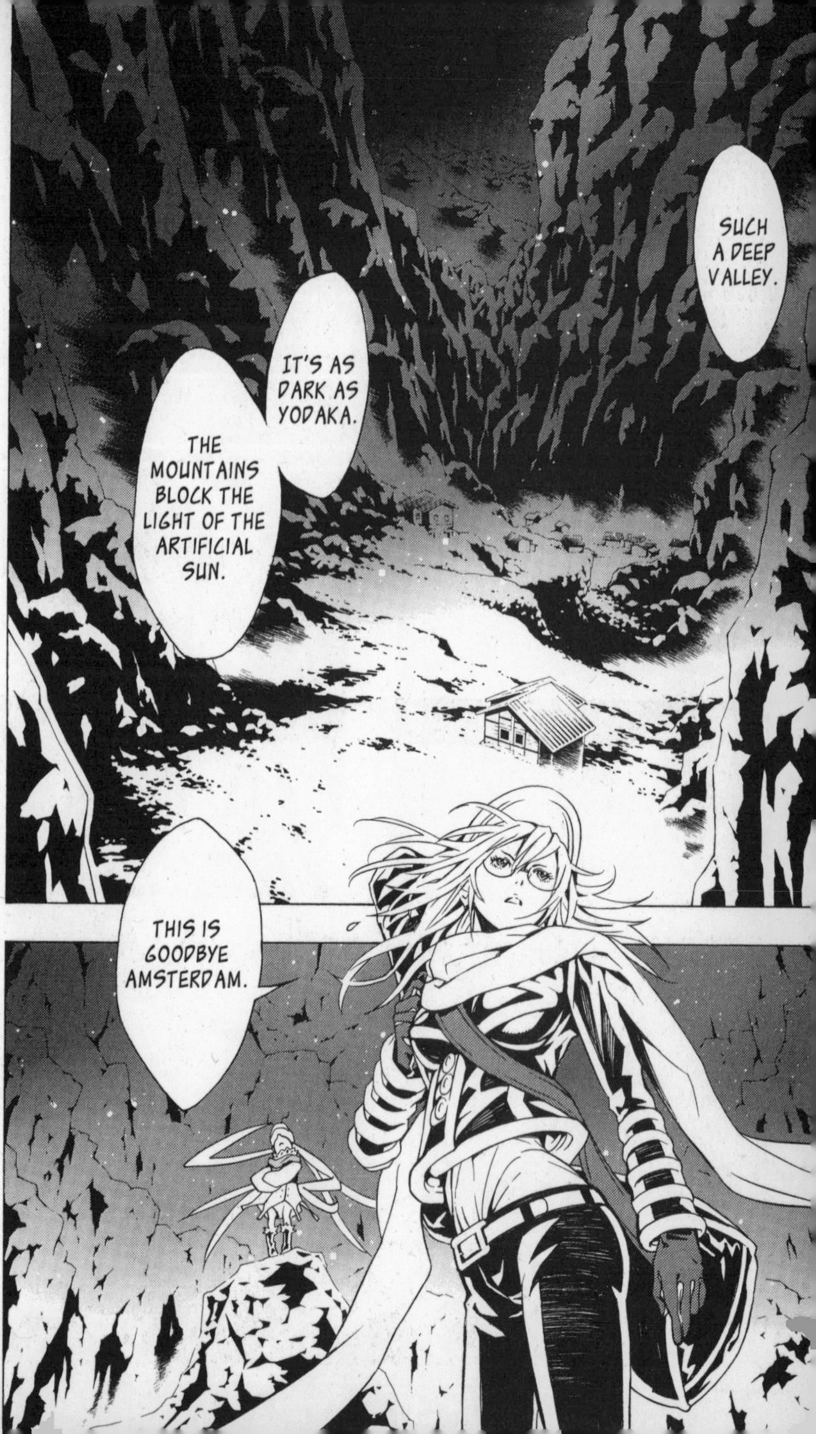
SUCH A DEEP VALLEY.
IT'S AS DARK AS YODAKA.
THE MOUNTAINS BLOCK THE LIGHT OF THE ARTIFICIAL SUN.
THIS IS GOODBYE AMSTERDAM.

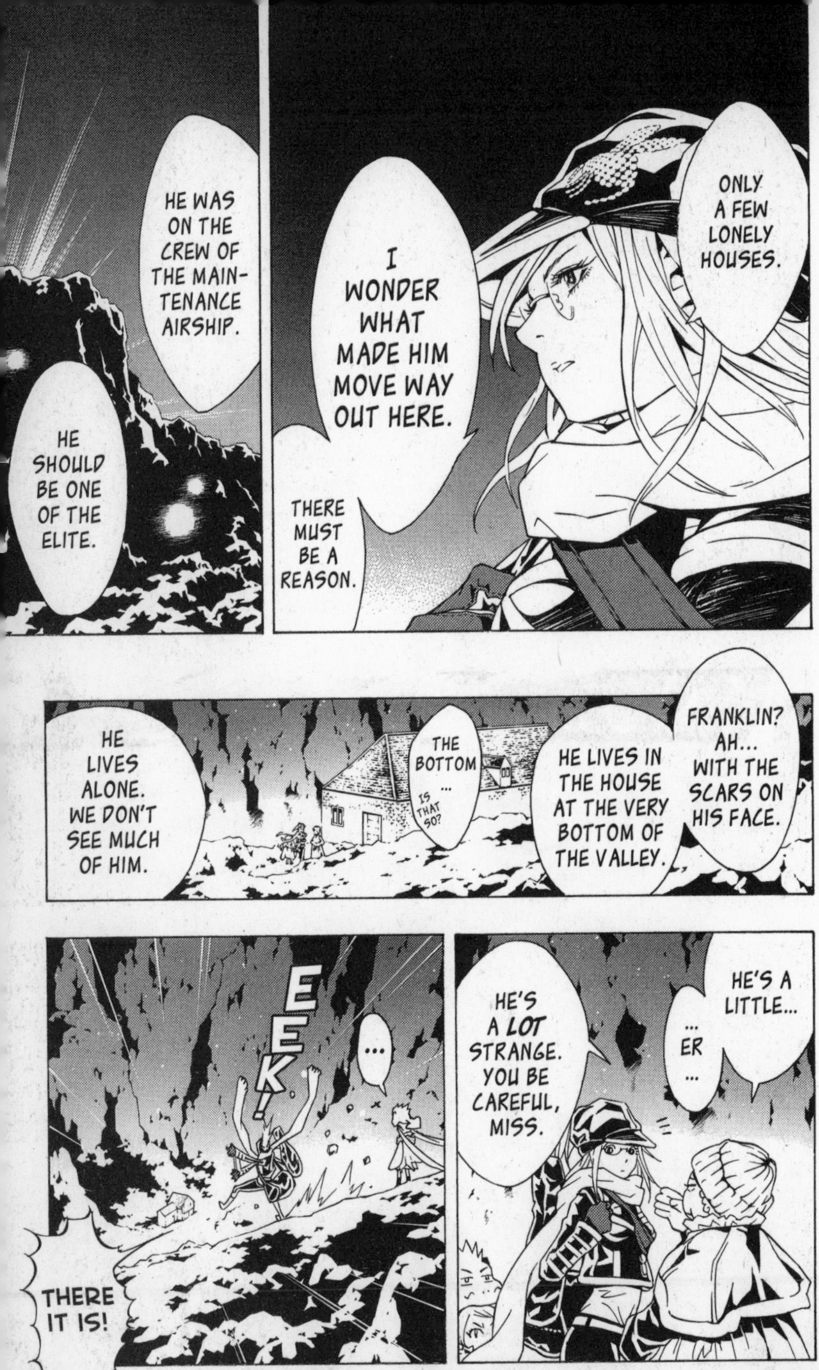

ONLY A FEW LONELY HOUSES.
I WONDER WHAT MADE HIM MOVE WAY OUT HERE.
THERE MUST BE A REASON.
HE WAS ON THE CREW OF THE MAIN-TENANCE AIRSHIP.
HE SHOULD BE ONE OF THE ELITE.
FRANKLIN? AH... WITH THE SCARS ON HIS FACE.
HE LIVES IN THE HOUSE AT THE VERY BOTTOM OF THE VALLEY.
THE BOTTOM ...
IS THAT SO?
HE LIVES ALONE. WE DON'T SEE MUCH OF HIM.
HE'S A LITTLE...
... ER ...
HE'S A *LOT* STRANGE. YOU BE CAREFUL, MISS.
...
EEK!
THERE IT IS!

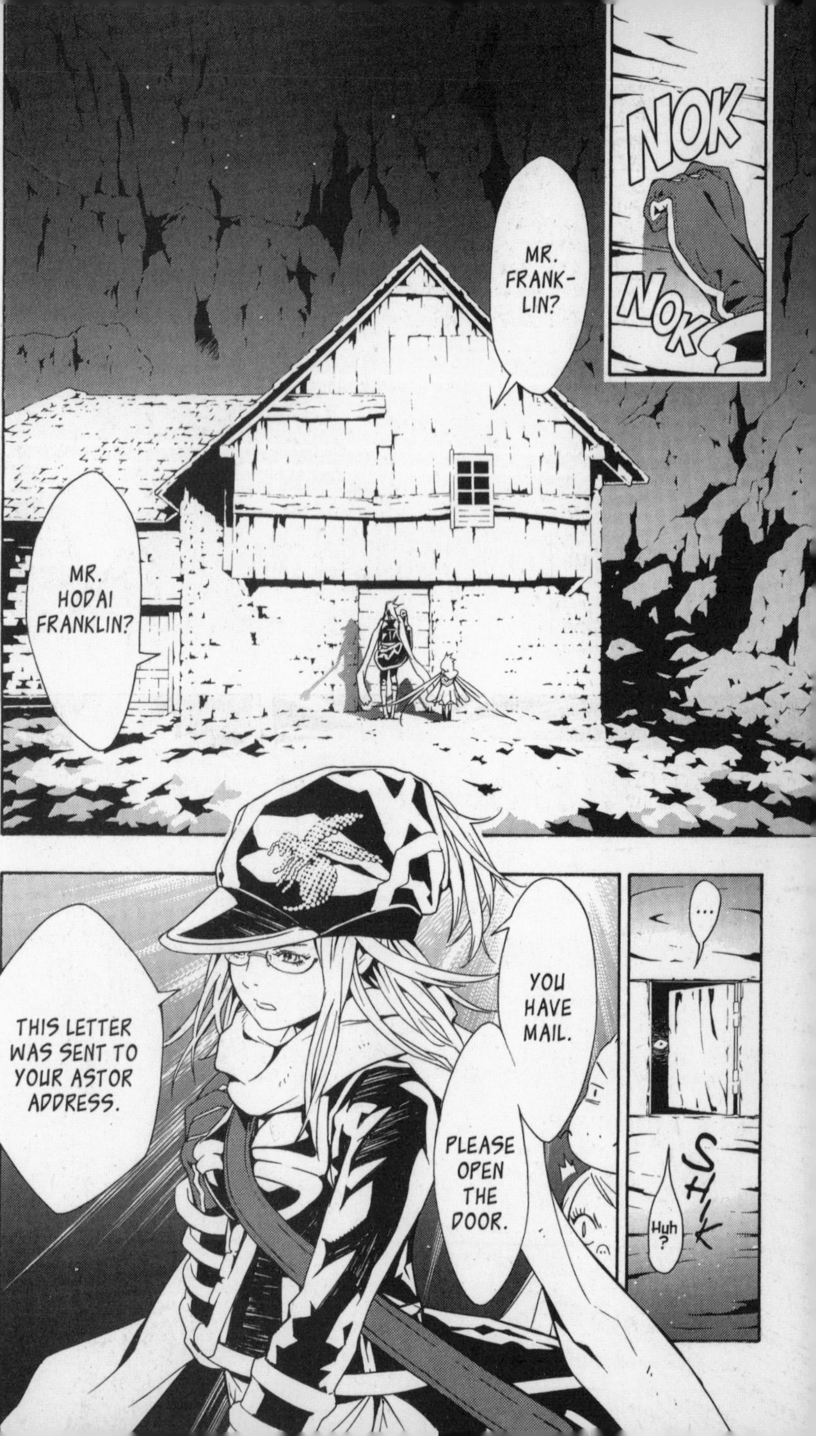
NOK
NOK
MR. FRANKLIN?
MR. HODAI FRANKLIN?
...
SHK
Huh?
YOU HAVE MAIL.
PLEASE OPEN THE DOOR.
THIS LETTER WAS SENT TO YOUR ASTOR ADDRESS.

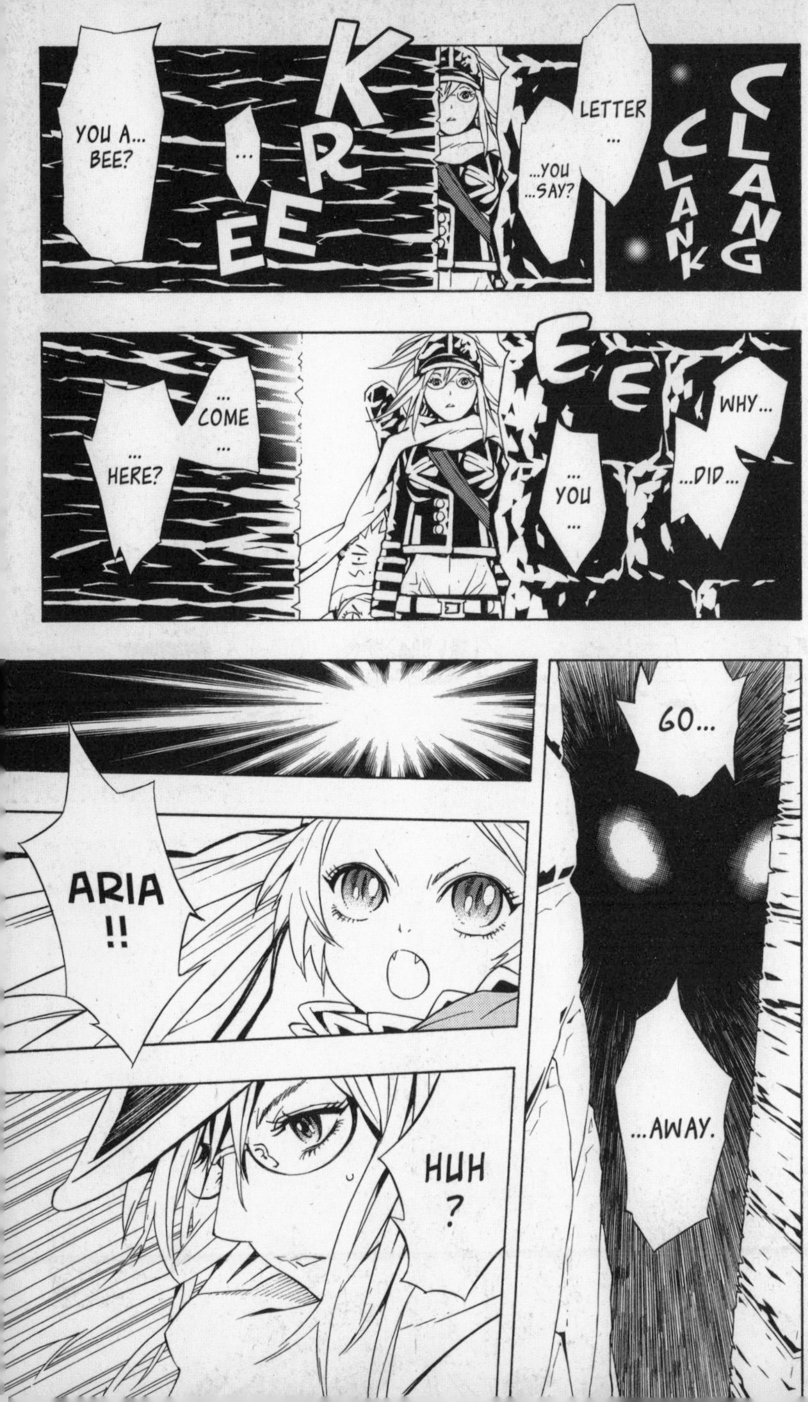
CLANG
CLANK
LETTER ...
...YOU ...SAY?
KREEE
...
YOU A... BEE?
EEE
WHY...
...DID...
... YOU ...
... COME ...
... HERE?
GO...
...AWAY.
ARIA !!
HUH ?

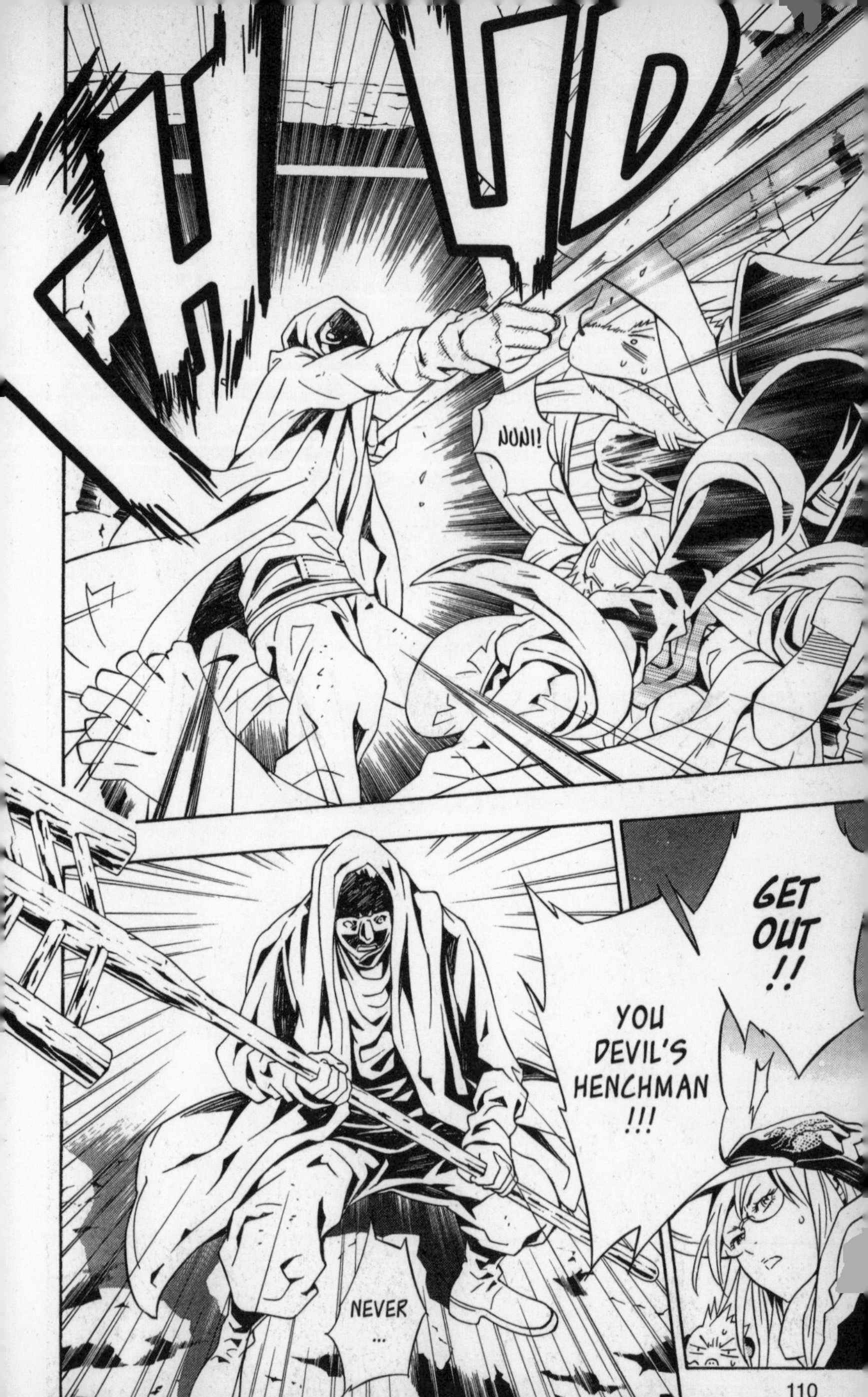
THUD
NUNI!
GET OUT!!
YOU DEVIL'S HENCHMAN!!!
NEVER...

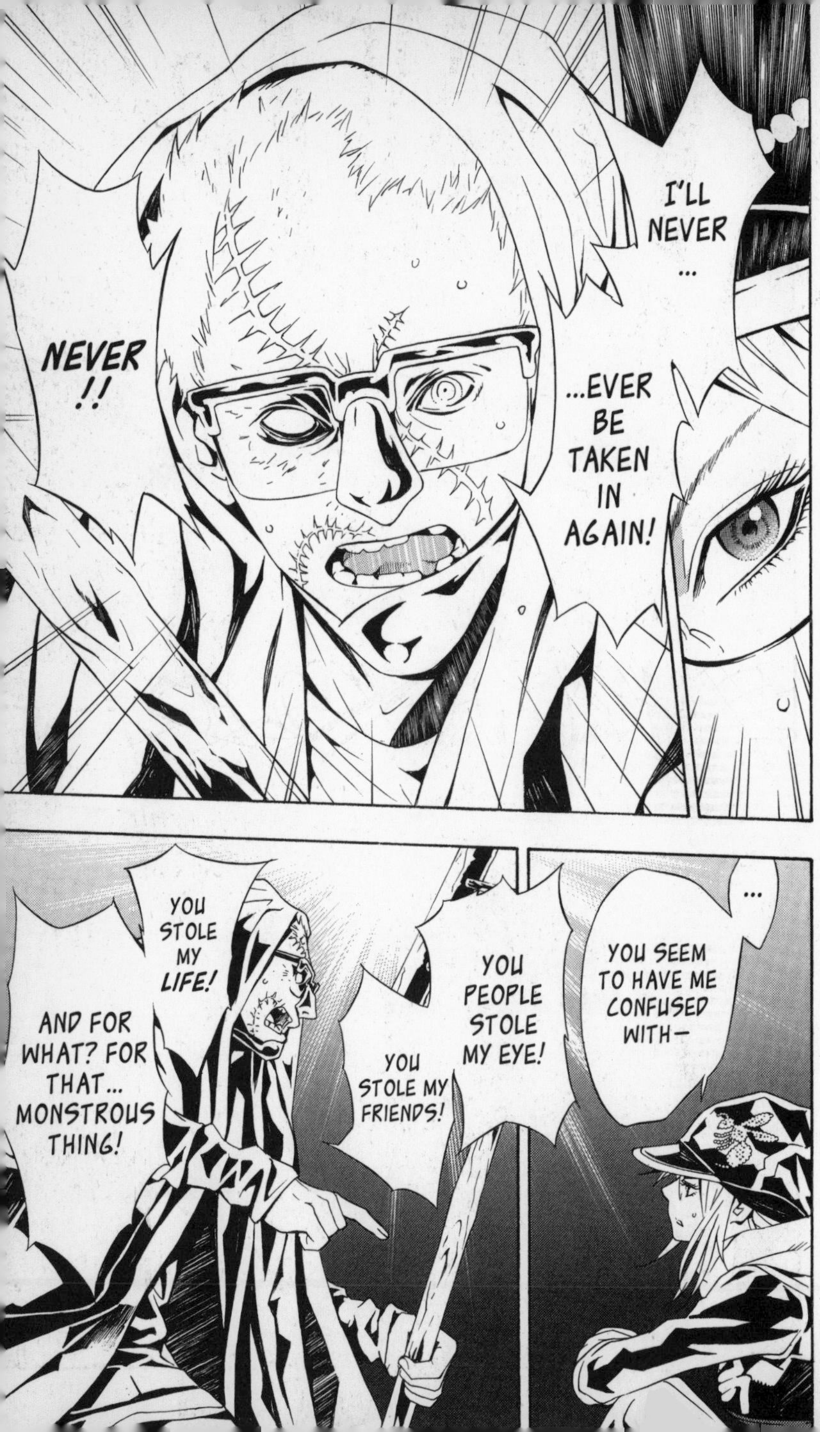
I'LL NEVER ...
...EVER BE TAKEN IN AGAIN!
NEVER !!
...
YOU SEEM TO HAVE ME CONFUSED WITH—
YOU PEOPLE STOLE MY EYE!
YOU STOLE MY LIFE!
YOU STOLE MY FRIENDS!
AND FOR WHAT? FOR THAT... MONSTROUS THING!

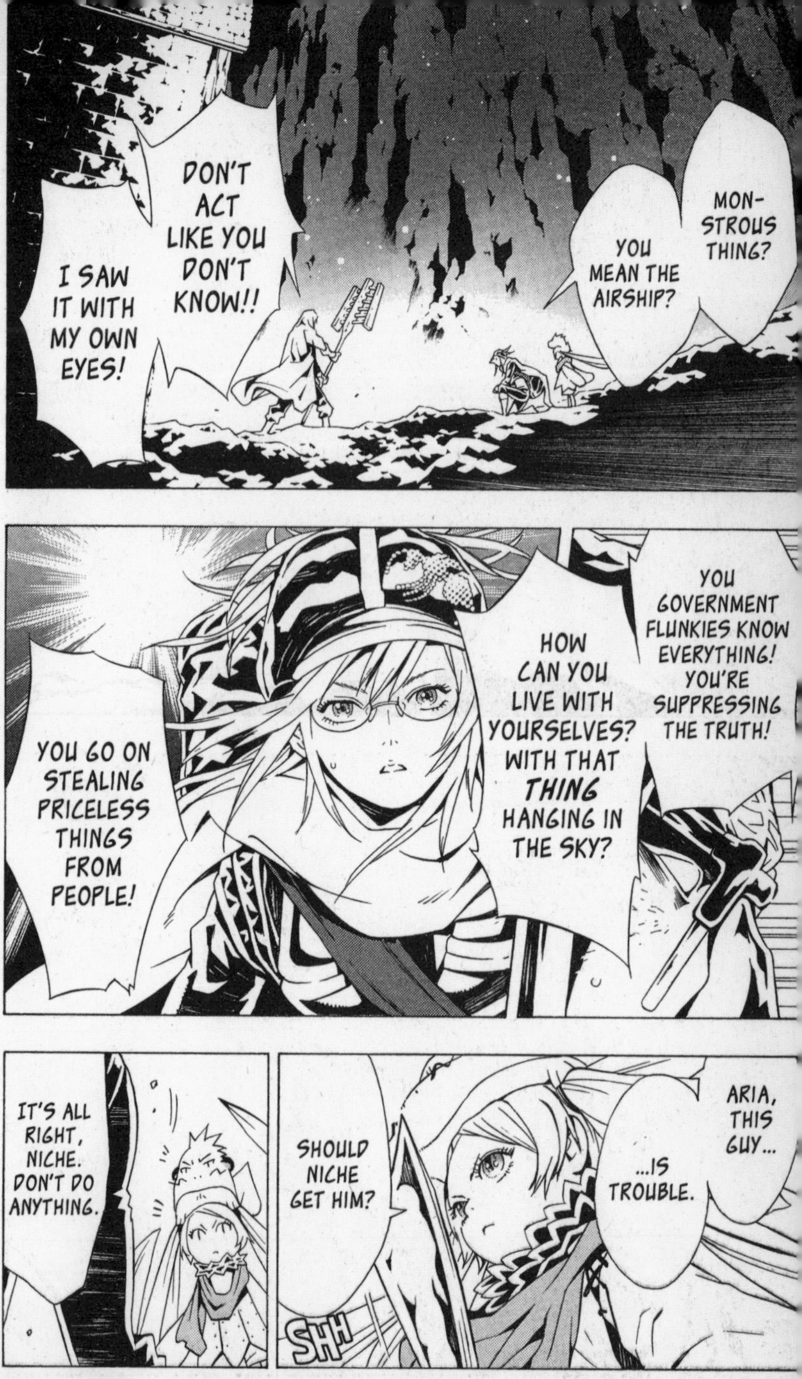
MON-STROUS THING?
YOU MEAN THE AIRSHIP?
DON'T ACT LIKE YOU DON'T KNOW!!
I SAW IT WITH MY OWN EYES!
YOU GOVERNMENT FLUNKIES KNOW EVERYTHING! YOU'RE SUPPRESSING THE TRUTH!
HOW CAN YOU LIVE WITH YOURSELVES? WITH THAT *THING* HANGING IN THE SKY?
YOU GO ON STEALING PRICELESS THINGS FROM PEOPLE!
ARIA, THIS GUY...
...IS TROUBLE.
SHOULD NICHE GET HIM?
SHH
IT'S ALL RIGHT, NICHE. DON'T DO ANYTHING.

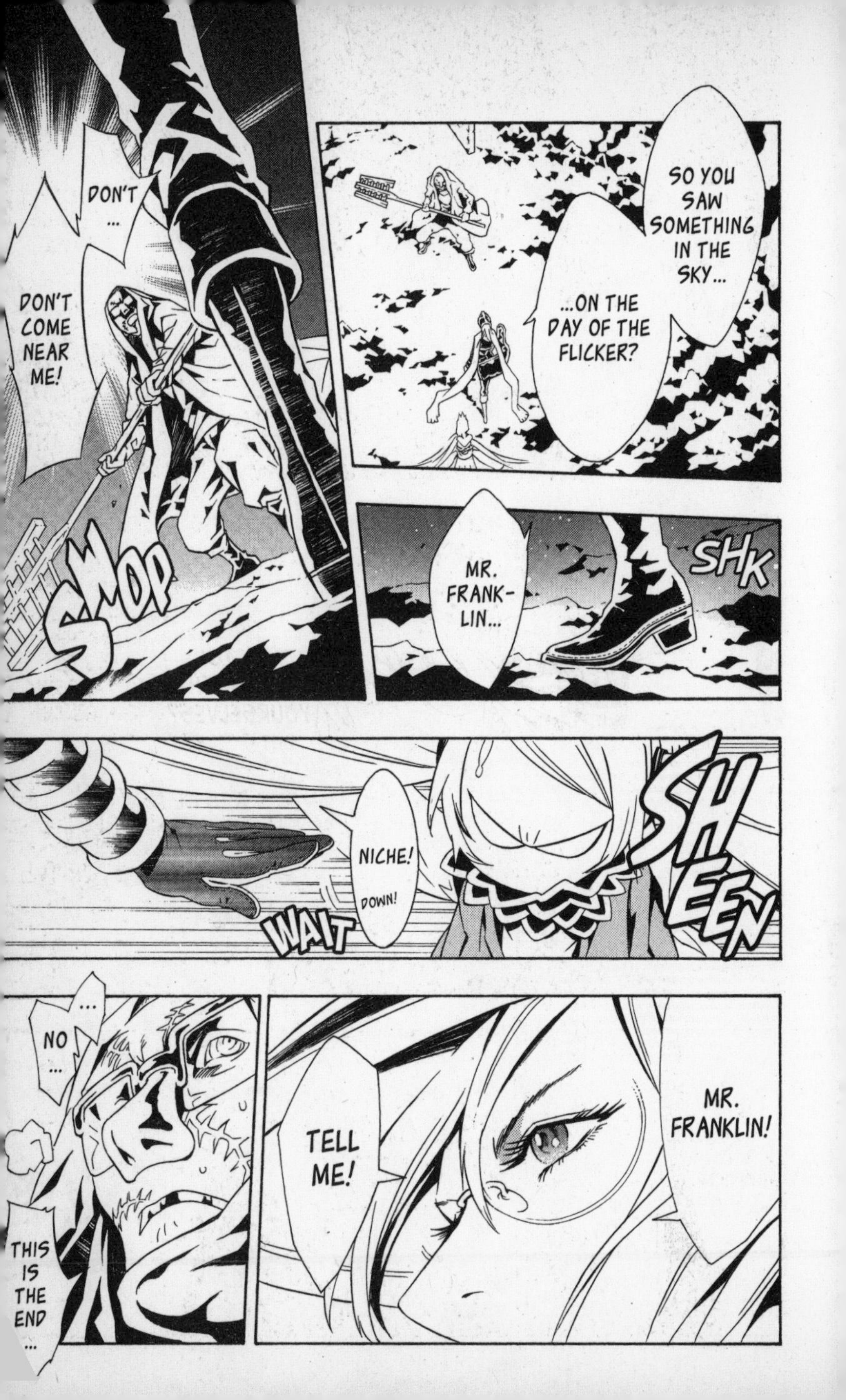

SO YOU SAW SOMETHING IN THE SKY...
...ON THE DAY OF THE FLICKER?
MR. FRANK-LIN...
SHK
DON'T ...
DON'T COME NEAR ME!
SHOP
SHEEN
NICHE!
DOWN!
WAIT
MR. FRANKLIN!
TELL ME!
...
NO ...
THIS IS THE END ...

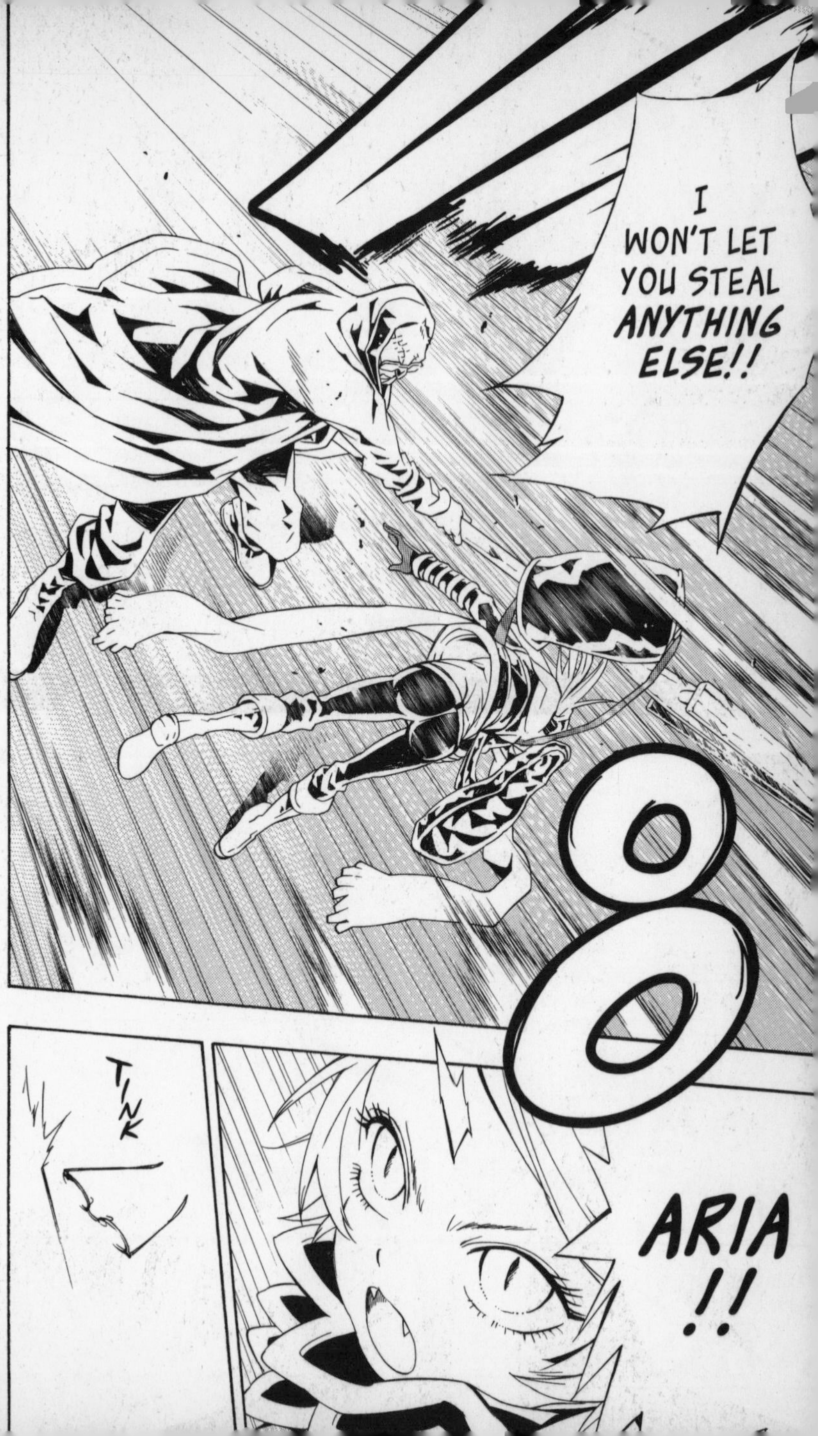
I WON'T LET YOU STEAL ANYTHING ELSE!!
ARIA!!
TINK

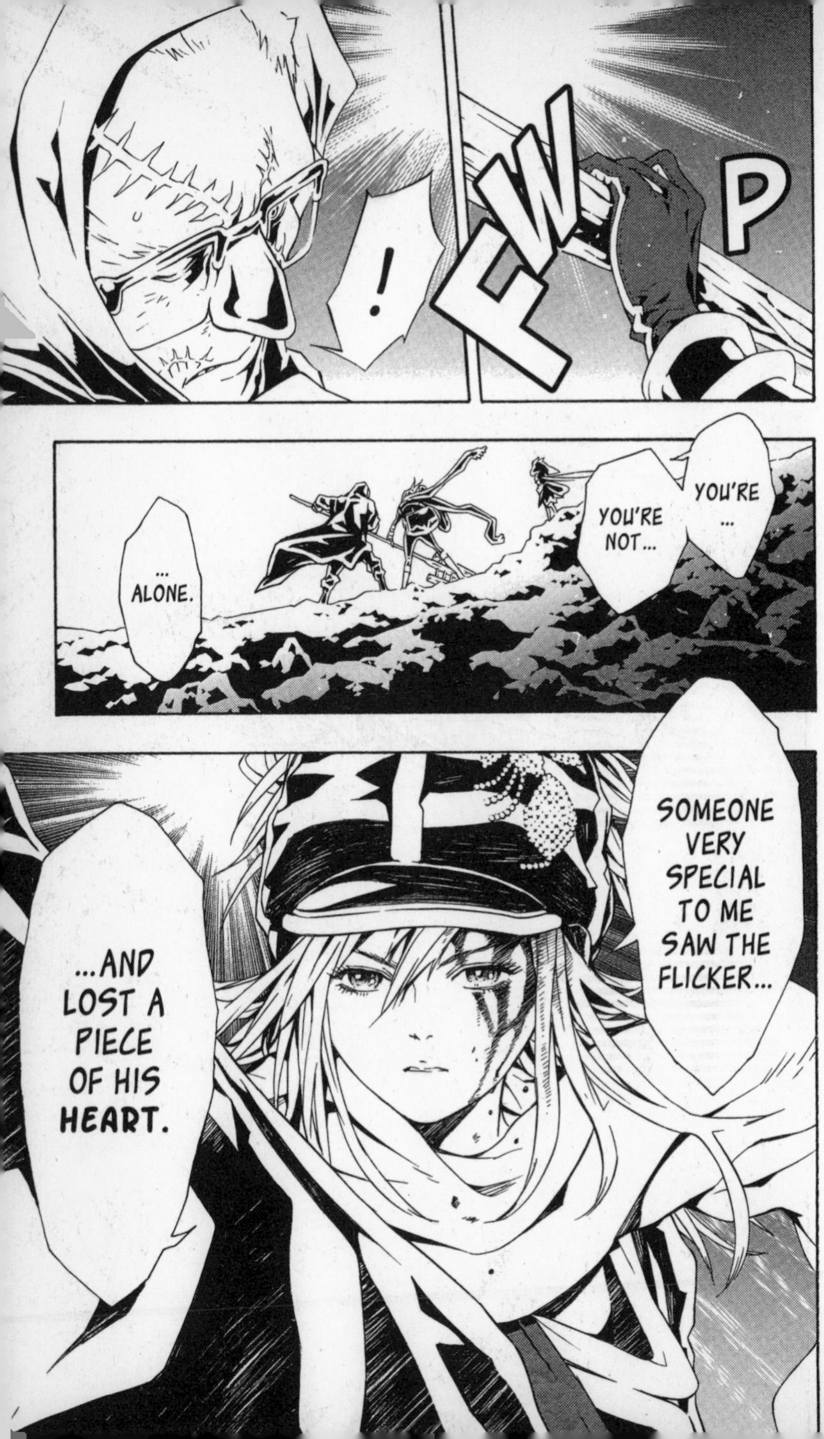
FWP
!
YOU'RE ...
YOU'RE NOT...
... ALONE.
SOMEONE VERY SPECIAL TO ME SAW THE FLICKER...
...AND LOST A PIECE OF HIS HEART.

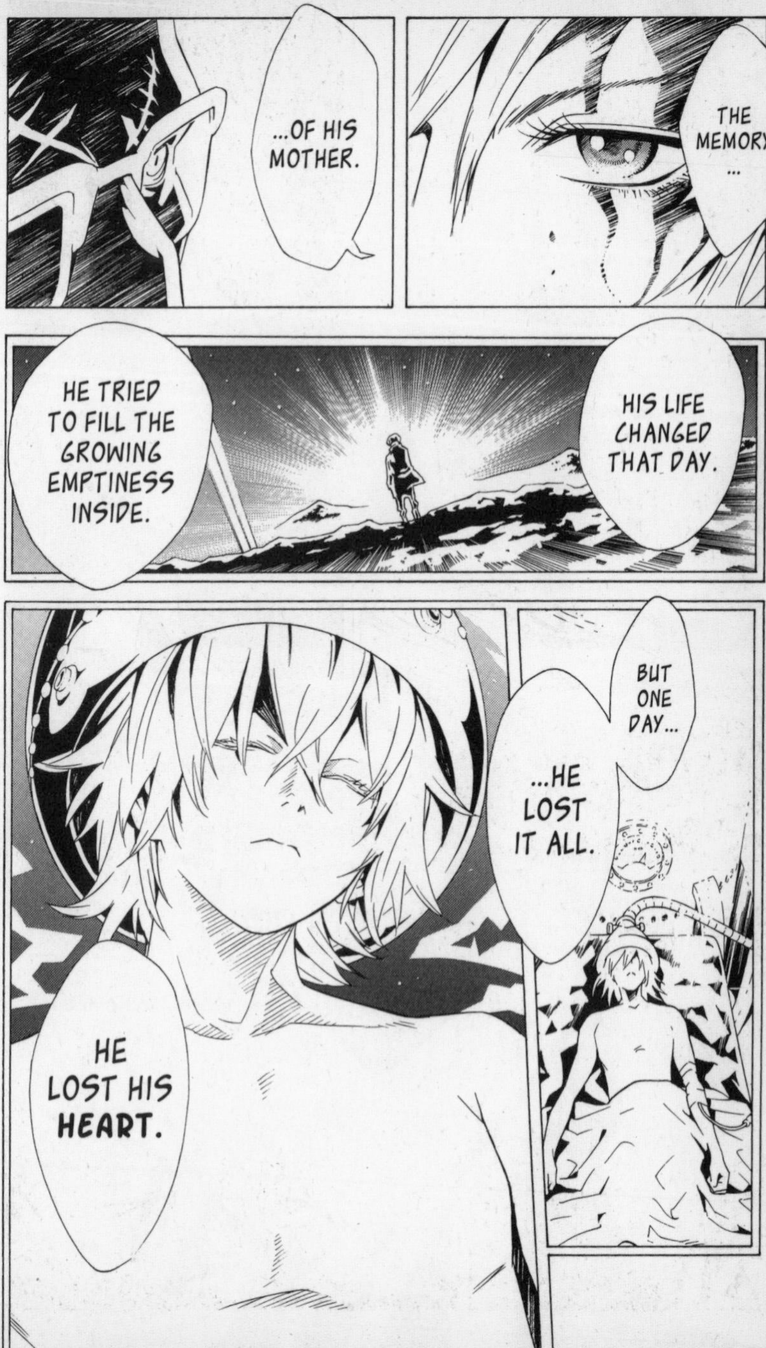
THE MEMORY ...
...OF HIS MOTHER.
HIS LIFE CHANGED THAT DAY.
HE TRIED TO FILL THE GROWING EMPTINESS INSIDE.
BUT ONE DAY...
...HE LOST IT ALL.
HE LOST HIS **HEART.**

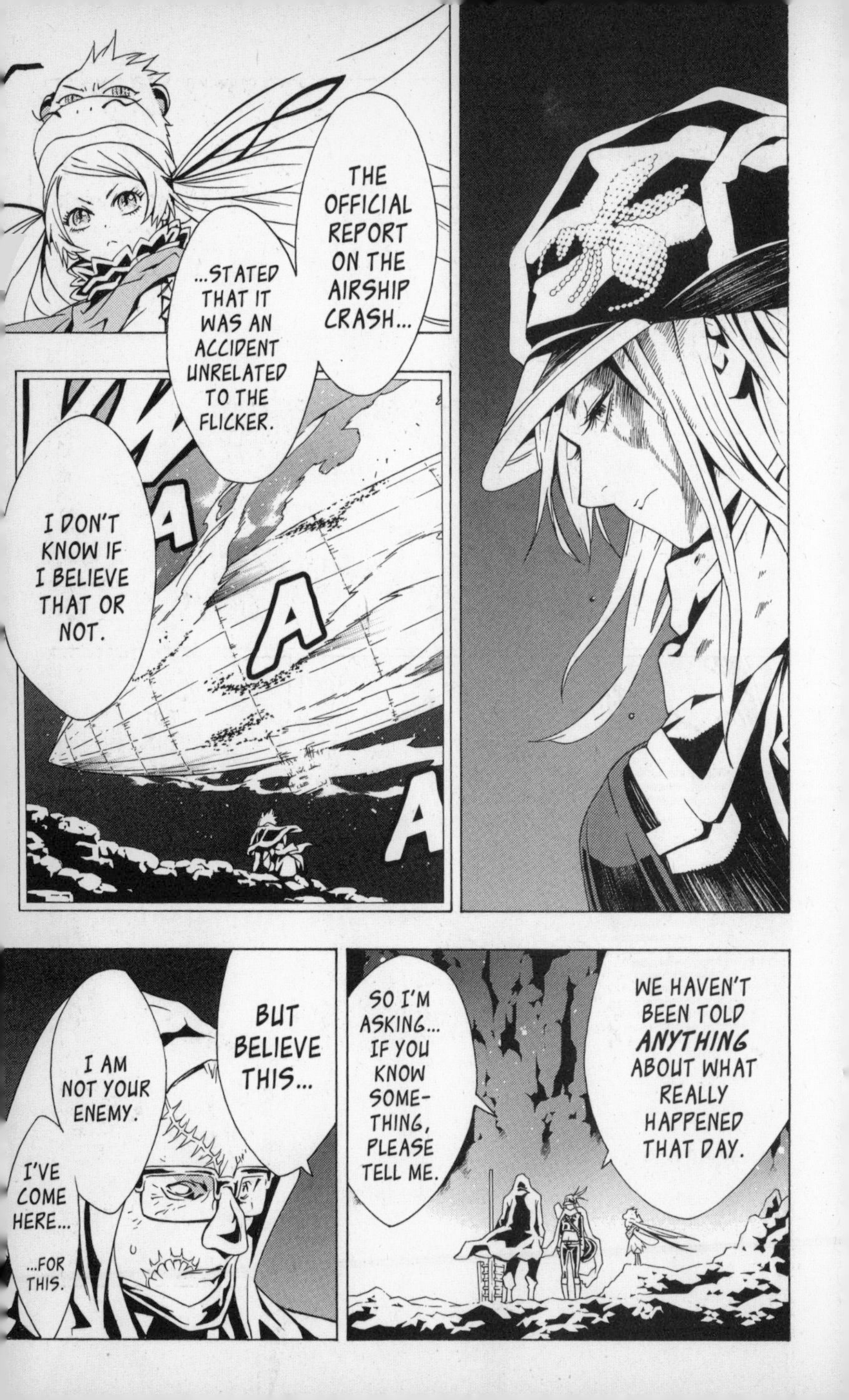
THE OFFICIAL REPORT ON THE AIRSHIP CRASH...
...STATED THAT IT WAS AN ACCIDENT UNRELATED TO THE FLICKER.
I DON'T KNOW IF I BELIEVE THAT OR NOT.
WE HAVEN'T BEEN TOLD *ANYTHING* ABOUT WHAT REALLY HAPPENED THAT DAY.
SO I'M ASKING... IF YOU KNOW SOME-THING, PLEASE TELL ME.
BUT BELIEVE THIS...
I AM NOT YOUR ENEMY.
I'VE COME HERE...
...FOR THIS.

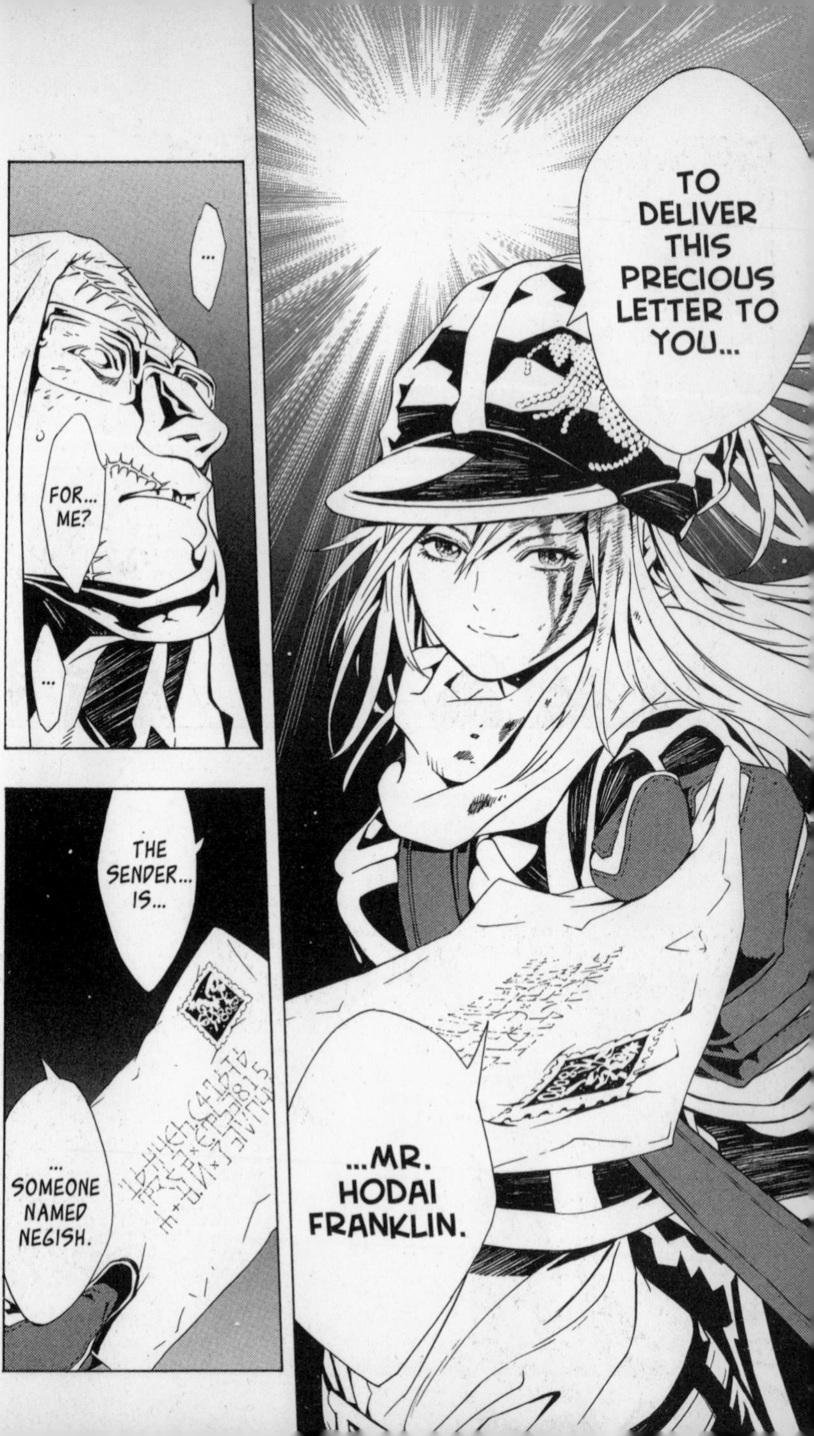
TO DELIVER THIS PRECIOUS LETTER TO YOU...
...MR. HODAI FRANKLIN.
...
FOR... ME?
...
THE SENDER... IS...
... SOMEONE NAMED NEGISH.

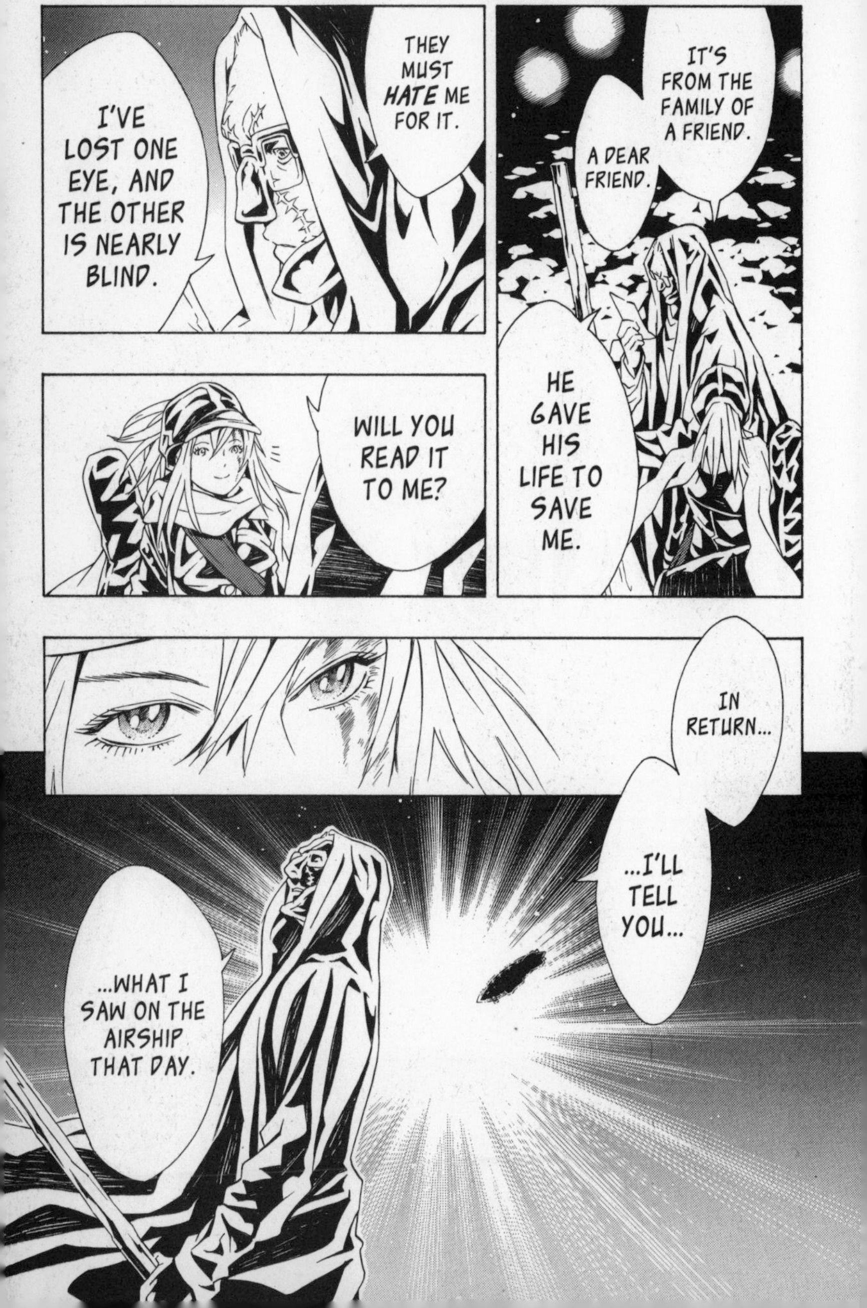
IT'S FROM THE FAMILY OF A FRIEND.
A DEAR FRIEND.
HE GAVE HIS LIFE TO SAVE ME.
THEY MUST *HATE* ME FOR IT.
I'VE LOST ONE EYE, AND THE OTHER IS NEARLY BLIND.
WILL YOU READ IT TO ME?
IN RETURN...
...I'LL TELL YOU...
...WHAT I SAW ON THE AIRSHIP THAT DAY.

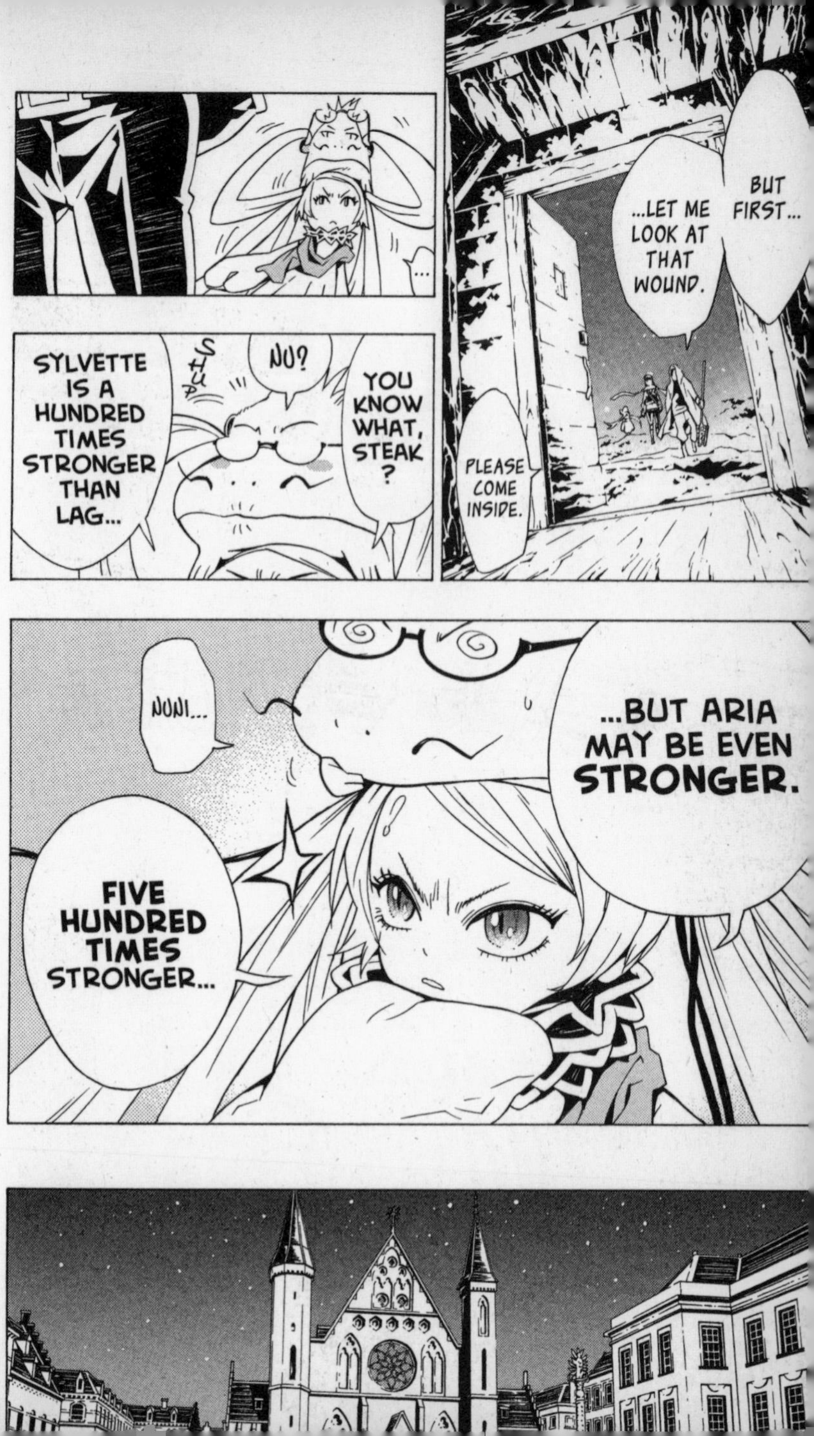
BUT FIRST...
...LET ME LOOK AT THAT WOUND.
PLEASE COME INSIDE.
...
YOU KNOW WHAT, STEAK?
NU?
SHUPA
SYLVETTE IS A HUNDRED TIMES STRONGER THAN LAG...
...BUT ARIA MAY BE EVEN STRONGER.
NUNI...
FIVE HUNDRED TIMES STRONGER...

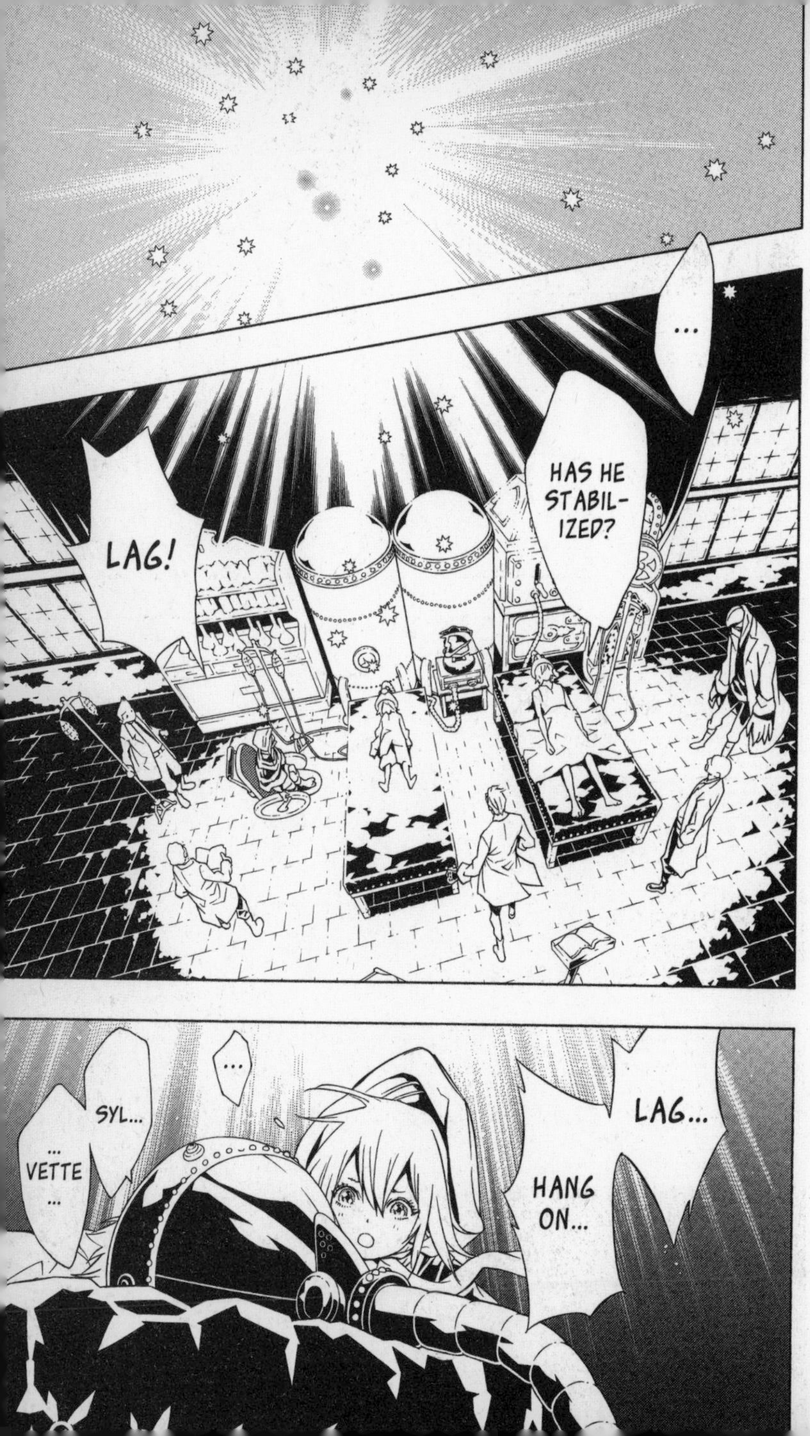
...
HAS HE STABILIZED?
LAG!
LAG...
HANG ON...
...
SYL...
... VETTE ...

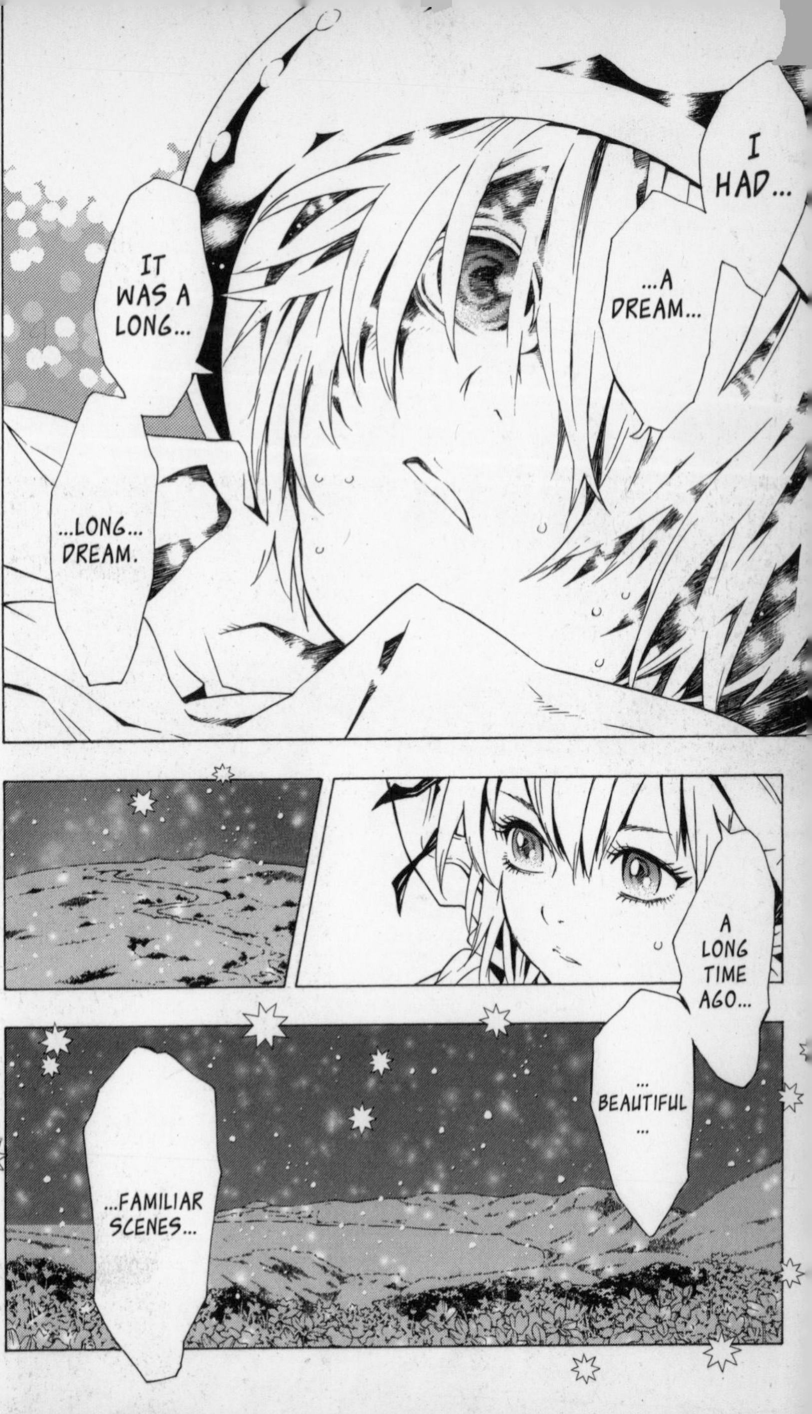
I HAD...
...A DREAM...
IT WAS A LONG...
...LONG... DREAM.
A LONG TIME AGO...
... BEAUTIFUL ...
...FAMILIAR SCENES...

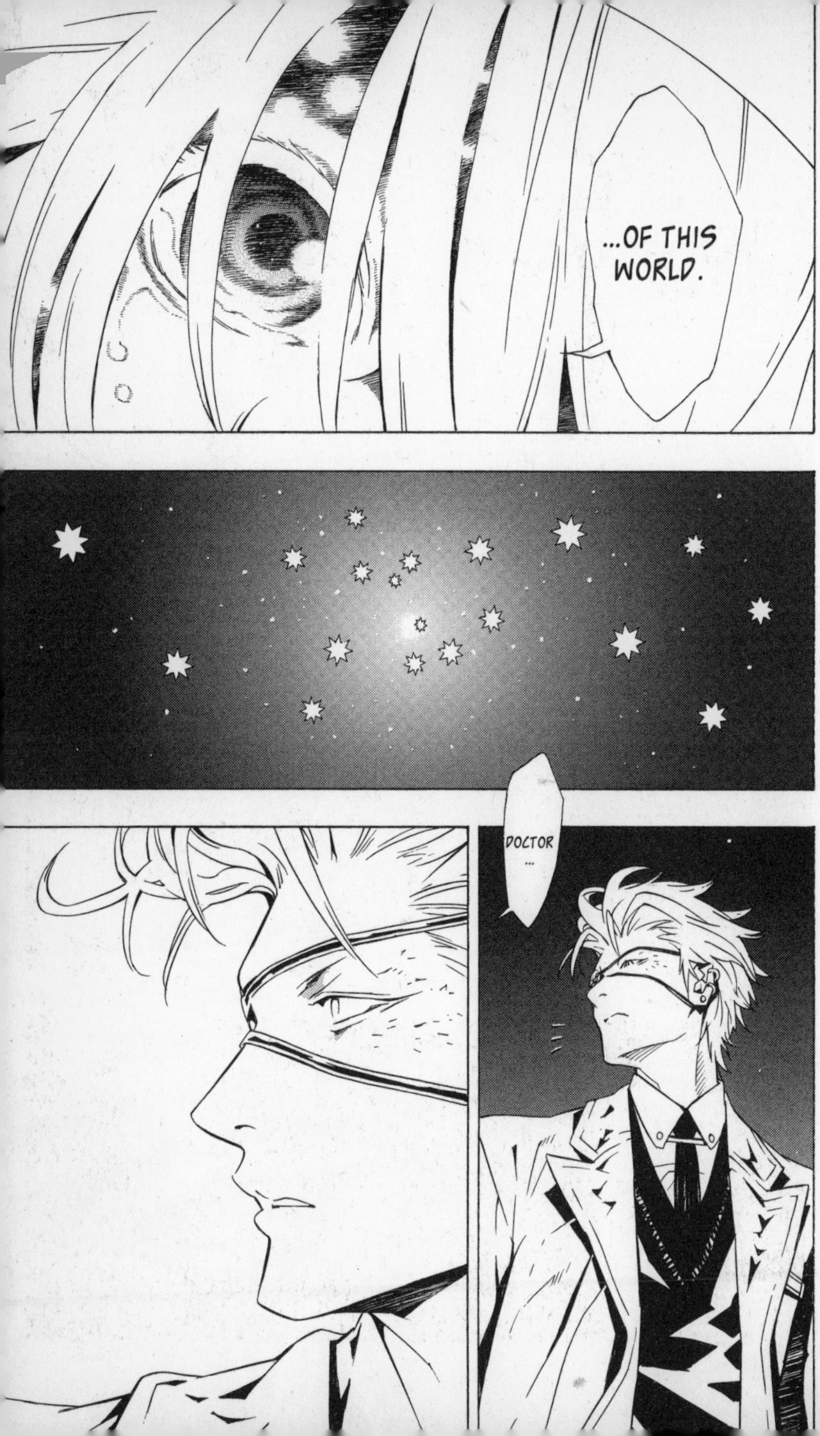
...OF THIS WORLD.
DOCTOR ...

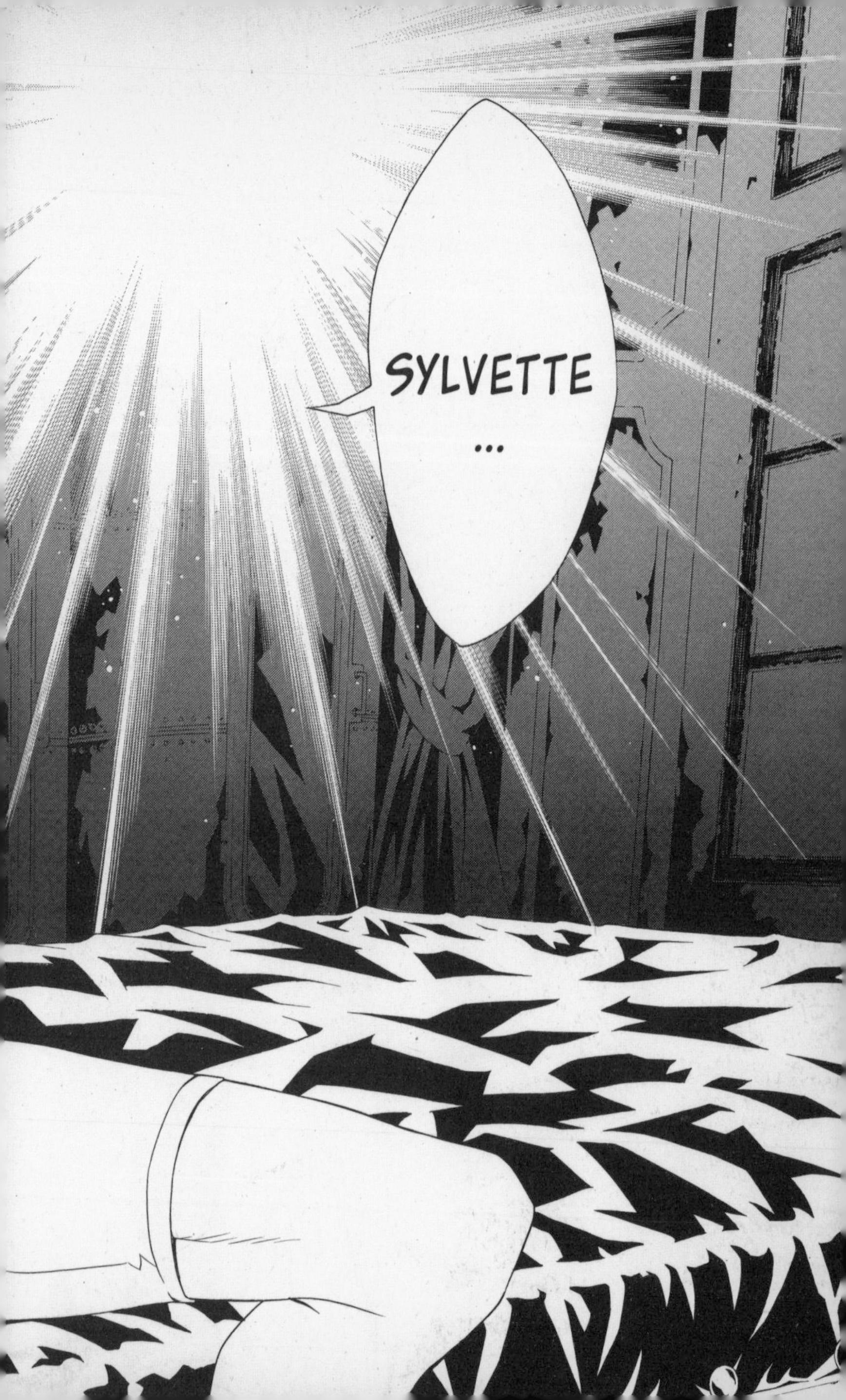
SYLVETTE
...

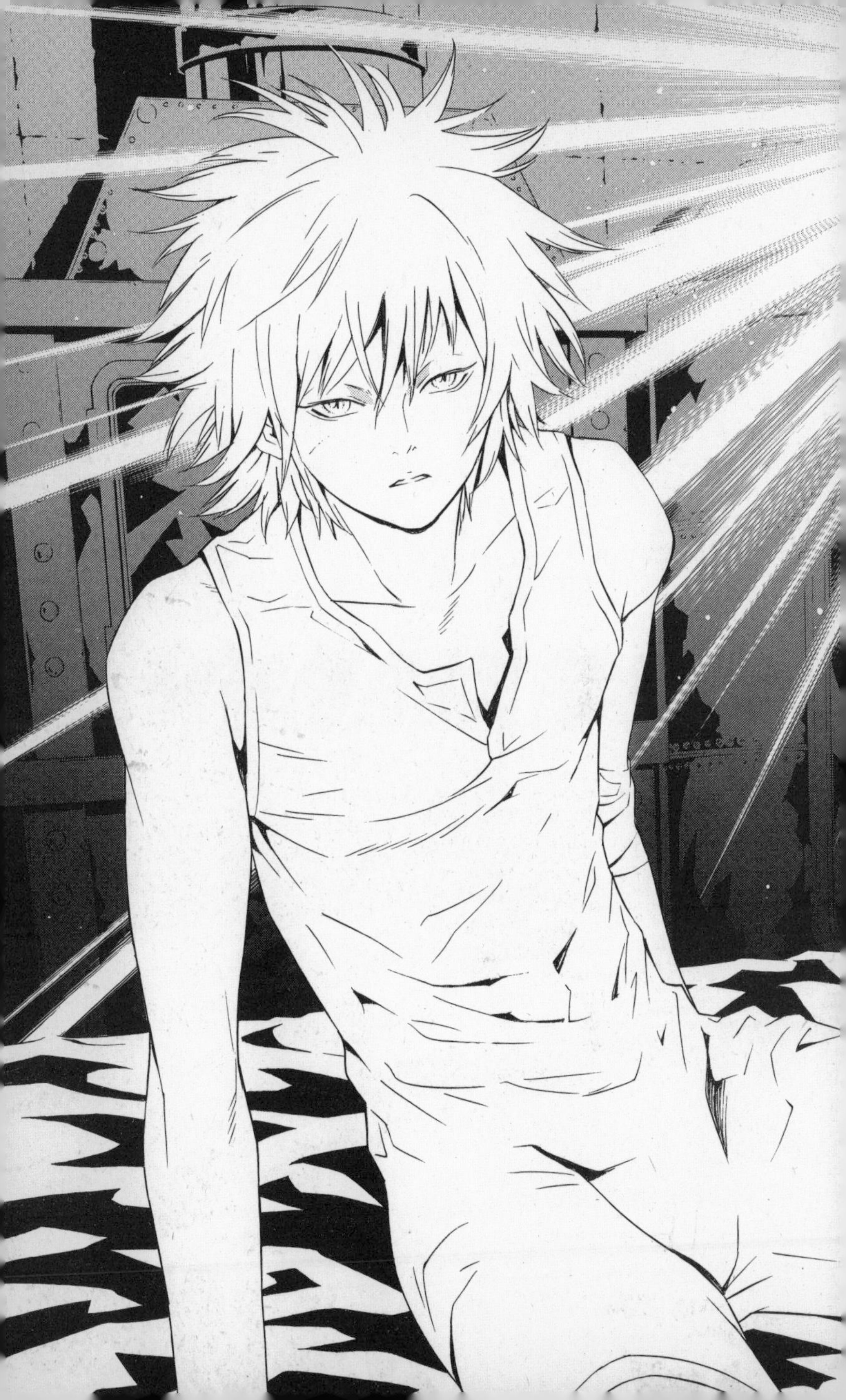

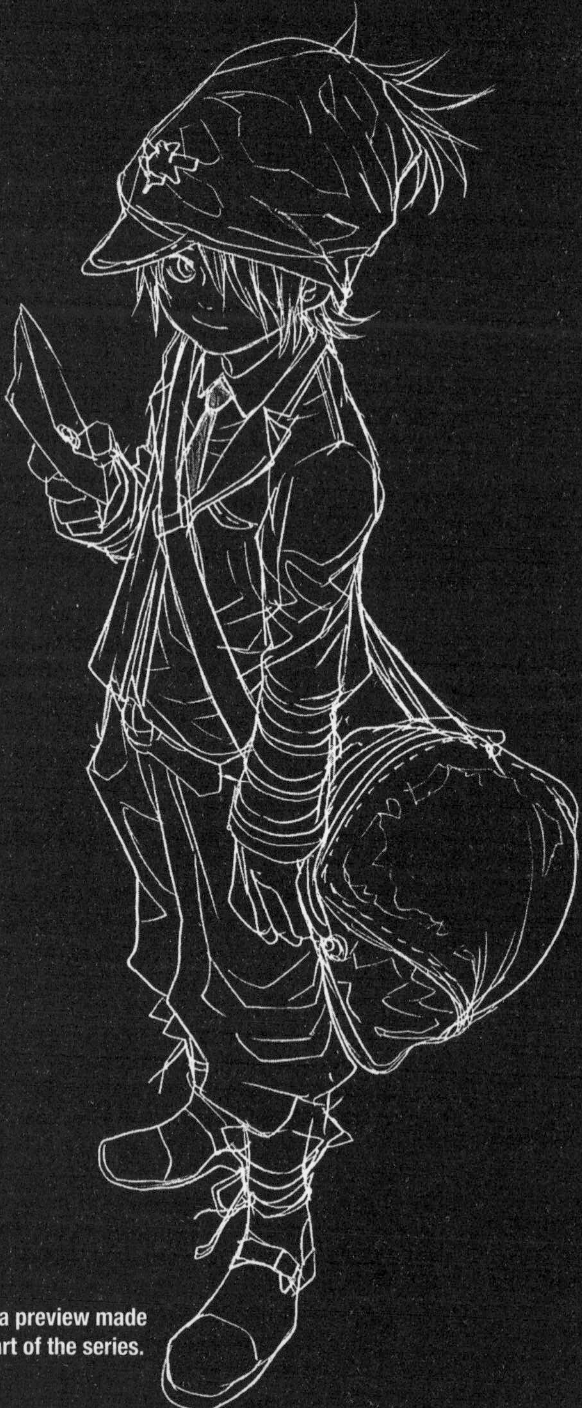

Rough sketch for a preview made
just before the start of the series.

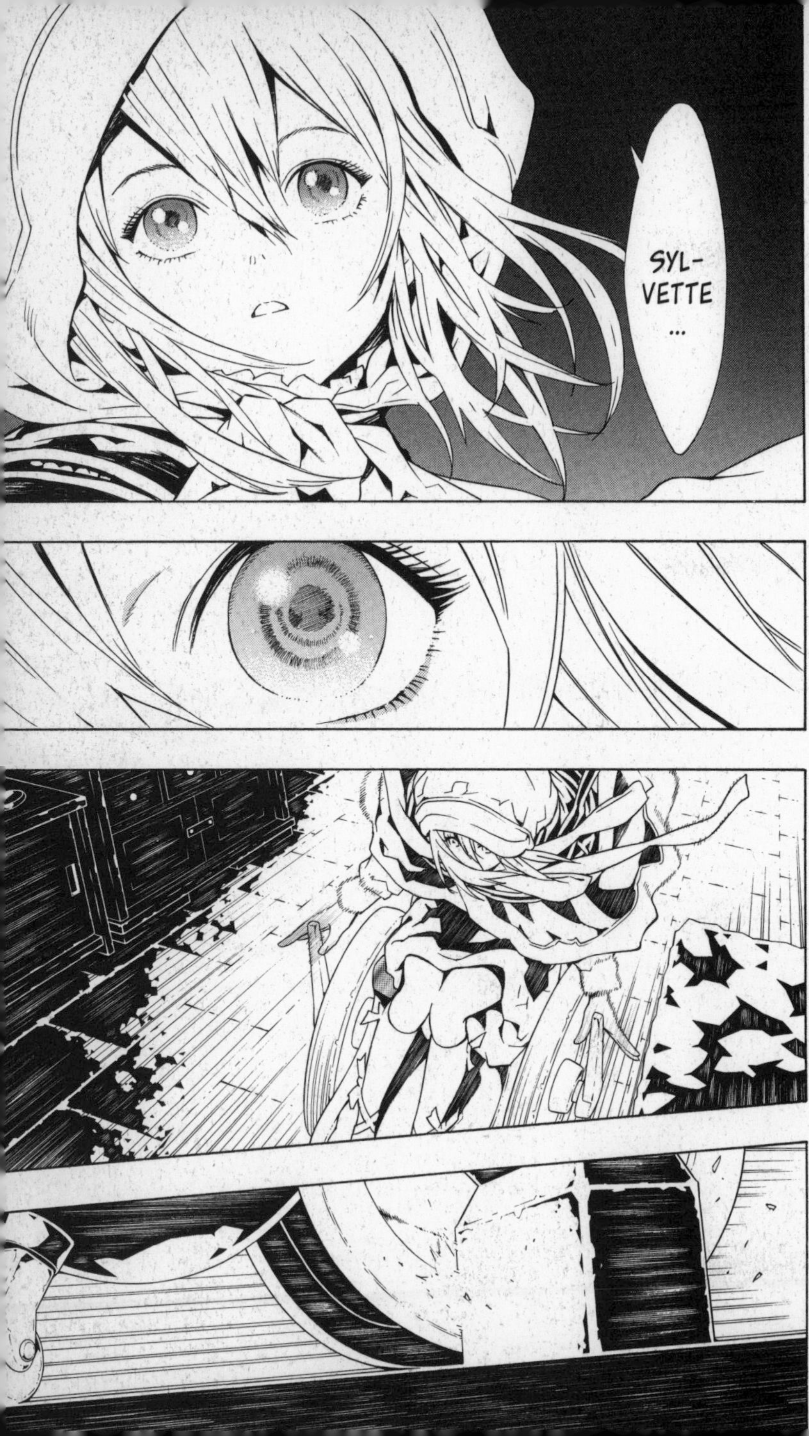
SYL-
VETTE
...

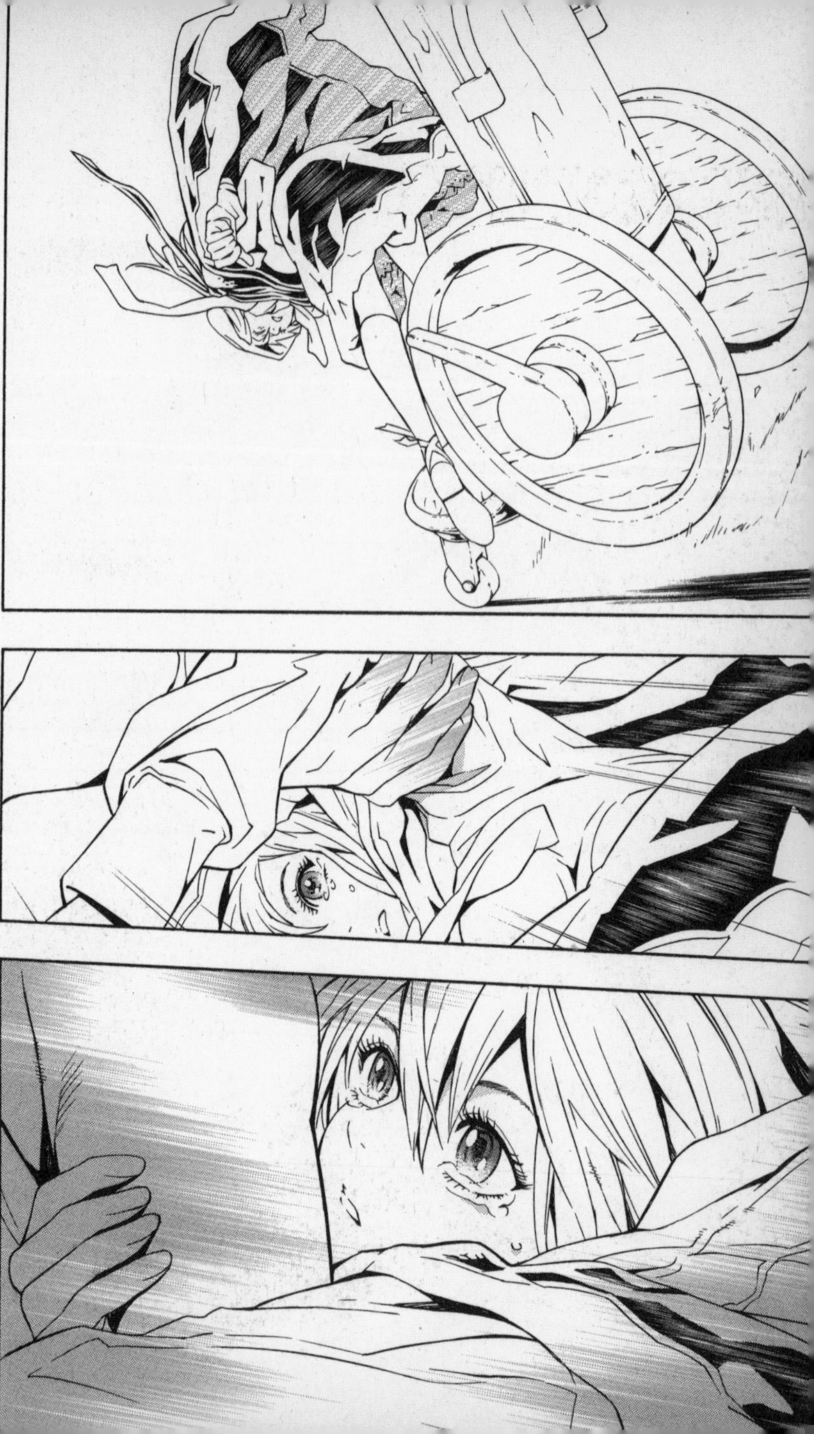

Chapter 38: Shining Eye

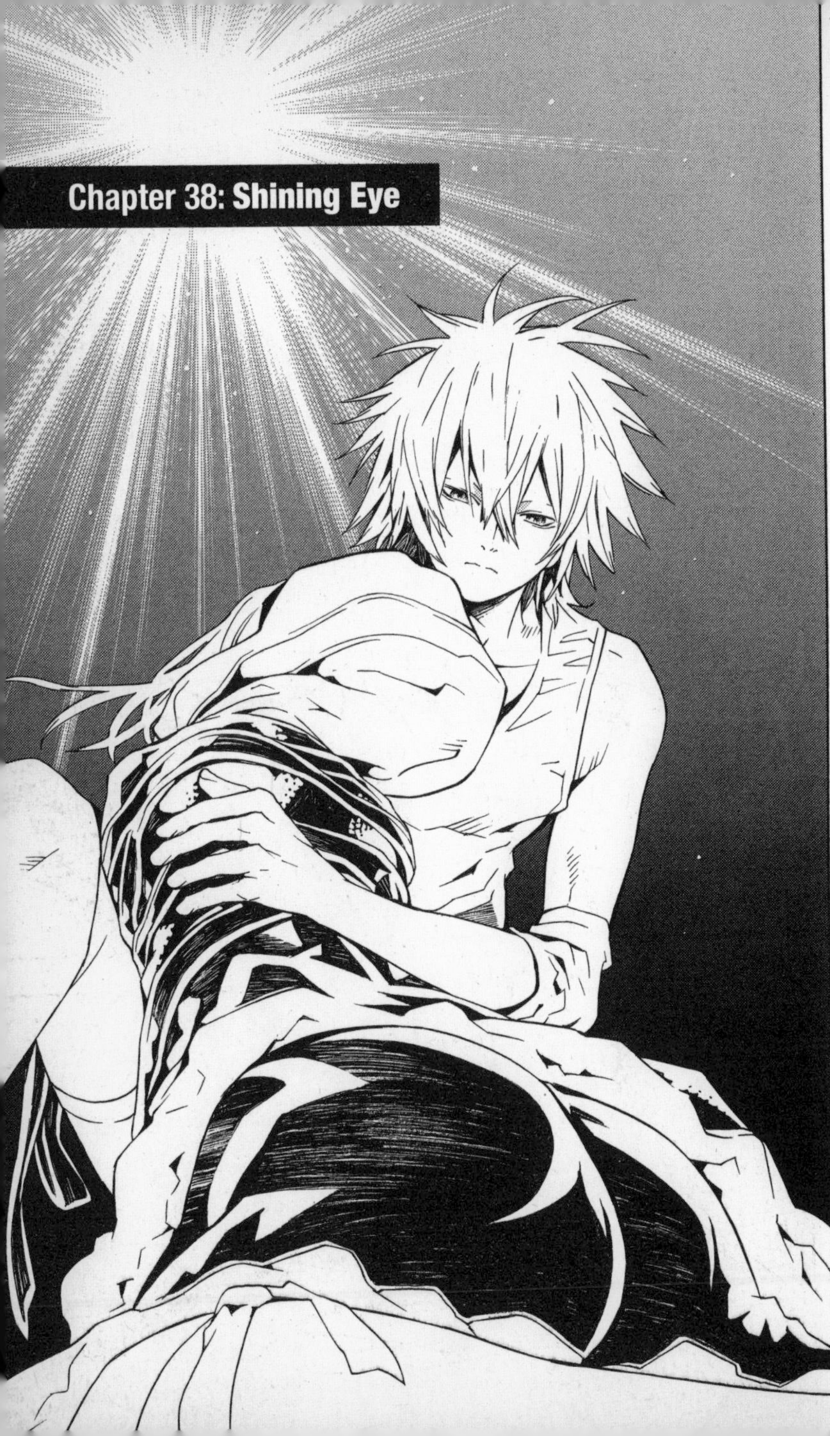

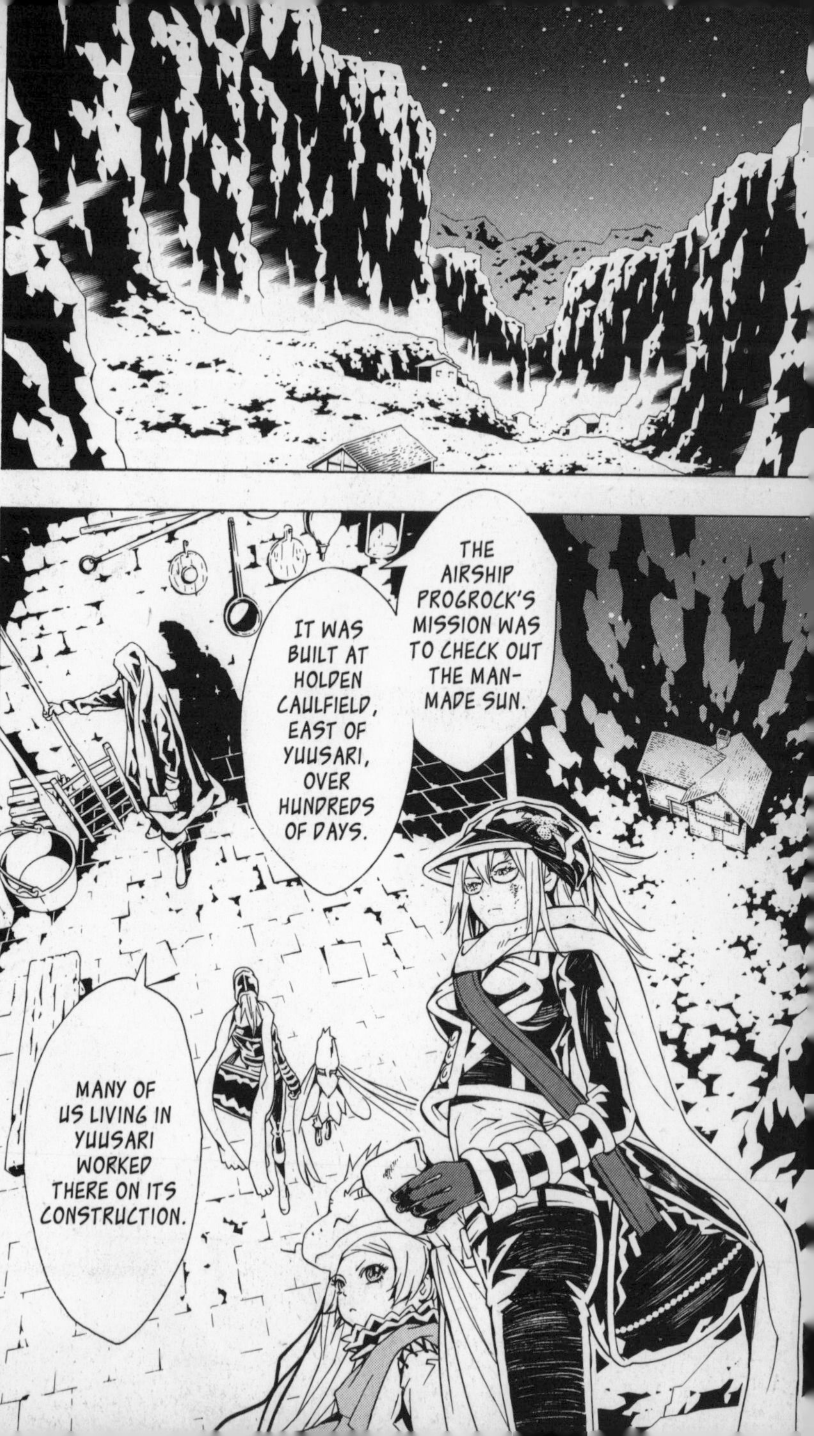
THE AIRSHIP PROGROCK'S MISSION WAS TO CHECK OUT THE MAN-MADE SUN.
IT WAS BUILT AT HOLDEN CAULFIELD, EAST OF YUUSARI, OVER HUNDREDS OF DAYS.
MANY OF US LIVING IN YUUSARI WORKED THERE ON ITS CONSTRUCTION.

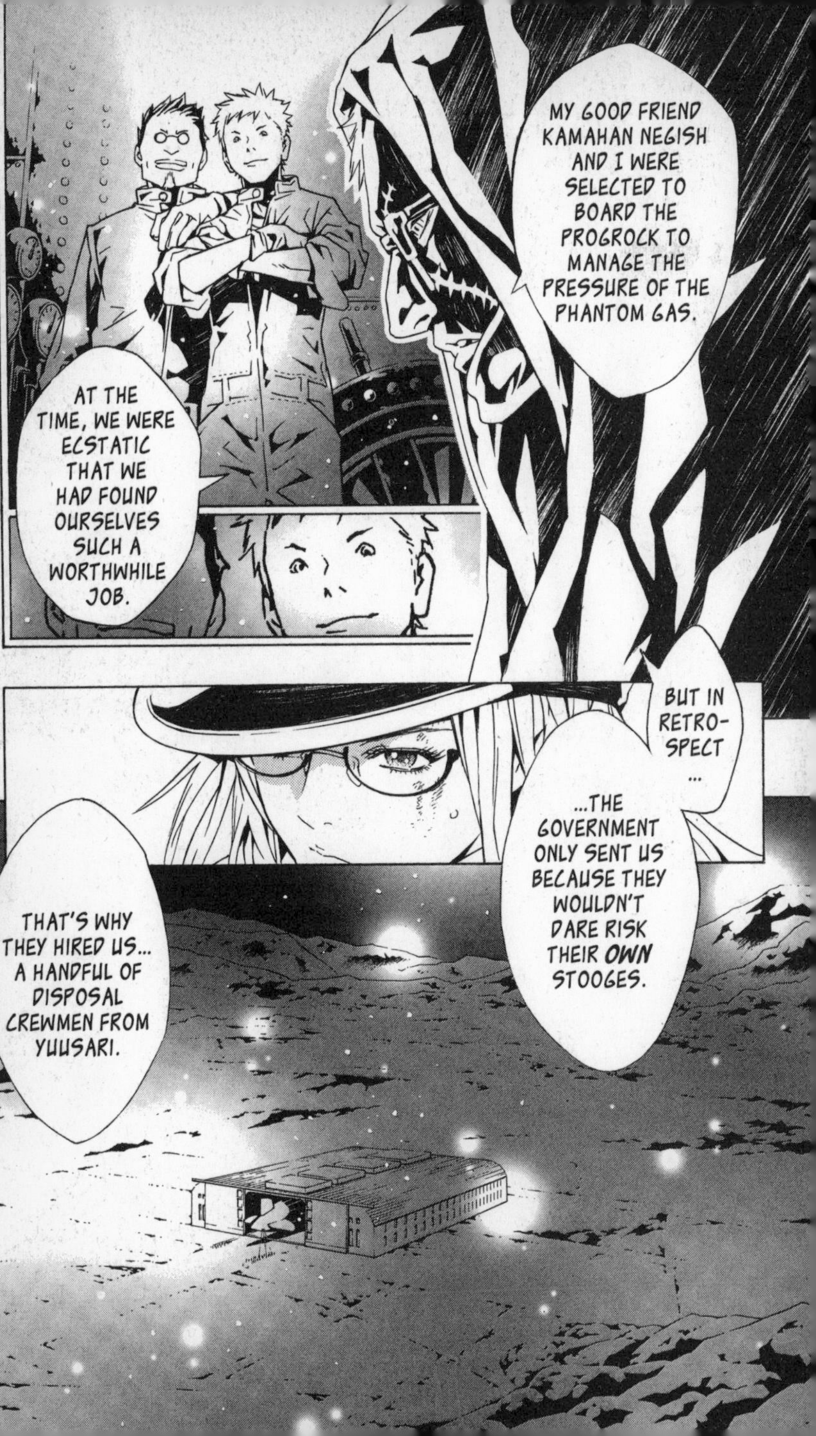

MY GOOD FRIEND KAMAHAN NEGISH AND I WERE SELECTED TO BOARD THE PROGROCK TO MANAGE THE PRESSURE OF THE PHANTOM GAS.
AT THE TIME, WE WERE ECSTATIC THAT WE HAD FOUND OURSELVES SUCH A WORTHWHILE JOB.
BUT IN RETRO-SPECT ...
...THE GOVERNMENT ONLY SENT US BECAUSE THEY WOULDN'T DARE RISK THEIR *OWN* STOOGES.
THAT'S WHY THEY HIRED US... A HANDFUL OF DISPOSAL CREWMEN FROM YUUSARI.

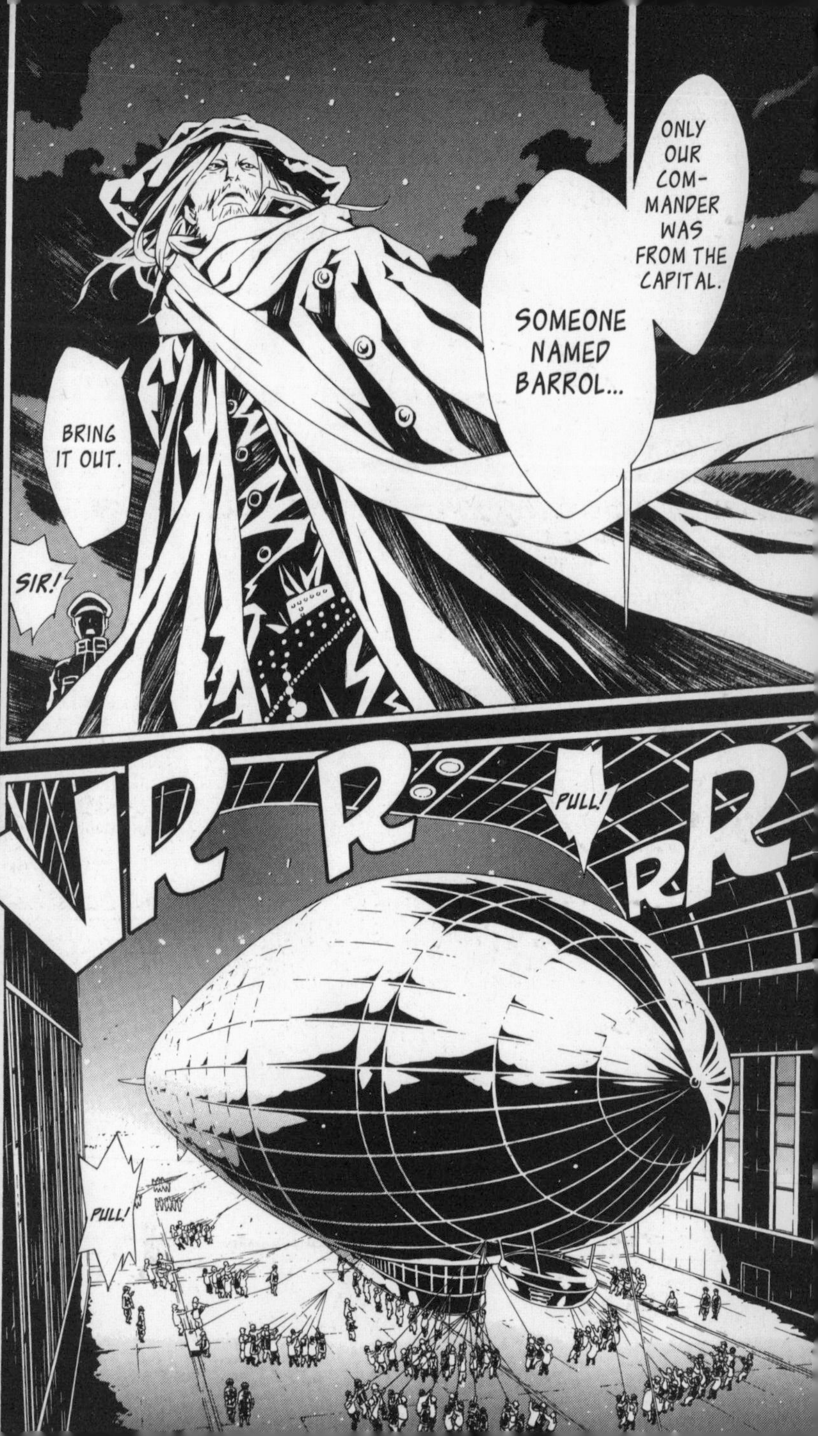
ONLY OUR COM-MANDER WAS FROM THE CAPITAL.
SOMEONE NAMED BARROL...
BRING IT OUT.
SIR!
VRRRRR
PULL!
PULL!

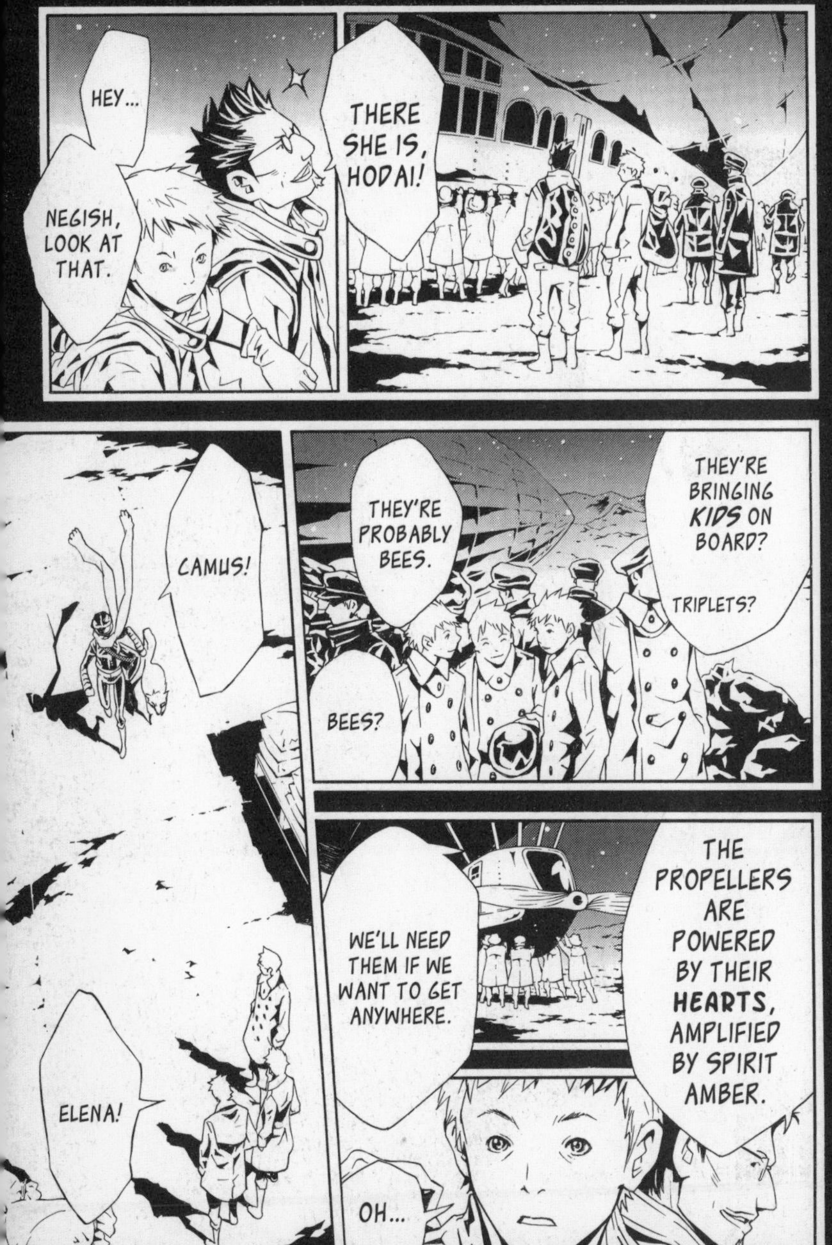
THERE SHE IS, HODAI!
HEY...
NEGISH, LOOK AT THAT.
THEY'RE BRINGING KIDS ON BOARD?
TRIPLETS?
THEY'RE PROBABLY BEES.
BEES?
THE PROPELLERS ARE POWERED BY THEIR HEARTS, AMPLIFIED BY SPIRIT AMBER.
WE'LL NEED THEM IF WE WANT TO GET ANYWHERE.
OH...
CAMUS!
ELENA!

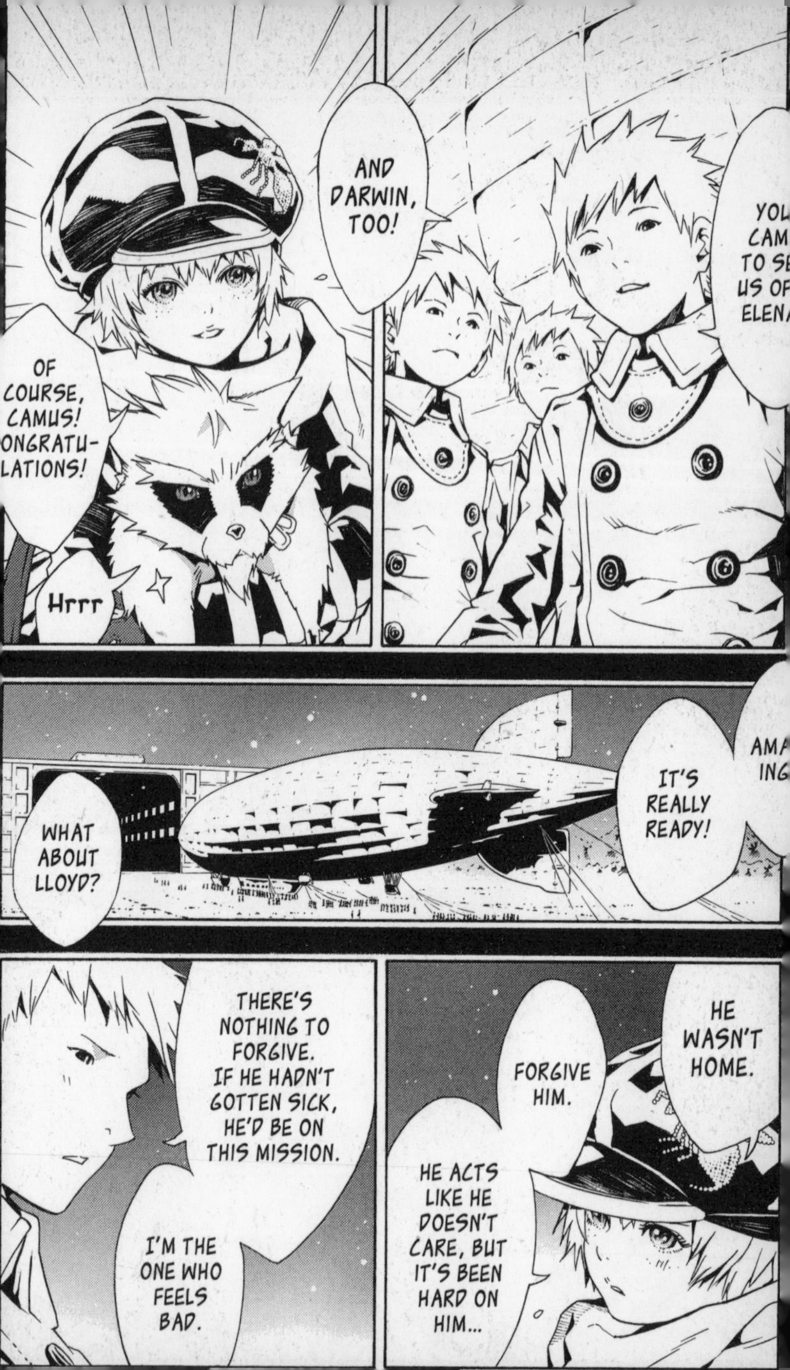
YOU CAM TO SE US OF ELENA
AND DARWIN, TOO!
OF COURSE, CAMUS! ONGRATU-LATIONS!
Hrrr
AMA ING
IT'S REALLY READY!
WHAT ABOUT LLOYD?
HE WASN'T HOME.
FORGIVE HIM.
HE ACTS LIKE HE DOESN'T CARE, BUT IT'S BEEN HARD ON HIM...
THERE'S NOTHING TO FORGIVE. IF HE HADN'T GOTTEN SICK, HE'D BE ON THIS MISSION.
I'M THE ONE WHO FEELS BAD.

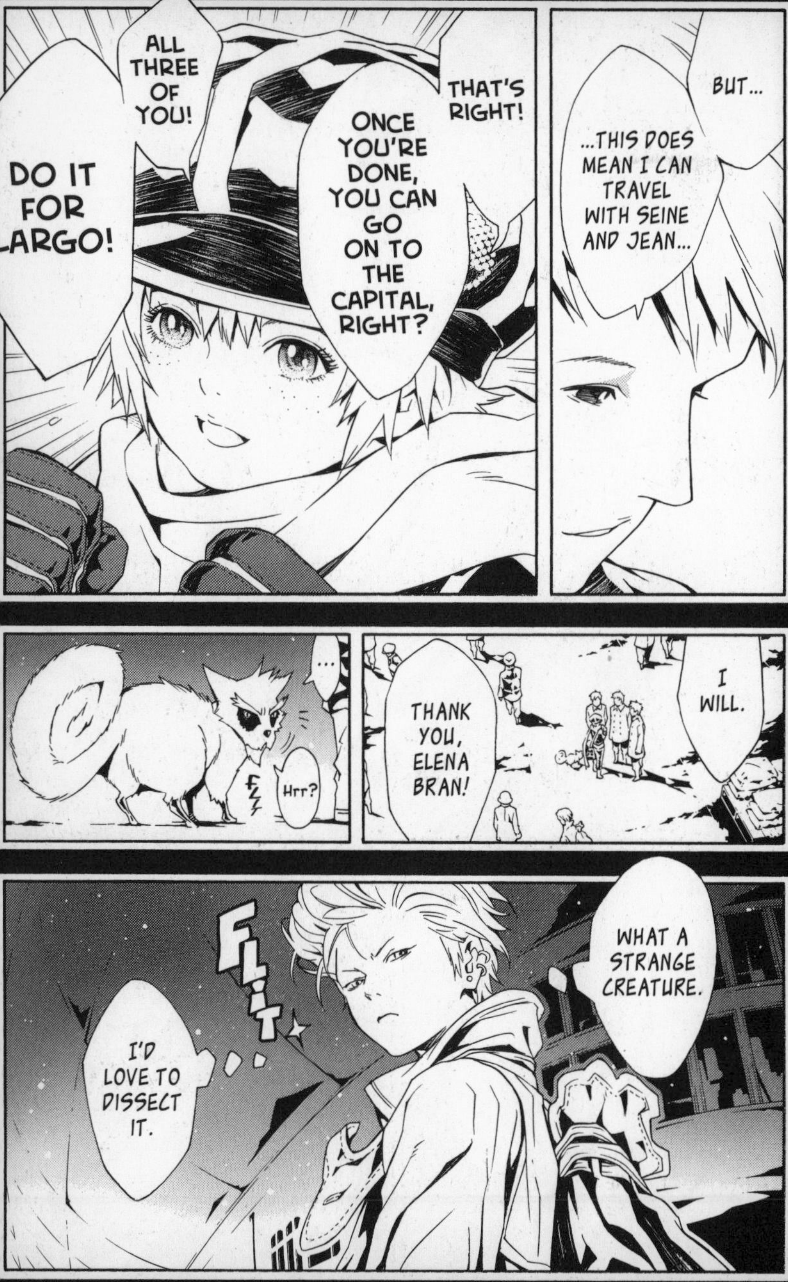
BUT...
...THIS DOES MEAN I CAN TRAVEL WITH SEINE AND JEAN...
THAT'S RIGHT!
ONCE YOU'RE DONE, YOU CAN GO ON TO THE CAPITAL, RIGHT?
ALL THREE OF YOU!
DO IT FOR ARGO!
I WILL.
THANK YOU, ELENA BRAN!
...
Hrr?
WHAT A STRANGE CREATURE.
FLIT
I'D LOVE TO DISSECT IT.

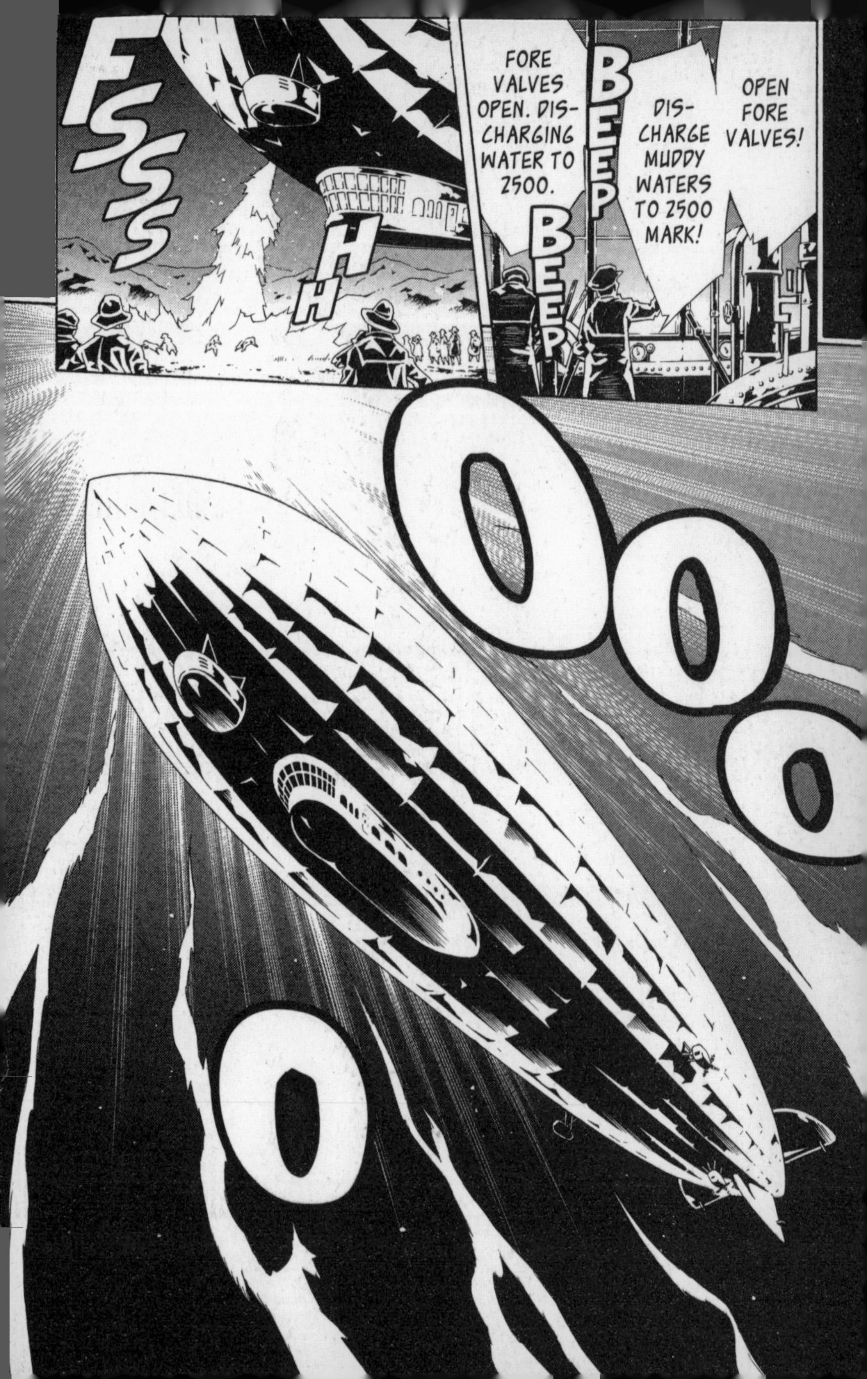
OPEN FORE VALVES!
DIS-CHARGE MUDDY WATERS TO 2500 MARK!
BEEP BEEP
FORE VALVES OPEN. DIS-CHARGING WATER TO 2500.
FSSSHH
OOOO

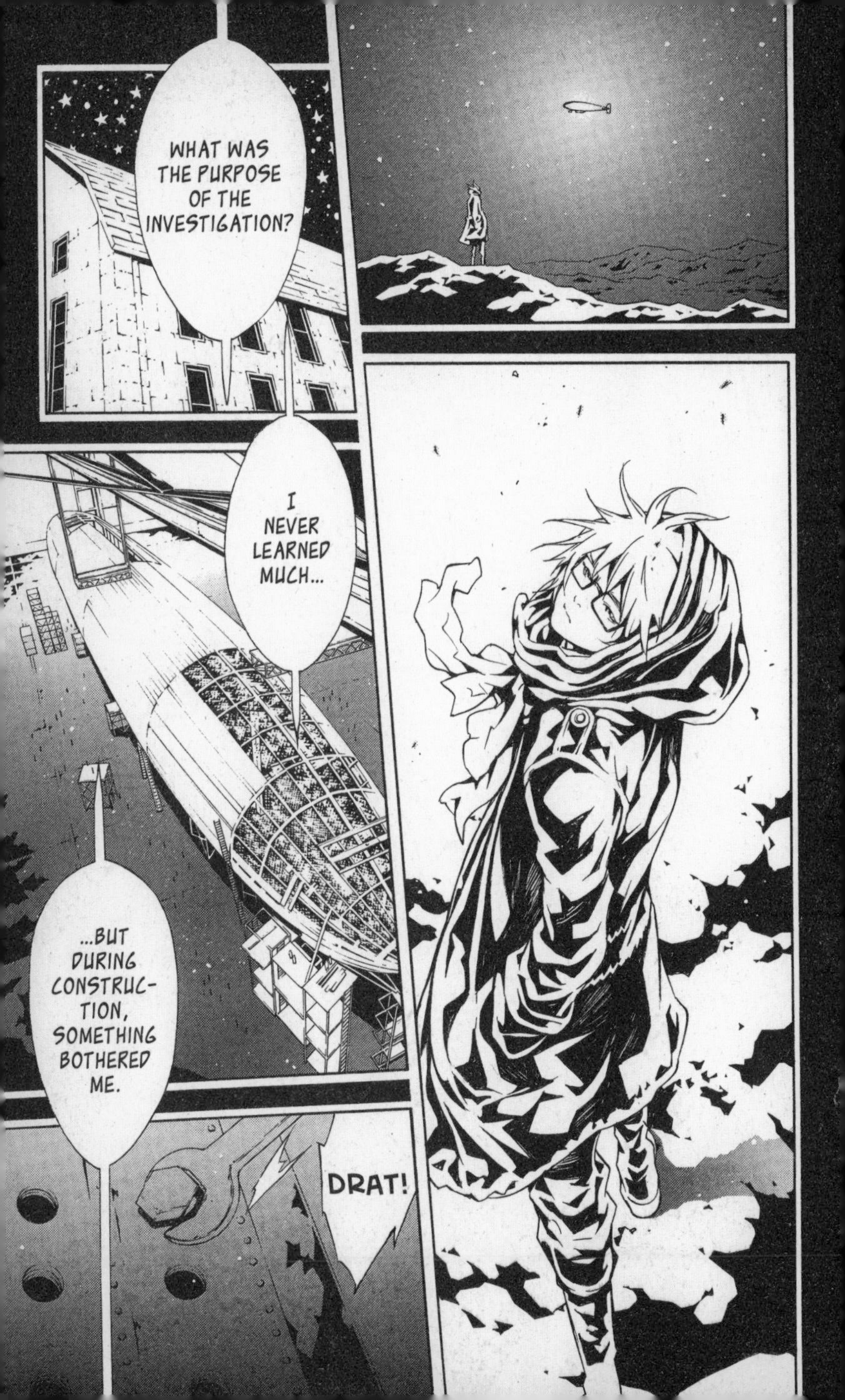
WHAT WAS THE PURPOSE OF THE INVESTIGATION?
I NEVER LEARNED MUCH...
...BUT DURING CONSTRUC-TION, SOMETHING BOTHERED ME.
DRAT!

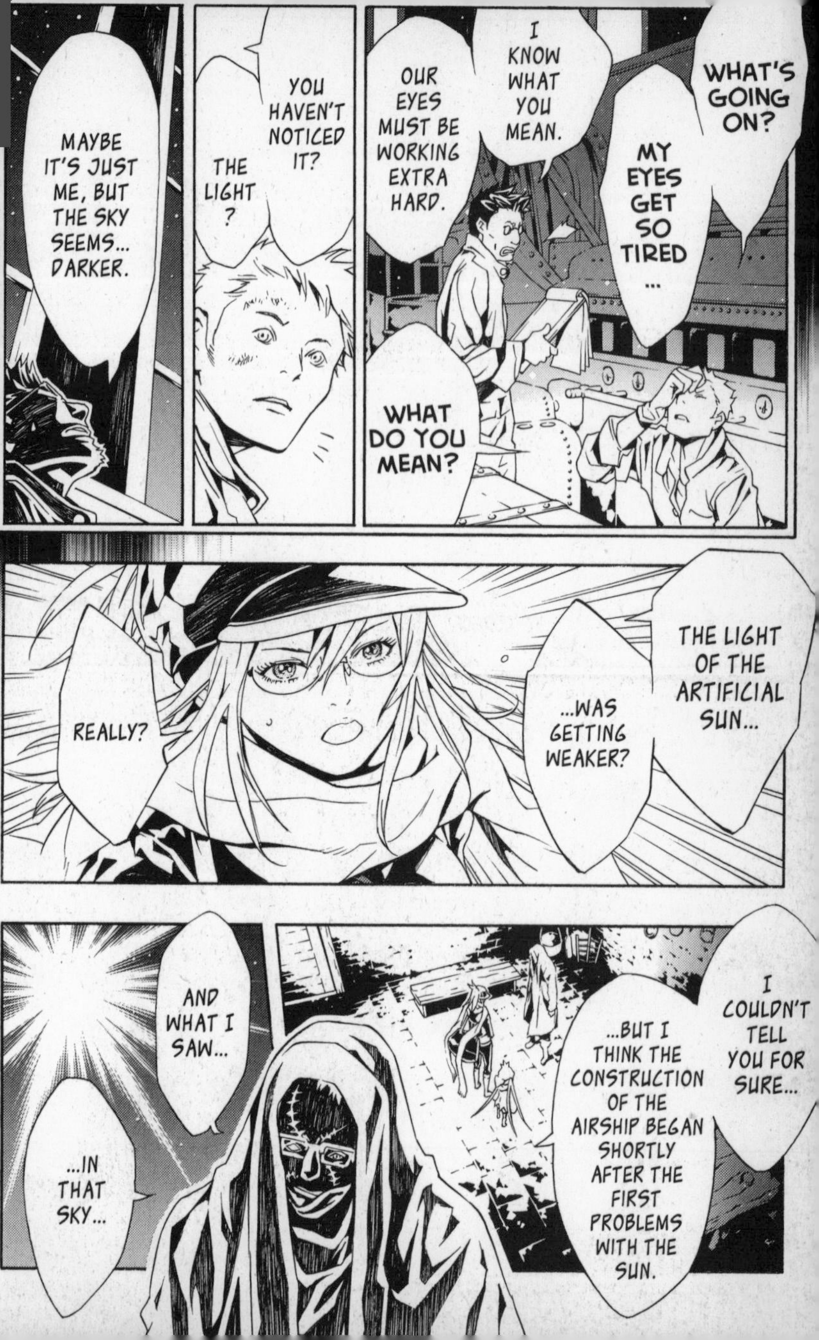
WHAT'S GOING ON?
MY EYES GET SO TIRED...
I KNOW WHAT YOU MEAN.
OUR EYES MUST BE WORKING EXTRA HARD.
WHAT DO YOU MEAN?
YOU HAVEN'T NOTICED IT?
THE LIGHT?
MAYBE IT'S JUST ME, BUT THE SKY SEEMS... DARKER.
THE LIGHT OF THE ARTIFICIAL SUN...
...WAS GETTING WEAKER?
REALLY?
I COULDN'T TELL YOU FOR SURE...
...BUT I THINK THE CONSTRUCTION OF THE AIRSHIP BEGAN SHORTLY AFTER THE FIRST PROBLEMS WITH THE SUN.
AND WHAT I SAW...
...IN THAT SKY...

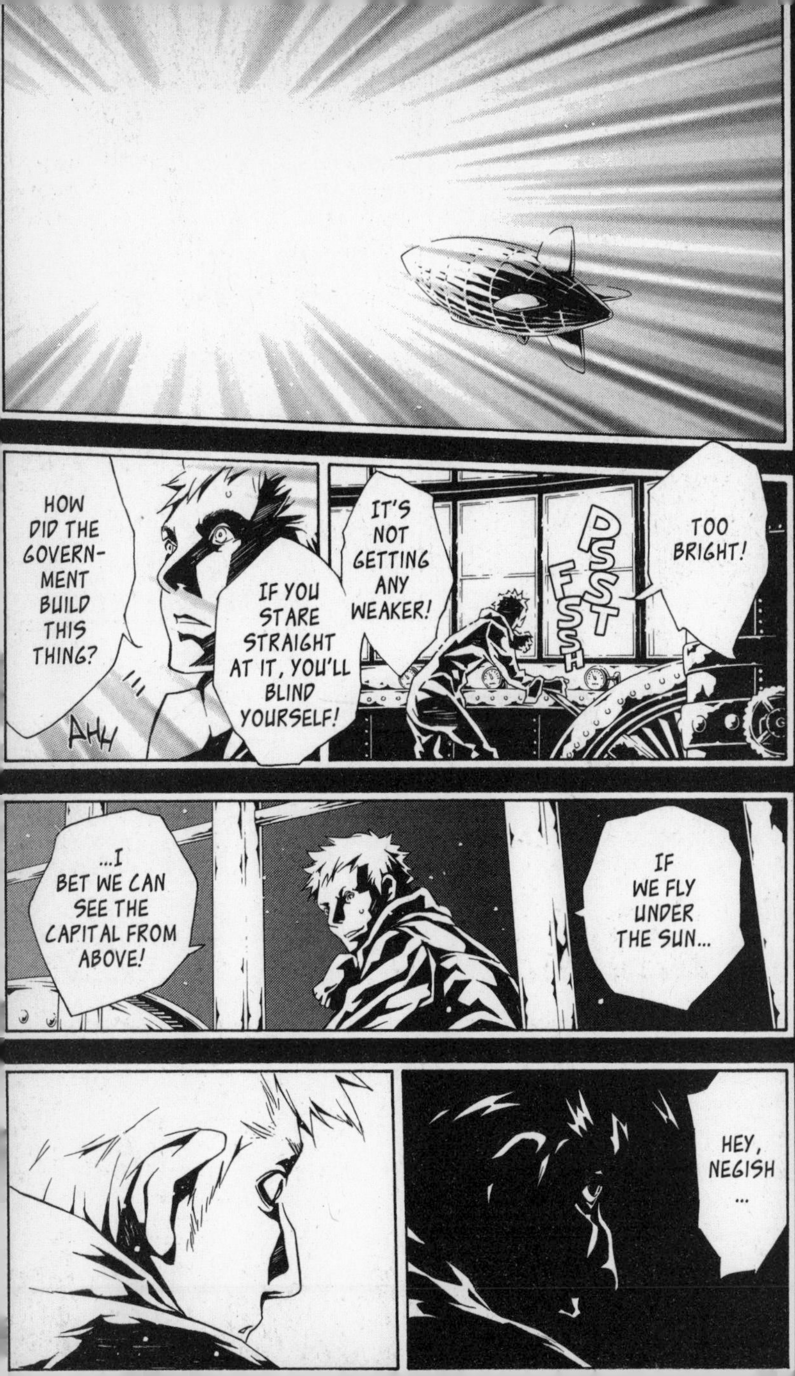
TOO BRIGHT!
PSST
FSSH
IT'S NOT GETTING ANY WEAKER!
IF YOU STARE STRAIGHT AT IT, YOU'LL BLIND YOURSELF!
HOW DID THE GOVERN-MENT BUILD THIS THING?
AHH
IF WE FLY UNDER THE SUN...
...I BET WE CAN SEE THE CAPITAL FROM ABOVE!
HEY, NEGISH ...

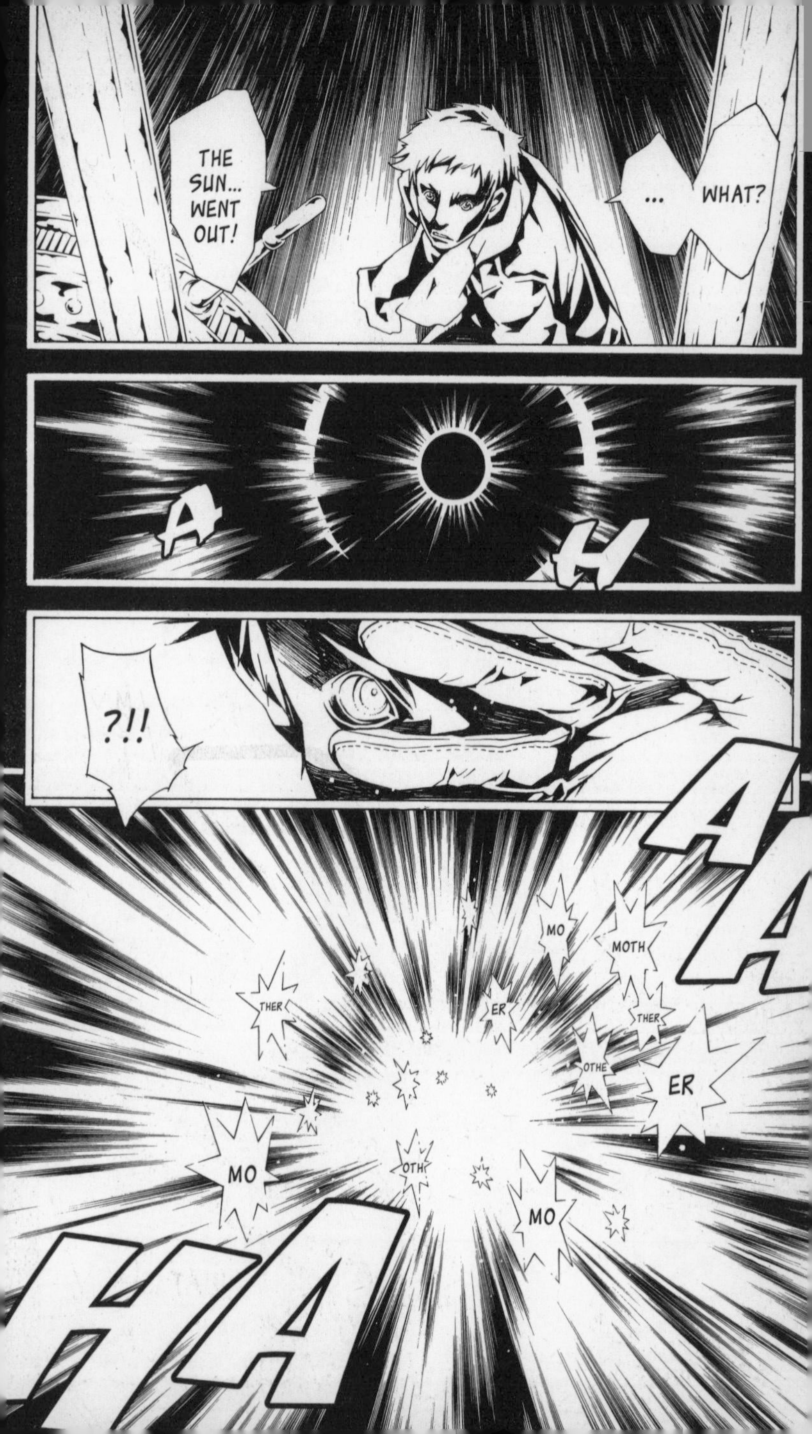
... WHAT?
THE SUN... WENT OUT!
A H
?!!
AA
MO
MOTH
ER
THER
OTHE
ER
THER
MO
OTH
MO
HA

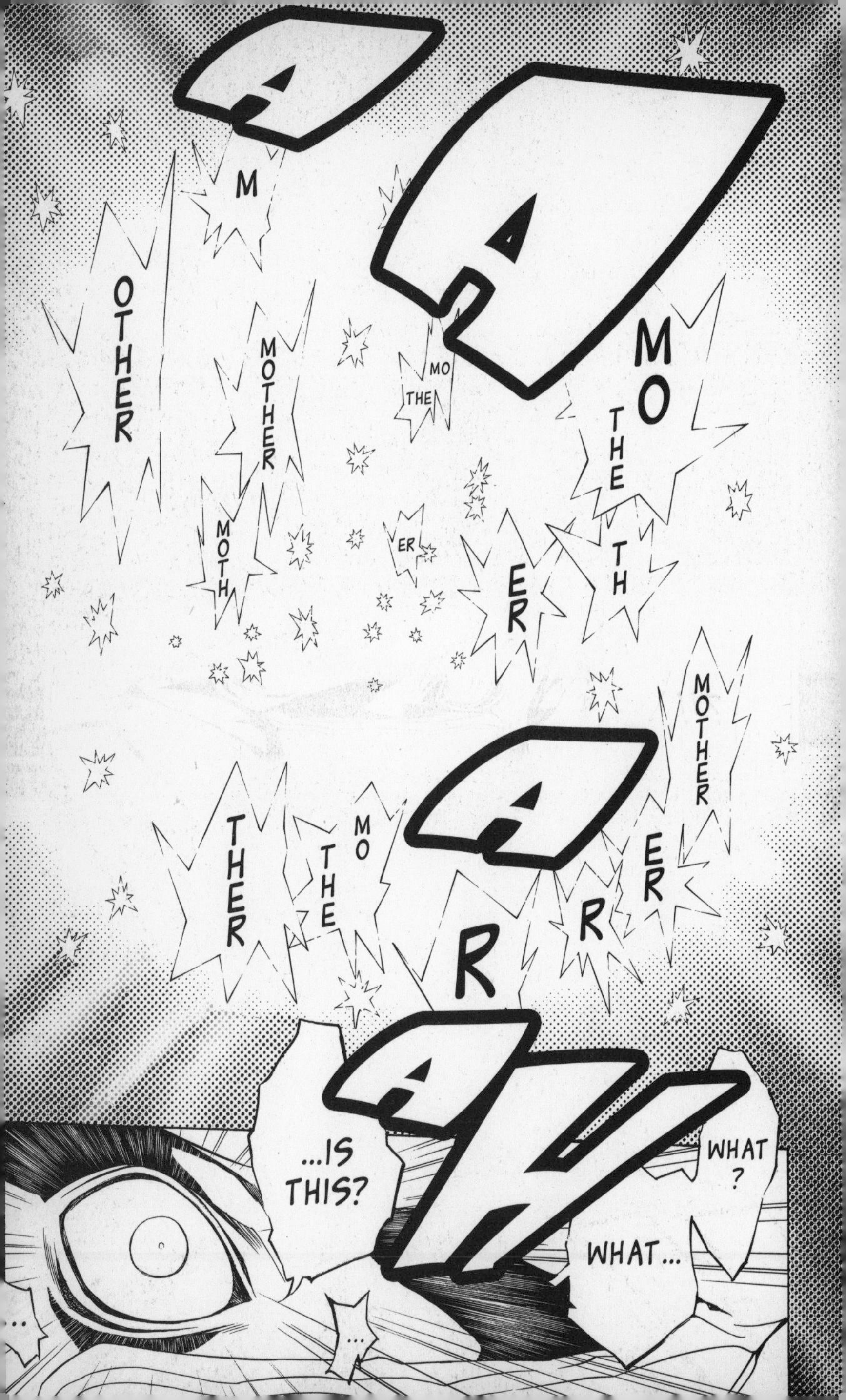

MO
THE
TH
ER
MO
THE
ER
M
MOTHER
MOTH
OTHER
MOTHER
ER
R
R
MO
THE
THER
WHAT
?
WHAT...
...IS THIS?
...
...

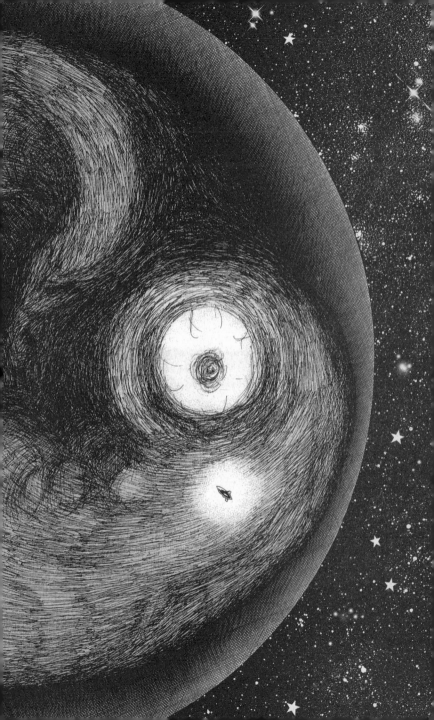

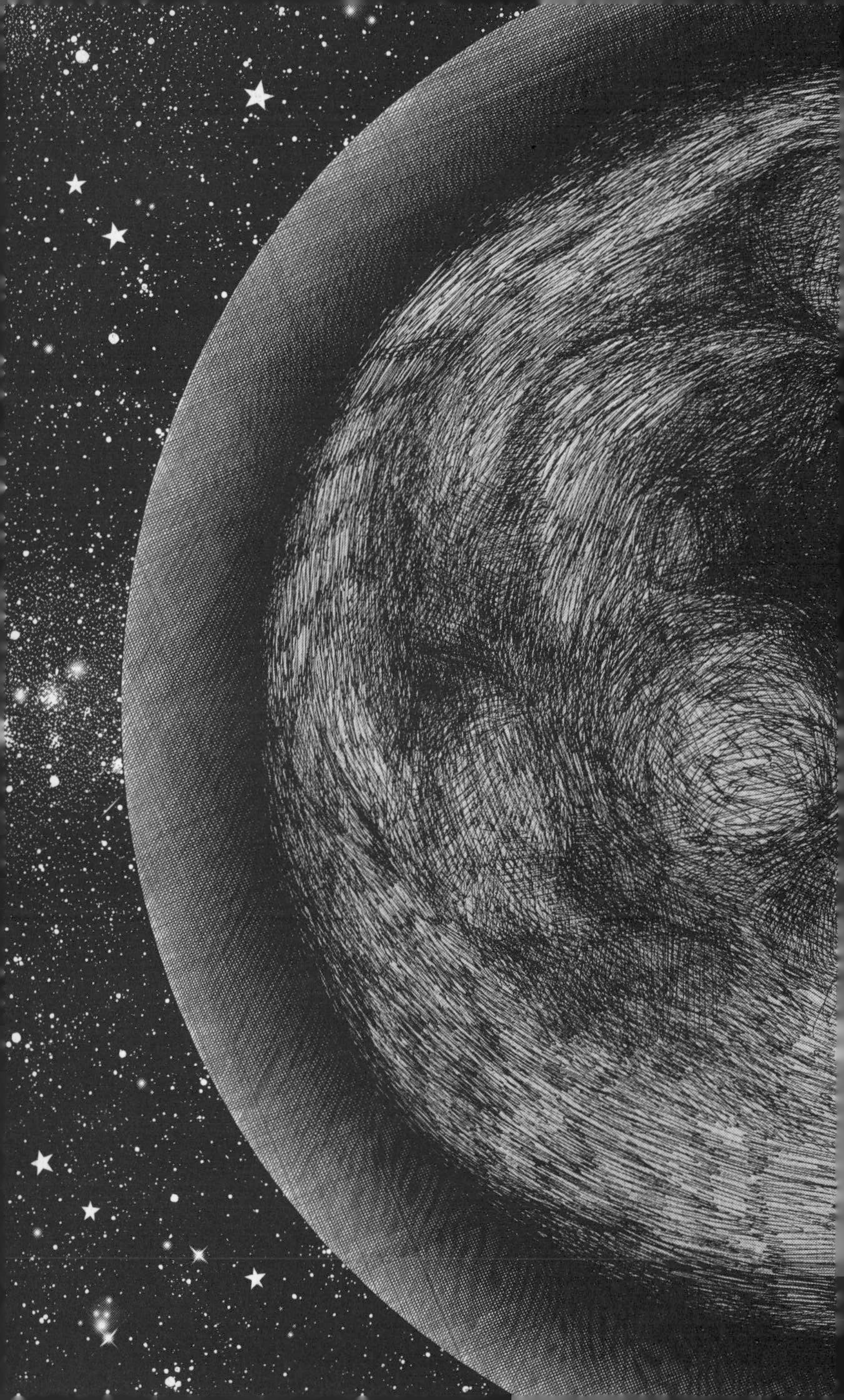

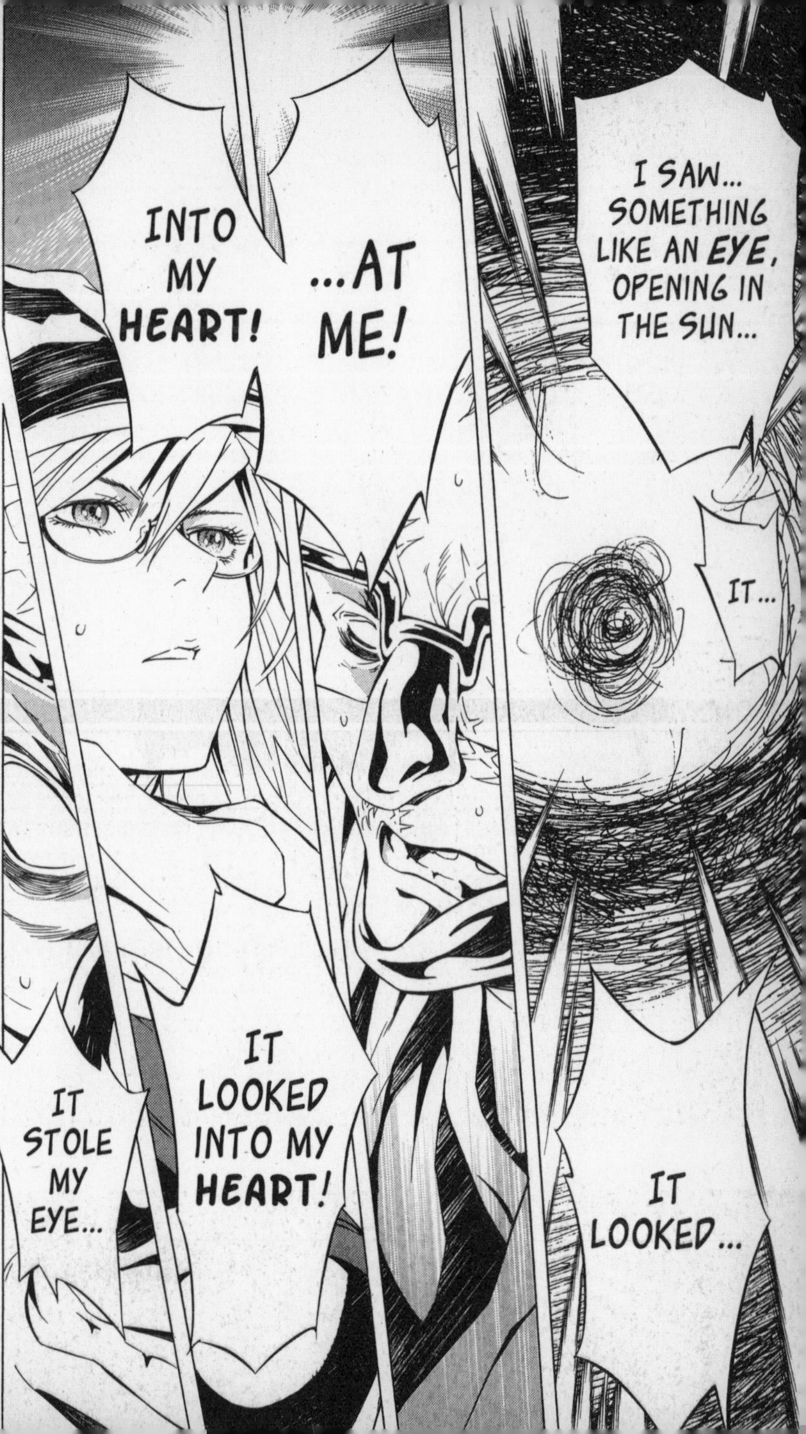
I SAW... SOMETHING LIKE AN *EYE*, OPENING IN THE SUN...
IT...
IT LOOKED...
...AT ME!
IT LOOKED INTO MY **HEART!**
INTO MY **HEART!**
IT STOLE MY EYE...

AAAAHHH!!!
AAAAAAH!!!
MY EYE!!!
BEEP BEEP
HODAI!
WHAT IS IT? WHAT HAPPENED?
BEEP
GAS PRESSURE'S CRITICAL, AND—
HEY!
BEEP
BEEP
WHAT ARE THOSE GUYS IN THE COCKPIT DOING?
BEEP

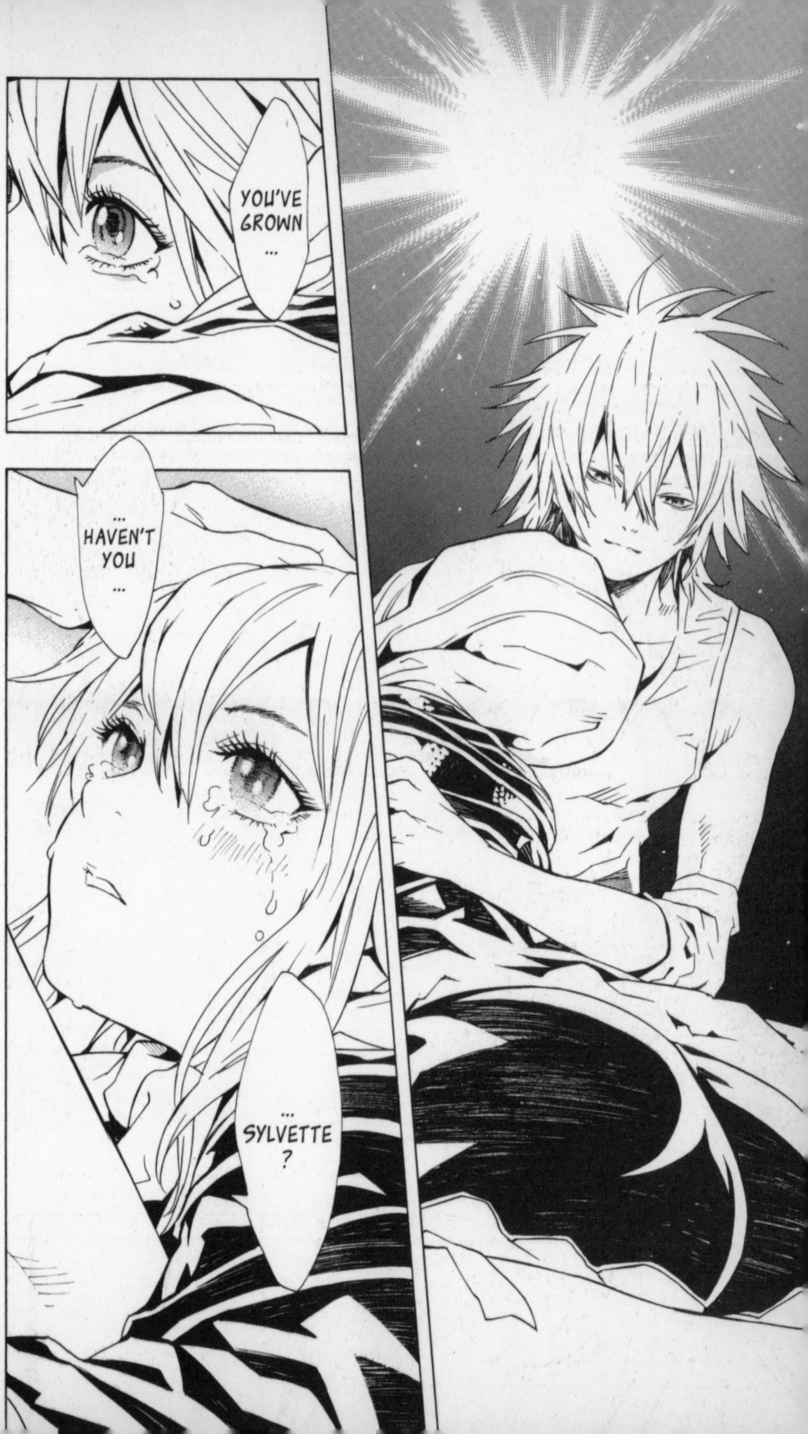
YOU'VE GROWN ...
... HAVEN'T YOU ...
... SYLVETTE ?

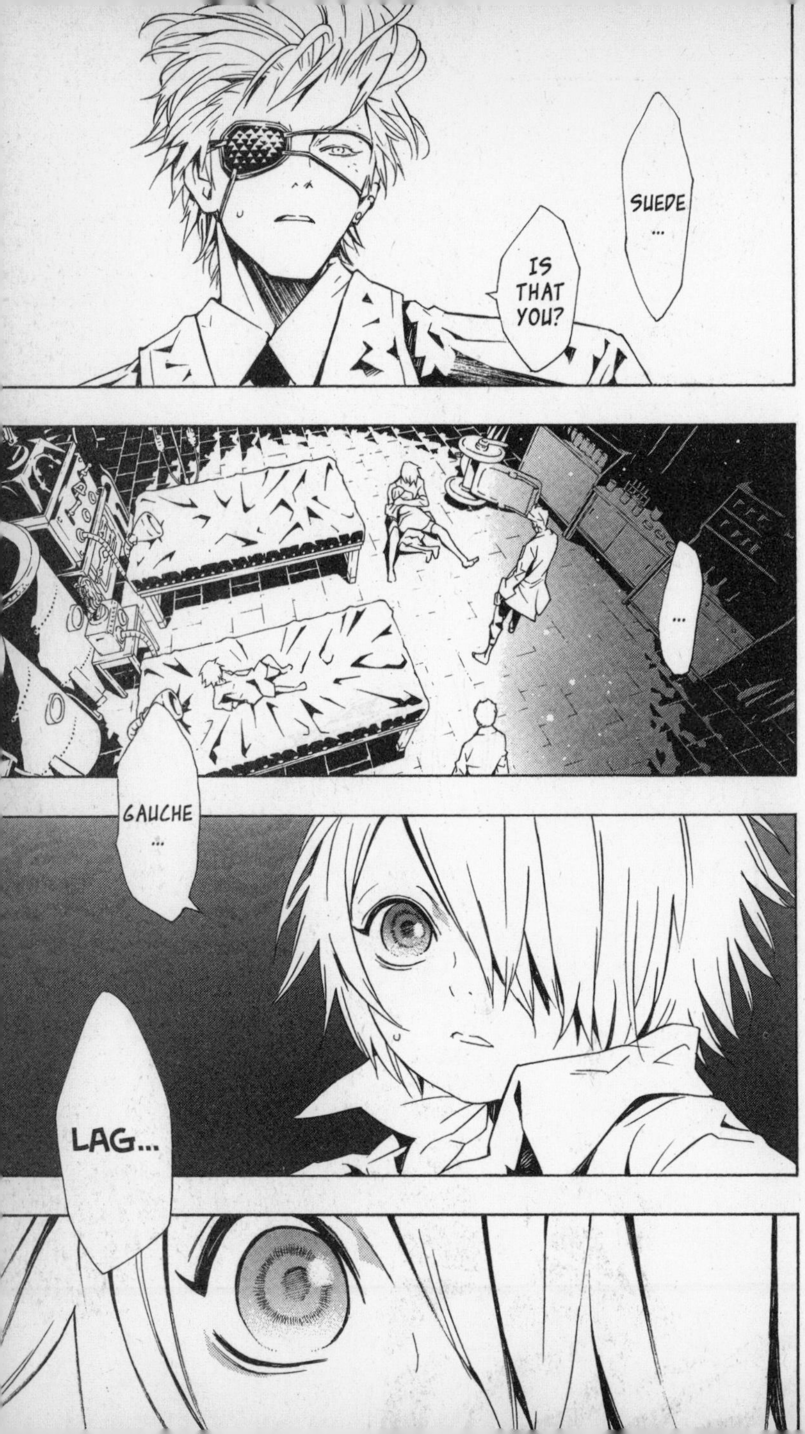
SUEDE ...
IS THAT YOU?
...
GAUCHE ...
LAG...

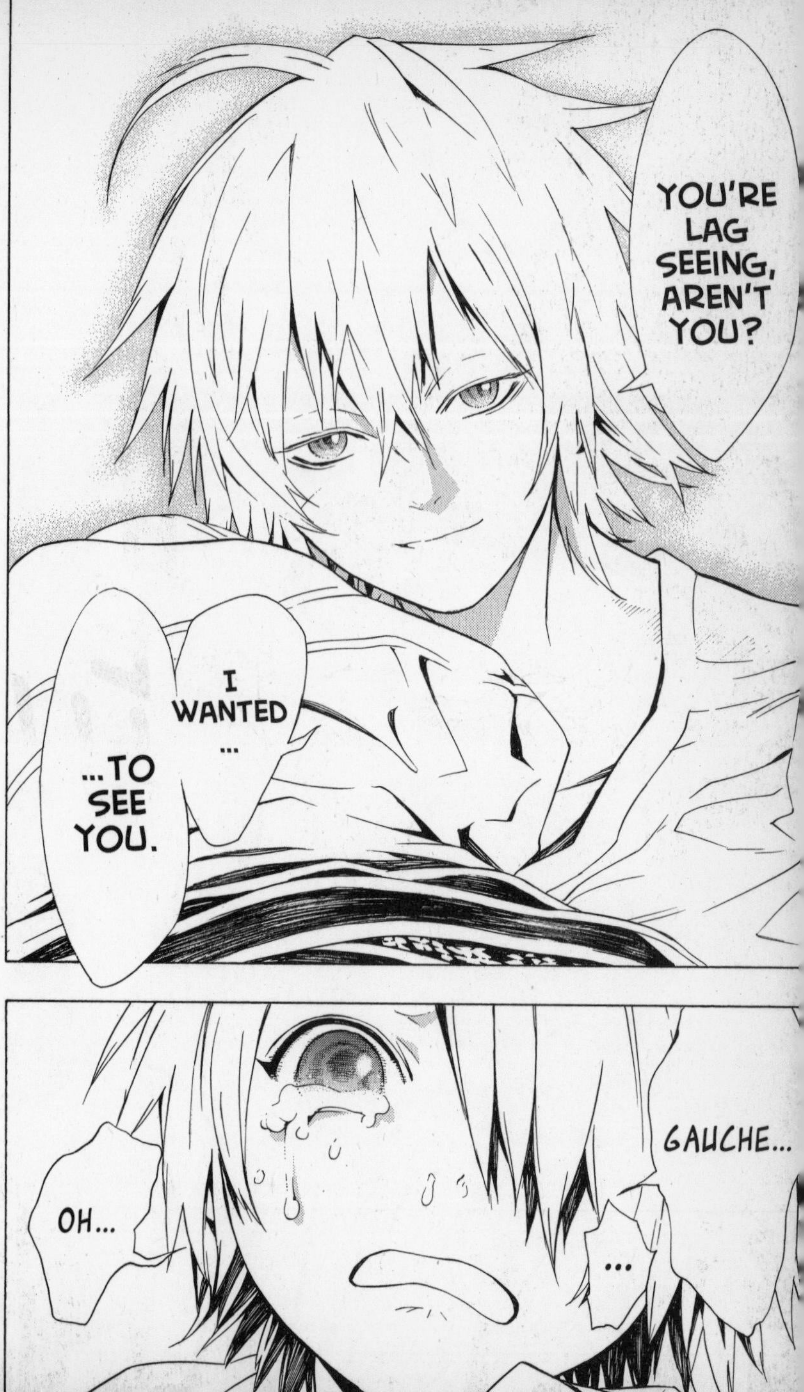
YOU'RE LAG SEEING, AREN'T YOU?
I WANTED ...
...TO SEE YOU.
GAUCHE...
...
OH...

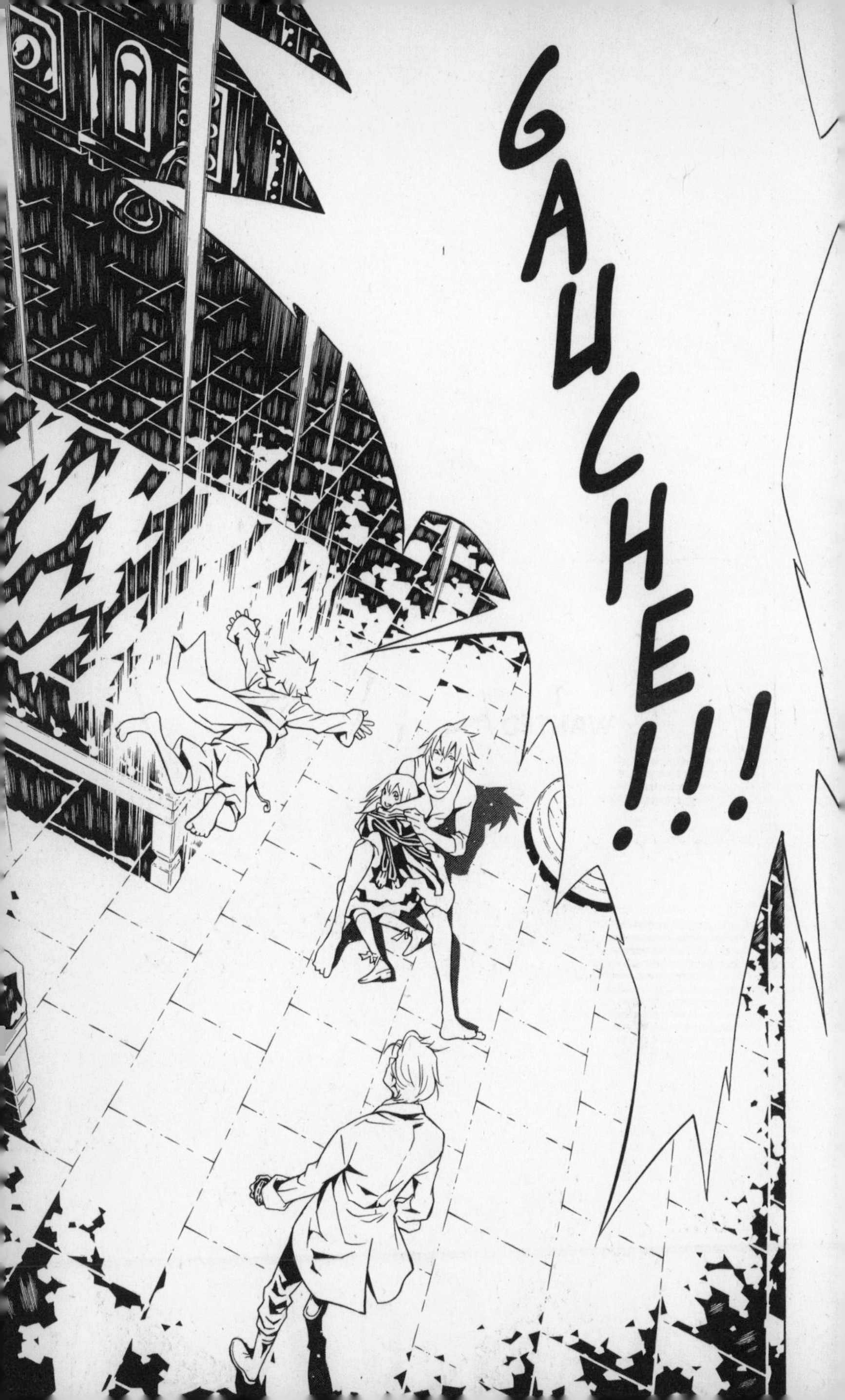
GAUCHE!!!

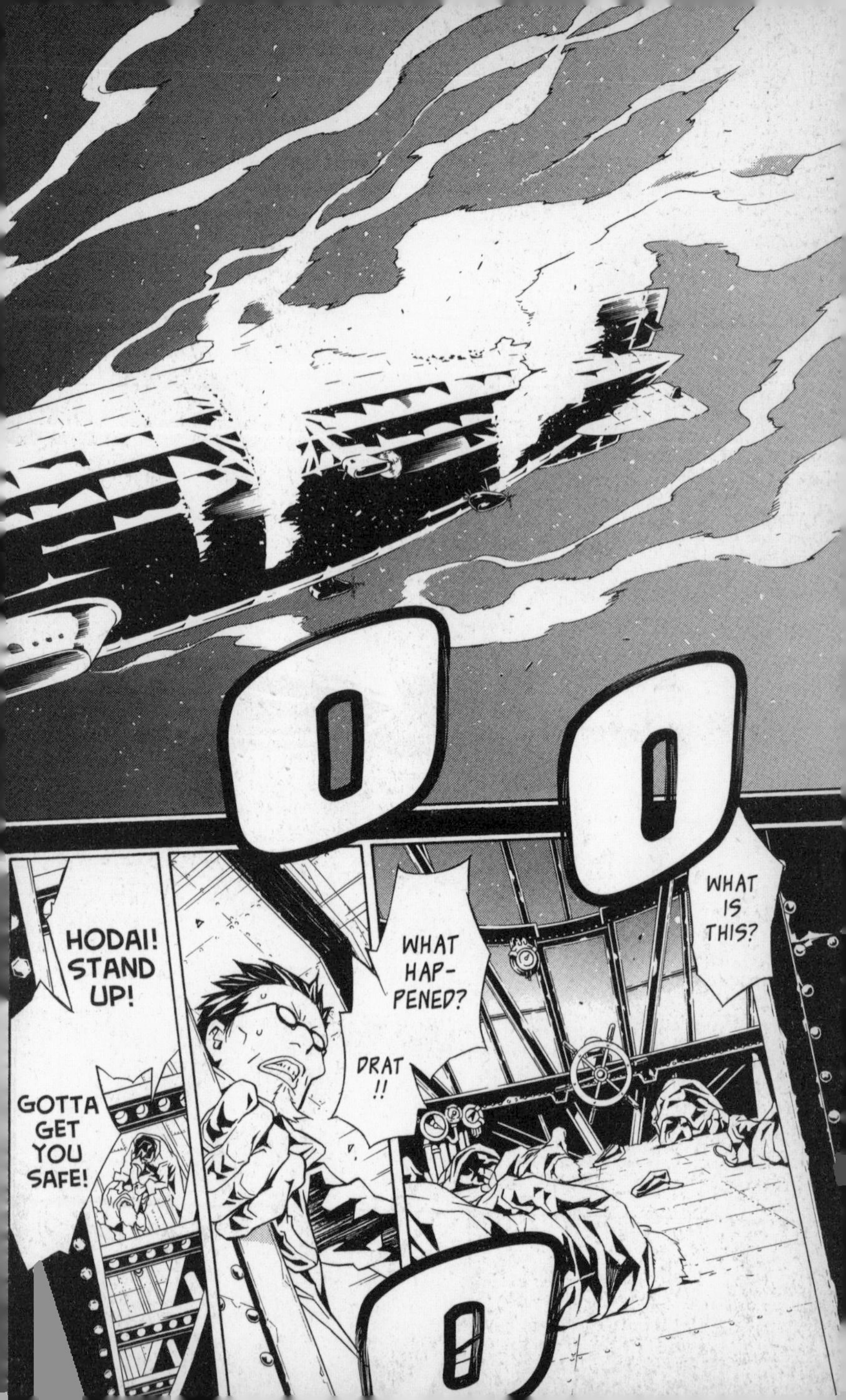
WHAT IS THIS?
WHAT HAP-PENED?
DRAT!!
HODAI! STAND UP!
GOTTA GET YOU SAFE!

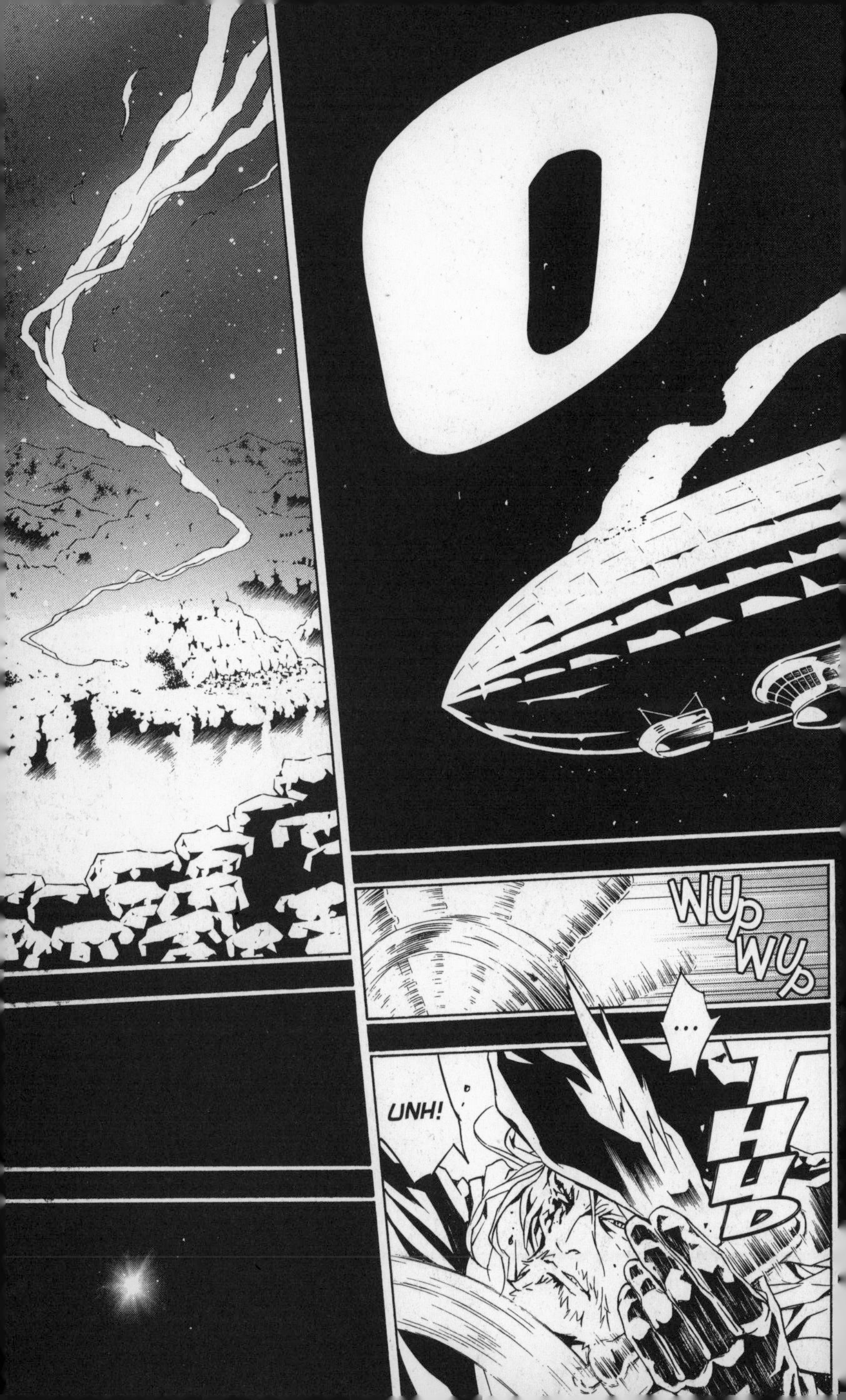
WUP WUP
...
THUD
UNH!

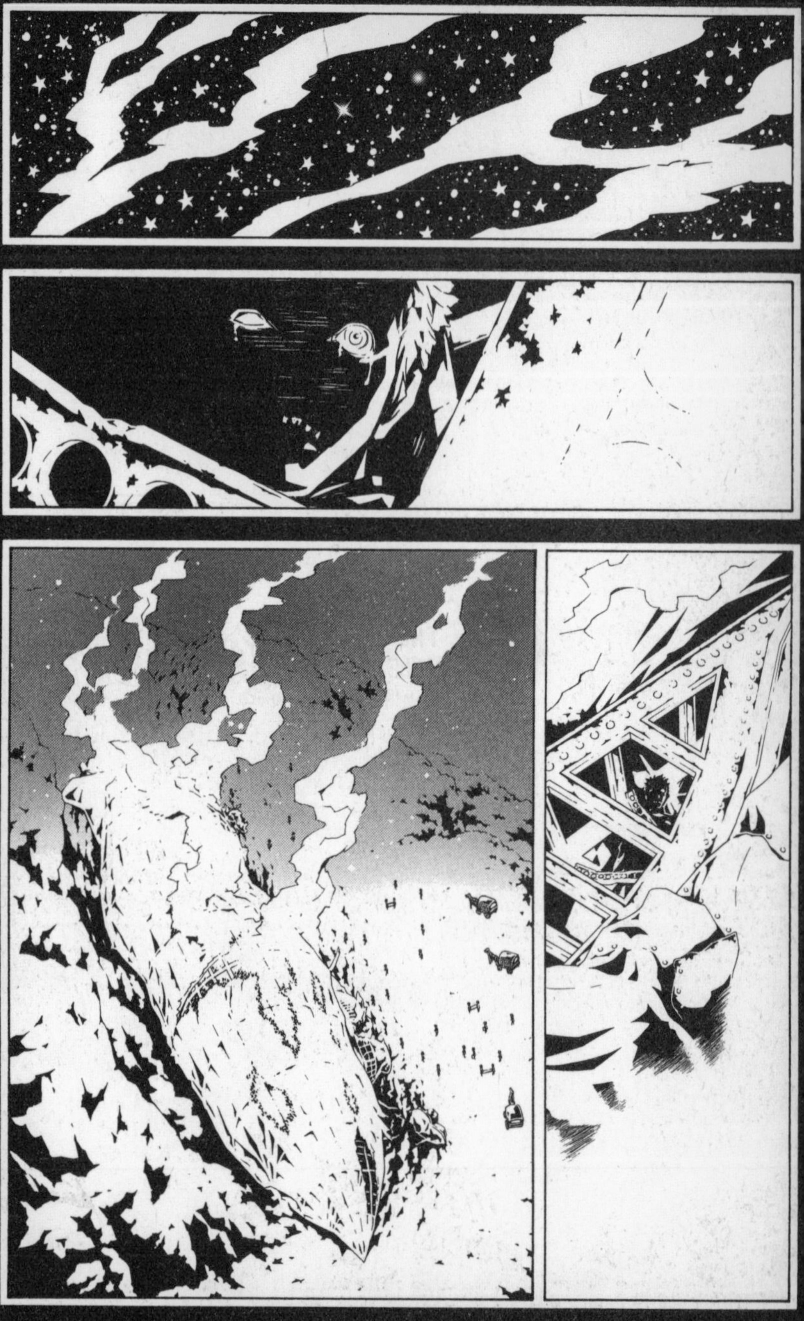

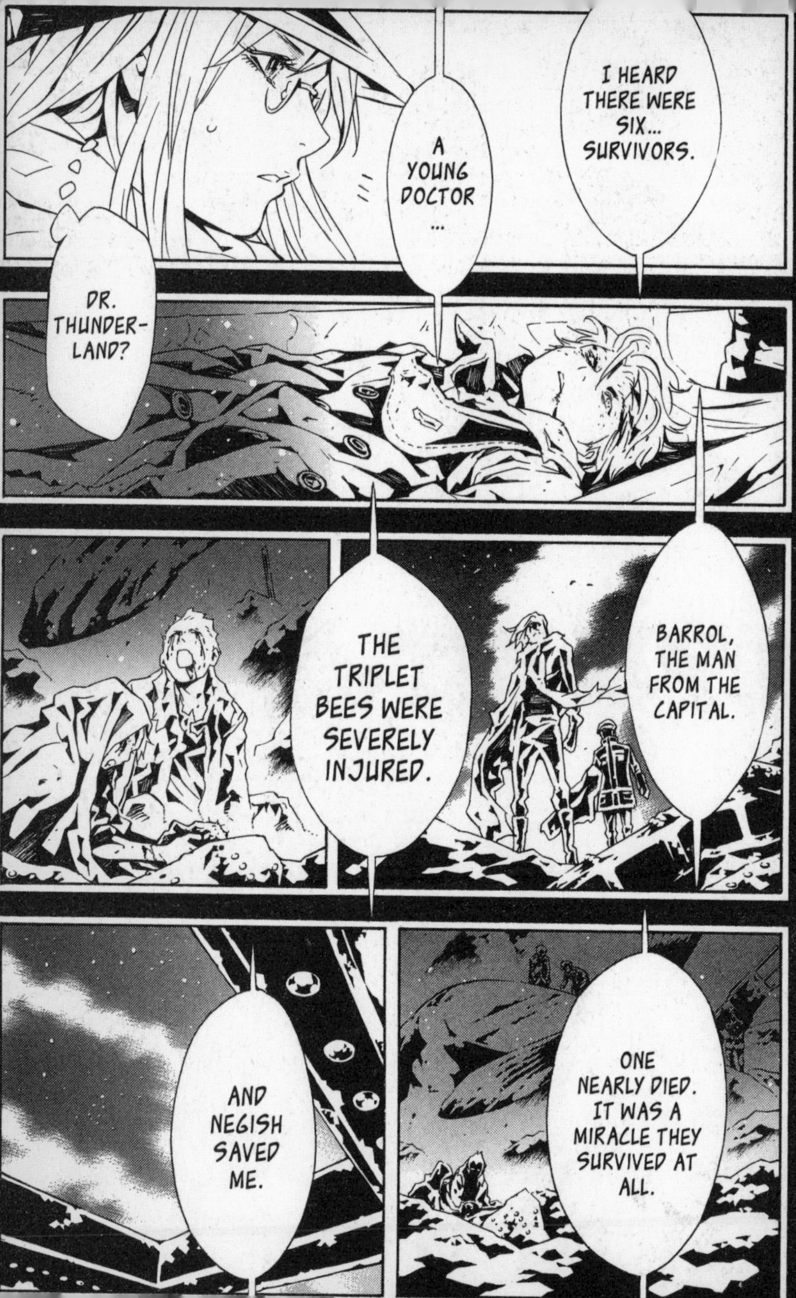
I HEARD THERE WERE SIX... SURVIVORS.
A YOUNG DOCTOR ...
DR. THUNDER-LAND?
BARROL, THE MAN FROM THE CAPITAL.
THE TRIPLET BEES WERE SEVERELY INJURED.
ONE NEARLY DIED. IT WAS A MIRACLE THEY SURVIVED AT ALL.
AND NEGISH SAVED ME.

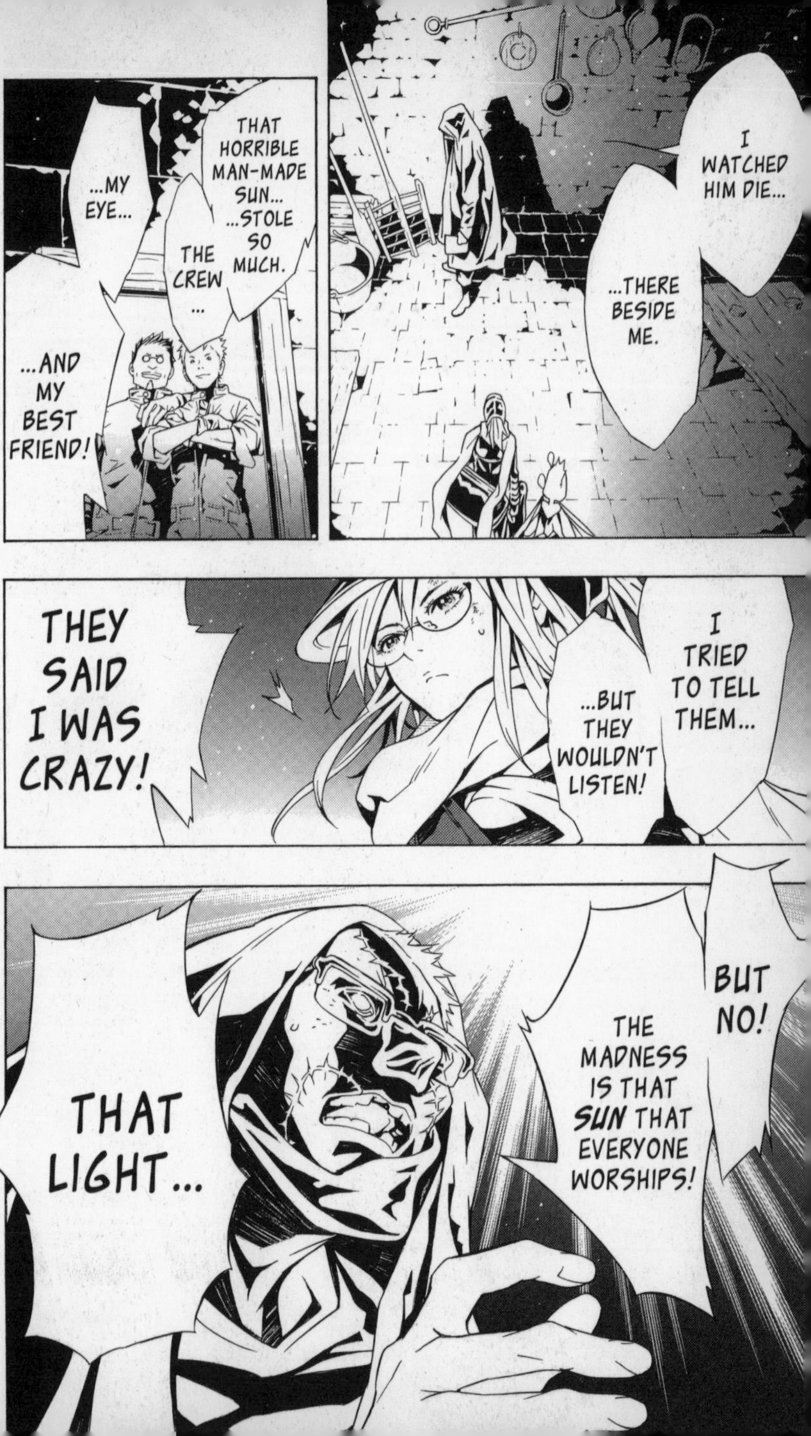
I WATCHED HIM DIE...
...THERE BESIDE ME.
THAT HORRIBLE MAN-MADE SUN... ...STOLE SO MUCH.
THE CREW...
...MY EYE...
...AND MY BEST FRIEND!
I TRIED TO TELL THEM...
...BUT THEY WOULDN'T LISTEN!
THEY SAID I WAS CRAZY!
BUT NO!
THE MADNESS IS THAT *SUN* THAT EVERYONE WORSHIPS!
THAT LIGHT...

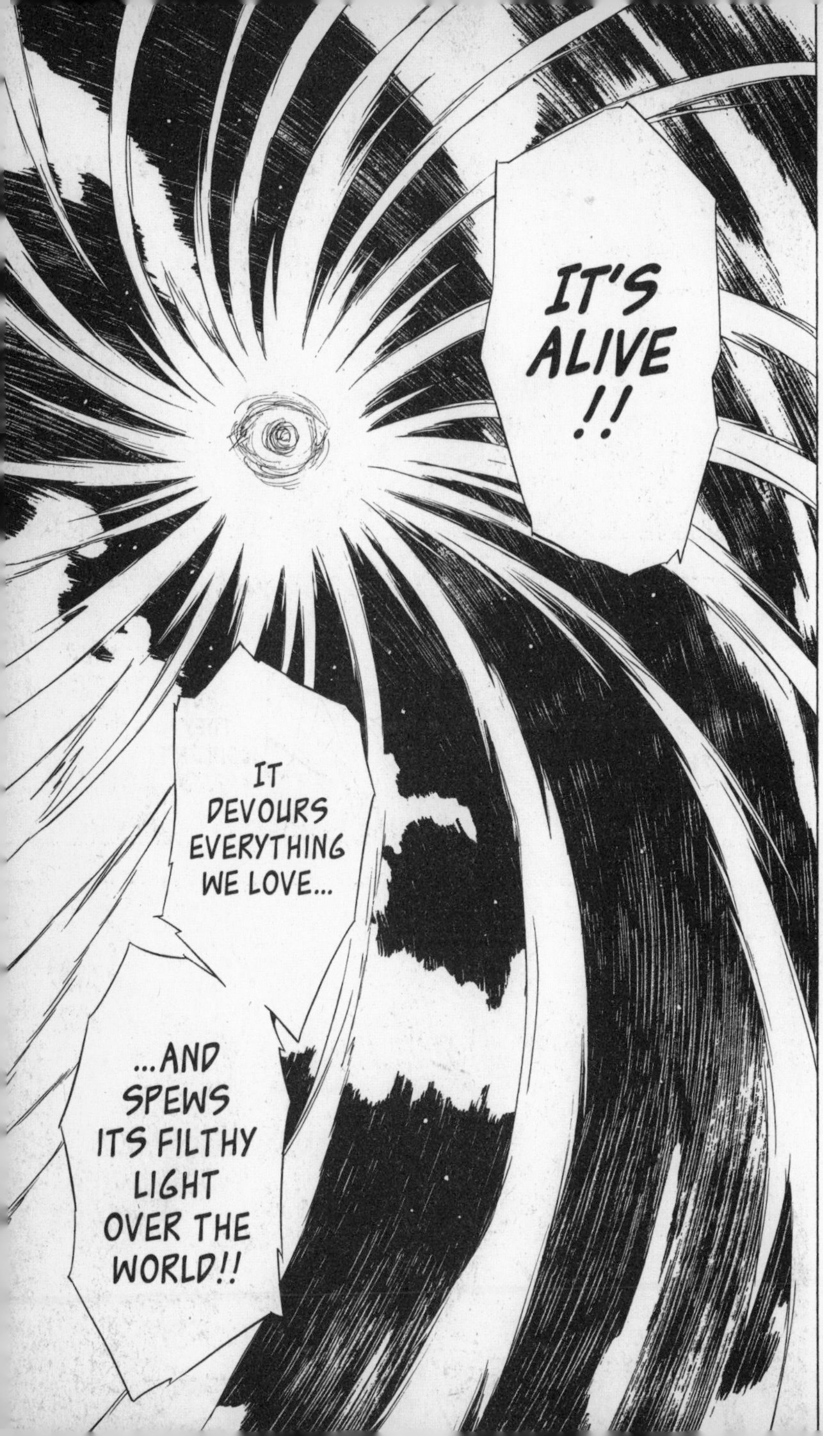
IT'S ALIVE!!
IT DEVOURS EVERYTHING WE LOVE...
...AND SPEWS ITS FILTHY LIGHT OVER THE WORLD!!

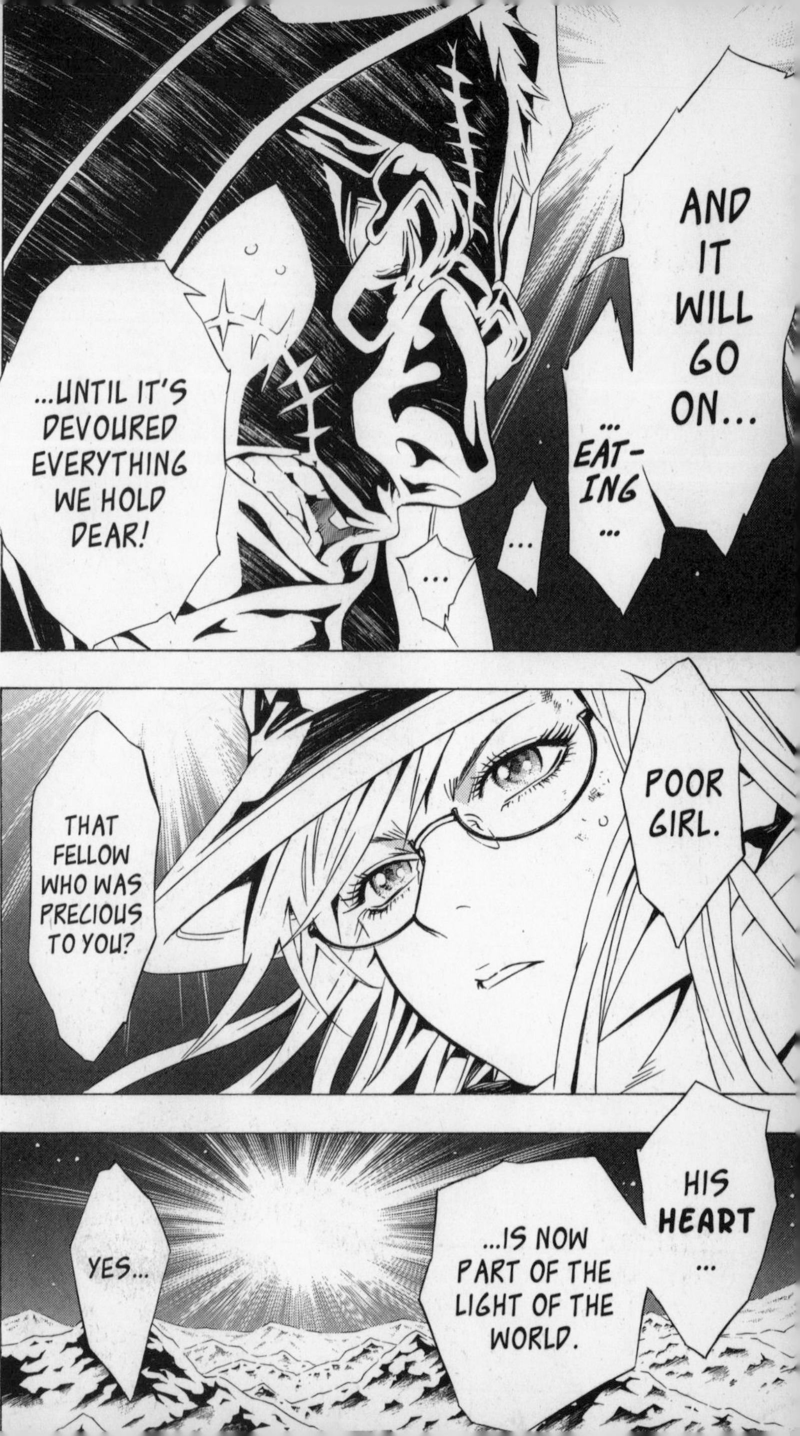
AND IT WILL GO ON...
...EAT-ING...
...
...
...UNTIL IT'S DEVOURED EVERYTHING WE HOLD DEAR!
POOR GIRL.
THAT FELLOW WHO WAS PRECIOUS TO YOU?
HIS **HEART**...
...IS NOW PART OF THE LIGHT OF THE WORLD.
YES...

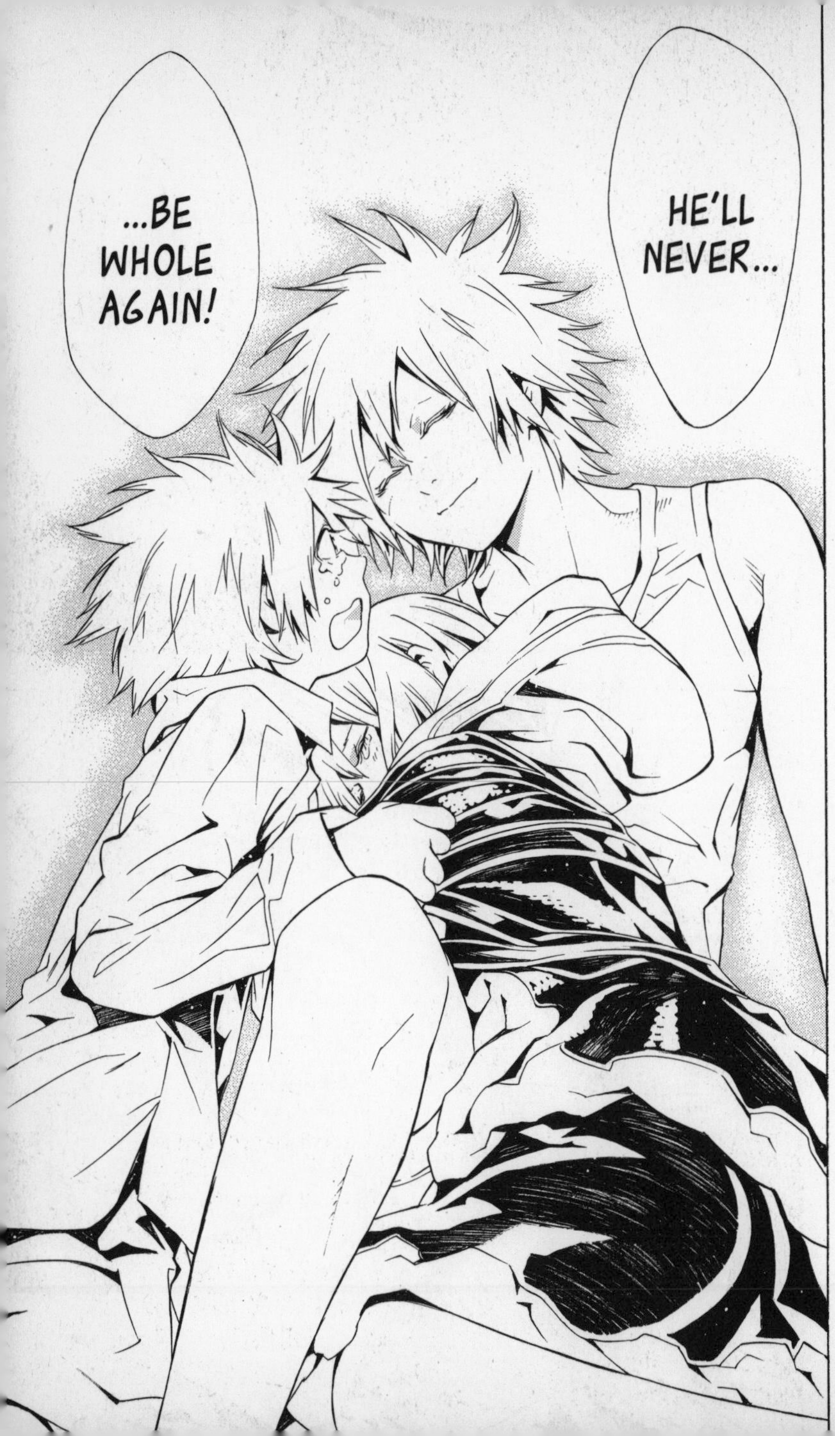
HE'LL NEVER...
...BE WHOLE AGAIN!

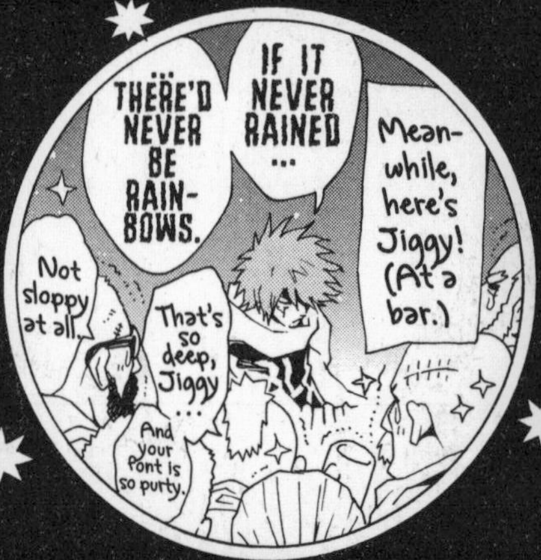
Mean-while, here's Jiggy! (At a bar.)
IF IT NEVER RAINED...
...THERE'D NEVER BE RAIN-BOWS.
That's so deep, Jiggy...
Not sloppy at all.
And your Pont is so purty.

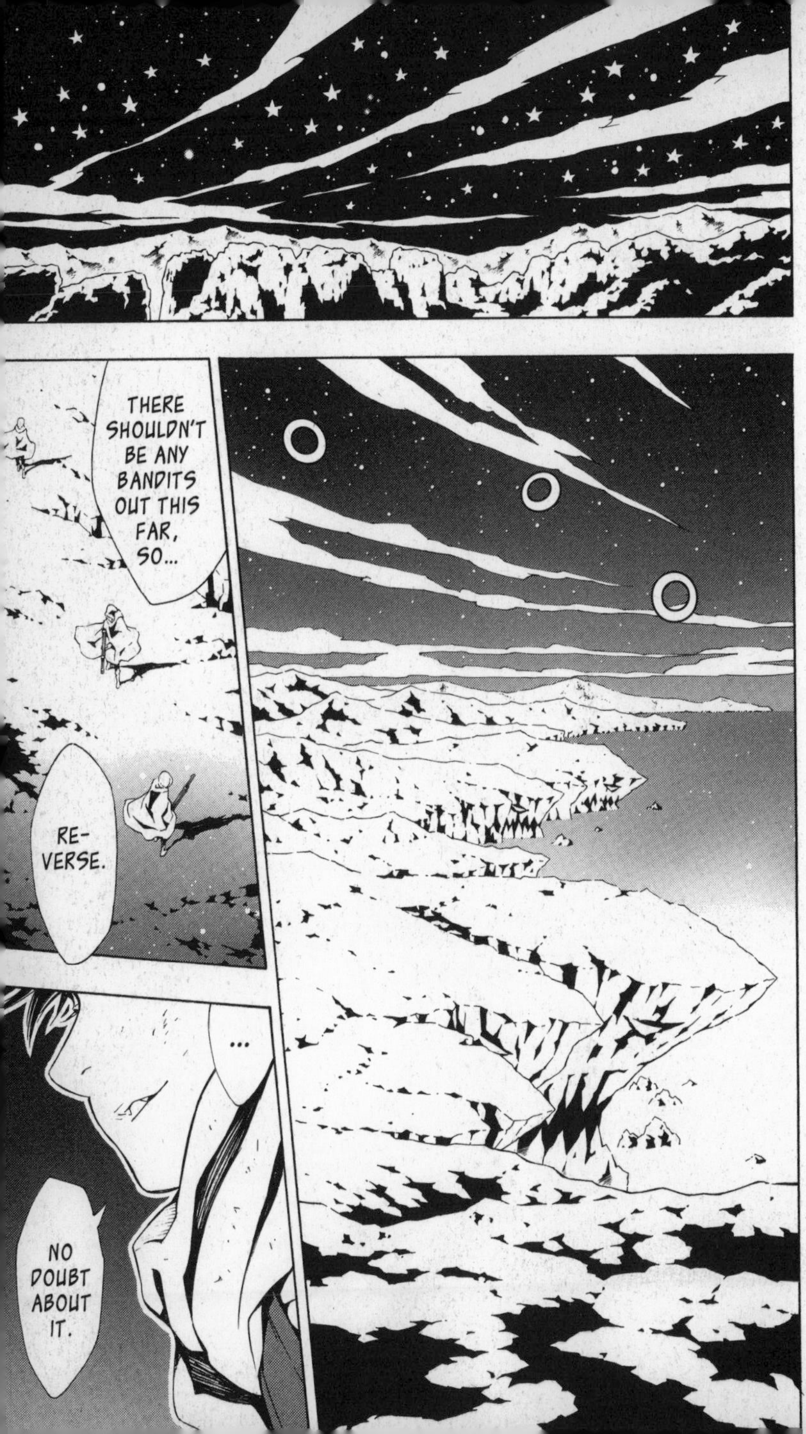
THERE SHOULDN'T BE ANY BANDITS OUT THIS FAR, SO...
RE-VERSE.
...
NO DOUBT ABOUT IT.

Chapter 39: The Wolf Who Could Not Become Spirit

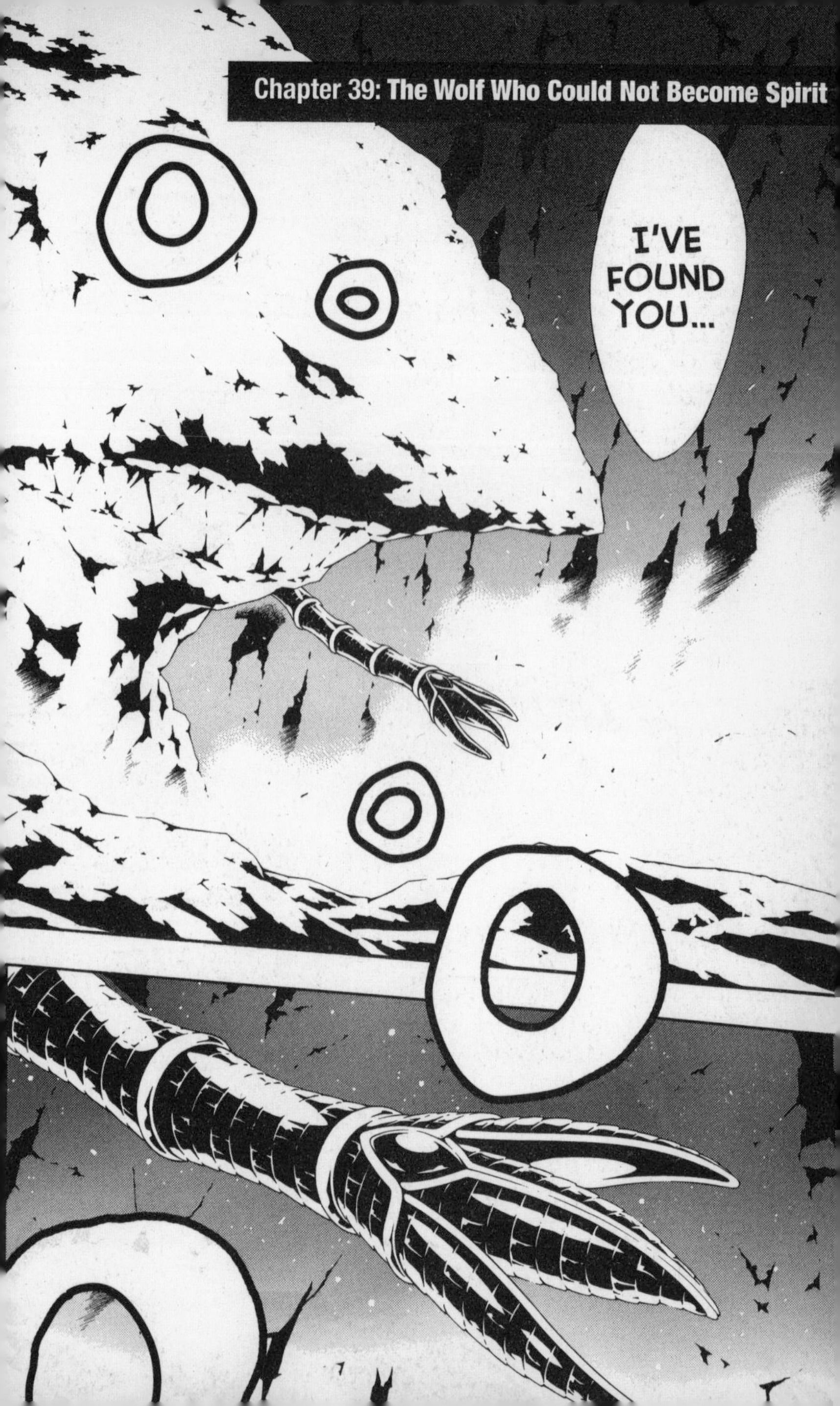
I'VE FOUND YOU...

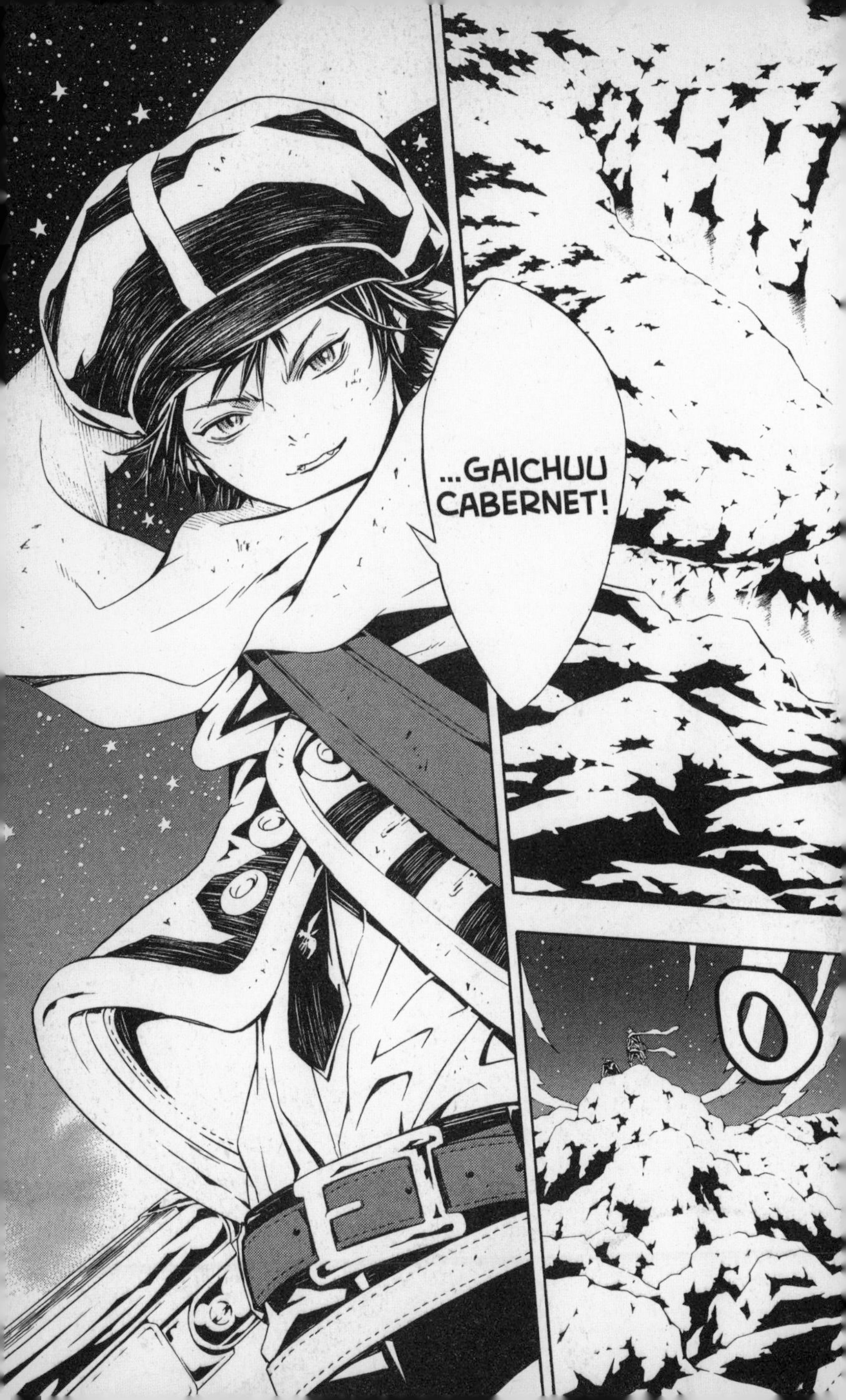
...GAICHUU CABERNET!

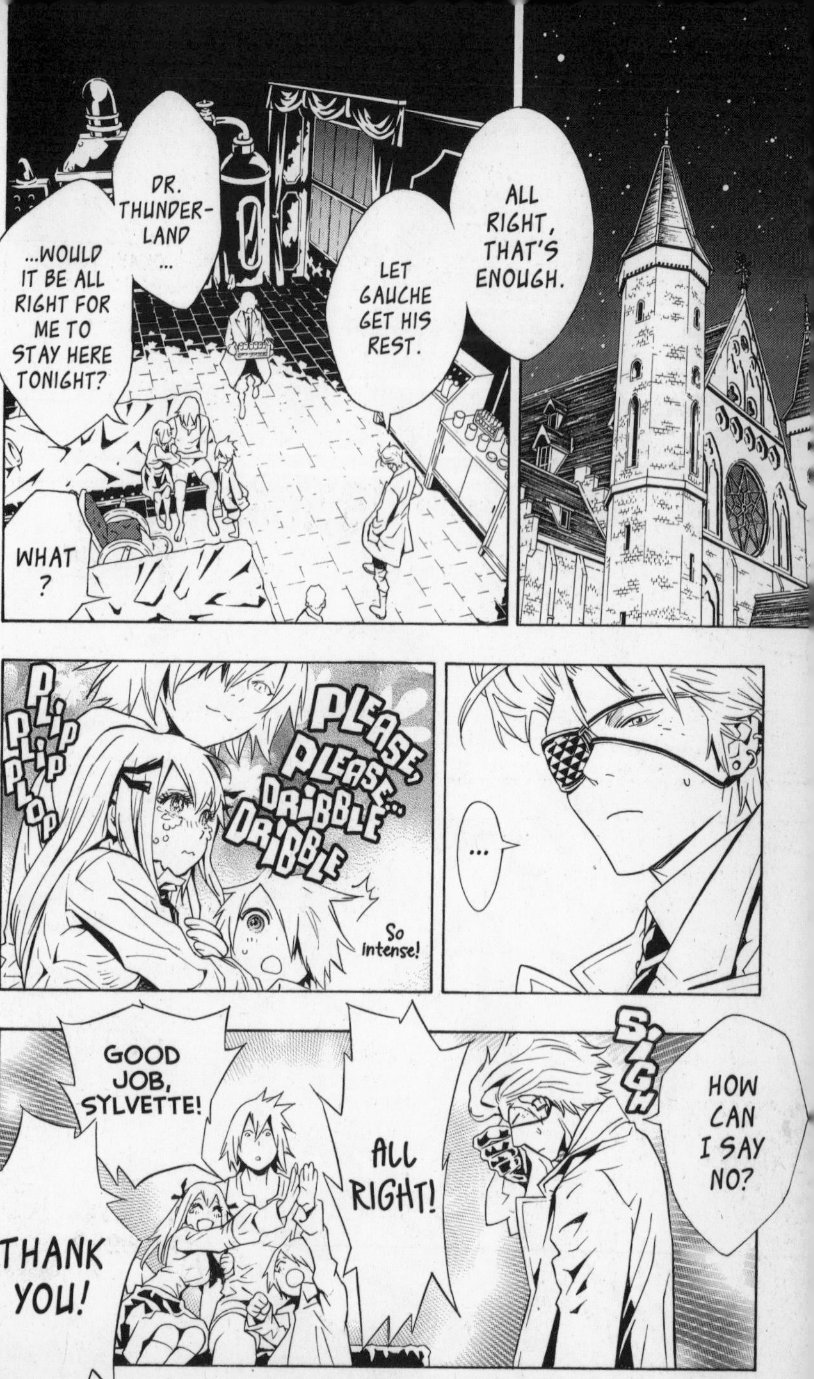
ALL RIGHT, THAT'S ENOUGH.
LET GAUCHE GET HIS REST.
DR. THUNDERLAND...
...WOULD IT BE ALL RIGHT FOR ME TO STAY HERE TONIGHT?
WHAT?
...
PLEASE, PLEASE... DRIBBLE DRIBBLE
PLIP PLIP PLOP
So intense!
SIGH
HOW CAN I SAY NO?
ALL RIGHT!
GOOD JOB, SYLVETTE!
THANK YOU!

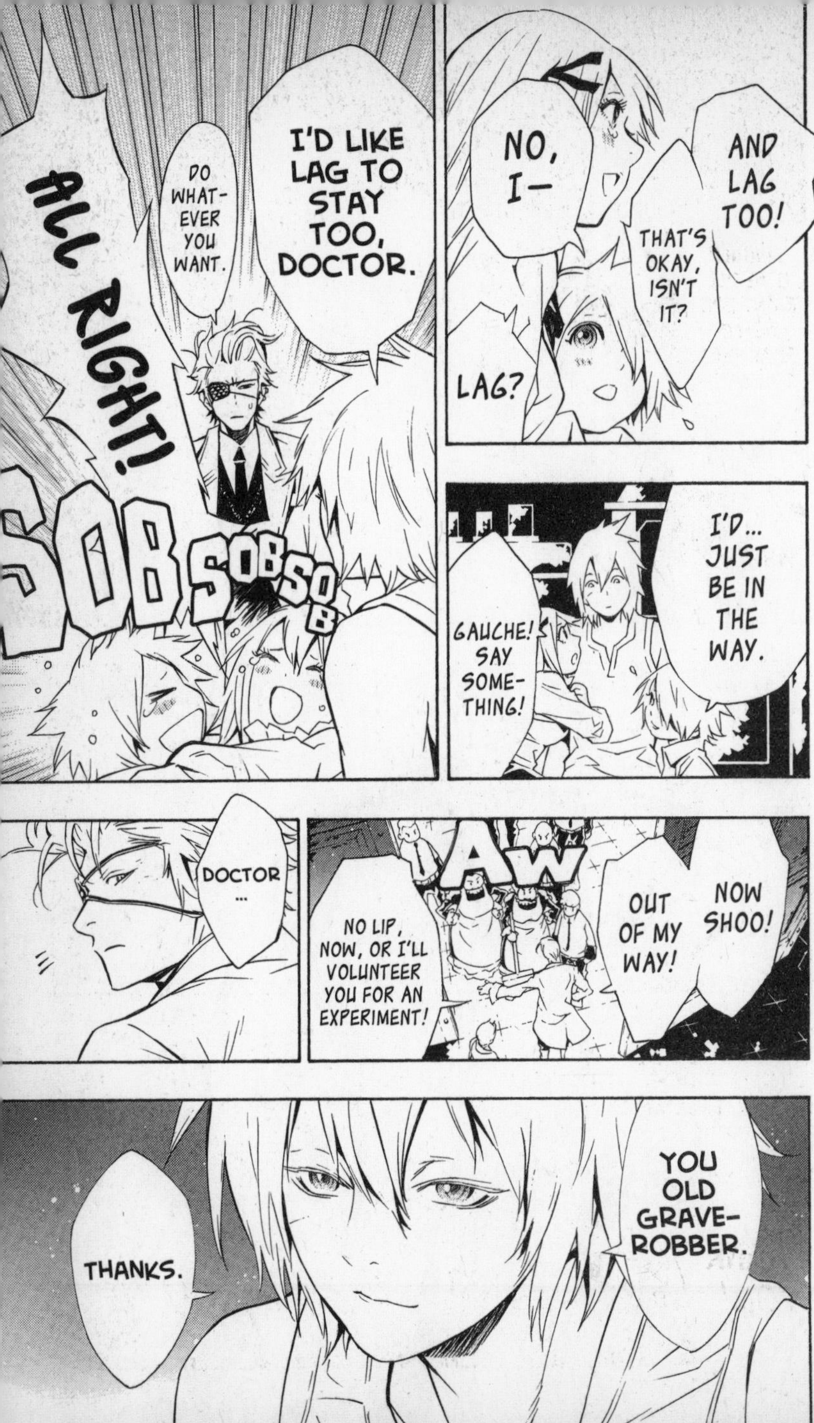
AND LAG TOO!
NO, I—
THAT'S OKAY, ISN'T IT?
LAG?
I'D... JUST BE IN THE WAY.
GAUCHE! SAY SOMETHING!
I'D LIKE LAG TO STAY TOO, DOCTOR.
DO WHATEVER YOU WANT.
ALL RIGHT!
SOB SOB SOB
NOW SHOO!
OUT OF MY WAY!
AW
NO LIP, NOW, OR I'LL VOLUNTEER YOU FOR AN EXPERIMENT!
DOCTOR ...
YOU OLD GRAVE-ROBBER.
THANKS.

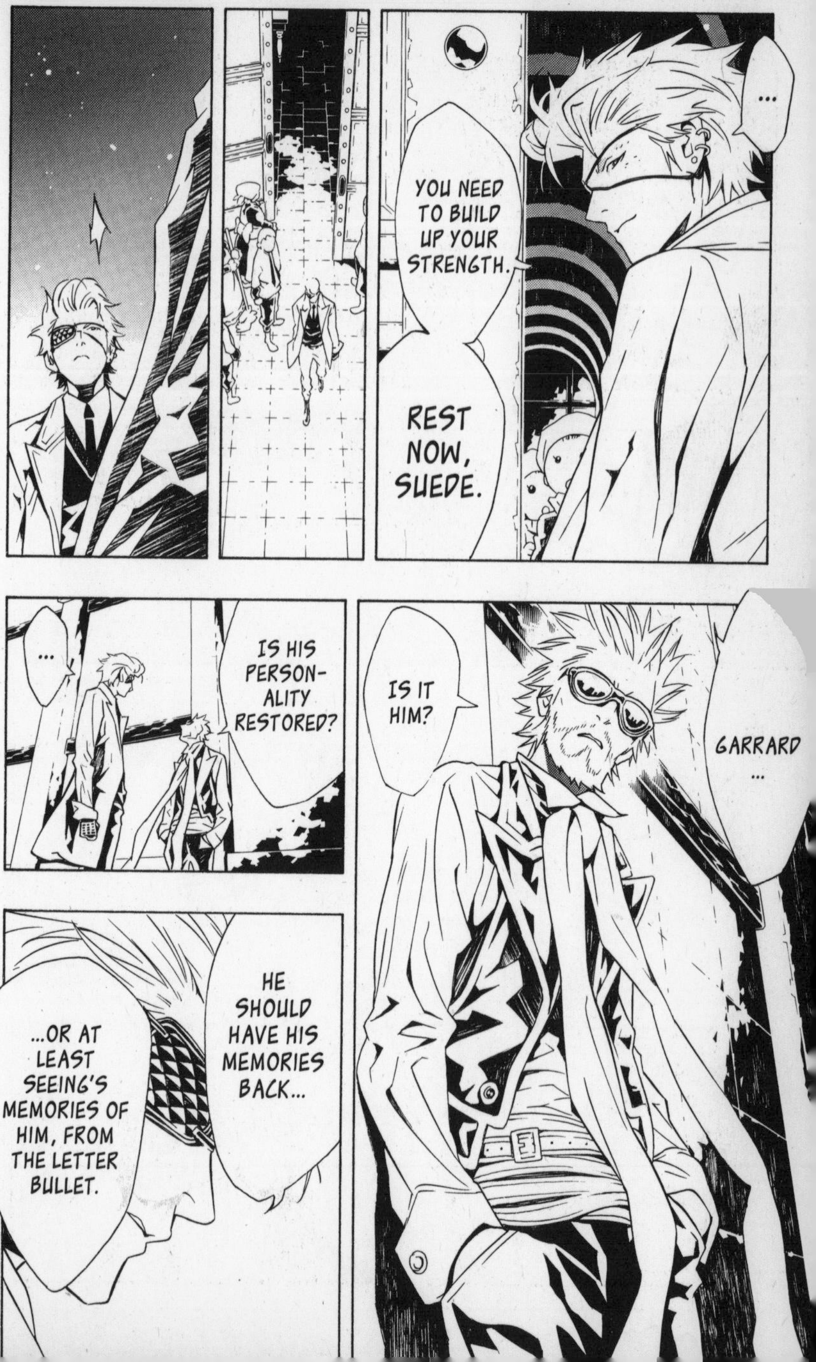
...
YOU NEED TO BUILD UP YOUR STRENGTH.
REST NOW, SUEDE.
GARRARD ...
IS IT HIM?
IS HIS PERSON-ALITY RESTORED?
...
HE SHOULD HAVE HIS MEMORIES BACK...
...OR AT LEAST SEEING'S MEMORIES OF HIM, FROM THE LETTER BULLET.

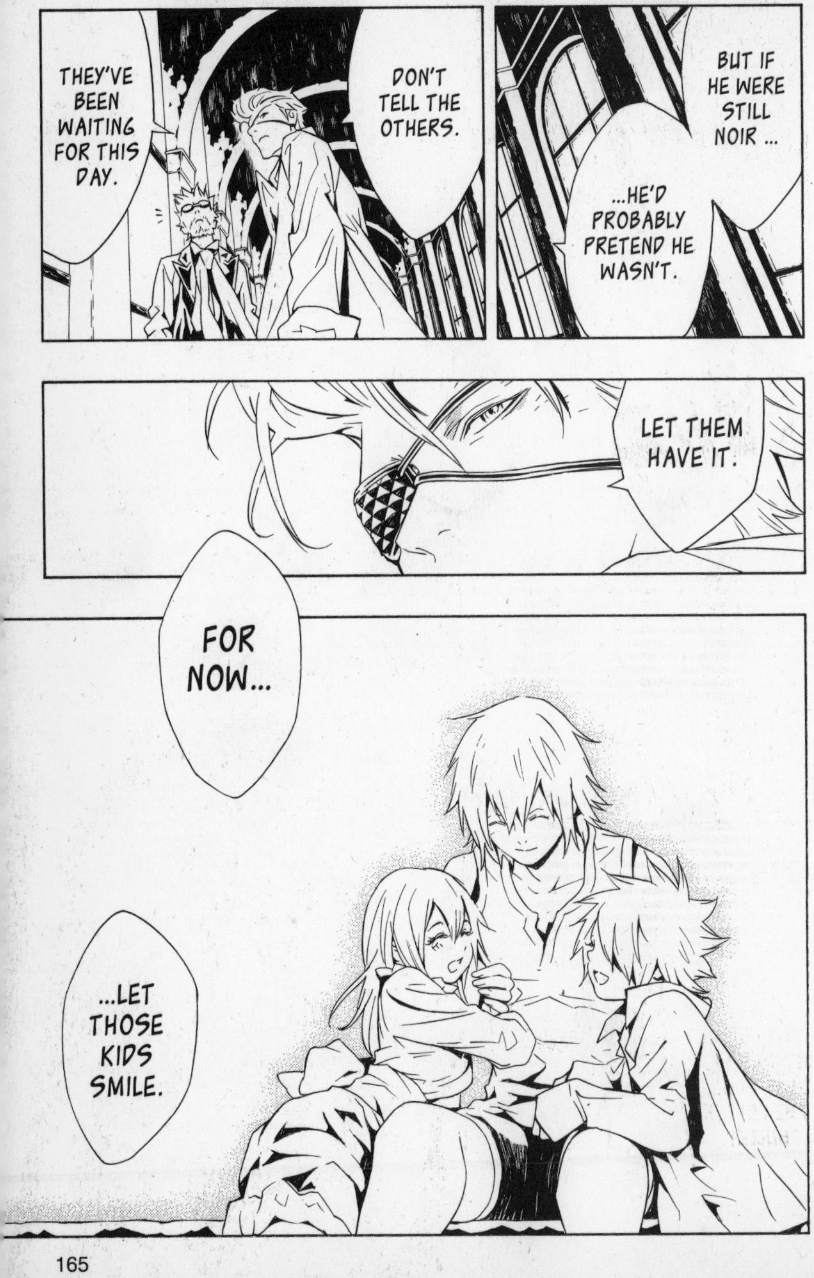
BUT IF HE WERE STILL NOIR ...
...HE'D PROBABLY PRETEND HE WASN'T.
DON'T TELL THE OTHERS.
THEY'VE BEEN WAITING FOR THIS DAY.
LET THEM HAVE IT.
FOR NOW...
...LET THOSE KIDS SMILE.

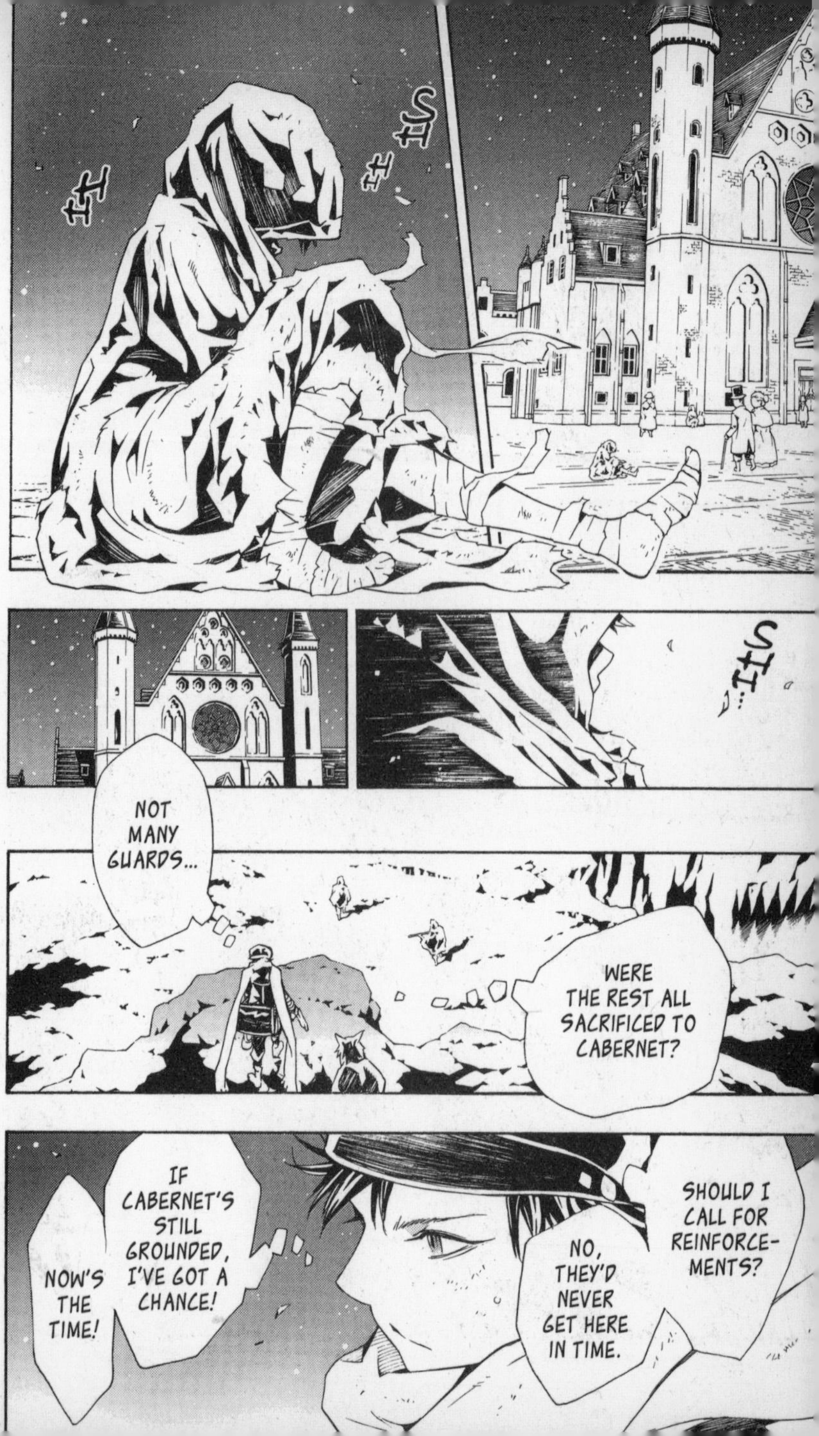
SH
SH
SH
SH...
NOT MANY GUARDS...
WERE THE REST ALL SACRIFICED TO CABERNET?
SHOULD I CALL FOR REINFORCE-MENTS?
NO, THEY'D NEVER GET HERE IN TIME.
IF CABERNET'S STILL GROUNDED, I'VE GOT A CHANCE!
NOW'S THE TIME!

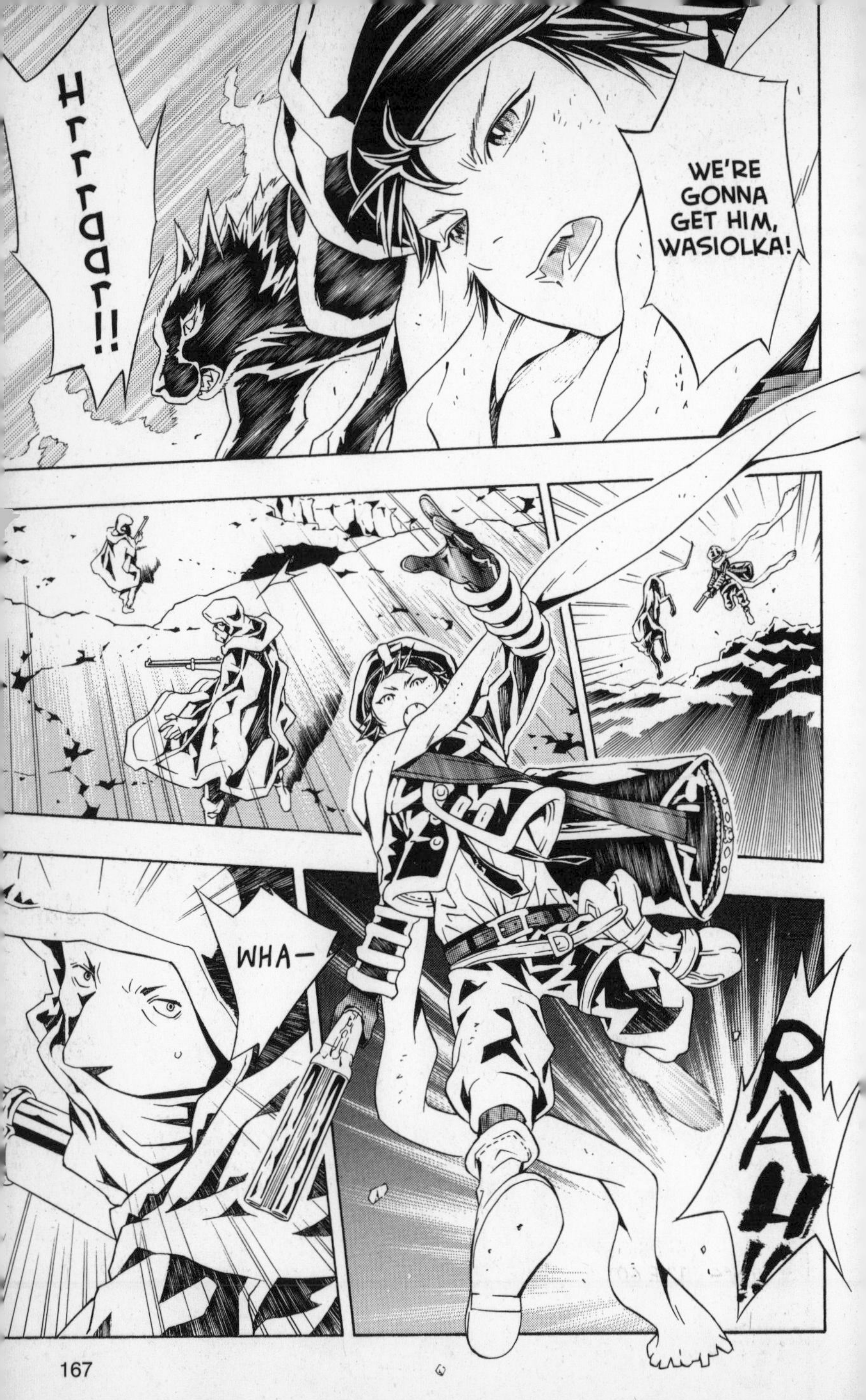
WE'RE GONNA GET HIM, WASIOLKA!
Hrrraar!!
RAH!!
WHA-

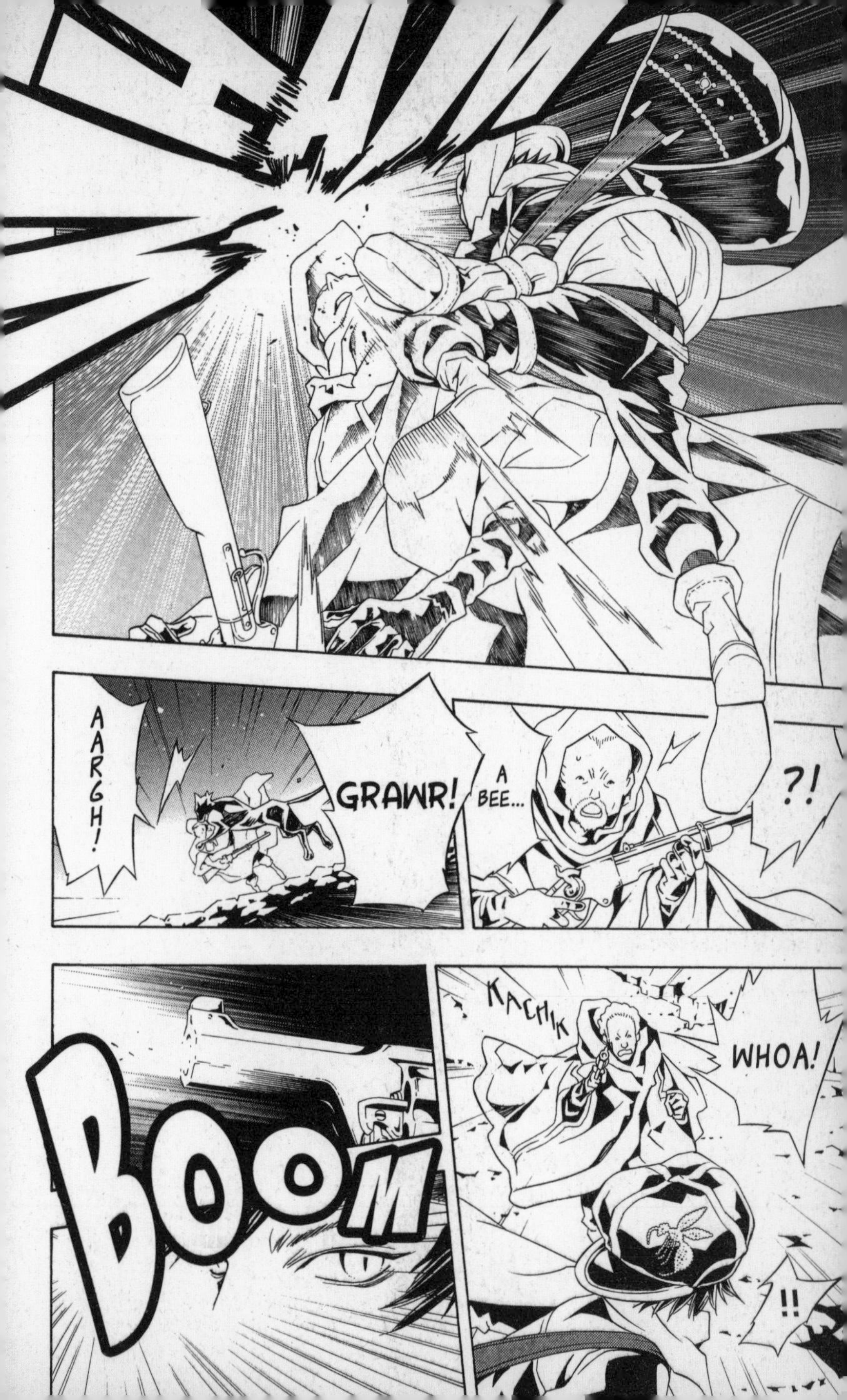
?!
A BEE...
GRAWR!
AARGH!
WHOA!
KACHIK
!!
BOOM

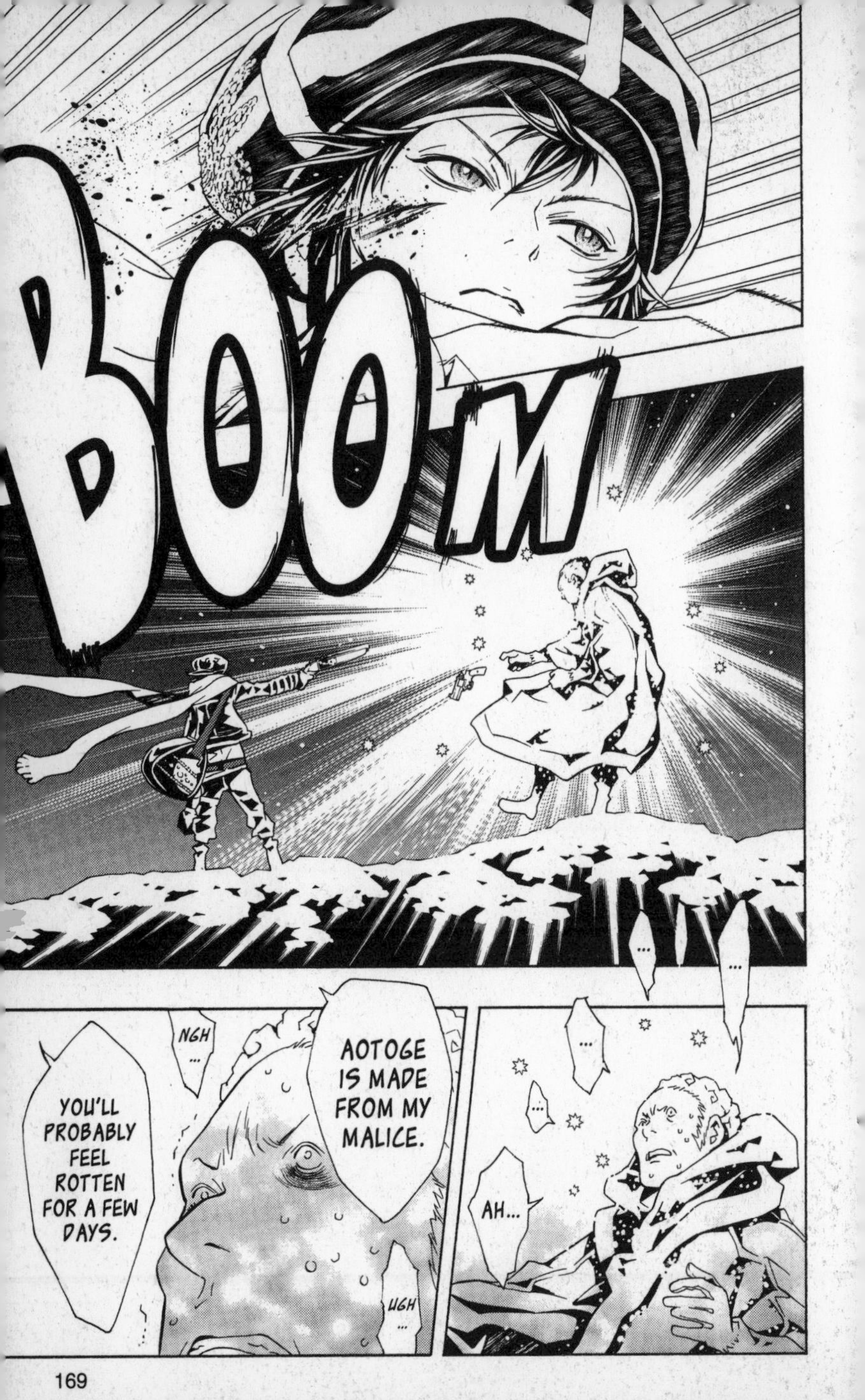
BOOM
...
...
...
...
AH...
AOTOGE IS MADE FROM MY MALICE.
NGH...
YOU'LL PROBABLY FEEL ROTTEN FOR A FEW DAYS.
UGH...

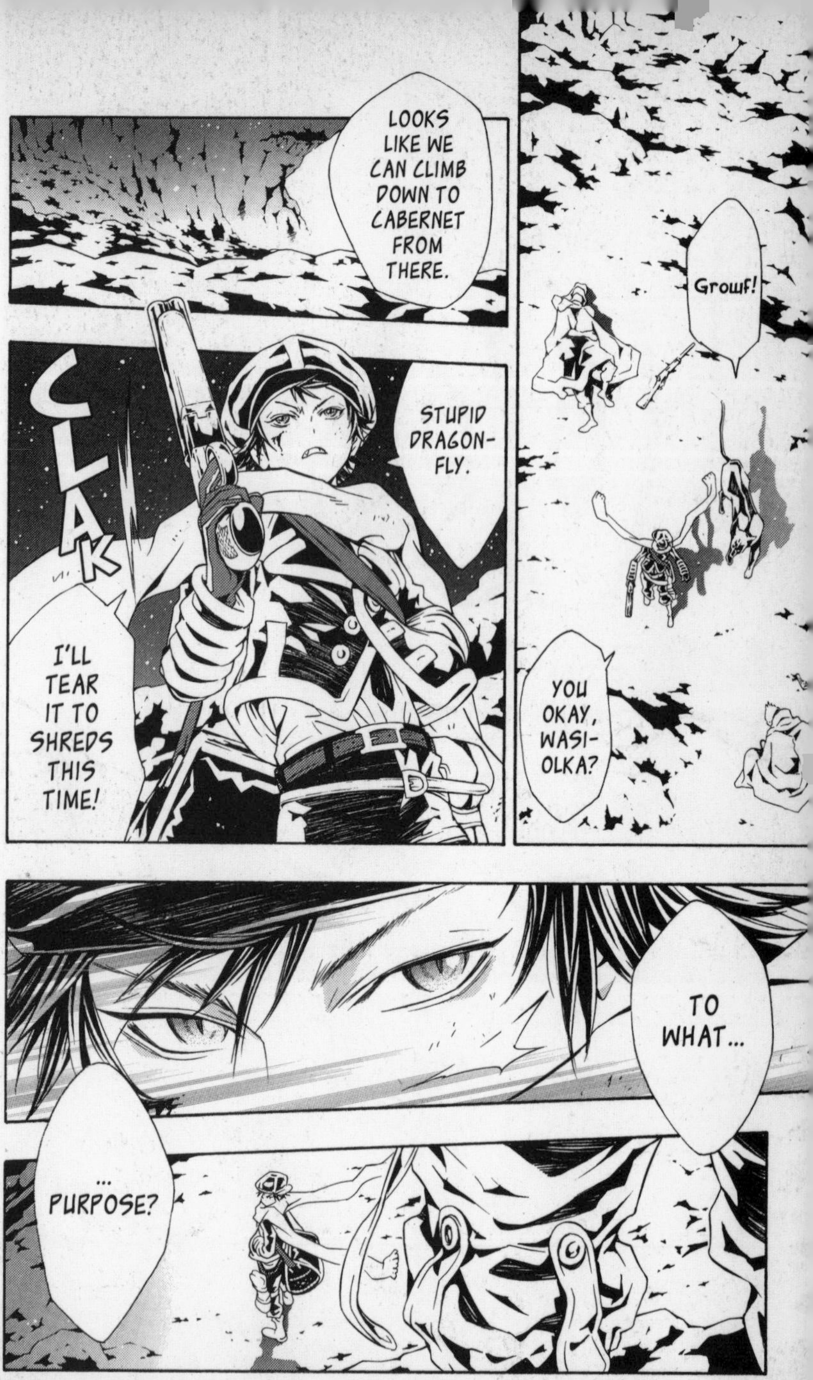
Growf!
YOU OKAY, WASI-OLKA?
LOOKS LIKE WE CAN CLIMB DOWN TO CABERNET FROM THERE.
STUPID DRAGON-FLY.
CLAK
I'LL TEAR IT TO SHREDS THIS TIME!
TO WHAT...
...PURPOSE?

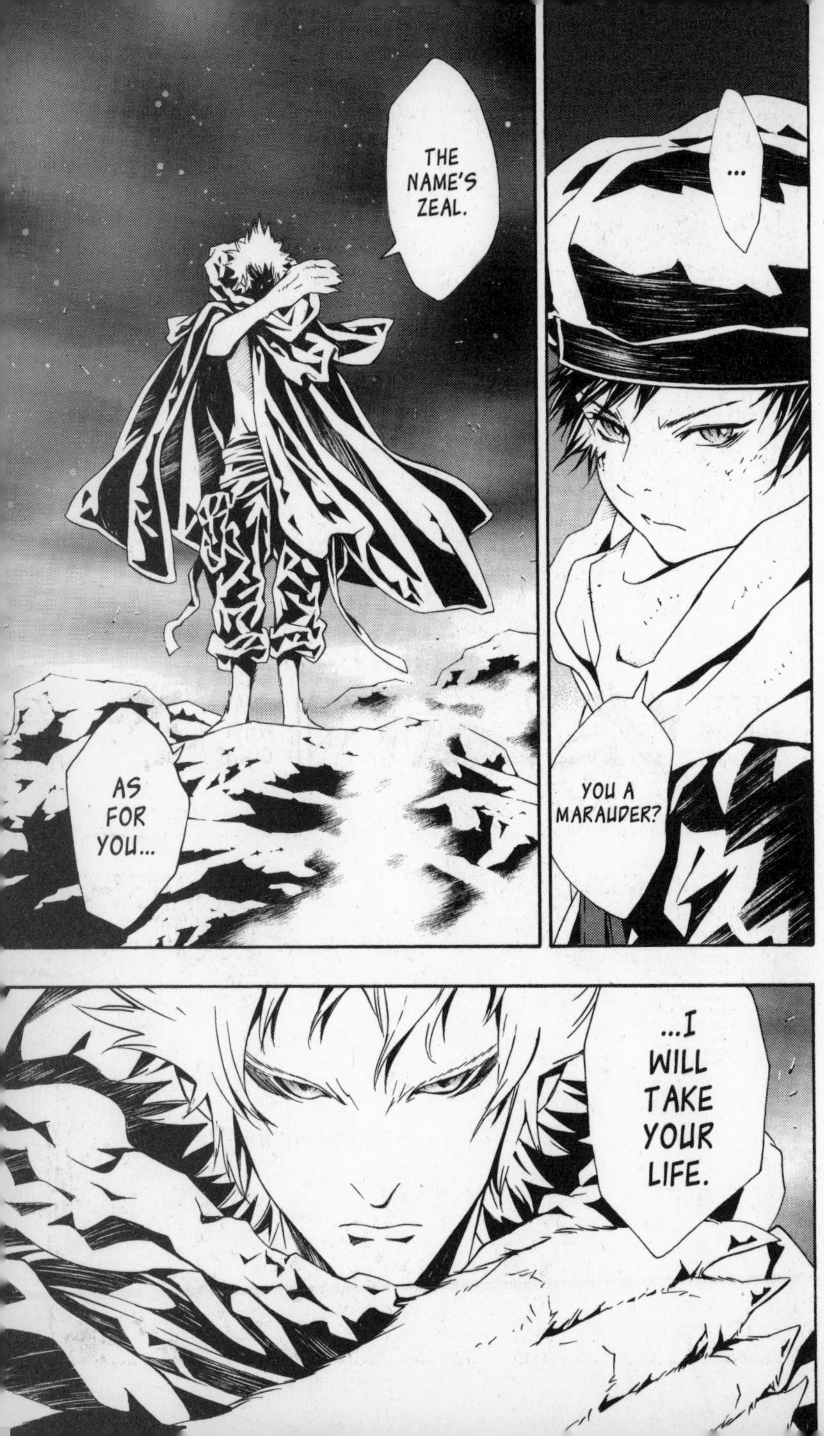
...
YOU A MARAUDER?
THE NAME'S ZEAL.
AS FOR YOU...
...I WILL TAKE YOUR LIFE.

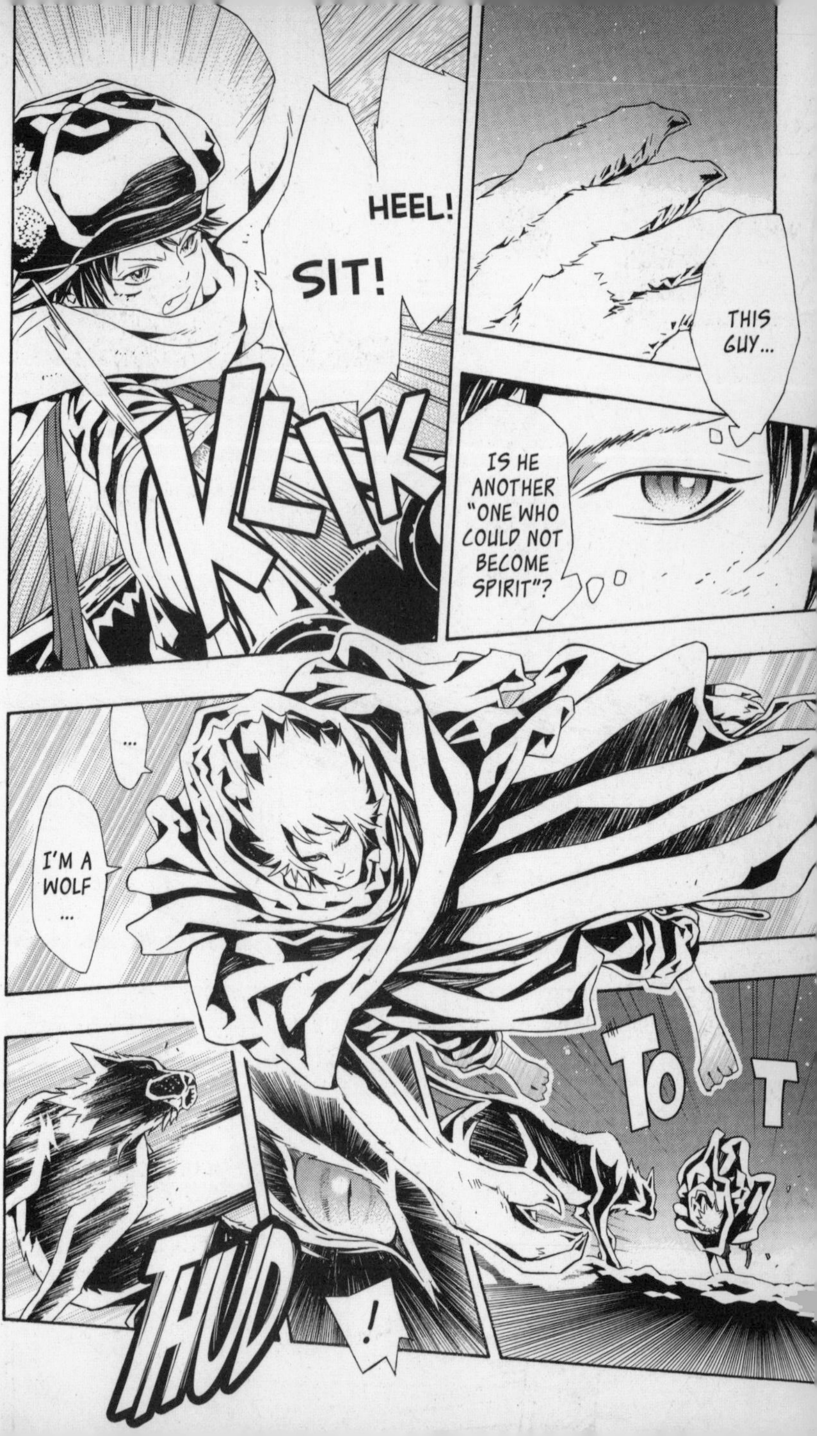
THIS GUY...
IS HE ANOTHER "ONE WHO COULD NOT BECOME SPIRIT"?
HEEL!
SIT!
KLIK
...
I'M A WOLF ...
TO T
THUD
!

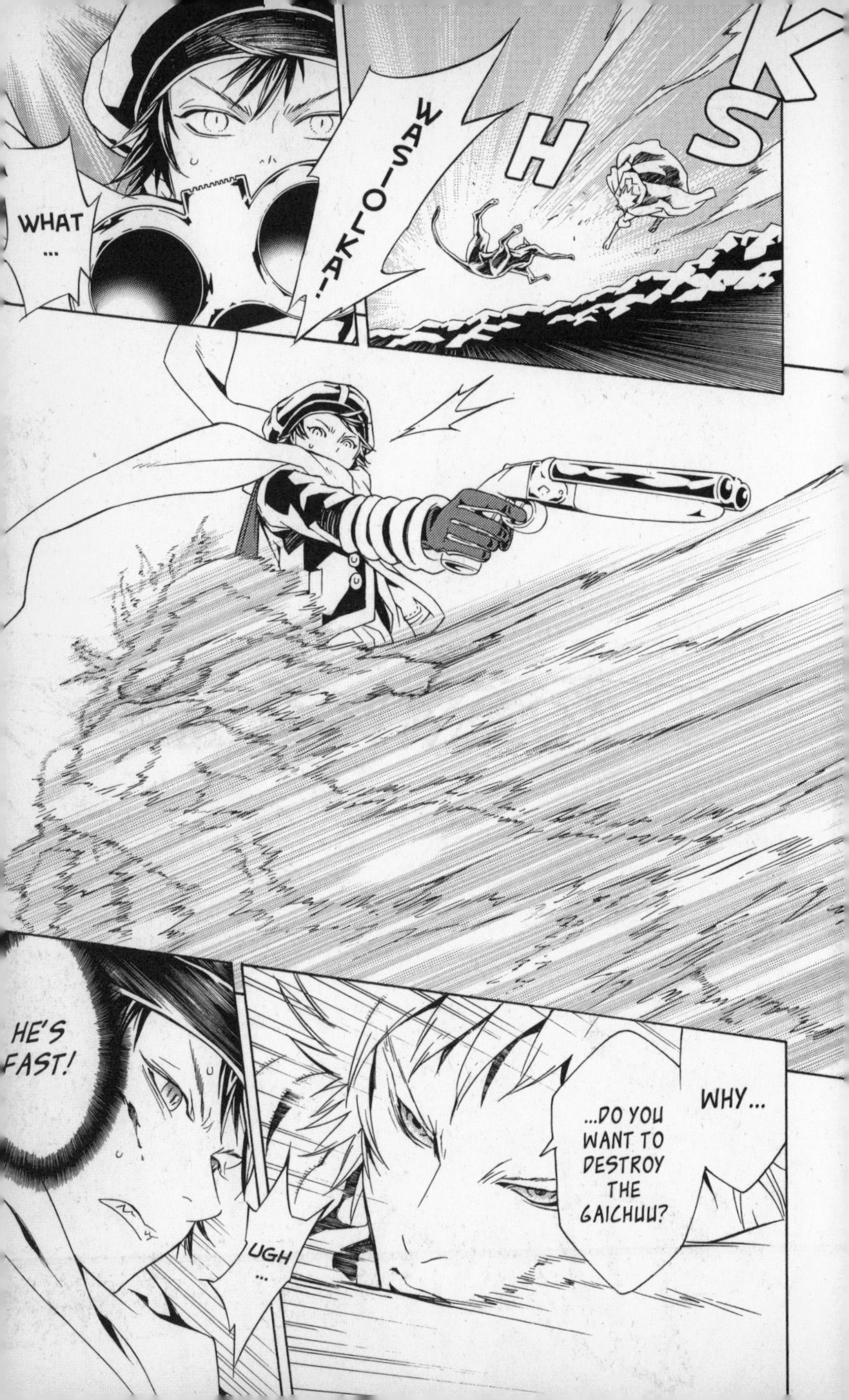
HSK
WASIOLKA!
WHAT ...
WHY...
...DO YOU WANT TO DESTROY THE GAICHUU?
HE'S FAST!
UGH ...

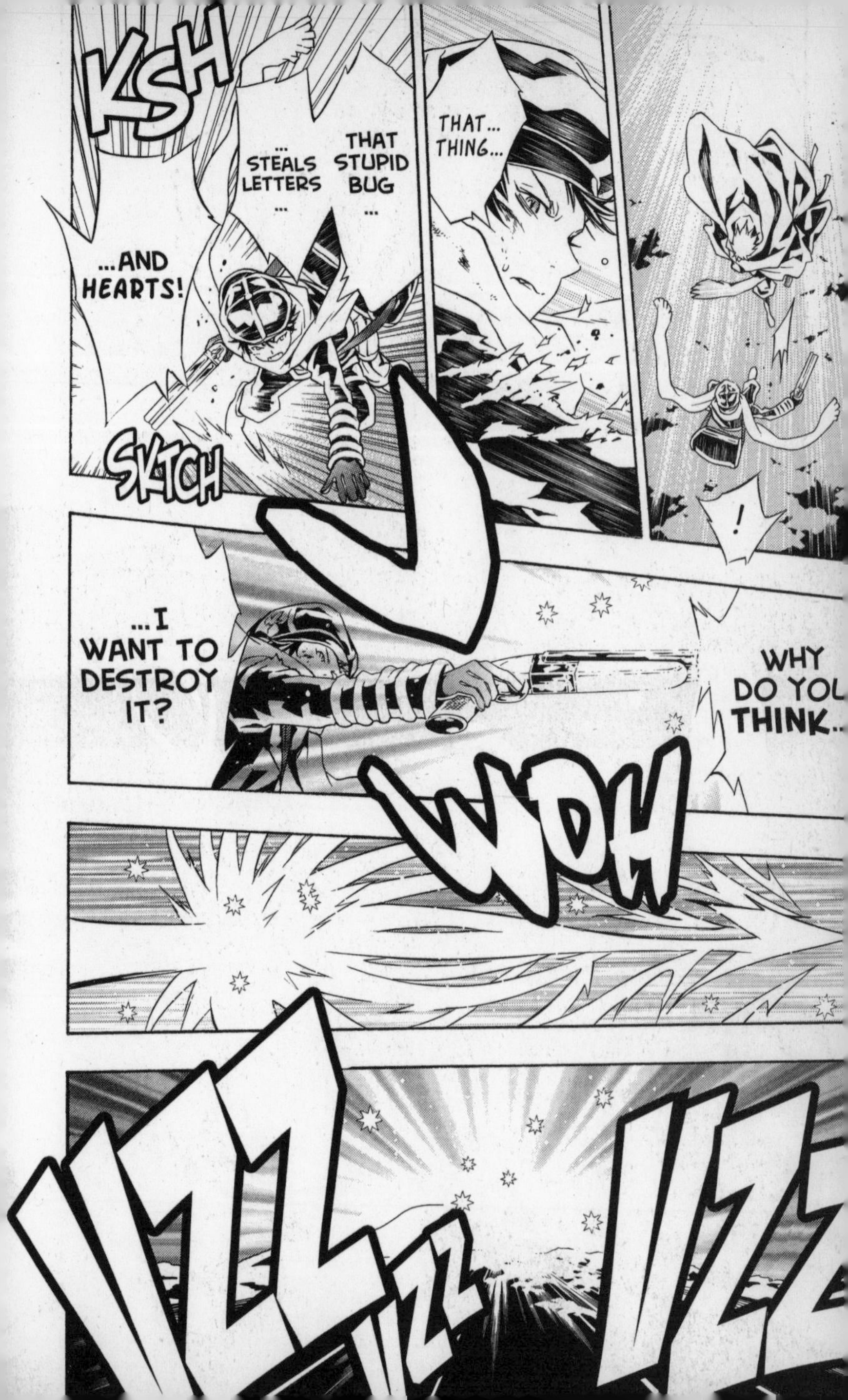
!
THAT... THING...
THAT STUPID BUG ...
... STEALS LETTERS ...
...AND HEARTS!
KSH
SKTCH
WHY DO YOU THINK...
...I WANT TO DESTROY IT?
WOH
VZZ
VZZ

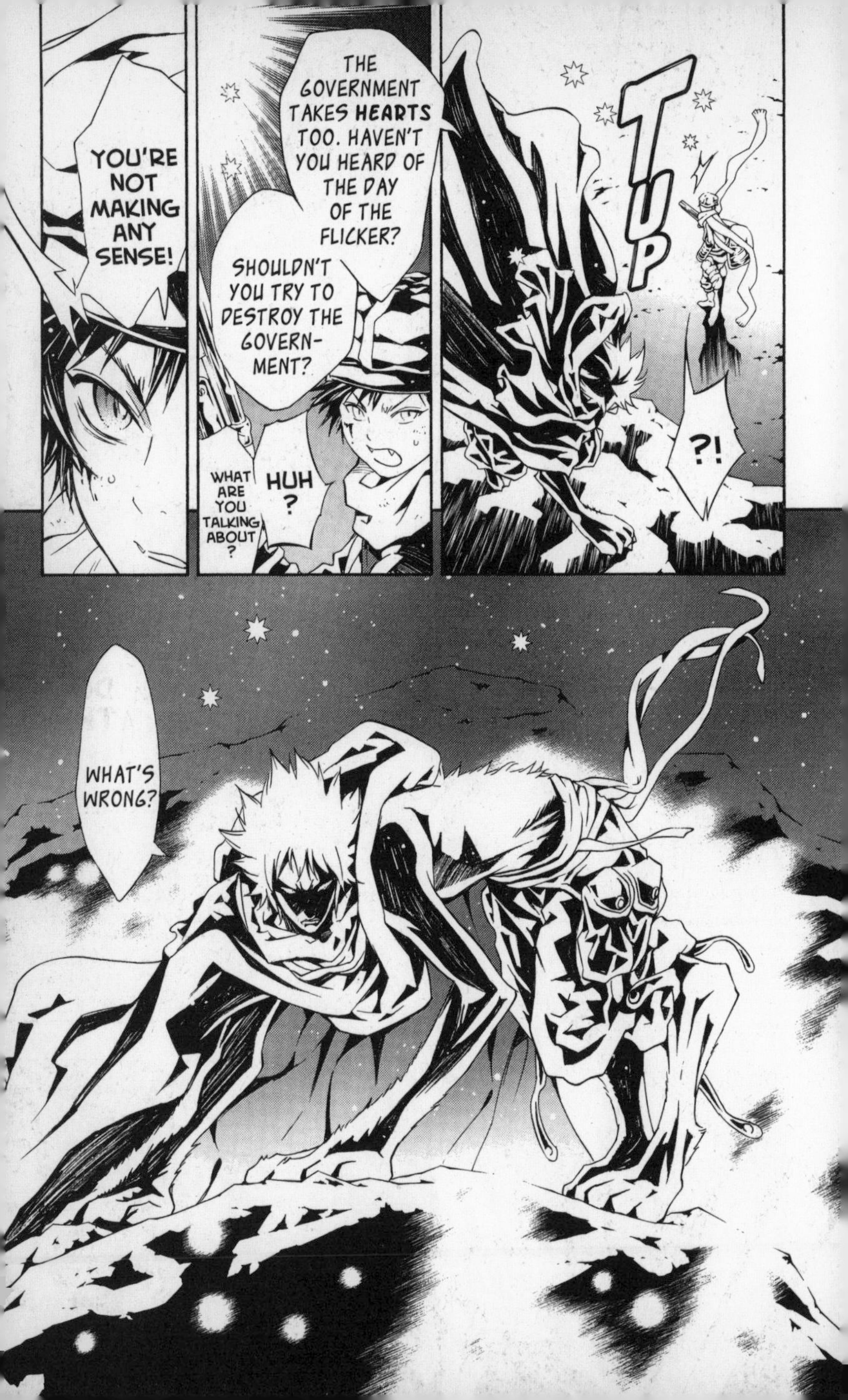
TUP
?!
THE GOVERNMENT TAKES HEARTS TOO. HAVEN'T YOU HEARD OF THE DAY OF THE FLICKER?
SHOULDN'T YOU TRY TO DESTROY THE GOVERN-MENT?
HUH?
WHAT ARE YOU TALKING ABOUT?
YOU'RE NOT MAKING ANY SENSE!
WHAT'S WRONG?

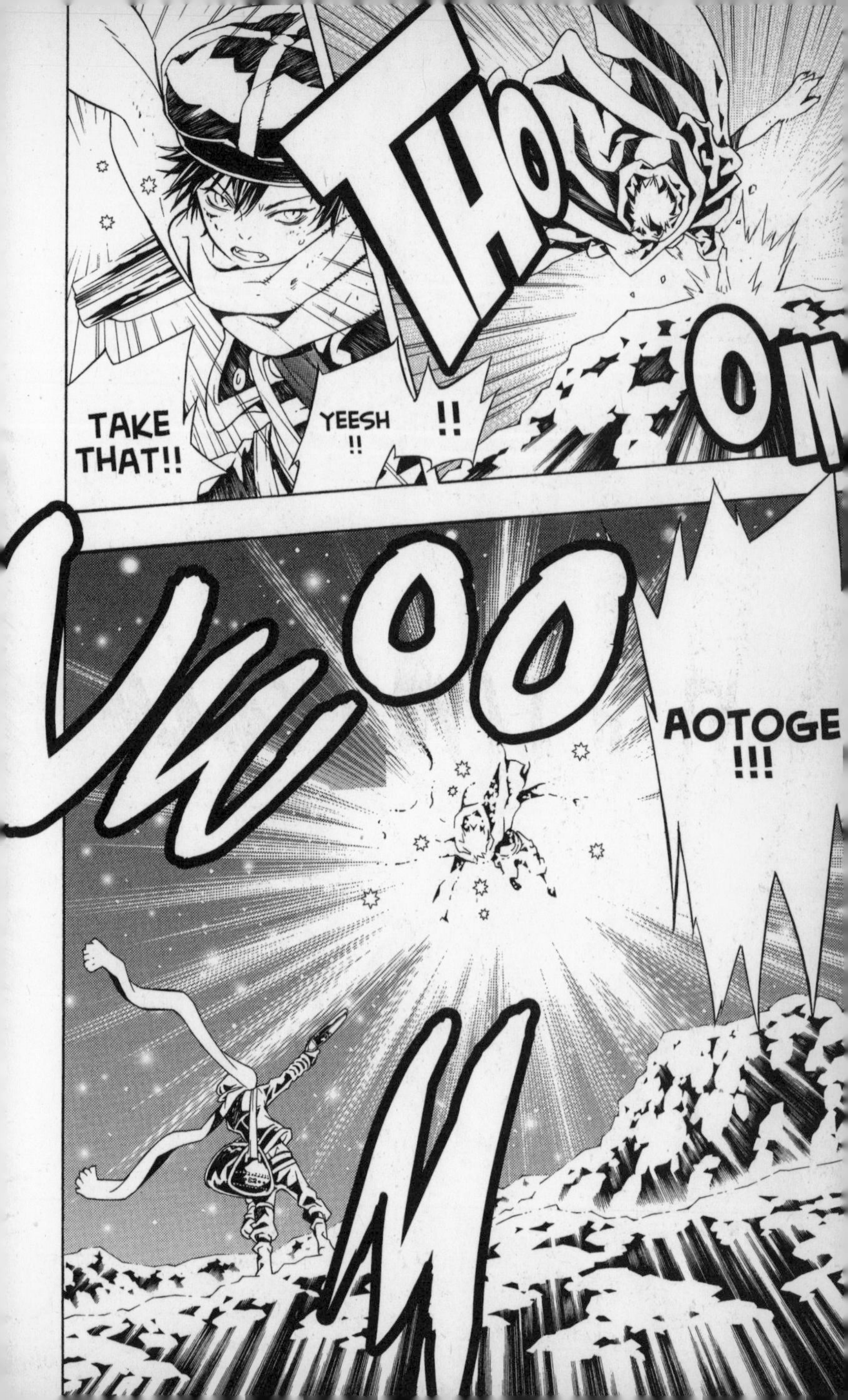
THOOM
!!
YEESH !!
TAKE THAT!!
AOTOGE !!!
WOOM

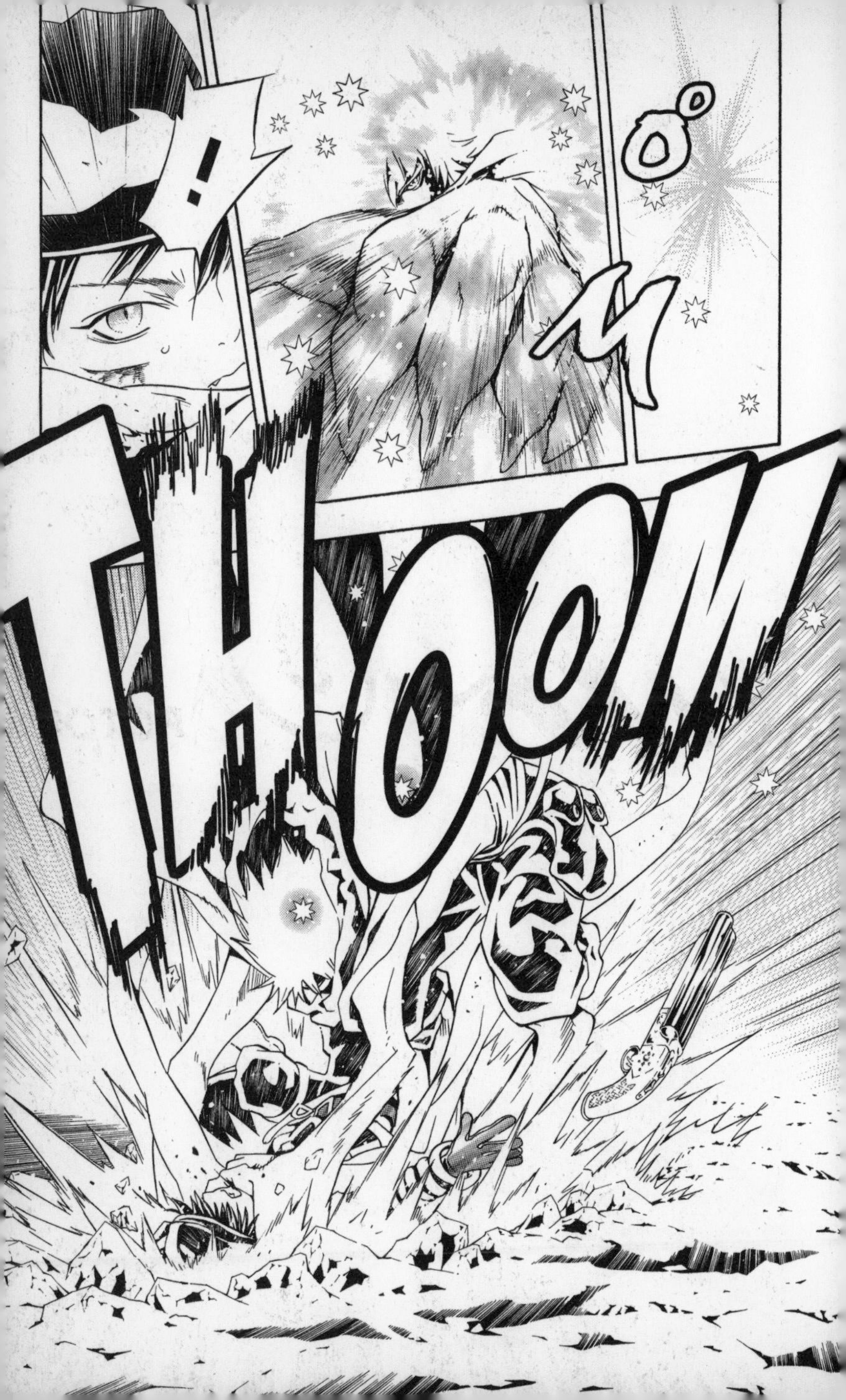
!
WHOOM

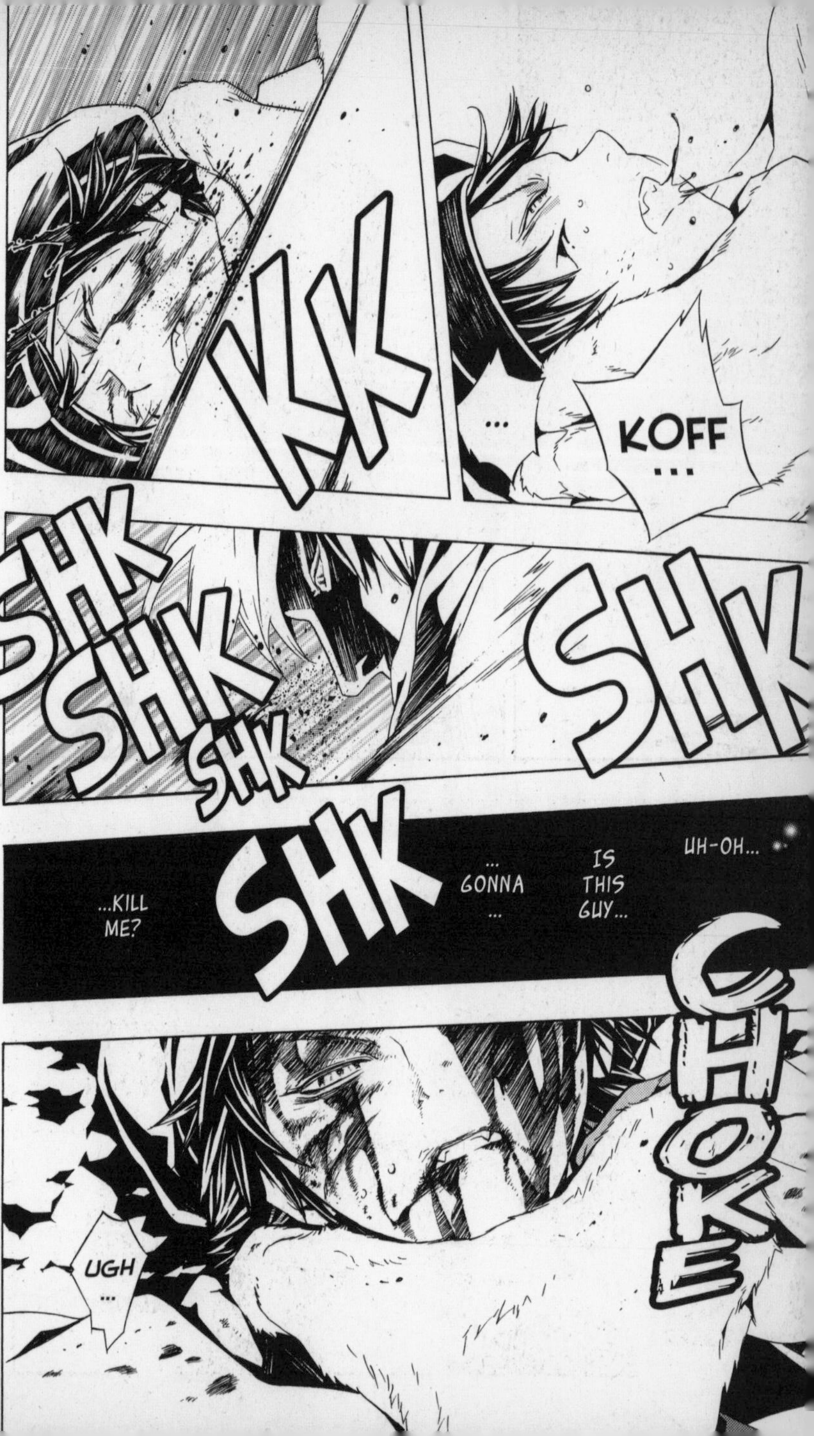
...
KOFF ...
KK
SHK
SHK
SHK
SHK
UH-OH...
IS THIS GUY...
... GONNA ...
SHK
...KILL ME?
CHOKE
UGH ...

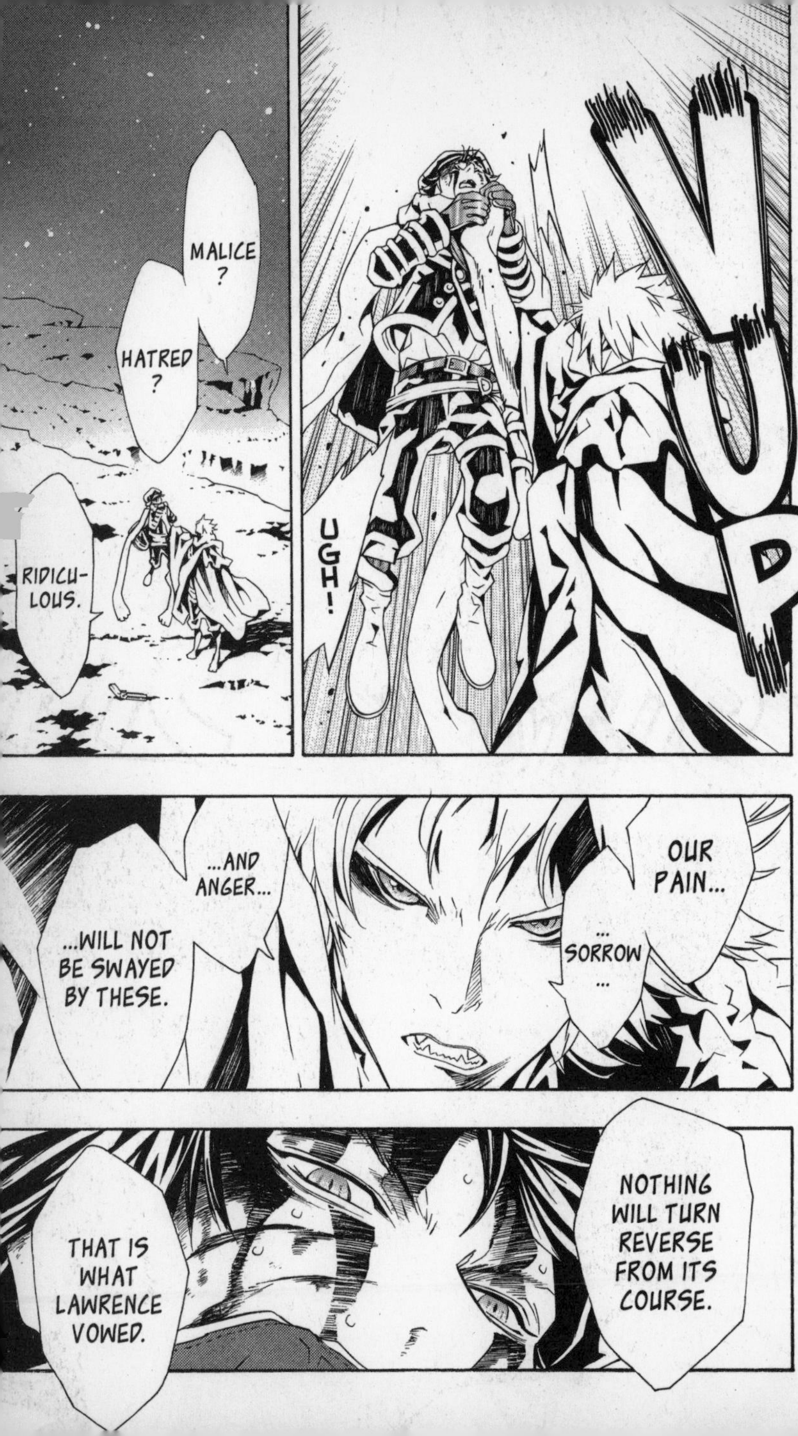
VUD
UGH!
MALICE?
HATRED?
RIDICULOUS.
OUR PAIN...
...SORROW...
...AND ANGER...
...WILL NOT BE SWAYED BY THESE.
NOTHING WILL TURN REVERSE FROM ITS COURSE.
THAT IS WHAT LAWRENCE VOWED.

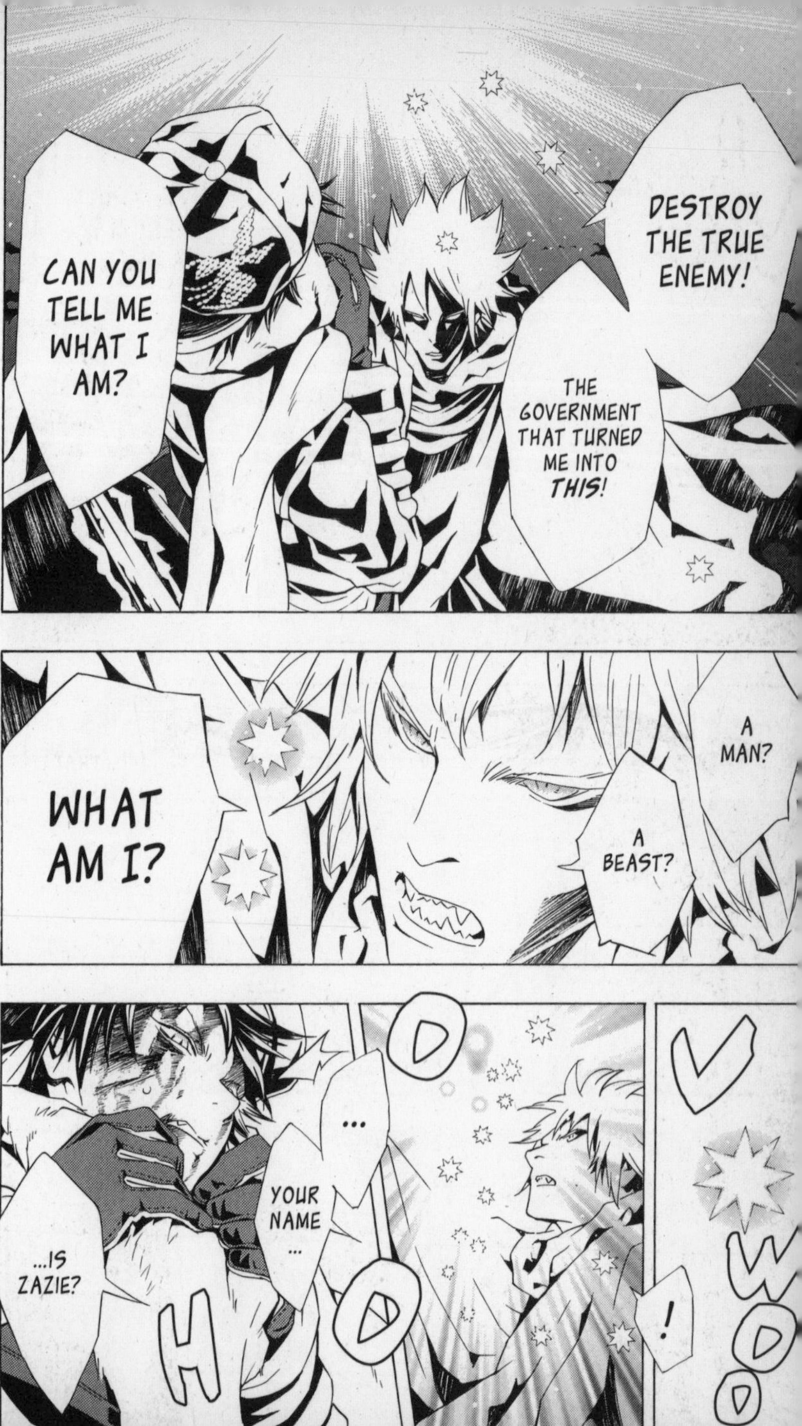
DESTROY THE TRUE ENEMY!
THE GOVERNMENT THAT TURNED ME INTO THIS!
CAN YOU TELL ME WHAT I AM?
A MAN?
A BEAST?
WHAT AM I?
VWOOO
!
...
YOUR NAME ...
...IS ZAZIE?

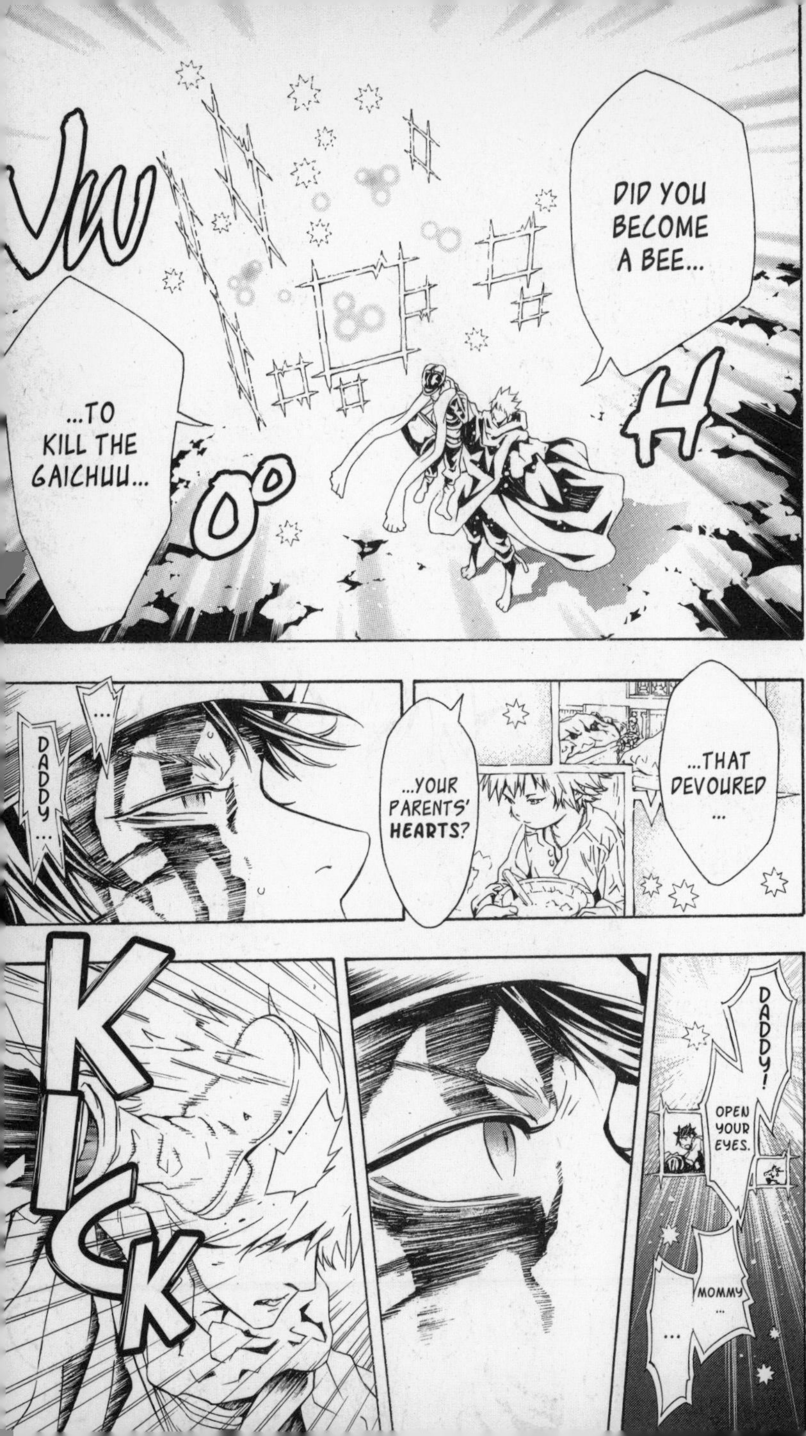

DID YOU BECOME A BEE...
...TO KILL THE GAICHUU...
...THAT DEVOURED ...
...YOUR PARENTS' **HEARTS**?
...
DADDY...
DADDY!
OPEN YOUR EYES.
MOMMY ...
...
KICK

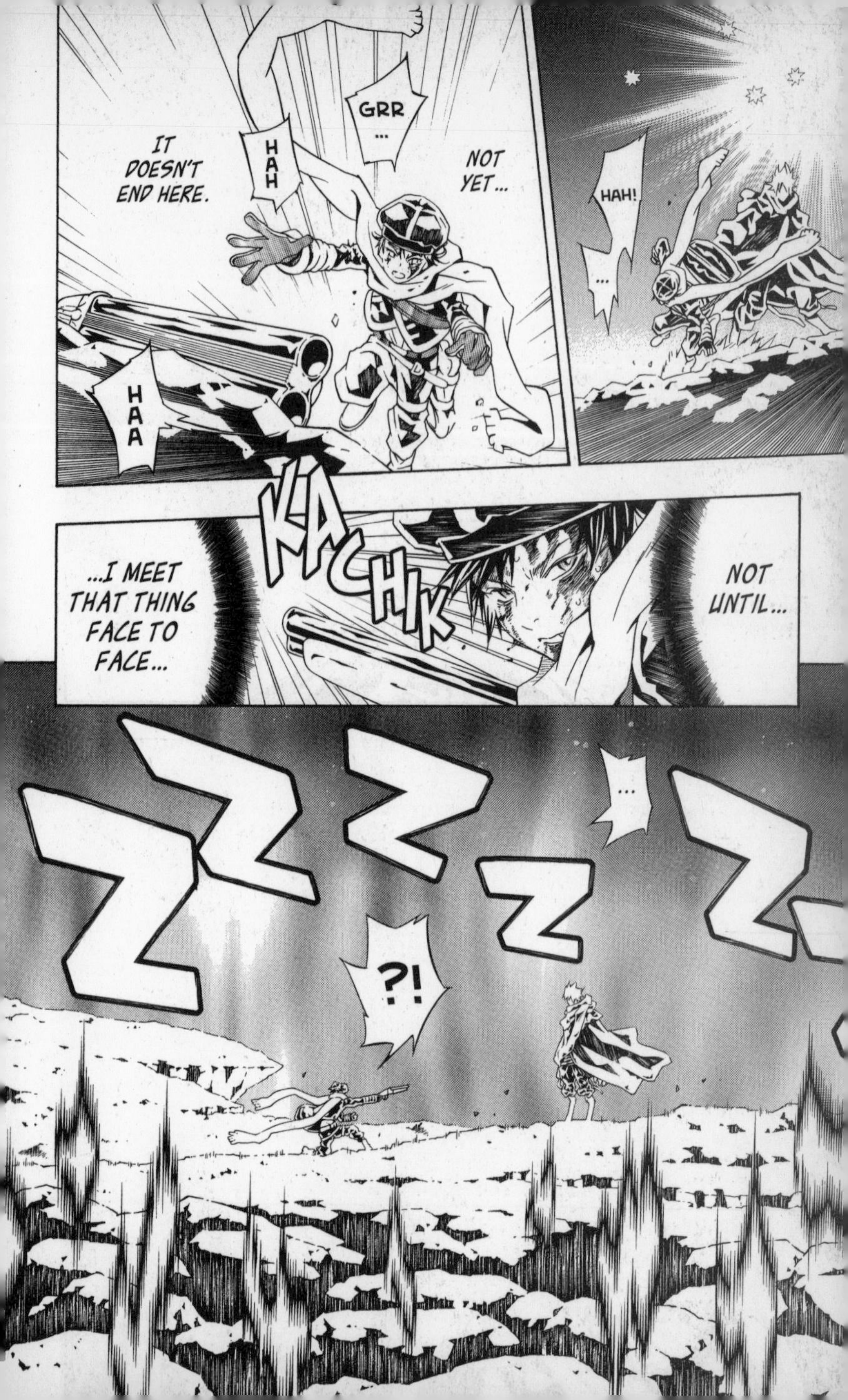
HAH!
...
NOT YET...
GRR ...
HAH HAH
IT DOESN'T END HERE.
HAA HAA
NOT UNTIL...
KA-CHIK
...I MEET THAT THING FACE TO FACE...
ZZZzZ
...
?!

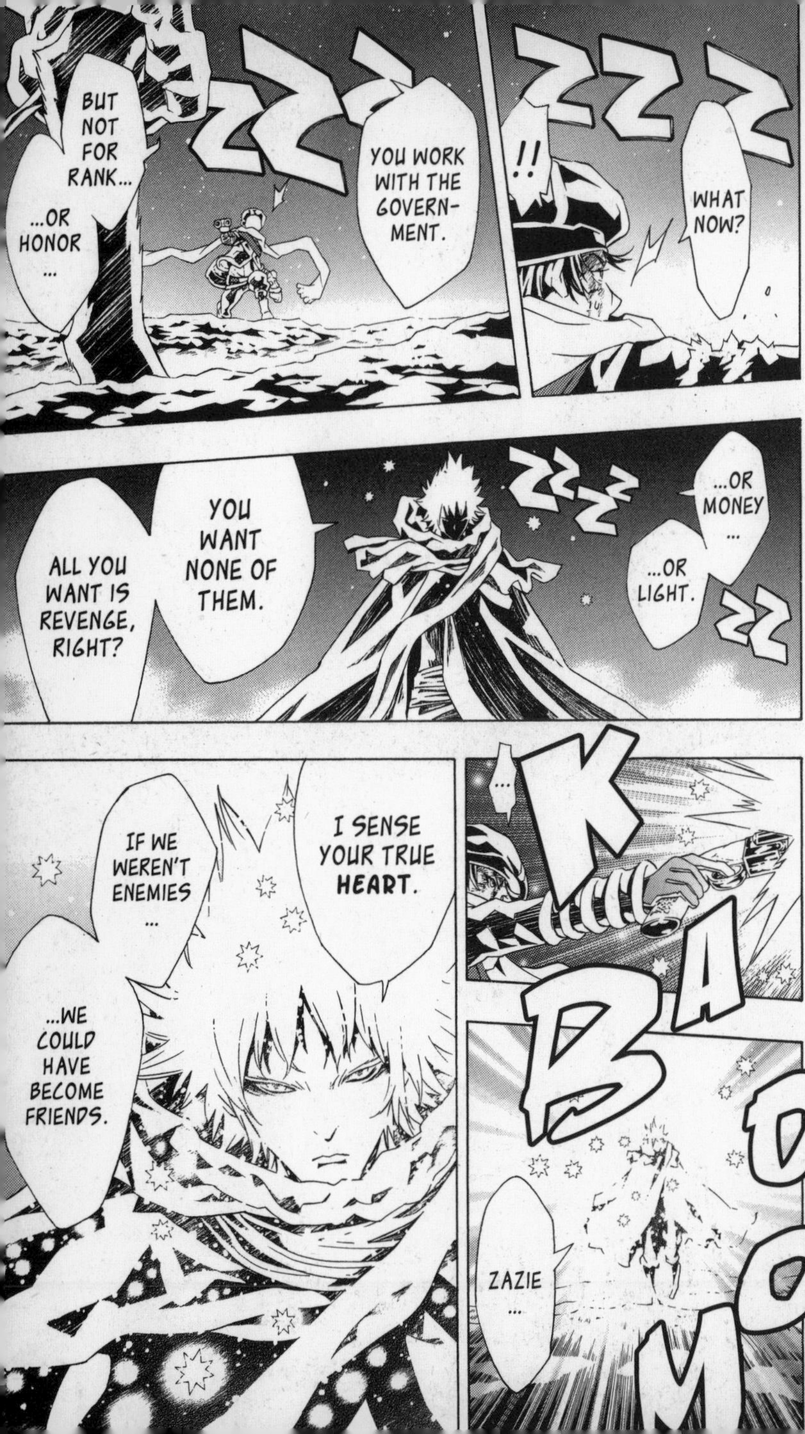
ZZZ
WHAT NOW?
!!
ZZZ
YOU WORK WITH THE GOVERN-MENT.
BUT NOT FOR RANK...
...OR HONOR ...
...OR MONEY ...
ZZZZ
...OR LIGHT.
ZZ
YOU WANT NONE OF THEM.
ALL YOU WANT IS REVENGE, RIGHT?
...
KABOOM
ZAZIE ...
I SENSE YOUR TRUE HEART.
IF WE WEREN'T ENEMIES ...
...WE COULD HAVE BECOME FRIENDS.

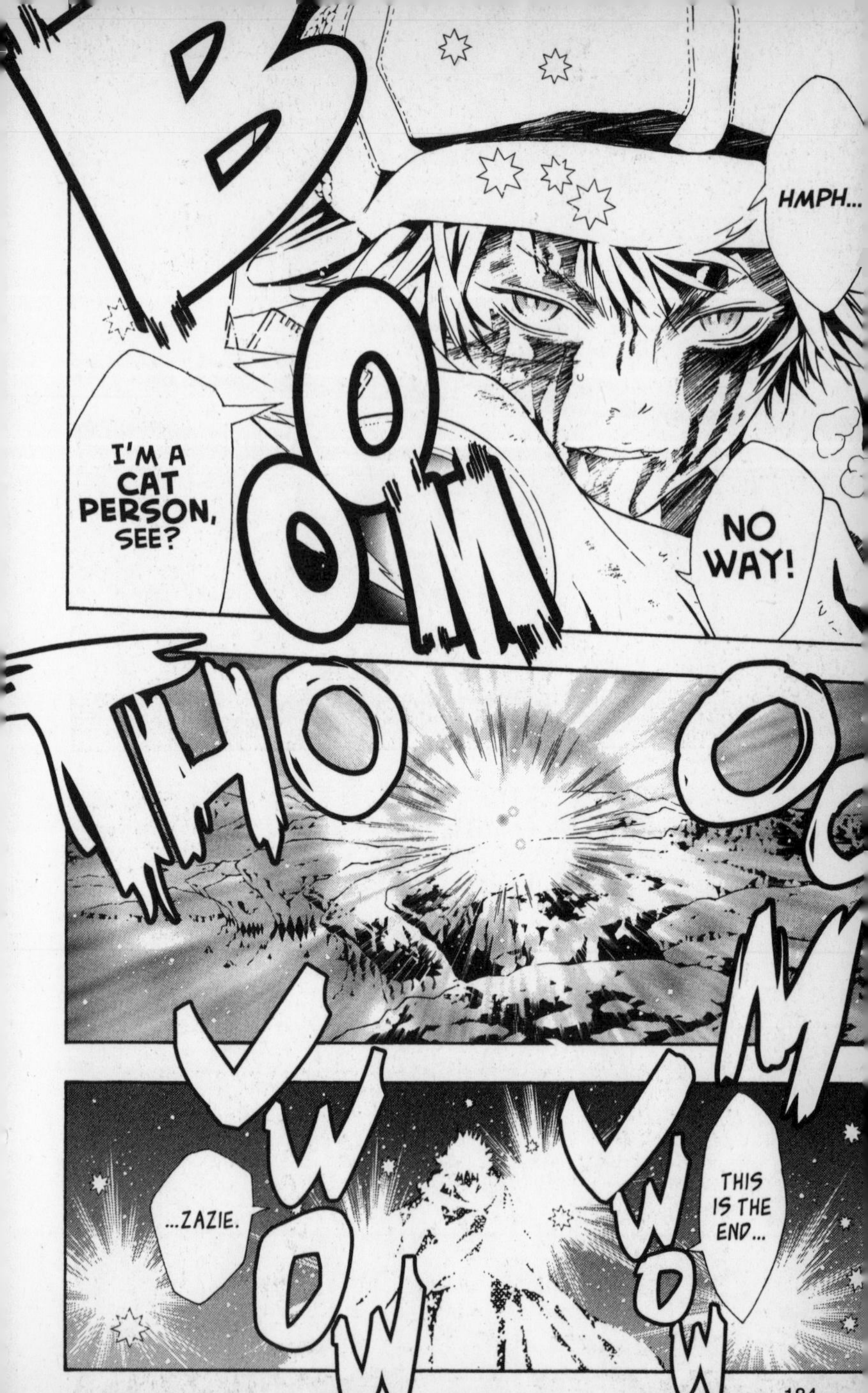
HMPH...
BOOM
NO WAY!
I'M A CAT PERSON, SEE?
THOOOM
VWOW
THIS IS THE END...
...ZAZIE.
VWOW

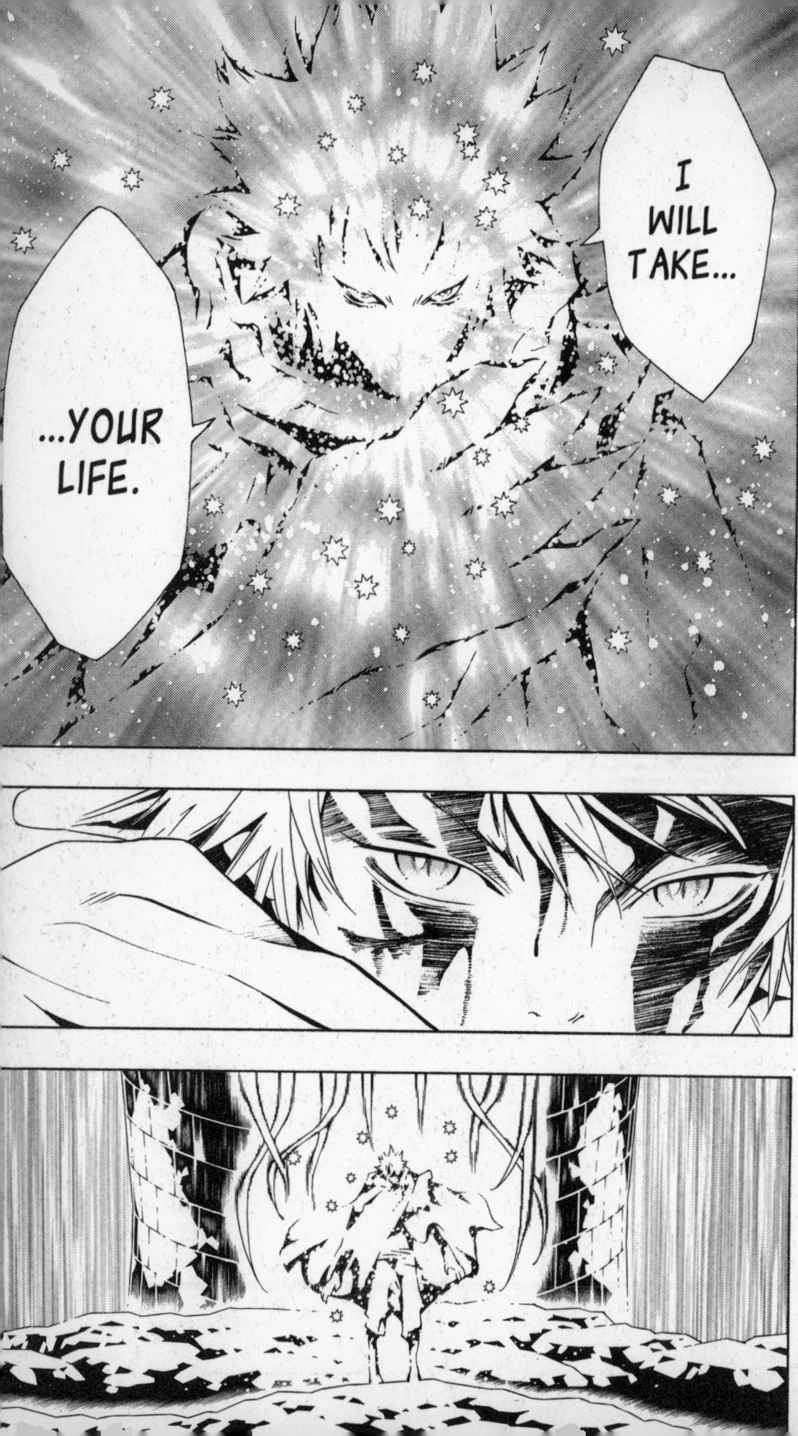
I WILL TAKE...
...YOUR LIFE.

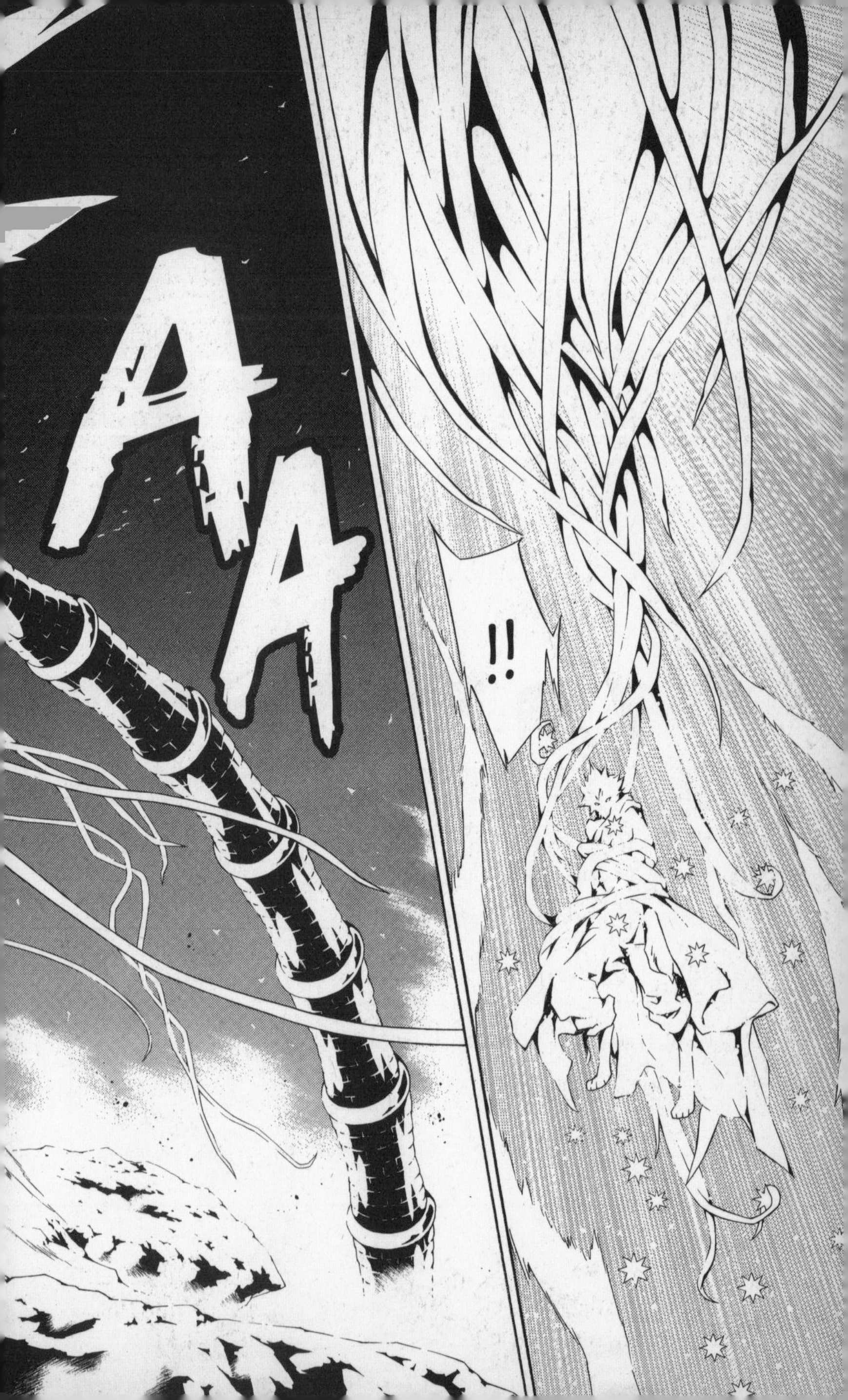
!!
AA

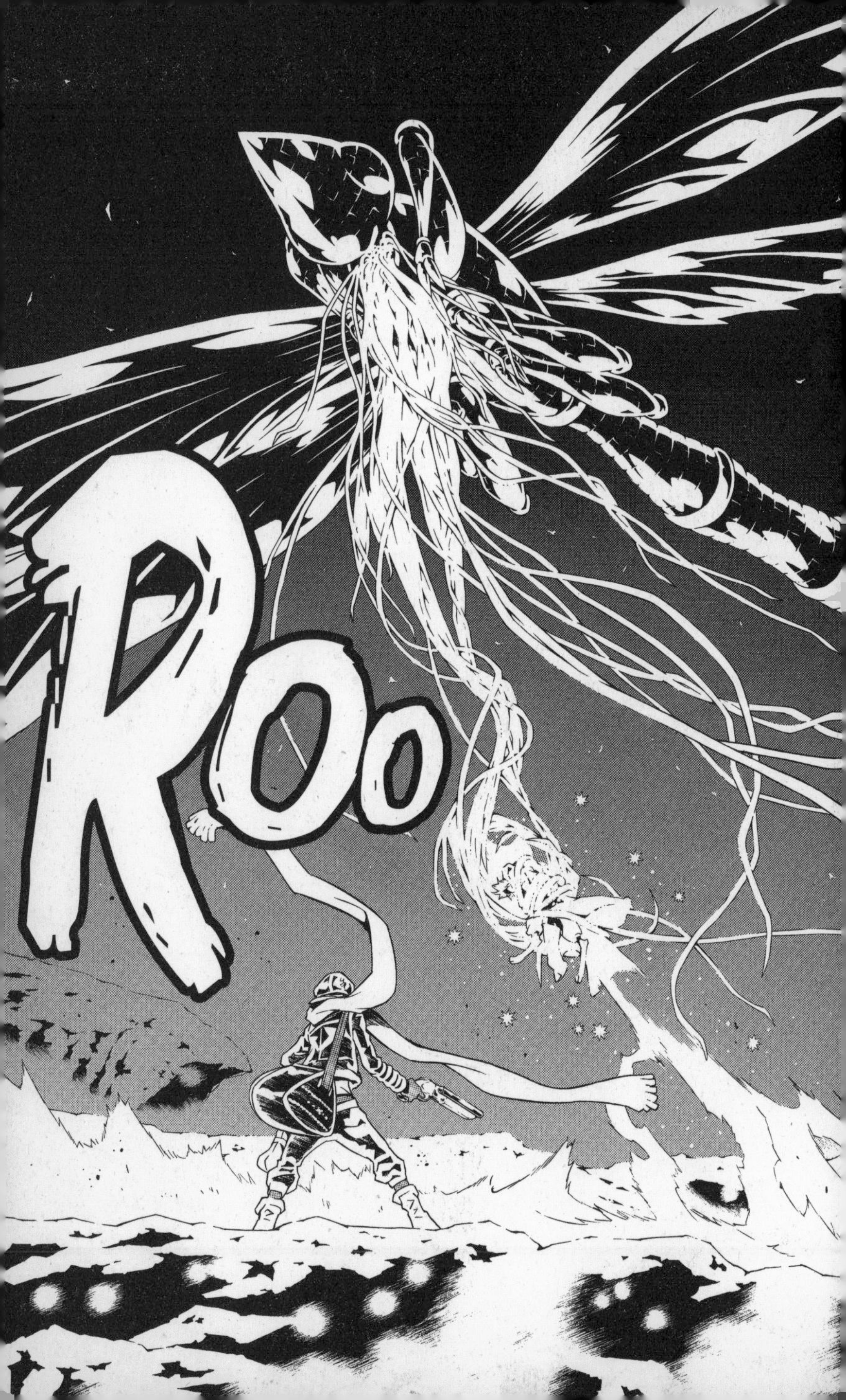
ROOO

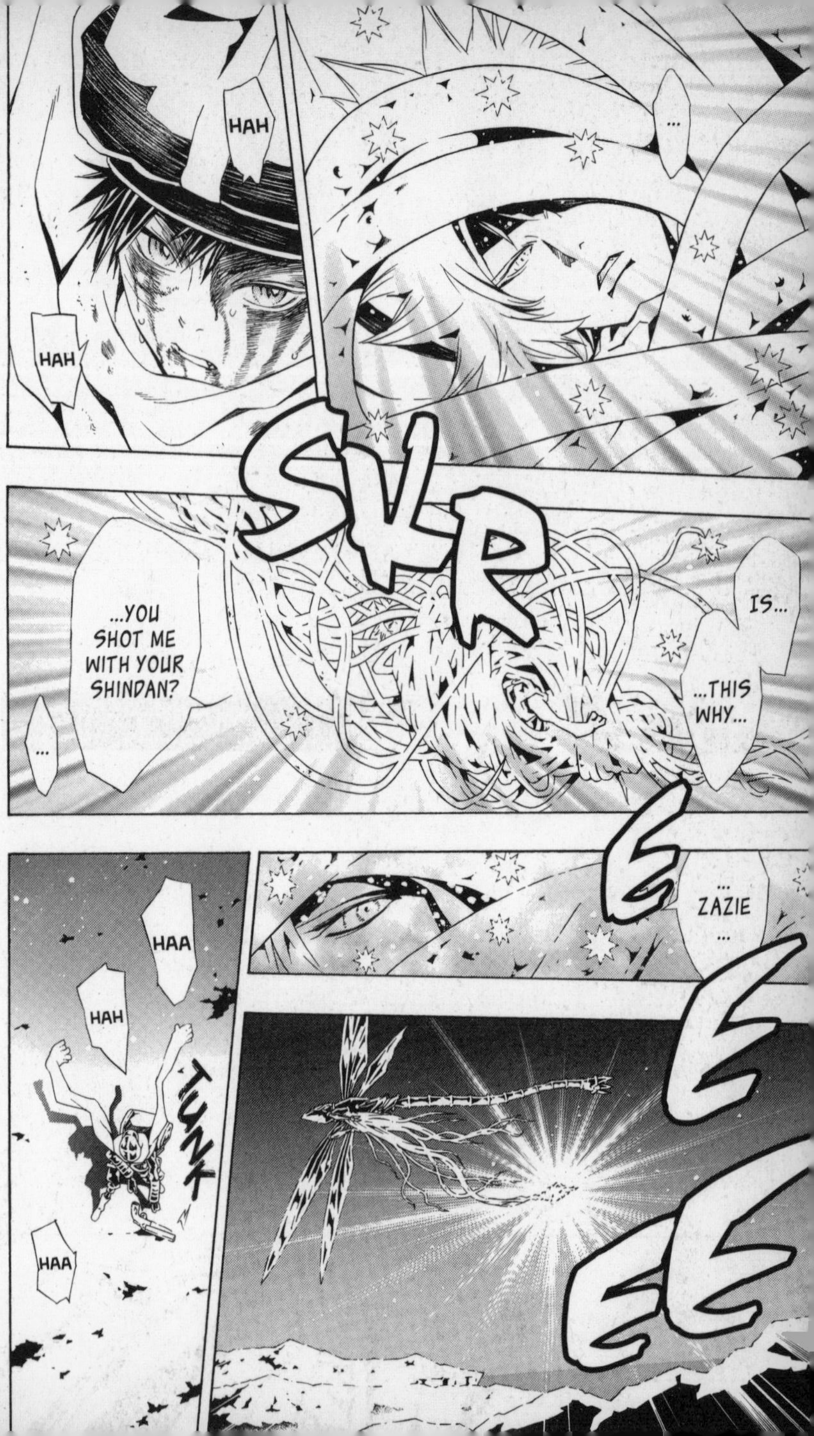
...
HAH
HAH
SKREEEEE
IS...
...THIS WHY...
...YOU SHOT ME WITH YOUR SHINDAN?
...
... ZAZIE ...
HAA
HAH
TUNK
HAA

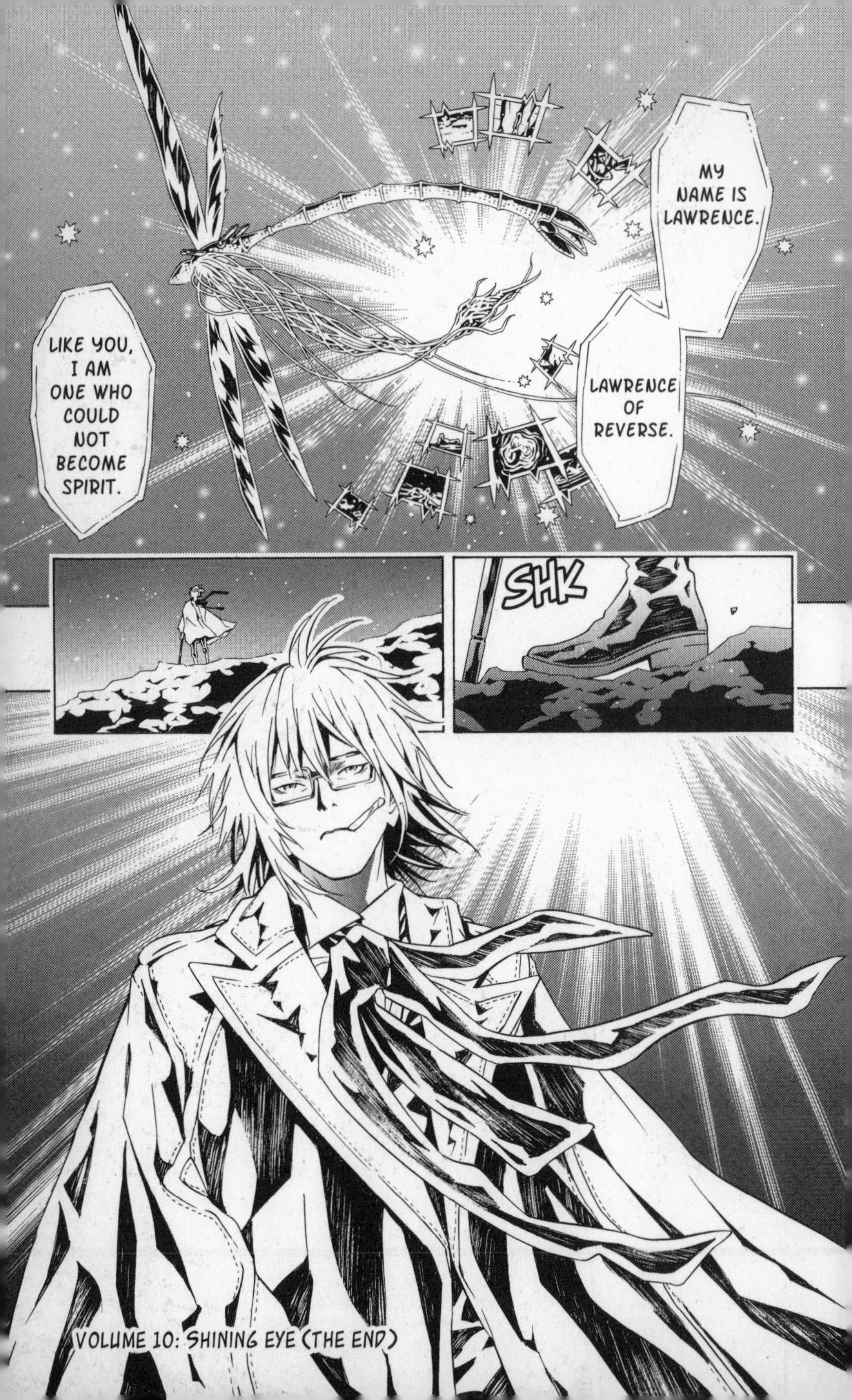
MY NAME IS LAWRENCE.
LAWRENCE OF REVERSE.
LIKE YOU, I AM ONE WHO COULD NOT BECOME SPIRIT.
SHK
VOLUME 10: SHINING EYE (THE END)

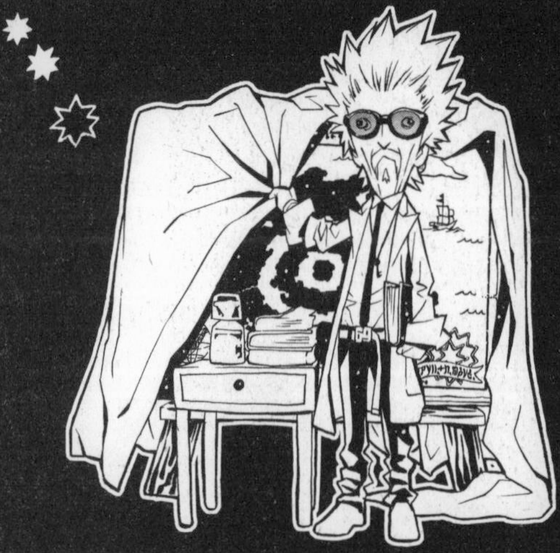

Dr. Thunderland's Reference Desk

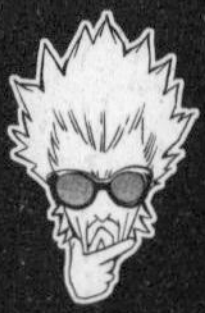

Hello, dear friends! I am Dr. Thunderland.

You sit right down in any seat you like. I work at the Beehive in Yuusari, spending my days on various sorts of research. Today I'd like to review some of the matters concerning this world as introduced in this volume.

...Hmm? I don't sound like my usual self? Heh heh heh. *Non non non, Monsieur...Mademoiselle...* What you see before you is my true self.

My calm, clear spirit always flows as smoothly as the gentlest brook...

Incidentally, Lag, the main character, hardly appeared at all in this volume! What? You think *that's* the reason for my calm demeanor?

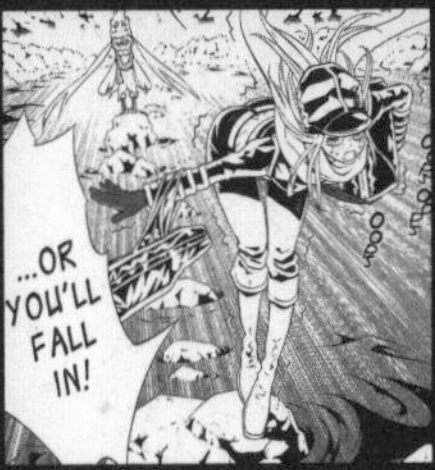
...OR YOU'LL FALL IN!

■ SHINDAN

At long last we see Aria's shindan! Her skintight uniform was quite a sight too. Who would've thought the oh-so-proper Aria was such a klutz? In the end, the Niche-Aria combo was not bad, not bad at all (as Niche might say), but it's much harder for adults like Aria to summon a shindan. To create a shindan that will resonate in a gaichuu, you need a heart that is true and almost impossibly pure.

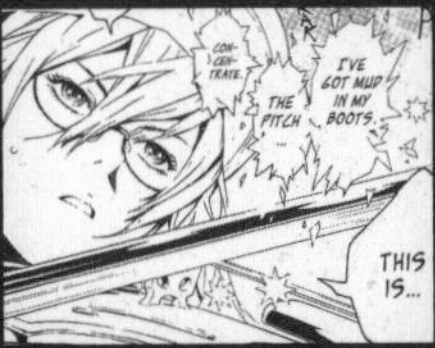
I'VE GOT MUD IN MY BOOTS.
CON-CENTRATE.
THE PITCH
THIS IS...

To be honest, if I tried to fire a shindan, not only would I fail to bring down a gaichuu, but the shards of my dirty-minded *heart* would horrify the entire nation. I'd get sued. I'm surprised Connor can do it. Is it because his appetite is true and pure? Speaking of Connor, I wonder if he's all right.

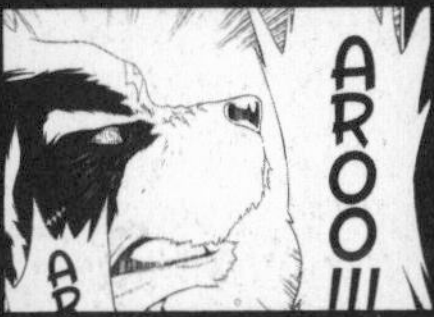
AROOO!!!

■ ASSISTANT DIRECTOR OF THE BEEHIVE

Her performance may have had something to do with it, but Aria quit her job as a Bee mainly for the sake of her dingo. Bolt still feels he is protecting her. Niche seemed happy to hear they were still together. Both Bolt and Niche serve with pride as dingos, defending their Bees. Each party is indispensable to the other. How nice! I'd love to have a busty, sexy-older-lady dingo! Wow!

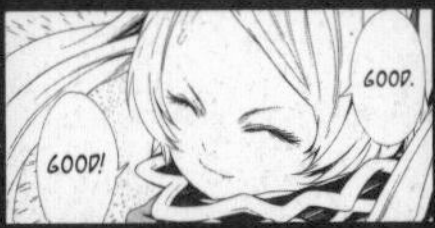
GOOD.
GOOD!

nb: Astor Piazzolla (1921-1992) / Argentine composer who created his own style of music incorporating tango, classical and jazz.

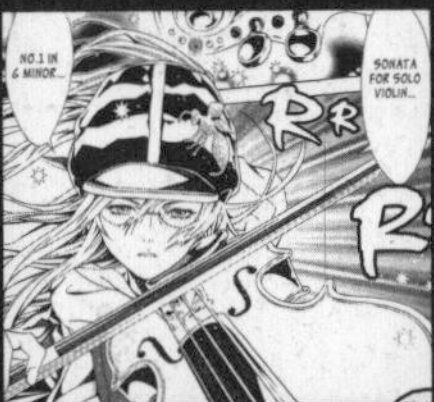
SONATA FOR SOLO VIOLIN...
NO.1 IN G MINOR...

nb: *Sonatas and Partitas for Solo Violin* / A set of six works consisting of three sonatas and three partitas composed by Johann Sebastian Bach.

■ INVESTIGATIVE AIRSHIP PROGROCK

Twelve years ago, on the Day of the Flicker, the whole world was thrown into darkness for an instant. The government claimed that it had been conducting routine maintenance of the man-made sun, but we scientists and researchers were not satisfied with that explanation. I say that, but...

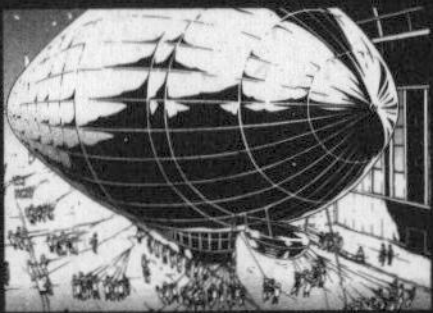

...I wasn't on the ship! Where the devil was I? Home sick? What a weakling!! *Sob*... Because of me, my son, who took my place, was injured. I feel terrible about that. It seems that Junior has lost all his memories of that day. Somehow, all those who witnessed the flicker lost parts of their minds and bodies...unbelievable. That government man Barrol looked suspicious, and what about the huge shining eye? There's still a veil of secrecy over the whole business...

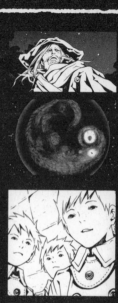

■ THE GATEKEEPERS

In one chapter of this volume, it becomes clear that the two gatekeepers at Bifrost were once Bees who had been on that airship. So that's why former Director Lloyd knew Signal's old name in volume 2. And there was another brother; they were triplets. It seems they were all severely injured, but I wonder where that third brother has gone. Is he the gatekeeper at Akatsuki, the capital?

nb: Hodai Yamazaki (1914-1985) / a vagabond poet. Injured during WWII, he lived out his life in a hut a friend in Kamakura built for him in his yard.

nb: Progrock / an abbreviation for "progressive rock," a category of advanced, avant-garde rock music born toward the end of the 1960s.

■ THE WOLF WHO COULDN'T BECOME SPIRIT

So far we've met several members of Reverse: Lawrence, the apparent ringleader, Roda, and now this third person, Zeal. It seems like there could be more out there... Could this man be another victim of the government's experiments? I'd like to learn more about the *heart* lost by Zeal.

In the next volume, Cabernet will finally take wing, the former director will reappear, Gauche will awaken, that man-killer and that young girl and even that soup will appear. I'm getting excited (although I'm always excited)! This one is not to be missed!

Route Map

Finally, I am including a map, indicating the route followed by Aria and the places Cabernet appeared in this volume, created at Lonely Goatherd Map Station of Central Yuusari.

A: Akatsuki B: Yuusari C: Yodaka

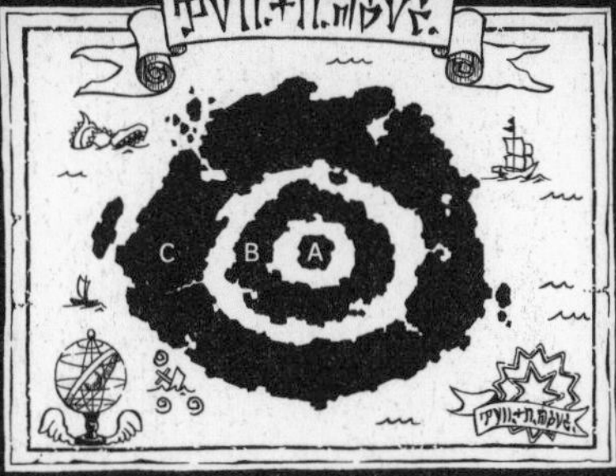

C
B
A

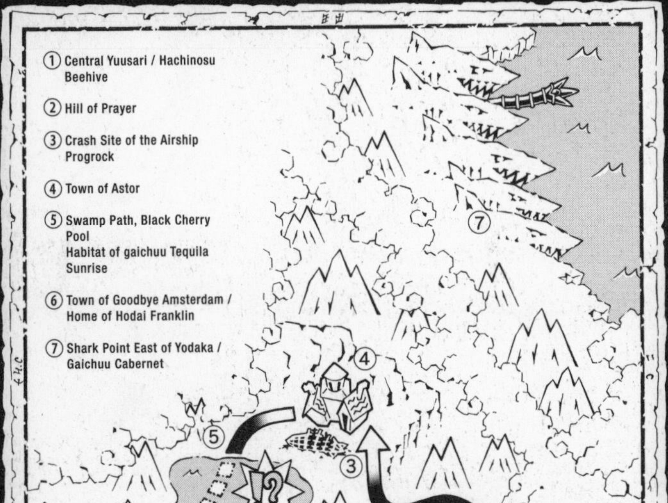

① Central Yuusari / Hachinosu Beehive
② Hill of Prayer
③ Crash Site of the Airship Progrock
④ Town of Astor
⑤ Swamp Path, Black Cherry Pool
Habitat of gaichuu Tequila Sunrise
⑥ Town of Goodbye Amsterdam / Home of Hodai Franklin
⑦ Shark Point East of Yodaka / Gaichuu Cabernet
!?

Lag's not on the cover? It's Aria and Niche instead? Whoopie!! Does this mean there is a chance of a cover featuring my son and me someday? Yes! Yes! Listen, everyone! Look for me on the cover of volume 11!!

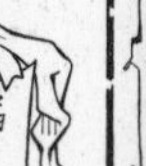

In the next volume...

A Bee's Bag

As Reverse prepares to attack, Largo Lloyd, ex-director of the Beehive, makes his way to the heart of the rebel organization. Meanwhile, Lag discovers that Gauche's awakening isn't quite the happy ending he'd hoped for...

Available November 2012!

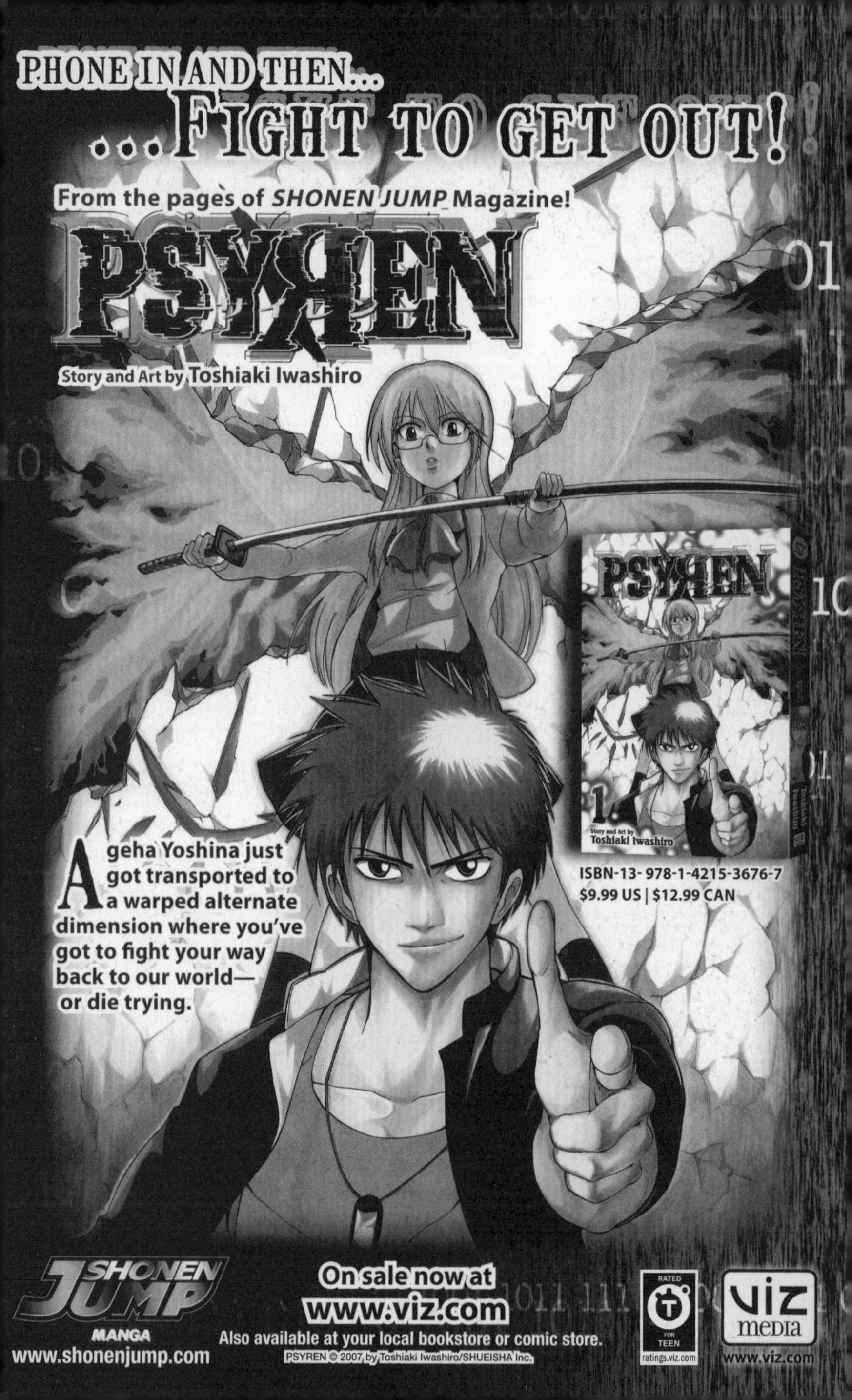

PHONE IN AND THEN...
...FIGHT TO GET OUT!
From the pages of SHONEN JUMP Magazine!
PSYREN
Story and Art by Toshiaki Iwashiro
PSYREN
1
Story and Art by
Toshiaki Iwashiro
ISBN-13- 978-1-4215-3676-7
$9.99 US | $12.99 CAN
Ageha Yoshina just got transported to a warped alternate dimension where you've got to fight your way back to our world—or die trying.
SHONEN JUMP
MANGA
www.shonenjump.com
On sale now at
www.viz.com
Also available at your local bookstore or comic store.
PSYREN © 2007 by Toshiaki Iwashiro/SHUEISHA Inc.
RATED
T
FOR
TEEN
ratings.viz.com
viz media
www.viz.com

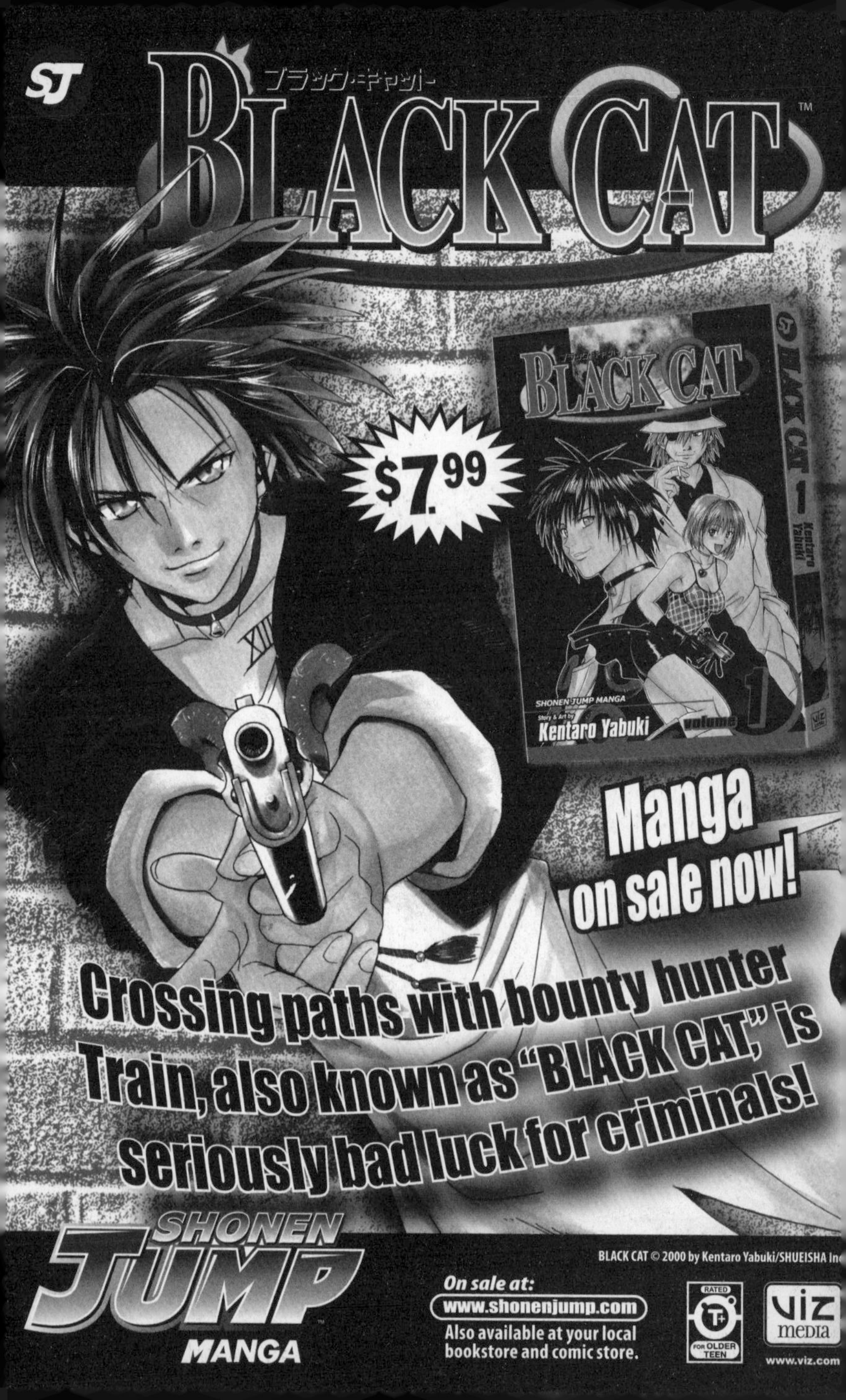
SJ
ブラック・キャット
BLACK CAT™
$7.99
BLACK CAT
SHONEN JUMP MANGA
Story & Art by
Kentaro Yabuki
volume 1
BLACK CAT 1 Kentaro Yabuki
Manga on sale now!
Crossing paths with bounty hunter Train, also known as "BLACK CAT," is seriously bad luck for criminals!
SHONEN JUMP MANGA
BLACK CAT © 2000 by Kentaro Yabuki/SHUEISHA Inc
On sale at:
www.shonenjump.com
Also available at your local bookstore and comic store.
RATED T+ FOR OLDER TEEN
viz media
www.viz.com

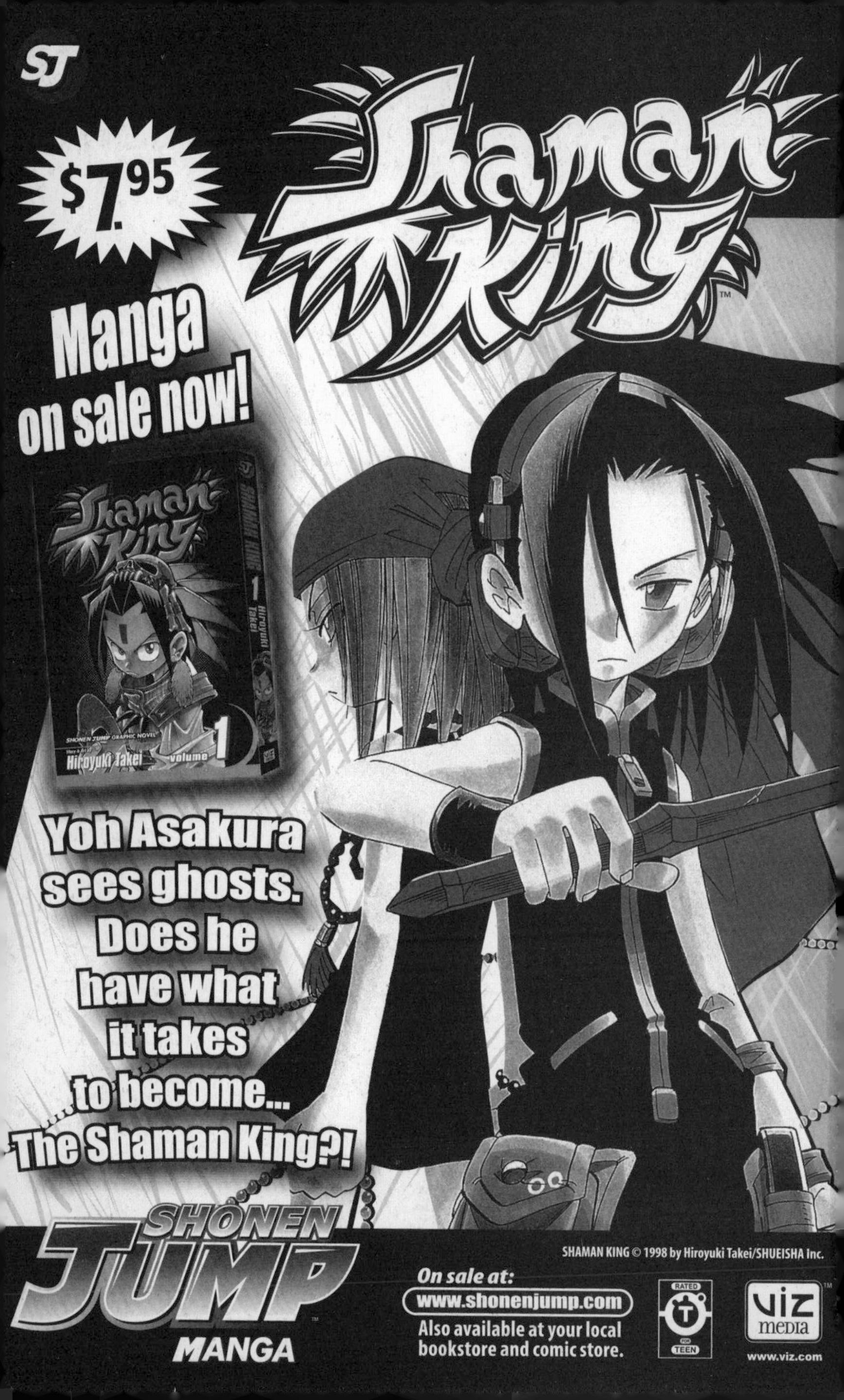
SJ
$7.95
Shaman King™
Manga on sale now!
Shaman King
SHONEN JUMP GRAPHIC NOVEL
Hiroyuki Takei
volume 1
Yoh Asakura sees ghosts. Does he have what it takes to become... The Shaman King?!
SHONEN JUMP MANGA
SHAMAN KING © 1998 by Hiroyuki Takei/SHUEISHA Inc.
On sale at:
www.shonenjump.com
Also available at your local bookstore and comic store.
RATED T FOR TEEN
viz media
www.viz.com

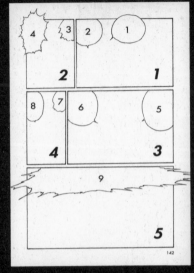

← Follow the action this way.

THIS IS THE LAST PAGE.

Tegami Bachi: Letter Bee has been printed in the original Japanese format in order to preserve the orientation of the original artwork.

Please turn it around and begin reading from right to left. Unlike English, Japanese is read right to left, so Japanese comics are read in reverse order from the way English comics are typically read. Have fun with it!